John Woodroffe Hill

The management and diseases of the dog

John Woodroffe Hill

The management and diseases of the dog

ISBN/EAN: 9783337814823

Printed in Europe, USA, Canada, Australia, Japan

Cover: Foto ©ninafisch / pixelio.de

More available books at **www.hansebooks.com**

THE MANAGEMENT AND DISEASES OF THE DOG

BY

JOHN WOODROFFE HILL

Fellow of the Royal College of Veterinary Surgeons,
Late Professor of Veterinary Science at the College of Agriculture, Downton.
Author of "The Principles and Practice of Bovine Medicine and
Surgery;" "The Relative Positions of the Higher and
Lower Creation; or a Plea for Dumb Animals,"
"Canine Distemper," etc.

WITH TEN PHOTOGRAVURE PLATES OF PRIZE DOGS, AND

THIRTY-NINE ILLUSTRATIONS ON WOOD.

THIRD EDITION.

PHILADELPHIA:
GEBBIE & COMPANY.

TO THE

MEMBERS OF THE VETERINARY PROFESSION

AND

ALL THOSE INTERESTED IN THE WELFARE OF

THE CANINE RACE

THE FOURTH EDITION OF THIS WORK IS

RESPECTFULLY DEDICATED BY

THE AUTHOR.

PREFACE TO THE FIRST EDITION.

Of all the domesticated animals subservient to man, the dog may, without fear of contradiction, be said to stand pre-eminent. His courage, fidelity, usefulness, and companionship attach him to the human race in bonds of lasting endurance.

The field upon which I have entered—"The Management and Diseases of the Dog"—is a large one, and, in comparison with other veterinary subjects, it must be confessed, to the discredit of our Profession, has been inexcusably neglected.

Man's best animal friend, until Blaine, Youatt, Mayhew, "Stonehenge," and one or two others interested themselves in his welfare, was left to the mercy of individuals who professed a knowledge of subjects of which they were, on all scientific points, totally ignorant.

If in the course of this work my feeble efforts to enlighten the public, and alleviate the sufferings of the canine race are attended with success, I shall feel more than amply rewarded for the labour I have bestowed on the various subjects herein treated of.

I have to acknowledge my obligations to my friend Mr. George Fleming, 2nd Life Guards, for many valuable suggestions offered to me while the work was passing through the press.

J. W. H

Wolverhampton,
March 20, 1878.

PREFACE TO THE THIRD EDITION.

In the third edition of "The Management and Diseases of the Dog," which extends to fifty pages beyond its predecessor, the Author has introduced upwards of thirty new subjects of importance, and, he ventures to hope, interest to canine veterinary surgeons and the dog-loving public.

Several of the original sections have also been enlarged upon, and additional prescriptions have been given in accordance with their value, as tested in the Author's practice, whose desire it is, having canine welfare at heart, that his work may still continue to merit support and deserve the generous reviews bestowed on its first production.

In the second edition the present appendix on "Poisons and their Antidotes" was merely added, the Author's health and duties at that date precluding any alteration or increase to the general text.

Hastings,

March, 20, 1888.

LIST OF FULL PAGE ILLUSTRATIONS.

PHOTOGRAVURES BY THE

Gebbie & Husson Photogravure Co., Limited.

CHAMPION ENGLISH MASTIFF, "MINTING." . FRONTISPIECE.
From a Photograph by Schreiber & Sons.

CHAMPION ST. BERNARD, "OTHO.". . . . . Page 33

CHAMPION ENGLISH BLOOD HOUND, "BARNABY." . " 65
From a Photograph by Schreiber & Sons.

PRIZE BULL TERRIER BITCH, "NORA." . . . . " 113
From a Photograph by Schreiber & Sons.

CHAMPION GORDON SETTER, "ROYAL DUKE." . . " 162
From a Photograph by Schreiber & Sons.

CHAMPION ENGLISH POINTER, "DONALD." . . . " 209
From a Photograph by Schreiber & Sons.

PRIZE ENGLISH SETTER, "RODERICK." . . . . " 257
From a Photograph by Schreiber & Sons.

CHAMPION COLLIE DOG, "SCOTILLA." . . . . " 305
From a Photograph by Schreiber & Sons.

PRIZE CLYDESDALE TERRIER, "CLYDESDALE LADY." " 353
From a Photograph by Phillips.

CHAMPION PUG DOG, "DUDE." . . . . " 401
From a Photograph by Schreiber & Sons.

ILLUSTRATIONS.

FIG.		PAGE
1.	KENNEL PLAN. (KINGDON)	11
2., 3.	STRONGYLUS CANIS BRONCHIALIS. ("VETERINARIAN")	31
4., 5., 6., 7., 8., 9., 10.	FRONT TEETH OF THE DOG IN VARIOUS STAGES OF GROWTH AND DECAY. (YOUATT)	48-49
11.	CYSTIC CALCULUS. ("VETERINARIAN")	124
12.	HILL'S OBSTETRICAL FORCEPS	150
13.	WEBER'S ,, ,, (FLEMING)	150
14.	DEFAYS' FORCEPS. (FLEMING)	152
15.	DEFAYS' WIRE EXTRACTOR, WITH THE TORSION RODS. (FLEMING)	152
16.	DEFAYS' WIRE EXTRACTOR APPLIED. (FLEMING)	154
17.	BREULET'S TUBE AND NOOSE. (FLEMING)	155
18.	BREULET'S NOOSE FIXED ON THE FŒTUS. (FLEMING)	155
19.	CROTCHET. (MAYHEW)	156
20.	EXTEMPORISED HOOK. (ORIGINAL)	158
21.	DOG WITH CANKER CAP. (ORIGINAL)	193
22.	SARCOPTES CANIS. (GERLACH)	201
23.	ACARUS FOLLICULORUM. (FLEMING)	201
24.	THE LIVER FLUKE OF THE DOG. (LEWIS)	219
25.	THE GIANT STRONGLE. (BLANCHARD)	224

FIG.		PAG
26.	Larvæ of the Gid Tapeworm. (Newman)	22
27.	Tapeworm-like Heads of the Gid Hydatid. (Newman)	22
28.	Larva of the Margined Tapeworm. (Goeze)	22
29.	Hydatid Tapeworm and Echinococcus Head. (Cobbold)	23
30.	Group of Echinococcus Heads. (Cobbold)	23
31.	Larval Pentastome. (Kuchenmeister)	23
32.	A Dog with Rickets, Sketched from Life. (Original)	34
33.	Heart of Dog affected with Rheumatic Chorea, showing Ante-Mortem Clot. (Original)	36
34.	Incomplete Fracture. (Original)	371
35.	Fracture of the Scapula. (Original)	373
36.	Ditto, with Bandage applied. (Original)	374
37.	Deformed Limb after Union of Fracture, necessitating Re-Fracture. (Original)	378
38.	Dislocation of the Shoulder-Joint. (Original)	380
39.	Throat Forceps. (Arnold)	400

CONTENTS.

CHAPTER I.
GENERAL MANAGEMENT.

Food.— Exercise.— Washing.— Grooming.— Kennel Arrangement.—Disinfection.—Administration of Medicine.—Nursing.   PAGE 1

CHAPTER II.
DISEASES OF THE RESPIRATORY ORGANS.

Catarrh.—Influenza.—Laryngitis.—Bronchitis.—Asthma.—Pleurisy.—Pneumonia.—Consumption.—Polypus.—Ozæna.   15

CHAPTER III.
DISEASES OF THE MOUTH AND TONGUE.

Dentition.—Decayed teeth.—Tartar.—Canker.—Aphthæ—Glossitis.—Ulcers.—Blain.—Paralysis.—Pharyngitis.—Salivation   48

CHAPTER IV.
DISEASES OF THE STOMACH.

Indigestion.— Vomiting.—Worms.— Husk.—Gastritis.— Inversion.—Calculi.—Foreign bodies   61

CHAPTER V.
DISEASES OF THE BOWELS.

Constipation. — Diarrhœa. — Dysentery. — Intussusception.—Hernia,—Worms.—Colic.—Enteritis.—Peritonitis.—Piles.—Prolapsus Ani.—Fistula in Ano.   71

CHAPTER VI.
DISEASES OF THE LIVER AND SPLEEN.

Hepatitis.—Jaundice.—Fatty Degeneration of the Liver.—Cancerous Deposit in the Liver and Spleen.—Biliary Calculi.—Splenitis   89

CHAPTER VII.
DISEASES OF URINARY ORGANS.

Nephritis.—Hæmaturia.—Renal Calculi.—Cystitis.—Cystic Calculi.—Retention of Urine.—Paralysis of the Bladder.—Rupture of the Bladder.   109

CHAPTER VIII.
DISEASES OF THE GENERATIVE ORGANS.

Balanatis.—Warts on the Penis.—Scrotal Irritation.—Enlarged Testicle.—Inversion of the Vagina.—Polypus in the Vagina.—Inflammation of the Uterus.—Inversion of the Uterus.—Ulceration of the Uterus.—Hernia of the Uterus.—Dropsy of the Uterus.—Fatty Degeneration of the Ovaries.   129

CHAPTER IX.
FUNCTIONS OF THE GENERATIVE ORGANS.

Œstrum.—Breeding.—Parturition.   141

CHAPTER X.
DISEASES IMMEDIATELY CONNECTED WITH PARTURITION.

Influence of Mental Emotion on Canine Lactation.—Agalactia—Parturient Apoplexy or Milk Fever.—Parturient Eclampsia.—Septikæmia Puerperalis.   164

CHAPTER XI.
DISEASES OF THE MAMMARY GLAND.
Mammitis.—Lacteal Tumour.—Cancer. 175

CHAPTER XII.
DISEASES OF THE EYE.
Ophthalmia.—Cataract.—Amaurosis.—Iritis.—Enlargement of the Haw.—Protrusion of the Eye-Ball.—Extirpation of the Eye.—Hairy Tumour on the Cornea.—Hydrophthalmia. . 180

CHAPTER XIII.
DISEASES OF THE EAR.
Canker.—Serous Abscess.—Polypus.—Deafness.—Scurfy Ears. 190

CHAPTER XIV.
DISEASES OF THE SKIN.—EXTERNAL PARASITES.
Mange (Sarcoptic).—Ditto (Follicular).—Eczema.—Erythema.—Ringworm.— Ditto (Honeycomb).— Alopecia.— Warts.—Fleas.—Lice.—Ticks. 200

CHAPTER XV.
INTERNAL PARASITES.
Distoma conjunctum.—Holostoma alatum.—Ascaris marginata. —Filaria immitis.—Estrongylus gigas.—Spiroptera sanguinolenta.—Dochmius trigonocephalus.—Trichosoma plica.—Tricocephalus depressiusculus.—Trichina spiralis.—Filaria hæmatica.—Filaria trispinulosa.—Filaria hepatica.—Hematozoon subulatum.—Tænia Cucumerina.—Tænia cœnurus.—Tænia marginata.—Tænia echinococcus.—Tænia serrata.—Bothriocephalus latus, B. cordatus, B. fuscus, B. reticulatus.—B. dubius.—Pentastoma tæmoides.—Maw Worms, or Segments of Tænia marginata, and Tænia serrata.—Cysticercus cellulosus. 219

CHAPTER XVI.
DISEASES OF THE NERVOUS SYSTEM.
Rabies.— Epilepsy.—Apoplexy,— Vertigo.—Chorea.—Paralysis. Concussion of the Brain.—Compression of the Brain.—Hydrocephalus.— Turnside. —Meningitis.— Dementia.—Nostomania.—Neuralgia. 239

CHAPTER XVII.
GENERAL DISEASES.
Abscess.— Tumours.— Cancer.— Bronchocele.— Diphtheria. — Distemper — Malignant Distemper.— Dropsy.— Leukæmia.—Anæmia.— Marasmus.— Plethora.— Obesity.—Rheumatism.— Rickets.— Ostitis.— Periostitis.— Scrofula.—Glanders.— Small-pox.— Measles.— Tetanus.— Cramp.—Heart Diseases.—Pericarditis.—Embolism.—Emphysema. . 288

CHAPTER XVIII.
ACCIDENTS AND OPERATIONS.
Fractures —Dislocations —Amputations.—Wounds.—Sprains.—Burns.— Scalds.— Umbilical Hernia.— Ventral Hernia.—Femoral Hernia. —Fistulæ. — Cyst Excision.— Choking.—Osophagotomy.— Lithotomy.—Urethral Obstruction. — Catheterism.— Vaginotomy.— Anti-conception Operation.—Sore Feet.—Soft Corns.—Overgrowth of Claws.—Removal of Dew-claws.— Cropping.— Rounding.— Tailing.— Worming.—Castration.—Spaying.—Vaccination.—Chloroform. . 370

Appendix.—Poisons and their Antidotes. 417

Index 425

THE MANAGEMENT AND DISEASES OF THE DOG.

CHAPTER I.

GENERAL MANAGEMENT.

FOOD, KENNEL ARRANGEMENT,
EXERCISE, DISINFECTION,
WASHING, ADMINISTRATION OF MEDICINE,
GROOMING, NURSING.

FOOD.

How much evil accrues from the want of a proper system and, in many cases, knowledge of administering food, and of the kind requisite, it is impossible to say. That many of the diseases to which the canine species are subject, and especially of the digestive organs, are due to ignorance and neglect of this subject, is no exaggeration.

The organism of the dog is peculiar: his digestive powers are undoubtedly great, but the process by which digestion is accomplished is slow. Hence, he does not require more than one, or, if in full exercise and work, two substantial meals per day. The food should be plain, wholesome, nutritious, and, as far as possible, compatible with the circumstances under which the animal exists.

Sugar, buttered bread, hot toast, muffin, preserves, fancy biscuits, tea, sweetmeats, and such like, are items never intended to enter a canine bill of fare. And yet how often is the reply given, when the attendant alleges his patient is suffering from indigestion: "But he has had nothing to disagree with him; the poor little dear eats most sparingly; a morsel of buttered toast or muffin, some tea and a lump of sugar, has been doggie's only diet for months." True, and therein lies the key to the mystery. The animal, contrary to Nature's laws, has been educated to mimic human beings: three or four meals a day, exclusive of kitchen-scraps, have taken the place of the prescribed one or two, and human delicacies substituted for the proper requirements of a carnivorous stomach.

Can it be wondered at, if the whole digestive machinery is in consequence put out of gear; if the once glossy-coated pet of cleanly habits becomes the bloated, waddling, unsightly animal so often seen, with teeth loose, discoloured, and decayed, breath foul, and excrements fœtid? And all the result of what? Ignorance and mistaken kindness. Ask the human mother the effect on the child of a continued diet of preserves, pastry, and sweet cakes, and she will tell you it is much the same.

Is it, then, reasonable to suppose that the stomach of the dog can properly digest and appropriate to the nourishment of its body and the maintenance of health that which mankind, for whom such is more in accordance, cannot take with impunity?

A proper system of feeding is, therefore, one of the great essentials of canine management.

Time of Feeding.—The food should always be given, if convenient, at a stated time: where only one meal is allowed, at midday; in the case of two, morning and evening. It should not be given immediately before exercise or work, or the process of digestion will be interrupted, and the foundation laid for ill health; but as soon as the animal comes home, has had sufficient time to rest, and become cool, then food may be proffered and will be relished considerably more. I am now alluding to dogs in health; invalids of course require a different system, and, under many conditions, require frequent support.

Quantity.—This should be exactly in proportion to the appetite, *i.e.*, until the animal is satisfied. Some individuals condemn the practice of permitting dogs to fill, or, as they put it, overgorge themselves. And where dogs have been previously starved, or have missed a meal or two, they are right, but otherwise not so. The cravings of the carnivorous stomach are not of the frequency found in herbivorous and omnivorous ones, owing to the slow process of digestion; and this being so, a larger stock of material is required to work on than when the intervals between the meals are shorter; otherwise long fasts would result, and eventually act prejudicially to the animal's health.

When the dog, after eating for some time, pauses, looks about, leaves the dish, returns to it and makes an attempt, as it were, to get a little more down, *then* it should be removed. Company will frequently induce the animal, from motives of jealousy, to take more than he really wants, and he will greedily devour, on the approach of another creature, that which a few moments before was rejected. This, of course, is hurtful; it may be likened unto the surplus oil on machinery, which cannot be utilized, and is therefore wasted, and does injury to other parts: so with the dog, the surplus food may pass into the intestinal canal undigested, and produce diarrhœa or constipation.

Kind of Food.—Many and various are the opinions on this point: horse-flesh, mutton, paunch, entrails, liver, greaves, and oatmeal are among the list of those advocated.

Flesh is undoubtedly the dog's natural food, but, on the other hand, we must look to the circumstances under which he is placed. For instance, toy-dogs or house-pets not used for sport do not require flesh-meat beyond an occasional bone and meat-gravy; bread or plain biscuit with milk, oatmeal-porridge, plain rice-pudding, or potatoes and gravy, with green vegetables once or twice a week, form the most suitable diet for this class of dog.

For those used in sport or kept on the chain, especially the former, flesh-meat used with discretion is suitable. Paunches or mutton are best adapted; the former should always be thoroughly washed, otherwise worms or their larvæ, which are frequently present, are likely to be swallowed, and develop in the dog into large tape-worms (see chapter on "Internal Parasites"); horse-flesh is heating, causes the animal to smell strong, and is a great producer of worms. Liver cooked is like so much leather—indigestible and innutritious; and, from its liability to flukes, which in the dog develop into the tæniæ proper, is also objectionable raw. Greaves I have observed frequently give rise to diarrhœa, probably from the amount of tallow often retained, and other foreign matters—as maggot-skins and mineral substances.

Sheep-heads, trotters, and ox-noses form a highly nutritious and valuable food, especially for invalid dogs; boiled down, they form a glutinous jelly, of which dogs are particularly fond. Whichever kind of flesh-meat is used, meal should form the basis, and none is better than the coarse Scotch oatmeal.

Bones are of great value to the Dog.—The dog has a natural fondness for bones, independently of which they are of great value to him. One should always be allowed at least once or twice a week. They assist in cleansing the teeth and aid digestion. The animal's instinct would appear to teach him this; for however good and savoury the meal may be, if there be a bone in it, he will immediately pick it out, strip it of its meat, if there be any, and store it safely away for after-use. It is best, however, to give bones after a meal; otherwise, when hungry, they are apt to eat as much of the bone as possible, to their own injury; as portions may get lodged in the œsophagus, and give rise to asphyxia, or, from being too hard to digest cause gastric or intestinal irritation.

Biscuits.—The example set by Spratt, of old, has been followed by others, and at the present time we have numerous canine biscuit manufacturers; but of the various kinds offered for sale none appear to have risen in public estimation to the extent of "Spratt's Patent." After an inspection of their works, the system adopted, and materials used, this appreciation is not difficult to understand. The biscuits are prepared with careful selection and adjustment, and abound in nutrient bone and flesh forming elements.

The recent introduction of a fish biscuit by the same firm is also likely to prove a boon to the canine fancy. Fish is an exceedingly nutritious food, forming an agreeable change in the diet, and to those unable to procure a sufficiency of fresh fish, a biscuit so constituted will be most acceptable. I should add that I have given the latter an extended trial with my own dogs and hospital patients and the results have been pleasing. Spratt's cod-liver oil biscuit is now well known. In cases of debility, light-feeding and delicate dogs, they are of especial service. Cod-liver oil is a highly nutritive and reparative agent; it builds up and improves the muscular and fatty tissues, and imparts tone to the digestive organs. Highly bred dogs (especially if tainted with the results of consanguinity) derive great benefit from cod-liver oil: its rapid assimilation renders it particularly valuable in nervous disorders and dyspeptic conditions. A biscuit, therefore, containing such an agent should find favour with members of the canine fancy as well as professional men.

A dog should never be induced to eat against its will, except under circumstances which will be named when considering diseases. Many are the dogs I have had sent me for advice, with no other complaint than want of appetite. As a rule, they are enormously over-fed. A week's spare, plain diet, and a dose of castor-oil, has generally produced the desired result.

Beer, wine, and spirits should never be allowed, except medicinally. Some dogs are particularly fond of the former. I recently had a mastiff-bitch (Duchess) who would greedily lap it whenever she had the chance.

Water.—There are few animals to which the denial of water is felt to a greater degree than the dog. Whether in health or disease, water is requisite in assisting the natural functions of the body.

With regard to the feeding of puppies, I have little to say; when weaning, milk is undoubtedly the most suitable diet, and to this, as time goes on, may be gradually added a little bread or boiled oatmeal-porridge, or Spratt's puppy food. Animal food (except an occasional bone) is not advisable in any breed of young dog, until four or five months old, and it should then be *gradually, not suddenly*, introduced into the diet.

EXERCISE.

Exercise is equally beneficial to canine as it is to human health. The mind is diverted not only in the performance of the act, but also in the novelty of fresh scenes, new faces and objects, bright weather and pure and bracing air.

To the young dog it is indispensable. Compare the animal, which, from a puppy, has had full freedom, with one cooped up until it has arrived at maturity; in the former Nature has asserted her right, and, unchecked, given symmetry, full development, and health; in the latter, crooked legs, deformed body, and stunted growth is the picture she presents of an interference with her laws. Who will deny the fact that some poor creatures are kept on the chain from one month's end to another after growth is complete, with the idea that it is then not hurtful? Fallacy! Out at the elbows and bowed arms, with spreading toes, will in time result, and become a permanent deformity. Again, loose such an one, and the exuberance of spirits immediately manifested, the wild scampers of delight until exhaustion takes place, will exhibit even to the doubtful mind the enjoyment of freedom and exercise.

Other tender little morsels of caninity are carried, protected from every breath of wind, in the arms of their mistress, and thus have, as it is termed *"their airing,"* the most invigorating and muscle-developing part of it being denied them; and so they go their way yelping and snarling, in all probability with envy at the gambols of those taking exercise in a natural manner.

Exercise should not be allowed so as to produce undue fatigue, as in carriage-followers and sporting-dogs; in the latter, I am aware, it is under certain circumstances unavoidable.

It should also, if possible, take place before feeding, or, if impracticable, not until some hours afterwards. Running, or long walks on a full stomach, is liable to produce fits of the worst kind, and many a dog have I seen so affected.

Again, as I have previously observed, the meal is relished far more after exercise than before it; of this we have proof in ourselves. Finally, locomotion is especially necessary in indoor dogs, for the performance of the natural evacuatory acts, and thereby continuance of health and purity.

Erasmus Wilson's remarks on the subject will not be misapplied here: " Well-directed exercise favours the preservation of the general health by calling into direct action the majority of the organs of the body; and it also acts powerfully on the skin by stimulating its functions, increasing its temperature, awakening its tone, and subjecting it to a current of atmosphere favourable for its respiratory offices."

WASHING.

Washing in moderation adds greatly to the health and comfort of the dog. I say in moderation, because some persons are never satisfied unless their favourites are submerged twice or three times a week in water, and lathered over with soft-soap (the latter to kill the fleas). This is a great mistake, and three results of such a custom are—blindness, deafness, and canker.

Long-haired dogs require ablution more than short-haired ones, and usually have a natural inclination for water. The frequency of washing will depend to some extent on the manner in which the coat is kept; if regularly brushed and combed, once a month is quite sufficient; under any circumstances a weekly bath is more than ample. The water should be a little more than tepid, and soap used merely enough to create a lather; as its alkaline properties, if used in excess, render it an irritant to the skin (where careful rinsing is adopted, the caution is almost needless). This, however, as I know from experience, is so frequently not carried out, that the soap in the process of wiping is rubbed in, and gives rise to the irritation named. When, then, thoroughly cleansed, the animal should be finally douched in cold water, rubbed dry before the fire, if the weather is raw, and immediately after allowed some brisk exercise. Outdoor dogs will dry themselves after their own fashion, and a good bed of straw will be sufficient to complete the toilet. In those breeds which have an inclination for water, as Newfoundlands, retrievers, and spaniels, the lake, river, or canal will afford the best means of ablution.

GROOMING.

This is especially advisable in all dogs where fineness of coat. kindness of skin, cleanliness, and health are desired.

Combing and brushing in long-haired dogs is absolutely necessary to prevent the hair matting, and to preserve its character. In large breeds, as the mastiff tribe, it is as requisite for good appearance as in the horse. Once daily, twice if possible, I have my mastiffs thoroughly groomed; they enjoy it, the sensation affords them pleasure, and the dog accustomed to the practice will look for it as regularly as he does his meals. The brush is a far better remedy for glossy coats than nitre, sulphur, antimony, or arsenic.

KENNEL ARRANGEMENT.

In dealing with this subject I shall merely make a few passing practical remarks on ordinary kennel-arrangement, though they are not particularly applicable to one breed more than another.

The kennel should neither have an easterly unsheltered aspect nor damp foundation. If dogs so placed escape kennel lameness and rheumatism, it is more from mere chance or constitution, than from the sanitary condition of the locality. Good air, dry atmosphere, and sunlight are as essential to health and spirits in the canine as the human subject. It is all very well to argue as what dogs are in a state of nature and what they are in the domestic state. Nature and art in kennel-management are not compatible. The South Sea Islander thrives in the hot humid atmosphere to which he is indigenous, and becomes fat upon the flesh of his own species; but he must be artificialised, so to speak, and civilised before he can accommodate himself to our colder latitudes and description of food. So with the dog; domestication produces in him a like result; he accommodates himself to it because he is artificialised; give him the bare ground for his bed, expose him to bleak cold winds, and allow no shelter from wet, and disease will inevitably follow.

The kennel, then, should be dry, sunny, and cheerful; this is especially necessary for puppies, for the circumstances under which they attain their growth, as will be hereafter mentioned, will influence their disposition when they arrive at maturity.

The benches should be elevated at least eighteen inches above the ground, and the planks either drilled with holes or placed an inch apart for the escape of wet, and for ventilation of the bed. A strip of wood along the edge will keep the bedding on, and prevent puppies from slipping off. To insure dryness of the walls, I nail boarding round, with shavings between.

With regard to the flooring, cement undoubtedly forms the best and cleanest. Many different opinions have been expressed as to what it should be covered with. Sand is not unfrequently recommended; this, however, is not good for dogs' feet, it creates irritation between the toes, and gives rise to what is known in cattle as "foul." Fine shavings or sawdust are decidedly preferable, and should be put down fresh every morning after first removing the soiled materials. A little clean bedding scattered over the latter to give it an appearance of cleanliness, is like wearing a clean shirt on a dirty body, or gloves on filthy hands—the evil is still there, disguised.

Washing or swilling down the floor is a necessary office, but it is often carried to extremes, and then becomes an evil by engendering a continual damp, and acting as a fruitful source of rheumatism and kennel-lameness. Once a week is quite often enough for this duty. After the place has been thoroughly swept and mopped, I always have ashes thrown over the floor; these absorb any wet that may have lodged in sunken places or between the bricks, and in old, somewhat uneven, and broken floors they are of great service. In half an hour they may be swept off, and a little crude carbolic acid dropped here and there, after which dress with the sawdust or shavings.

Mr. H. D. Kingdon, whose experience in the management of dogs, particularly mastiffs, is considerable, ranging over a period of forty years, and for whose sound opinion I entertain the highest respect, informs me his kennels are constructed in stables and shedding, and formed into loose boxes; the flooring is composed of asphalte, and is sloped from the sides to the centre, and outwards to communicate with the common drain. On this flooring he has a slight sprinkling of air-slacked lime, and this is littered over with fern. The bench is composed of a loose wooden floor, on planks separated a short distance, and nailed across joists. (Fig. I.)

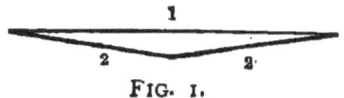

FIG. I.

The top line 1 is the bench, the oblique lines 2 2 the sloping asphalte-floor.

For full-grown dogs he uses four-legged bedsteads similar to a table, with a ledge round the outside to prevent them getting their legs between it and the wall, and sufficient space is left to walk on two sides of the said table.

DISINFECTION.

The disinfection of a kennel is a matter of great importance, for unless the habitation and ground is sweet and clean we cannot expect our dogs to be healthy and pleasant companions.

An agent which possesses an overpowering smell, concealing an offensive one without destroying its disease-producing power, is not a true disinfectant. The infective principle of contagion or infection must be met by a stronger and exterminating force.

When disease invades a kennel, especially if it be of an infectious or contagious character, the employment of genuine disinfectants is imperative. Amongst those chiefly in use may be mentioned Condy's Fluid, Sir Wm. Burnett's, Chloride of Lime, various carbolic and coal tar preparations, and last, but not least, " Sanitas." The latter apart from its powerful deoderizing properties, possesses not only a fragrant, but a refreshing odour, and has therefore attractions—especially for the pet house-dog's toilet. At canine exhibitions, where on other occasions the effluvia from the urine and intestinal excreta have been controlled only by an objectional amount of carbolic disinfectant, almost equally overpowering, Sanitas has been found to do its work pleasantly and effectually. I have long used it in various forms in my practice, especially the post-mortem department, in which I should feel incomplete without at least possessing Sanitas soap, which I also recommend to be used in washing dogs after suffering from skin disease, especially mange.

ADMINISTRATION OF MEDICINE.

This is often a troublesome process with canine patients; the usually affectionate, obedient, and harmless pet becomes (*through fear and mental excitement*) snappish and resistful. And a general complaint the veterinary attendant hears is: " It's no use, sir, we can't give him the medicine; the more we try, the more he struggles, fights, and bites." This in the majority of cases is so. The reason for which is that, as a rule, strength *versus* system is the plan adopted. As with ourselves, so with the dog, there is a right and a wrong way in the taking or administering of medicine.

The medicine is in the form of a pill or draught. The former may be given one of two ways; first, taking the animal in the lap, or rearing him up between the knees, the upper part of the mouth is then grasped with the hand

and the lips on either side thrust between the teeth; security against the operator being bitten is gained by the dog being afraid of biting and hurting himself. The head is then elevated, the pill is dropped into the posterior part of the mouth, and the jaws immediately closed and held so; and if the animal refuses to swallow it, placing the fingers on or compressing the nostrils will speedily compel him to do so. Pushing the pill down with the finger is injudicious and unnecessary. The other and more advisable way, if it can be contrived, is by deception—*i.e.*, clothing the pill in a little meat, and throwing it to the animal to bolt.

With regard to draughts, they should be administered as follows:—The animal being placed in the same position as for the pill, the angle of the mouth is drawn away from the teeth, and into the pouch thus formed the medicine may be poured; the same means as recommended in the former will, if he refuses, compel him to swallow it.

Some forms of medicine, more or less tasteless from the minuteness of the dose, may be given in a little milk or broth, which the animal laps voluntarily.

NURSING.

It is, I think, necessary before entering on the general subject of diseases, that I should say a few words about nursing.

As in human, so in canine practice, good nursing is one of the greatest helps the medical attendant can have: indeed, it may almost be said to be indispensable in the treatment of disease.

Warmth, comfort, cleanliness, pure air, good food, and water, regularity in the administration of medicine where it has to be given, kindness, watchfulness in the progress or abatement of certain symptoms, are all matters requiring the supervision of the nurse.

In short, the health of the patient is in the majority of cases quite as much in the hands of the nurse as of the professional attendant, and the fault so often, in all classes of practice, attached to the medical treatment would generally be more correctly placed to the lack of attention on the part of those on whom the general care of the patient devolves. It is always, therefore, advisable to let the latter know the full extent of his or her responsibility; and that though the charge is, as they may express it, "*but a dog*," it is endued with imagination, instincts, and thought, has a language of its own, is sensible of neglect, harshness, yea, even cross looks on the part of those ministering to it, and to a degree rarely exhibited in other of the lower animals.

The two then—the practitioner and nurse—acting in combination, and working to the same end, if they do not reap the desired reward of their labours, have at least the satisfaction of knowing they did their best for the patient under their care.

CHAPTER II.

DISEASES OF THE RESPIRATORY ORGANS.

CATARRH,	PLEURISY,
INFLUENZA,	PNEUMONIA,
LARYNGITIS,	CONSUMPTION,
BRONCHITIS,	POLYPUS,
ASTHMA,	OZÆNA.

CATARRH,

Or what is commonly known as "a cold," consists of a febrile or inflammatory condition of the mucous membranes. When confined to the eyes and nostrils it its termed *Coryza*, from Καρα, the head, and ζεω, to boil; signifying a fevered condition, or cold in the head. If it extends to the mucous membrane of the bronchial tubes, it gives rise to what is termed *bronchitis*. If to the alimentary tract, we have an enteritic or gastro-enteritic catarrh. The two latter are not unfrequent in distemper.

The usual causes of common or simple catarrh are damp, cold, or contagion.

Symptoms.—Increased secretion of mucus from the membranes affected, eyes watery, nose hot and dry, shiverings, sneezing, and sometimes cough, languor, fever, and consequent thirst.

As the disease proceeds, these symptoms increase in severity, the mucous secretion becomes thicker, respiration impeded, the shiverings more frequent, languor greater, urine high-coloured, bowels constipated, and stools coated with slime.

Treatment.—Fortunately for the patient, the old system of depletion by bleeding and physic is with men of science no longer in use. The administration of diffusible stimulants at the onset, with careful attention to warmth and comfort generally suffices to effect a cure.

>   Spt. Camphor .... 1 ounce.
>   Spt. Æther Nit. .... 2 ounces.
>   Liq. Ammon. Acetat. .... 4 ,,

A teaspoonful twice or three times a day for a small dog, double for a large one.

Where the fever runs high, tartar emetic, ½—1 grain, or Dover's powder, 5—10 grains, may be given daily; but this usually in the dog is uncalled for. If the mucous discharge has a tendency to lodge in the facial sinuses, which a rattling respiration with frequent snuffling will denote, steaming the head will encourage its outward flow, and afford considerable relief.

The diet requires very little alteration, warm broth, beef-tea, or milk, are most suitable. The liability of catarrh to extend to other structures must not be overlooked. Undue and premature exposure to damp and cold during the attack should therefore be avoided. If much debility attends the complaint, from 5—10 drops of tinct. ferri in 1—2 teaspoonfuls of cod-liver oil should, after the first three or four days, take the place of the first prescribed medicine. Constipation is best relieved with enemas, or a little salad oil—purgatives are strongly contra-indicated.

INFLUENZA,

Or epidemic catarrh, is similar in character to the foregoing disease, but it is attended with greater prostration, and is more highly contagious. The direct cause is unknown; it was supposed by the Italians to be due to some stellar influence, hence the term *Influenza*, signifying influence. It is now generally believed to arise from a peculiar condition of the atmosphere, but in what that condition consists is still a mystery. Dogs are liable to it at any age, and at all periods of the year. Spring and autumn are, however, the seasons in which it is most frequently seen, and this tends to prove that if cold and damp do not actually produce influenza, they may be certainly looked upon as predisposing agents.

Symptoms.—These vary somewhat in their manifestation. Frequently the disease is ushered in with scarcely any premonitory symptoms, beyond extreme lassitude. In some sneezing, redness of the eyes, and flow of tears are the first observed. In others sore throat, loss of appetite, nausea and vomiting, are alone present. Whilst in others, again, cough, expectoration, and muco-purulent discharge from the nostrils almost immediately follow the first signs of lassitude. Whatever form, however, it primarily assumes, it invariably terminates in the one which is diagnostic of influenza, and the symptoms named become more or less associated; and added to these, we have hurried respiration, increased weak pulse, scanty and turbid urine, fæces dry and slimy, hot skin, dry furred tongue, internal temperature high, and in the latter stages an œdematous condition of the limbs. In severe types that are allowed to run on unchecked, pleurisy and effusion in the chest become complicated with it.

Treatment.—Bodily warmth, proper ventilation, and diffusible stimulants are first indicated.

The medicine prescribed in the preceding disease is equally adapted to this; and where there is extreme debility the tinct. ferri should follow, or if œdematous, the iodide of iron in the same proportions. Linseed-meal poultices, or mustard or ammonia embrocation, may be applied to the throat if swollen or sore, and steaming the head will be attended with benefit. Purgatives should on no account be resorted to. Impaction of fæces can best be removed by means of plain enemas.

The diet must be nourishing and easy of digestion, as broth, beef-tea, gruel, or milk. For chest complications, refer to treatment under their respective heads.

LARYNGITIS.

Inflammation of the larynx, the upper or vocal part of the windpipe, is an affection very commonly met with in canine practice. Highly pampered dogs, particularly pugs and yard dogs with deficient shelter, are most liable to laryngitis. I have also observed what may be designated a temporary or simple form of it, in sheep-dogs when gathering flocks together, and the same is not uncommon at and after dog-shows, due to incessant barking.

Predisposing Causes.—Frequent and long-continued barking; a previous attack of the same disease.

Exciting Causes.—Exposure to wet and cold, the presence of foreign matter, injuries, irritating inhalations, or extension of neighbouring inflammation.

Symptoms.—Hoarseness, cough easily induced by external pressure, increased respiration and salivary secretion, frothy discharge from the nostrils, difficulty in swallowing, and pyrexia; pulse small, hard, and frequent. These symptoms, if not checked, rapidly increase, and the patient dies from suffocation.

Treatment.[*]—Of course removal of the cause is primarily

---

[*] (*Œsterreichische Vierteljahresschrift*, 1873.) Harms injected 0·07 grammes of morphine hydrochlorate, in solution, beneath the skin of a dog which had been suffering from a dry laryngeal cough for four weeks. For two hours after the injection, the animal exhibited every symptom of complete narcotism, with total loss of consciousness and sensibility. In the course of eight hours it manifested sensibility

necessary, and then treatment should be directed to the effect. If the disease is early recognised, mild counterirritants to the larynx externally, hot fomentation or linseed-meal poultice, an emetic, and a warm moist atmosphere, will generally effect a cure. In fact, a dog with laryngitis requires much the same treatment as a child with croup. Where the symptoms have become so aggravated that suffocation is threatened, tracheotomy is indicated, and all further treatment must be external. Attempting to drench a dog at this stage is attended with great danger, from the extremely irritable condition of the throat. A violent fit of coughing, ending in asphyxia, would, in all probability, be the result of such a proceeding. (For the extraction or removal of foreign matters, see "Choking.")

The diet should consist entirely of slops of a mucilaginous nature, as broth, beef-tea, or milk thickened with isinglass.

CHRONIC LARYNGITIS

Is not an unfrequent sequel of the former. It is characterised by continued hoarseness, with periodical exacerbations, specially induced by over-exertion, or the sudden inhalation of cold air, a dry husky cough, and mucous expectoration. We may relieve the symptoms, but when finally established the disease is incurable. Iron, cod-liver oil, and an occasional dose of tartar emetic are the best medicinal agents. Local treatment is often beneficial. Biniodide of mercury—1 part to 16 of lard—applied twice

---

when pricked with a pin, and could raise itself on its four limbs. In twenty-four hours it was able to stagger into its kennel, but it had no appetite. In two days and a half it was as lively as before the injection; and until it left the hospital a week afterwards, the cough had not returned.—(*Veterinary Journal*, Sept., 1875.)

weekly, until sufficient irritation is produced, or the insertion of a small seton, is advisable.

BRONCHITIS.

Bronchitis is an affection to which dogs are very liable. It may exist as a primary or secondary disease—*i.e.*, it may be present alone, or as an extension of catarrh or other respiratory affections. Likewise it may be acute or chronic.

Causes.—Cold, damp, irritating inhalation, neglected or protracted catarrh, or extension of other respiratory affections.

Symptoms.—These will depend on the extent of the bronchial inflammation; if the malady is only confined to the larger branches of the bronchi, the breathing will be much less disturbed than when the subdivisions are involved, particularly the smaller ones. The cough in the former will also be less frequent, louder and more sonorous, with little or no expectoration. This form is, however, rarely seen in the dog; or, if so, only to be quickly succeeded by the more complicated one. I shall therefore describe the general symptoms of the latter in its acute stage.

The respiration is hurried and difficult, the breath hot, an incessant wheezing cough (which ultimately becomes dry and short), succeeded by expectoration and vomiting accompanying it. The expectoration is usually frothy, and sometimes mingled with blood. The eyes are red and inflamed, the nose dry and hot, mouth devoid of moisture, tongue parched and coated with brown fur. The pulse is quick and small, and the heart's action jerking. On auscultation, the latter emits a thumping noise, and the diagnostic mucous rattle of bronchitis is very distinctly heard. A thin mucous discharge from the nostrils usually takes place soon after bronchitis sets in, and, as the disease proceeds, this becomes copious, muco-purulent, and accompanied by violent sneezing.

As the malady advances all these symptoms increase in severity, and the poor animal dies either from sheer exhaustion, acute inflammatory fever, or asphyxia.

Treatment.—Immediately symptoms of acute bronchitis are observed, it is advisable to place the animal in a moderately warm, sufficiently ventilated, and dry habitation. With regard to medicinal agents, from 1 to 3 grains of tartar emetic, in proportion to the size of the patient, is at the onset very beneficial. If the disease proceeds, the following mixture may be used:

    Spt. Camph. .... ½ ounce.
    Spt. Æther Nit. .... 1 „
    Liquorice Extract......................... 4 „

A teaspoonful for a small dog, double for a full-sized terrier, treble for a large dog, twice or three times a day.

When the cough is very troublesome, a dose of the following every now and then, in the same proportions as the above, will afford relief:

    Tinct. Opii .... 20 drops.
    Essence of Anisi .... 30 „
    Liquorice Extract .... 1 ounce.
    Linseed Tea .... 2 „

                  or

    Chlorodyne .... 1 drachm.
    Chloroform .... 1 „
    Glycerine .... 2 ounces.

Similarly administered.

When it fails to do so, an emetic is generally beneficial. Counter-irritation is also very useful in the shape of hot linseed-meal poultices to the front of the chest, or, in severe cases, mustard-plasters or turpentine embrocations. With small dogs considerable benefit arises from moistening the atmosphere with steam, which is easily accomplished in a room with an ordinary bronchitis kettle, and if the symptoms are unusually urgent, the steam may be rendered sedative by putting a few bruised poppy-heads in the water.

Warm broths or bread and milk form the most suitable diet.

From the susceptibility of a return of the malady, unnecessary exposure to cold or damp should be avoided, and, until a thorough restoration to health is established, the animal should not be allowed to return to his natural and ordinary life.

CHRONIC BRONCHITIS.

This is usually a sequel of the acute form, and is more generally met with in old animals. It rarely leaves the patient, and increases in severity in the cold seasons of the year.

The symptoms are invariable; cough of a husky character, shortness of breath, increased with exertion, expectoration, and retching.

Treatment.—This consists in alleviating the symptoms, and avoiding unnecessary exposure to cold and damp. Occasional stimulants combined with iron form the best medicinal treatment, and the cough mixture prescribed in acute form is also useful.

VERMINOUS BRONCHITIS IN DOGS.[*]

"Early in the month of January I was asked by Principal McEachran, F.R.C.V.S., to aid him in the investiga-

---

[*] A Paper read before the Montreal Veterinary Medical Association, March 29th, 1877, by William Osler, M.D., L.R.C.P. Lond.; Fellow of the Royal Microscopical Society, London; Vice-President of the Montreal Veterinary Medical Association; Professor of Physiology in McGill University, and in the Veterinary College, Montreal.

tion of a disease which had broken out among the pups at the kennels of the Montreal Hunt Club, and which was believed to be of a pneumonic nature. On proceeding to the place we found that the affection was confined almost exclusively to animals under eight months' old, and that it had already proved fatal in several instances. At the time of the visit only one pup was ill, presenting symptoms of diminished air-space in the chest. In order to ascertain the exact condition of the lungs, one of the pups, which had died a day or two previously, and had meanwhile frozen stiff, was ordered to be sent to the Veterinary College for dissection. On the following day it was found at the autopsy that, in addition to the pneumonia, there were numerous small parasitic worms in the trachea and bronchial tubes. Knowing how subject many of the lower animals are to bronchial strongyles, I did not think it very remarkable that they should occur in the dog. On referring, however, to Dr. Cobbold's list of entozoa infesting the dog, I was surprised not to find a bronchial strongyle mentioned, and a further search through the standard works on veterinary medicine and helminthology proving fruitless, I then wrote to the editors of the *Veterinarian* asking for information on the subject. They very kindly replied in a short editorial note in the March number, stating 'that,' so far as their knowledge extends, 'no such cases have been placed formally on record,' but Dr. Cobbold tells them 'that one such instance has been verbally brought under his notice, though not in such a way as to be thoroughly convincing.'

"I shall proceed now to speak of the symptoms and pathology of the disease, then give a description of the parasite itself, and make a few general remarks.

"*Symptoms.*—Only five of the diseased animals were seen during life, and that rather irregularly, on account of the distance of the kennels from the city. However, I have obtained some important details from the keeper, and a case which was brought to the infirmary and kept for some time was made the subject of clinical study.

"Among the initial symptoms disinclination for food and exercise, together with an unsteadiness of gait, amounting in some of the cases to a subparalytic condition of the hinder extremities, were the most evident. In fully half of the cases convulsions occurred. There was rarely diarrhœa or any other symptom referable to gastro-intestinal disorder. Cough was not a prominent symptom, being absent in many of the cases. When present, it was short and husky, 'not,' as the keeper said, ' the regular distemper cough.' In the case brought to the infirmary the cough was well marked, and was dry and short. The pulse and respirations were increased, and the temperature elevated. Towards the close all food was refused, and even when fed the soup given was commonly vomited. Death took place in most instances quietly, though sometimes during a convulsion, and the keeper noticed that the pups which lasted the longest had the most fits. The duration of the disease ranged from three days to a week or even ten days. The whole epidemic lasted about seven weeks.

"Altogether fifteen couples were attacked, all of which, with the exception of three couples of old dogs, were under eight months old. Of the old dogs three had the disease badly, but only one died. Of the total number affected four and a half couples recovered, so that twenty-one animals were lost. The dogs which recovered are now in their usual health, though not in such good condition as they were before.

"With regard to the hygienic surroundings of the animals it may be stated that, at present, the kennels are in an old house which stands by itself on the Government property known as Logan's Farm, at the east end of the city. It is isolated, being at some distance from any other building, and is situated on an elevated ridge overlooking the Quebec suburbs.

"The disease showed itself during a remarkably cold spell; indeed, for the first three weeks of the epidemic the thermometer was almost constantly below zero. It was first observed in two or three pups of four conples which were kept by themselves in a separate room, 14ft. by 8ft.; the floor being covered with straw, which was changed every week. There was a cupboard in the room, and in this the pups slept. This room was on the exposed side of the house, and, according to the keeper, was always very cold. The rest of the animals were kept in tolerably roomy quarters, though at night, with the doors closed, I do not think the ventilation would be sufficient. During the day they had free access to a large yard. The food consisted of porridge and cooked horseflesh, which were given either separately or boiled together. They got nothing else. The oatmeal was of good quality, nor did I find in portions of the food removed from the feeding-pans anything which afforded the slightest clue to the origin of the disease.

"*Pathology.*—*Post-mortem* examinations were made in eight cases. The following notes were dictated at the time:

"CASE I.—Autopsy eighteen hours after death. Body that of a well-nourished, half-grown, fox-hound bitch. On opening the thorax the lungs only partially collapse; the lower borders of the lobes are firm to the touch and dark in colour. The vessels in the lower mediastinum look full, and the tissues in that region are blood-stained. Pericardium natural; heart appears of normal size; right auricle filled with dark grumous clots, which extend into the vessels and are here decolourised. Right ventricle distended with dark, semi-coagulated blood; the conus arteriosus is filled with a perfectly decolourised clot, which passes into the pulmonary artery to the third and fourth divisions. The left auricle contains a small coagulum. The left ventricle contains no blood, but the whole cavity is occupied by a firm milk-white thrombus, which is connected through the mitral valve with the one in the auricle, while a prolongation from it extends into the aorta.

"*Lungs.*—After removal, on inverting them, a quantity of dirty brown frothy fluid escapes through the larynx.

"The anterior and middle lobes and the anterior half of the posterior lobe of the right lung are solidified, being of a dark reddish-brown colour, and contrasting strongly with the unaffected parts. The pleural surfaces are smooth, and there is no exudation. On section the lung-tissue is of a dark red colour, the surface of the section finely granular, and bathed with a quantity of reddish-brown serum. On close inspection it is seen that the air-cells are uniformly filled with a solid exudation; attempts at inflation of the affected portions with air are unsuccessful. Portions excised sink at once when placed in water. In the left lung the apex of the anterior lobe, the whole of the middle, and the root of one of the posterior lobes are in the same condition. The portions of the organs not diseased are of a rosy red externally, and on section contain much blood and frothy serum. Between the healthy and diseased parts there is a zone of intense hyperæmia.

"*Trachea.*—On slitting up the windpipe the mucous membrane is found covered with a dark frothy mucus. The membrane looks pale and natural to within an inch of the bifurcation, but at this point it becomes reddened, and uneven from the projection of irregular little masses of a greyish-yellow colour, which on close inspection are found to be localised swellings of the membrane, containing small parasitic worms, the white bodies of which can be seen lying upon and partially imbedded in these elevations. They are most abundant just at the bifurcation, at the lower part of which several have emerged, forming an elevation three or four lines in height. About the orifices of the second divisions these little masses are also seen, and the whole mucous membrane of this region is deeply congested, and somewhat swollen. Very few of the worms are found lying free on the mucous membrane; almost all of them are attached to the masses or buried in them. The smaller tubes, especially those leading to the diseased portions of the lungs, are filled with a dirty brown fluid, and on squeezing any portion of the organ quantities of it can be expelled.

"The *bronchial glands* are swollen and enlarged.

"The *spleen* appears healthy.

"The *left kidney* contains a large amount of blood; otherwise looks natural. Nothing unusual in the right one.

"The *stomach* contains a few ounces of dark brown fluid; mucous membrane is pale. Large veins full.

"The *duodenum* contains a bile-stained mucus, and on pressing the gall-bladder, bile flows from the papilla biliaria.

"*Jejunum* and *ileum* contain a dirty black material adhering to the mucous membrane.

"One tænia elliptica and one ascaris marginata are found in the jejunum.

"Large bowel healthy.

"*Liver* firm, dark red in colour, lobules indistinct, hepatic veins full, gall-bladder contains a small amount of bile. There is a clot in the portal vein.

"*Brain.*—Nothing abnormal about the membranes. Substance of good consistence and apparently healthy.

"In the following cases I have condensed the original account.

"CASE 2.—A five months old dog pup, which had been ill a week.

"Extensive pneumonic consolidation of the lungs, involving the lower part of the anterior lobe, and scattered patches in the middle lobe on the left side, and half the posterior lobe on the right. On section the solidified parts presented the appearance already described in the preceding case, and the unaffected portions are in a state of engorgement. On slitting up the trachea and bronchial tubes much frothy blood-tinged serum escaped, but no trace of any parasites can be found either in the tubes or parenchyma of the lungs. No ova or young parasites can be found in the blood of the cavities of the heart or of the pulmonary artery.

"Abdominal viscera appear healthy, though, owing to the obstruction in the lesser circulation, the blood-vessels are engorged. A few ascarides in the intestine and one small tænia elliptica.

"CASE 3.—Dog pup, six months old.

"In the left lung there are scattered patches of pneumonia in the anterior lobe, one or two are in the middle lobe, and half a dozen, the size of marbles, closely set together in the upper part of posterior lobe. In the right lung the anterior lobe is solid in an area 3″ by 1″, extending along the lower free border, and through the whole thickness. Small patches occur here and there over the other lobes. In this instance the inflamed spots are smaller, and not so extensive as in the other cases. On slitting up the trachea the mucous membrane looks healthy to within 2″ of the bifurcation, when it becomes swollen, dark red in colour, and thickly scattered over with the elevated granular masses noticed in the first case, attached to and in which numerous small white worms can be seen. A stream of water of considerable force does not wash them away, but shows that each little elevation consists of a nest of the parasites. They extend to the tubes of the second order, and are specially abundant at the bifurcation itself, and about the orifices of the first tubes given off from the main bronchi. The small tubes are filled up with a frothy serum. Two of the worms are found far in the mucus.

"Stomach and intestines appear healthy, except the lower portion of the ileum, which is congested.

"In this region ten specimens of dochmius trigonocephalus occur, and further up in the bowel eight ascarides.

"CASE 4.—A six months old dog pup brought to the infirmary and died the next day.

"In the left lung the anterior and middle lobes and the lower free border of the posterior lobe are solidified.

"In the right lung the lower three-fourths of the anterior and middle lobes, and the lower fourth of the posterior lobe, are in the same condition. Pleural surfaces involved. The posterior half of the windpipe contains upon the mucous membrane of its lower wall about a dozen small red patches, which extend in the axis of the tube; some appearing like linear streaks due to the injection of a few vessels. In all of them the presence of parasites can be determined, though in some of the smaller only one is found. They become more numerous about the bifurcation and in the main bronchi, occupying chiefly the lower wall. The masses are isolated and the mucous membrane between them intensely injected. None are found in the second divisions of the tubes.

"Abdominal organs contain a good deal of blood. Mucous membrane of stomach and intestines looks healthy. The large bowel contains a quantity of consistent fæces. Six ascarides in the duodenum; six specimens of dochmius trigonocephalus in the jejunum, and ten specimens of tricocephalus affinis in the cæcum.

"Blood of heart and veins examined; nothing abnormal found.

"CASE 5.—Seven months old bitch pup. Considerable emaciation. Scattered areas of pneumonia throughout both lungs; not quite so extensive as in Case 4, but presenting similar characters. From an inch in front of the bifurcation of the trachea to the bronchi of the second order, the whole mucous membrane is transformed into an irregular greyish-yellow granular structure, upon which the bodies of numerous white worms can be plainly seen. Two sizes may be distinguished, one longer and of a more opaque white, which subsequent examination showed to be the female, the other shorter, thinner, and paler. In this case, even about the orifices of the third division of the bronchi, a few nests of the parasite can be seen. In the mucus from the smaller tubes a few of the adult worms occur, and on spreading it out on glass slips, and examining with a low power, a few ova and free embryos are seen.

" Blood of heart and veins contains no parasites.

" Nothing abnormal in the stomach or intestines; a large specimen of tænia elliptica in the latter, also a few ascarides.

" CASE 6.—A thin, badly nourished dog pup, six months old. Lungs present numerous patches of consolidation, involving on the right side the lower half of the anterior lobe and a large piece of the posterior lobe. On the left side the free borders of the anterior and middle lobes for almost two inches from the margin, and a broad strip along the upper part of the posterior lobe.

" Trachea and bronchi healthy; mucous membrane of the tubes in the affected parts congested, but no parasites in the membrane or in the lung-tissue.

" Stomach and intestines appear natural; a few ascarides in the latter. Nothing abnormal found in the blood.

"CASE 7.—Dog pup, seven months old. The autopsy, which was made at the same time as the previous case, reveals a similar condition of the lungs, and an entire absence of any parasites either in the tubes or in the parenchyma of the lungs. Nothing unusual in the abdominal organs. The tænia elliptica and five or six ascarides in the jejunum.

" CASE 8.—A fine, well-grown dog pup, eight months old. Had been ill a week.

" Lungs contain pneumonic areas of considerable extent; in the right involving the entire apex with the dependent border, and a small portion of the posterior lobe near the diaphragm. In the left lung almost the whole of the middle lobe, and the root of the posterior, are especially affected.

" On opening the windpipe the discrete elevations above

described upon the mucous membrane about the bifurcation are very distinct, and the worms can be seen in them. The appearance is very like that met with in Case 4, and the description need not be repeated. No parasites in the intestines. Nothing abnormal found in the blood.

"The general and specific characters of the worm may be defined as follows :

"*Strongylus canis bronchialis.*—A slender nematode helminth, body filiform, the female measuring about one-fourth of an inch in length, the male smaller, measuring one-sixth to one-eighth of an inch ; head conical, mouth simple, unprovided with papillæ; tail of female obtuse, anal and generative orifices terminal, opening by a cloaca ; ovarian tube containing one row of eggs, which, in the mature species, have developed into slender-coiled embryos ; tail of the male somewhat pointed ; penis consists of a double spiculum of a yellowish-brown colour ; mode of reproduction viviparous.

"Only occasionally, as stated above, were the worms found lying free upon the bronchial membrane ; as a rule, they lay imbedded in a localised granular swelling of the mucosa,

 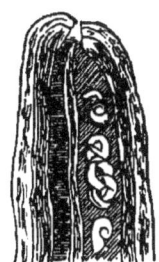

FIG. 2.
Head of Male Worm.

FIG. 3.
Tail of Female Worm, showing the young Embryos.

from which portions of them protruded. They could readily be pulled out with a pair of fine forceps, but a stream of water did not wash them away. In several of the cases examined (more especially Case 4) the whole mucous membrane of the affected part appeared rough and irregular, as if ulcerated, and innumerable parasites lay upon and in it. The mature females could easily be distinguished, not only by their larger size, but by the opaque whiteness of their bodies. The majority of the female worms examined were immature, and did not contain developed ova. The males were not nearly so numerous as the females. Forms intermediate between the adult worms and the young embryos (some of which, as already mentioned, existed free in the mucus) were not met with.

"The occurrence in the bronchial tubes of the lower animals of nematoid worms belonging to the genus strongylus is by no means uncommon. Owing to the irritation caused by their development in the mucous membrane an inflammation of the tubes is produced, hence the affection is known by the names of parasitic or verminous bronchitis, popularly called 'husk' or 'hoose.' It is not altogether unknown in man, but very few instances are on record. Infesting the domestic animals there are three well-recognised species of strongylus: the S. filaria of the sheep and goat; S. paradoxus of the pig; and S. micrurus of the calf, more rarely of the horse and ass. In calves and lambs parasitic bronchitis often constitutes a serious and fatal epidemic, so much so that in the latter it goes by the name of *the lamb disease.* So far as I know, no epidemic of the kind has been noticed in Canada. The species I have here described differs in several particulars from either of the above mentioned, and is most probably new to science.

"The origin of the epidemic must, I am afraid, like that of so many other diseases, remain obscure. We have absolutely nothing to aid us in forming an opinion on the subject. There had been no change in the locality nor in the food. The straw upon which the dogs slept was of the ordinary kind, and the usual attention had been paid to

changing it and also to the general sanitary condition of the place. The disease broke out, too, during a spell of very severe weather, when the food left in the pans froze quickly. The course of the epidemic was short, lasting between six and seven weeks, a sufficient time, however, to destroy almost all the pups in the kennels.

"The mode of invasion in parasitic disease of the bronchial tubes has been, and still is, a matter of much dispute, some observers maintaining that 'the ova and young parasites taken up with the food in the first place gain access from the alimentary canal to the circulation;' others hold the view that they pass directly from the mouth to the trachea, or that the ova are inhaled by the breath. The former view is the one most generally entertained, and it is urged in its favour that the presence of the worms has been determined in the cavities of the heart and in the blood-vessels, as well as in the intestines. Now, in the epidemic under consideration, I think this view does not meet the case. Supposing the young embryos to have been ingested and to have gained access to the branches of the portal vein, they would then be carried to the right side of the heart, and from thence to the lungs, by the pulmonary artery, the capillaries of which ramify in the lung-substance alone, a situation in which the parasites did not occur. To get to the bronchial mucous membrane they must be returned by the pulmonary veins to the left side of the heart, enter the aorta, and pass out by the small bronchial arteries which supply the tubes—an exceeding roundabout and somewhat improbable route. It is to be remembered that young strongyles have been found capable, like many other nematoid worms, of reviving on the application of moisture after a desiccation of a month or more, and even after immersion in spirits of wine and solutions of corrosive sublimate and alum (Williams), so that their chance of survival under adverse circumstances is unusually good. It seems quite as reasonable to suppose that the dried embryos were inhaled with the breath, and, lighting in the mucous membrane, found suitable conditions for development. The position of the parasites about the bifurcation of the trachea, at the angles of division of the main bronchi, and most abundantly in the lower wall of the tubes, just the localities where small particles would be most likely to lodge, favours an infection through the air rather than by the blood. The negative evidences in the heart and blood-vessels do not go for much either way, as the examination in all the cases was made after the invasion of the parasites, and consequently at a time when they could scarcely be found in the circulation.

"It is a somewhat remarkable fact that verminous bronchitis prevails to a much greater extent and is more fatal in young animals than in adults. Thus lambs and calves are the chief victims in epidemics of 'hoose,' whereas it is only occasionally that adult animals succumb to the disease. In lambs the worms are usually found in the bronchial tubes, while in sheep they are more commonly encysted in the lung-tissue itself where they do not appear to cause much irritation. It seems to me that in the anatomical peculiarities of the lungs in young animals we have an explanation of the fatality of the disease among them. If the bronchial tubes of a young animal be compared with those of an adult, they are seen to be softer, much less rigid ; the mucous membrane is lower, not so thin, nor so closely attached to the tissues beneath. Hence it happens that in inflammation of the tubes from any cause, swelling and tumefaction of the mucous membrane readily occur, and constitute elements of danger which are directly proportionate to the calibre of the tubes attacked. In the cases above reported the swelling of the membrane in the larger tubes was considerable, and, though not sufficient to prevent the access of air, must have interfered greatly with the expulsion of mucus from the smaller tubes, not only by decreasing and narrowing the orifices of exit, but also by destroying, over an important area, the ciliary action so useful for this purpose. The same difference is met with in human practice. Ordinary acute bronchitis in the adult is not at all a dangerous affection, while in young children it is the reverse; and for the very reason that in them the bronchial mucous membrane swells easily, and there is not the same expulsive power to enable them to get rid of the mucus which, in consequence, accumulates, and may cause collapse or inflammation of the lung tissue. In the 'lamb disease' death occurs from asphyxia, caused by the collection of mucus in the tubes. I have no records at hand of the state of the lung tissue in these cases, whether it is in a condition of collapse or of inflammation; probably the latter, for I see the expression 'verminous pneumonia' used by some authors.

"With reference to the pneumonic condition of the lungs of the dogs in this epidemic, it will be remembered that in three of the *post-mortem* examinations the inflammation of the lungs was found without the occurrence of parasites in the bronchial tubes; the pneumonia being quite as extensive as in the cases accompanied with strongyles. I must confess that this circumstance has puzzled me not a little, and I see no very satisfactory explanation of the fact. It appears natural to refer the diseased condition of the lung-substance in the parasite cases to the accumulation of the mucus in the smaller tubes producing collapse of the air-cells in certain areas, which subsequently became inflamed—a sequence of events sometimes observed in children. The appearance of the lungs in several of the cases corresponds with this view; for the pneumonia was lobular, affecting small and isolated portions of the lung-tissue.

Mr. James Moore, in his work on the homœopathic treatment of the dog, in his section on "Internal Parasites in the *Air-Passages*," gives the following:—

"*Pentastomum Tænioides.*—This worm occupies that part of the respiratory tube which lies anterior to the larynx, and especially inhabits the nasal sinuses, etc. Obstruction more or less marked is the consequence of its presence in this region.

"Chobart first discovered it in the frontal sinus of the horse and the dog. He confounded it with the tænia, and christened it the *tænia lanceole.*

" Blanchard examined many dogs without finding it, and states that the helminthological collection at the Jardin des Plantes contains only two specimens. It has been found in dogs in different parts of the Continent, and also in other animals. Leuchart introduced the *Pentastomum denticulatum* of the rabbit into the nostrils of a dog, where he afterwards found the *Pent. tenioides.* He concludes that the former, which lies encysted in the viscera of several species of animals, is the larval form of the latter. He states that mature ripe eggs are thrown off from this parasite, and discharged with the nasal mucus of its host in the act of sneezing. These embryonic forms manage somehow or other to get introduced into the bodies of other animals, where they become fully developed. Fürstenberg has found the immature or a sexual form in the mesenteric glands of the sheep, as developed from the eggs of this parasite, which are swallowed by the sheep with its food. When a dog or wolf eats the entrails and mesenteric glands of such sheep, the embryonic parasite sticks to the nose and lips, and afterwards passes up the nostrils, where it becomes firmly fixed by its hooks. Here the embryo gradually increases in size, is endowed with sexual organs in about two months, and attains its full development in twelve. Colin introduced fifty immature parasites into a Newfoundland dog. Eight months afterwards the dog was killed, and eleven mature parasites, nine males and two females, were found in the ethmoidal cells and about the turbinated bones. The males moved about; the females were fixed by their hooklets to the pituitary membrane, and had their copulative sacs filled with spermatozoa, and their oviducts crammed with eggs.

"*Symptoms.*—As to the symptoms produced by the worm, whilst Rudolphi found a dog which he examined perfectly well, and Dujardin, Miram, Colin, etc., make no reference to any disorder in their cases; on the other hand, Chobart gives rather a dark account of the effects produced. 'The animal,' he says, 'is subject to convulsions, during which it is violently agitated, stops short, hits itself on the head, rolls over, rubs its nose on the ground, and the jaws are convulsively champed. It devours everything within reach, such as wood, straw, etc., discharges a large quantity of saliva, passes urine involuntarily, and sneezes without ceasing. Death sometimes ensues.'

"The mucous membrane of the nose is found to be red, blackish, ecchymosed, thickened, and ulcerated; the sinuses more or less filled with pus; and even the ethmoid bone sometimes partially carious.

"*Treatment*—Trephine the nostrils and inject with water. Inhalations of chlorine and tobacco smoke. Chloroform?"

ASTHMA (CONGESTIVE).

This disease is due to congestion of the mucous membrane of the bronchial tubes, and chiefly affects aged, highly fed, pampered house-dogs, and those in the same condition out of doors.

Predisposing causes.—Hereditary disposition, indigestion, gastric and intestinal irritation.

Exciting Causes.—Sudden changes of temperature; flatulency; obstructed pneumonic circulation; large accumulations of fat, especially about the heart and large blood-vessels; pungent effluviæ, especially ammoniacal: hence dogs continually kept in foul stables being asthmatical.

Symptoms. — Thick, laboured, wheezing respiration; husky bark; distress after exertion, with excessive panting, and frequently palpitation; Schneiderian membrane injected; flatulency and constipation.

Treatment.—Remedial measures can only be adopted with a view to alleviating the symptoms: an absolute cure is out of the question. The digestive organs demand special attention; rich food, and that which is likely to produce flatulency, must be strictly avoided. Vegetable charcoal and iron, 1 scruple of the former and 10 grains of the latter, made into a pill and given three times a week, with an occasional oleaginous aperient, form as a rule the most effectual medicinal treatment. If the animal is gross, and the breathing difficult, an ordinary emetic may be administered with benefit; and to ensure prolongation of life a gradual reduction of obesity, and when reduced proportionately, a fixed standard maintained, is most necessary. If out of doors, the dryness, drainage, and kennel situation are matters of importance. (See "Kennel Arrangement.")

ASTHMA (SPASMODIC)

Differs from the former in that it comes on in paroxyms, often of almost a tetanic nature, and is usually unaccompanied by any inflammatory symptoms. It is more amenable to treatment than the previous form, but is liable to return suddenly and without warning.

Predisposing Causes.—A previous attack, or hereditary disposition.

Exciting Causes.—Prolonged dyspepsia; flatulence; anterior spinal irritation; sudden changes of temperature; irritating effluviæ.

Symptoms.—Sudden and laboured respiration, occurring at intervals; dry cough during the paroxysm, with or without expectoration; exertion frequently produces retching and vomiting.

Treatment.—An emetic at the onset is advisable. If the paroxysms continue, small doses of stimulants should be administered. as a teaspoonful of brandy and water, with three or four drops of spirits of camphor. If no relief attends these measures, five grains of iodide of potassium and five minims of tincture of belladonna given in a desertspoonful of water will frequently be found effectual in relaxing the bronchial spasm. Idoform 2-4 grains and chlorodyne 7-12 minims are also useful. When the attack occurs after a meal an aperient is indicated.

The instructions given for the preceding form regarding diet will apply to spasmodic asthma. Overloading the stomach and exertion after a meal, should specially be avoided.

PLEURISY,

Or inflammation of the investing membrane of the lungs, and that lining the thoracic cavity, may be associated with pneumonia (pleuro-pneumonia) or exist as an independent disease.

Predisposing Causes.—Debility, disease of the lungs, or any of the predisposing causes of inflammation.

Exciting Causes.—Cold ; inflammation of neighbouring textures ; injuries, as fracture of or wounds penetrating between or external to, the ribs.

Symptoms.—These generally commence with shivering and febrile disturbance ; respiration quickened ; the inspiration is remarkably short, being suddenly interrupted almost immediately the breath is taken ; this is due to the pain caused by the movement of the ribs in dilatation, or the inflation of the lungs on and against the pleura ; the abdominal muscles are in consequence called in to aid respiration, hence the bellow-like heaving movement at the flank. There is a dry suppressed cough, and the usual indications of fever; nose hot and dry, tongue white and slimy, eyes bright and watery, conjunctival membrane injected, pulse hard, jerking, and frequent. As these symptoms advance, the animal becomes exceedingly distressed frequently sitting on his haunches with the fore legs wide apart; pressure over the ribs causes acute pain; the cough is more frequent, the breathing shorter and more difficult, and an anxious haggard look pervades the whole countenance.

Terminations.—Resolution, adhesion, effusion, or the chronic form.

In the lower animals, recovery from acute pleurisy usually terminates in adhesions, while effusion is generally the forerunner of death. When the latter (effusion) takes place, a considerable and marked alteration is immediately manifested in the symptoms—the breathing becomes more and more laboured, threatening suffocation; on auscultation the natural respiratory murmur is absent so far as the fluid reaches, whilst above it is considerably increased; percussion gives a dull dead sound over the region of effusion; as the fluid increases the intercostal spaces become bulged, and towards the latter stage the dependent parts of the animal are more or less œdematous. The pulse is feeble and quick, and as the end approaches becomes imperceptible. Asphyxia closes the scene.

Post-mortem Examination.—Effusion of serum, with pus and bands of lymph across the walls of the chest; recent adhesions, and considerable thickening of the pleura, coated with lymph.

Treatment.—Pleurisy, from the acuteness of its character and rapidity of its progress, demands prompt and active measures: bleeding, advocated by other authors, is not, in my opinion, admissible, or in accordance with the character of the disease, which is excessively lowering in itself, and weakening the volume of blood would have a tendency rather to promote what of all things we should wish to avoid—effusion—than check the inflammatory process and prevent its occurrence. Purgatives are equally inadmissible, and, of the two, more dangerous, for if excessive action of the bowels is excited in any inflammatory chest affection, it is with the utmost difficulty it can be checked; more often it is the case, of which I have had painful experience, that its abatement has not been accomplished, and death has been hastened thereby.

The remedial measures best adapted to this disease are diffusible stimulants and counter irritation.

    Spt. Æther Nit. .... 2 ounces.
    Liq. Ammon. Acetat. 4   „

A teaspoonful every four hours in twice the quantity of linseed tea for a small dog, and double of each for a large one.

Counter-irritation may be applied to the chest in the form of mustard-plasters, ammonia or terebinth embrocation, or hot linseed-meal poultices. The temperature of the body should be equalised as much as possible, but due regard to the observance of proper ventilation is necessary. Many persons wrongly imagine that a warm room and the exclusion of fresh air is equally necessary to the lower animal as to the higher—a fatal error.

Where the debility rapidly increases, and there is danger of effusion taking place, tinct. of ferri, 5 to 10 minims, should be added to each dose of the stimulant. This, from its constringent power, is undoubtedly one of the best agents we have for the prevention of dropsies. Where effusion is present the ferri iodidum should be substituted, active counter-irritation applied to the sides, and a seton may be inserted with benefit in front of the chest. It is necessary, however, to observe that where the latter measure is adopted, increased support is needful, from the weakening tendency of the agent. Where the effusion increases, and the case appears hopeless unless the fluid is removed, tapping the chest by means of the insertion of a small trochar between the eighth and ninth ribs may be had recourse to. The operation affords immediate relief in removing the compression on the lungs and the displacement of the heart. It is, however, as a rule, but a temporary respite. Secondary secretion follows, and usually more rapidly than that which preceded it, and we may tap again with the same result. There are, nevertheless, exceptional cases: in the horse I have seen recovery follow the operation, and also in the dog.

CHRONIC PLEURISY

May, as I have stated, be a termination of the former, or it may begin as a chronic affection, *i.e.*, it may assume a sub-acute form from the commencement. Pain on the affected side, cough, increased pulse, and respiration considerably accelerated by exertion, and more or less fever, are the symptoms generally present. Effusion, or lymph and adhesions are usually present; as the lymph becomes organized, the fluid absorbed, and the adhesions firmer, the walls of the chest become flattened; dulness on percussion, feebleness of the respiratory murmur, and an occasional rasping sound attend this condition.

Treatment.—This consists in endeavouring to promote absorption of the effused fluids, and in giving strength to the patient. The sulphate of iron, in from 5 to 15 grains, in proportion to the size of the animal, with cod-liver oil, forms the best and, I have found, the most successful medicinal treatment.

Mild continued counter-irritation to the sides of the chest is also advisable. The application of the tincture of iodine, after first shaving off the hair, is exceedingly useful, and the insertion of a seton in front of the chest for a month or six weeks is most valuable.

The diet should be nourishing, and every means adopted which is calculated to impart vigour.

PNEUMONIA,

Or inflammation of the substance of the lungs, is a complaint to which dogs are exceedingly liable.

Predisposing Causes.—Hereditary disease, as scrofula or phthisis, an anæmic or plethoric habit of body, sudden and frequent changes of temperature.

Exciting Causes.—Exposure to cold and damp (especially in toy or house-dogs, frequently washed and not carefully dried, and who are used to a warm atmosphere), violent exertion, penetrating lung wounds.

Symptoms.—The stages of pneumonia are usually three : 1st, that of engorgement, or congestion ; 2nd, red hepatization ; 3rd, yellow or grey hepatization, or purulent infiltration.

The early stage is generally ushered in with shiverings, followed by fever ; the pulse is increased, the respiration becomes quickened, there is an occasional short cough, the head is extended, the eyes bloodshot, nose hot and dry, tongue protruded and furred, edges of a deep red ; the animal assumes a sitting posture, with the fore-legs wide apart.

Ausculation reveals a crackling or crepitating sound, which is circumscribed according to the amount of lung involved ; this sound obscures to a great extent the respiratory murmur in those portions not diseased, and as the malady proceeds this murmur becomes quite obliterated, the crepitus general and more defined, and the other symptoms all increased in severity.

If the malady is not checked at this stage, it quickly passes on into the second. The crepitus on auscultation is absent, and no sound, except it be a slight wheezing or whistling noise, can be detected ; hepatization has then taken place, and inflation is but a cypher. The sound emitted on percussion at this stage is very characteristic of consolidation being flat and dead.

The cough now is frequent, and accompanied with red or rusty expectoration ; the eyes have a sunken appearance ; respiration is performed with great effort and pain ; the cheeks are inflated in the act, nostrils dilated, and the general expression is haggard and pitiful in the extreme. The position on the haunches is still maintained, or, if changed, it is but momentarily, to stand with the fore-legs propped apart to allow more room for the abdominal muscles to aid respiration.

When the third stage arrives and suppuration commences —in other words, when the lung-structure breaks down, auscultation discovers a new sound—a bubbling or gurgling crepitation caused by the passage of air through pus.

On placing the hand flat upon the side, much the same sensation will be communicated; it is as though fluid was boiling underneath, and I have been painfully struck with this phenomenon both in the human and canine subject. The appealing look for relief in this stage is most affecting; acutely is the weakness of human aid now felt by the attendant—petting, caressing, words of comfort and pity are all that he has to dispose of.

The cough is now loose, and accompanied with copious expectoration; the mouth and lips are coated with sticky slime; the breath has a peculiar fœtid cadaverous odour, and is taken in short gasps; the ears and extremities are cold and clammy; the pulse is imperceptible, and death closes the scene. Such, briefly, may be described as the leading symptoms in the several stages of pneumonia.

Treatment.—Pneumonia admits of no delay in treatment; immediately symptoms of the malady are presented, our course must be promptly decided. The same remarks as to the advisability of bleeding and physic in pleurisy are equally applicable here. Stimulants and counter-irritation are decidedly indicated; in protracted pneumonia the latter may be carried to the extent of a cantharidine application, and the seton is especially serviceable; the necessity of bodily warmth, the admittance of a reasonable amount of fresh air, and a nutritious diet must not be forgotten. Iron and cod-liver oil, after the more active symptoms have abated, will materially assist in promoting convalescence.

It is now pretty generally acknowledged that consolidated lung is capable of regeneration, and I have had myself practical experience of the fact. Dr. Chambers observes: "I have no doubt, in my own mind, that the way in which consolidated lung recovers is by the exudated fibrin breaking down into pus, and being expectorated, whilst the obstructed air vesicles regain their elasticity and capacity for performing their functions. This is a strong argument for an ample supply of nutriment during the regenerative process."

CONSUMPTION.

This decimating disease of mankind extends to the lower animals, and dogs are frequently subjects in which its fatal seeds are sown.

Predisposing Causes.—Hereditary taint, close confinement, bad air, unwholesome food, and breeding in and in

Exciting Causes.—Preceding diseases, as distemper, pneumonia, catarrh, scrofula, asthma. Sudden changes of temperature; damp habitation.

Symptoms.—Occasional cough; short respiration, accelerated during exertion, with increased cough; failing appetite; loss of flesh. As the disease proceeds, profuse expectoration takes place, the breath becomes fœtid, great prostration is manifest, the hair falls off, diarrhœa sets in, and the animal dies much in the same way as our own unfortunate species do.

Treatment.—This can only be adopted so far as the alleviation of suffering and the prolongation of life are concerned: cure is impossible. In the early stages a seton in the chest, cod-liver oil and iron, nutritious diet, and the avoidance of exposure to damp and cold, will often arrest the progress of the disease; in fact, if thus checked early, it will assume a quiescent state, and remain so for a long time, or even the natural period of canine existence.

It is almost needless to add that a dog so affected should never be used for breeding purposes.

POLYPUS.

Polypus within the nose is occasionally met with in canine practice. At times the tumour is visible externally, protruding from the nostril; whilst at others, and when small, it may be situated high up and out of sight.

Symptoms.—The animal frequently sneezes, and from the obstruction to the free passage of air the respiration is stuffy and difficult, and, if the obstruction has existed some time, is accompanied with nasal discharge. Examination reveals the presence of polypus.

Treatment.—This consists in removal by ligature or forceps, and the nostril may be syringed for a few days afterwards with a weak solution of alum.

OZÆNA,

Though of common occurrence in the horse, is rarely seen in the dog. The disease consists of a copious and fœtid discharge from one or both nostrils.

Causes.—Prolonged catarrh, irritation, from the presence of foreign substances in the nasal chambers or frontal sinuses, ulceration of the Schneiderian membrane, disease of the turbinated bones, unsound teeth.

Symptoms.—Discharge, as already described, which may be continuous or periodical, obstructed breathing, having a rattling sound from the ingress and egress of air through the said discharge; frequent sneezing and occasional cough.

Treatment.—The nostrils should be daily syringed with warm water, and where there is ulceration or diseased bone, either of the following lotions may be injected :

1.—Alum	5 grains
Aqua	1 ounce
2.—Zinc chloride	5 grains
Aqua	1 ounce
3.—Nitrate of silver	5 grains
Aqua	1 ounce

The second recipe, where there is much fœtor, is most useful.

If the disease proceeds from a diseased tooth, removal will be at once necessary. If from polypus, the same course must be adopted.

Mineral tonics, and generous diet, and free out-door exercise, are essential adjuncts to the treatment.

CHAPTER III.

DISEASES OF THE MOUTH AND TONGUE.

DENTITION,	ULCERS,
DECAYED TEETH,	BLAIN,
TARTAR,	PARALYSIS,
CANKER,	PHARYNGITIS,
GLOSSITIS	SALIVATION.

DENTITION.

ACCORDING to the dentition of the dog by M. Girard, and Linnæus, the following is the acknowledged formula:

Incisors, $6/6$; canines, $\frac{1-1}{1-1}$ molars, $\frac{6-6}{6-6} = 42$.

The following cuts exhibit the front teeth of the dog in various stages of growth and decay:

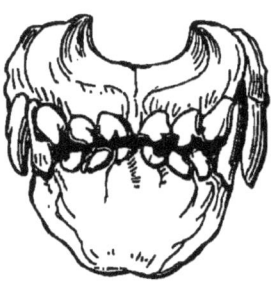
FIG. 4.

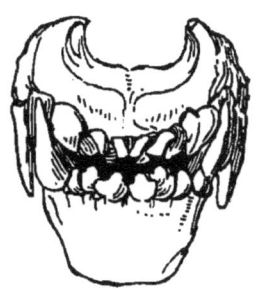
FIG. 5.

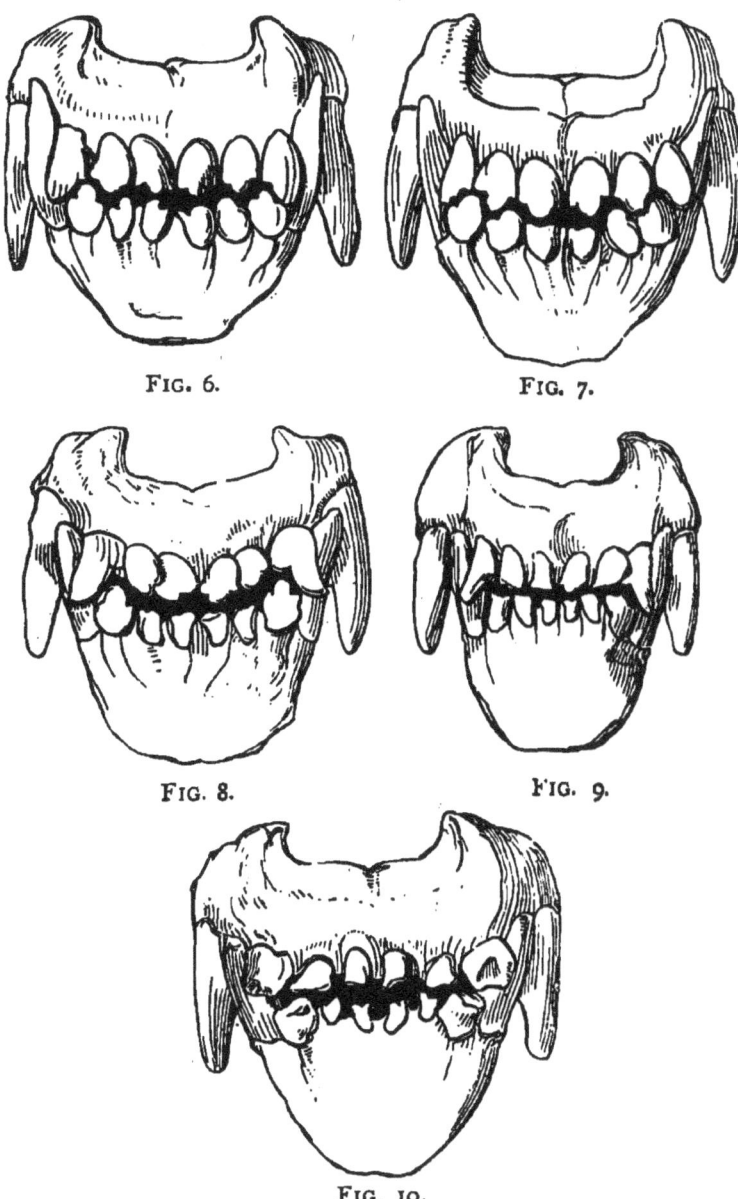

Fig. 6.

Fig. 7.

Fig. 8.

Fig. 9.

Fig. 10.

The full-grown dog has usually twenty teeth in the upper and twenty-two in the lower jaw, with two small supernumerary molars. All of them, with the exception of the tushes, are provided with a long neck covered by the gums, and separating the body of the tooth from the root. The projecting portion of the teeth is more or less pointed, and disposed so as to tear and crush the food on which the dog lives. They are of moderate size when compared with those of other animals, and are subject to little loss of substance compared with the teeth of the horse. In most of them, however, there is some alteration of form and substance, both in the incisors and the tushes; but this depends so much on the kind of food on which the animal lives, and the consequent use of the teeth, that the indication of the age by the altered appearance of the mouth is not to be depended upon after the animal is four or five years old. The incisor teeth are six in number in each jaw, and are placed opposite to each other. In the lower jaw, the pincers, or central teeth, are the largest and the strongest; the middle teeth are somewhat less, and the corner teeth the smallest and the weakest. In the upper jaw, however, the corner teeth are much larger than the middle ones; they are farther apart from their neighbours, and they terminate in a conical point, curved somewhat inwards and backwards.

As long as the teeth of the full-grown dog are whole, and not injured by use, they have a healthy appearance, and their colour is beautifully white. The surface of the incisors presents, as in the ruminants, an interior and cutting edge, and a hollow or depression within. This edge or border is divided into three lobes, the largest and most projecting forming the summit or point of the tooth. The two lateral lobes have the appearance of notches cut on either side of the principal lobe, and the union of the three resembles the *fleur de lis*, which, however, is in the process of time effaced by the wearing out of the teeth. (Figs. 6 and 7.)

While the incisors are young they are flattened on their sides, and bent somewhat backwards, and there is a decided cavity, in which a pulpy substance is enclosed. This, however, is gradually contracted as the age of the dog increases.

"M. F. Cuvier speaks of certain supernumerary teeth occasionally developed in each of the jaws. There is much irregularity accompaning them, and they have even been supposed to have extended to seven or eight in number."—*Youatt.*

The following notes are extracted from Professor Simonds' lecture on this subject:—"The dog, at birth, as a rule, has no teeth, but if we examine the gums we may plainly see the outline of them, and easily count the number, and the same applies to the molars. When about one month old the temporary teeth seem to be all complete, and cut through the gums. After that period very little is to be observed except the growth of them. In the course of a very short time the temporary teeth may be observed giving way. It is difficult to say which permanent ones come first, but he (Professor Simonds), from his observations, believes the corner incisors and tushes do so, and not unfrequently it is the same with the temporary ones. The cutting of the permanent teeth commences at the age of four months, and at about six months the animal generally has them all, and at eighteen months dentition is complete. Perhaps up to about a year old there is not much difficulty in telling the age of the dog. If properly kept the teeth will be sharp and white, without wear, because if fed on soft food they would be preserved much longer (?); while on the other hand, if the meal consists of bones and hard food, they will be worn away much sooner, and seeing these things, we must judge accordingly. At three years old, as a rule, they will present a worn surface; beyond this we have nothing more to guide us.

DECAYED TEETH.

Sound teeth are essential to the comfort, health, and

pleasurable companionship of the dog as they are to mankind. Unfortunately, however, in our canine friends these useful agents are liable to become decayed, and the once nursed pet is, by the fœtor of his breath, rendered offensive and ordered to a distance.

Decayed teeth are the cause of many diseases, especially of the mouth and digestive organs. Painful swellings, abscesses and sinuses of the cheek, structural changes in the jaw-bone—leading to tumour, laceration of the tongue, canker, constitutional irritation, indigestion, and intestinal disease.

There can be no doubt that the dog at times is a martyr to toothache, the slobbering manner in which he partakes of his food, and often his refusal to do so, with the head held on one side, denote this to the observant eye.

Decayed teeth are dependent, to a great extent, upon the system of feeding (see "Feeding"). They should at all times be removed. Occasionally hæmorrhage will follow extraction. In such a case a little cotton wool steeped in tincture of myrrh, iron, or solution of alum, and packed in the cavity, will have the desired effect of arresting it.

TARTAR.

The deposit of tartar on the teeth is likewise prejudicial to health, and is usually the result of injudicious feeding and gastric derangement.

The accumulation, especially in aged dogs, is often very considerable. In consequence of the irritation produced on the gums, they become congested, swollen, and spongy, the teeth loosen and decay, the breath is disgustingly fœtid, and constitutional disease follows such a condition if long maintained. Teeth so affected should be "scaled," and afterwards brushed with soap and water and a little charcoal, or a few drops of simple tincture of myrrh.

The reception of deposit may frequently be prevented, by allowing the animal occasionally large bones to gnaw.

The food must be plain, not stimulating; luxuries are especially to be avoided; a mild dose of aperient medicine and subsequently a little iron and quinine, will aid in restoring tone to the system.

CANKER.

Canker of the mouth is a result of the foregoing affections; it is exceedingly painful, and, if long neglected, very troublesome.

Symptoms.—The gum is congested, swollen and spongy, and bleeds on the least pressure. Abscesses not unfrequently form on the jaw, and discharge disgustingly fœtid pus; hæmatoid granulations follow, and the poor animal is reduced, from inability through pain to lap or masticate, to a mere skeleton, while a considerable amount of inflammatory fever is present.

Treatment.—This primarily consists in the removal of the cause. Rotten stumps, loose or over-crowded teeth, should be extracted; if necrosis of the bone is present, that likewise must be removed. Small doses of alterative medicine daily, for a few days, should follow. The food should be soft, nutritous, and plain; animal food is, for a time, best avoided.

The following gargle will have a beneficial effect on the condition of the gums :

Alum .... 10 grains.
Tinct. Myrrh Co. .... $\frac{1}{2}$ drachm.
Acid. acetic .... $\frac{1}{2}$ „
Aqua .... 6 ounces.

A little to be used twice a day.

APHTHÆ OF THE MOUTH.

This is an exudative form of stomatitis, commonly known

as "thrush." Aphthæ is most frequently seen in young animals, and occurs from disorder of the digestive organs or impaired nutrition. It is also common in unweaned puppies, especially when the parent or foster-mother is unhealthy. In old animals it occasionally arises from debilitating diseases and indigestion.

Symptoms.—Numerous small white specks covering the mucous membrane of the mouth (most abundant in sucking whelps on the edges and insides of the lips), especially on the inner surface of the cheeks, tongue, and fauces, and sometimes down the œsophagus. Profuse salivation, difficulty in swallowing, vomiting, diarrhœa, cough, and general debility.

Treatment.—Borax and glycerine, carbolic or salicylic acid, tincture of myrrh, alum, sulphite of soda.

Internally.—Chlorate of potash, carbonate of soda, iron, cod-liver oil.

Nutritious food, good hygiene (with puppies, change of milk, or bottle-feeding with goat's or cow's milk).

AFFECTIONS OF THE TONGUE.
GLOSSITIS.

Dogs are very liable to injuries of the tongue, resulting in severe inflammatory action of its membrane or substance (glossitis). This frequently occurs from its being bitten during an attack of epilepsy, in devouring sharp substances, or from irritation and laceration produced from broken teeth, stings, or the contact of acrid matters.

Symptoms.—Pain, swelling, increased salivation, difficulty of deglutition, intense thirst, and more or less constitutional disturbance.

Treatment.—Warm fomentations, scarification, or, if possible, the application of leeches—which in small dogs, when gagged, is not difficult. If from the teeth, filing or removal. A dose of aperient medicine should be administered, and the food consist of warm slops.

ULCERS.

These usually arise from excessive deposit of tartar on, or decay of, the teeth, or from gastric derangement.

Treatment.—If from tartar, the teeth should be scaled ; if from decay, removed. Where they are due to gastric derangement, aperient medicine, with restricted plain diet, must be prescribed. If the ulcers do not disappear under this treatment, they may be occasionally touched with lunar caustic.

BLAIN,

Or enlargement of the tongue, with the presence of vesicles on its lateral and under surface, is a disease to which the lower animals are very subject. The dog, however, is not so in proportion to horses and oxen. Blain is more frequent in spring and autumn, and often assumes an epidemic form.

Symptoms.—These come on suddenly, without any traceable cause or warning. The tongue is considerably swollen and red, and has the appearance of being engorged with blood ; its sides and under surface are studded with large livid vesicles. The salivary secretion is considerably increased, and rapidly changes from its normal character to a purulent, bloody, and foetid discharge, due to the formation of unhealthy or gangrenous ulcers at the base of the vesicles.

Treatment.—In the earlier stages the malady will generally yield to aperient medicine, and astringent washes to the mouth. When the disease has become advanced, ulcers succeed the vesicles, and a foetid discharge accompanies them. A weak solution of chloride of zinc should be used to the mouth, and the ulcers occasionally touched with nitrate of silver.

Tonics are the most suitable medicinal agents.

Ferri Sulph. .... } aa 5 to 10 grains.
Zingib. .... }
Treacle .... Sufficient.

One pill to be given twice a day.

Or,

Tinct. Ferri Mur. .... } aa 30 drops
Tinct. Gentian Co. .... }
Aqua................................. 1 ounce

A teaspoonful twice a day; double for a large dog.

The food should be soft, and chiefly liquid, owing to the soreness of the mouth.

PARALYSIS OF THE TONGUE.

A partial paralysis of the tongue is not unfrequent in dogs, and particularly those of the bull bred. In some this lolling side protrusion is a congenital deformity; but it more often occurs from injury, long-continued chorea or debility.

Symptoms.—The organ hangs generally from one side of the mouth. Its condition rarely interferes with lapping, but it gives rise to other undesirable results. From its protrusion and long exposure to air it becomes dry, coated with fur, more or less indurated, and is, to say the least of it unsightly.

Treatment.—If the paralysis be of recent date, nux vomica 1 to 2 grains, and ferri sulph. 5 to 10 grains, twice daily, will often, if not absolutely remove it, considerably reduce it. Where the affection has been of long existence, the same treatment is still applicable, with the addition of a small seton in the submaxillary space; but the latter cases are far from satisfactory ones to deal with. The tongue should be frequently placed back in the mouth, and, if possible, kept there for a time; this will tend to prevent, to a considerable extent, the condition named from its long exposure to air.

The diet is best composed of slops, and these should be placed within reach of the animal, so that he may lap whenever inclination prompts him.

PHARYNGITIS.

Inflammation of the pharynx, unassociated with other disease, is of rare occurrence in the dog. It is usually due to an immediate exciting cause—as the lodgment of some foreign body, or contact of acrid and irritating substances.

Symptoms.—A dry, irritable cough, such as would lead one to suppose an effort was being made to dislodge some irritant matter. The membrane has a congested and swollen appearance; there is considerable difficulty in deglutition, and the act, or attempt to perform it is followed with retching. The throat is sensitive to external pressure, and cough is easily excited by it.

If the disease proceeds, a purulent discharge takes place from the nostrils, the salivary secretion is increased, and considerable constitutional disturbance follows.

Pharyngitis may terminate in resolution, ulceration, and abscess, or pharyngeal stricture.

Treatment.—In the first place, it is necessary to ascertain the cause. If it arises from the presence of a foreign body, its removal at once is indicated; and the same will apply to the contact of acrid or irritating substances. External fomentations with warm water, or the application of linseed poultices, and the exhibition of bland, warm drinks, should form the after treatment.

If the inflammatory action has a tendency to become chronic, a weak solution of nitrate of silver is the best local application, particularly if there is ulceration; and tonics, particularly iron and quinine, are the most suitable medicinal agents.

Pharyngeal abscess is generally denoted by a fluctuating

tense swelling, with difficulty in swallowing. The head is carried stiffly, and the nose poked out. Treatment consists in the evacuation of the matter with the lance or trochar.

Pharyngeal stricture usually proceeds from protracted inflammatory action; and is manifested by repeated attempts at deglution, with considerable difficulty in performing the act when eating the food, particularly solid matter. Treatment, as in other strictures, is by dilatation. The food should be fluid and stimulating.

SALIVATION.

Salivation, when unassociated with any local affections of the mouth or neighbouring structures, is usually an indication of mercurialism. Unfortunately for the canine race, mercury, in some one of its compounds, whether for internal or external use, forms one of the pet remedies of "dog doctors." The red and green iodides are especial favourites for external use, and for diseases often requiring very opposite treatment these preparations are prescribed. To wit, skin diseases—all of which in the vocabulary of the quack are mange. While for alterative, aperient, or emetic purposes, calomel is used most indiscreetly.

Symptoms.—In mercurialism, the salivary secretion is unusually abundant, the teeth are loose and discoloured, the gums spongy, swollen, and tender, and of a deep red, often approaching a purple hue. The breath is singularly fœtid; the tongue loaded with brown fur, and red down the sides. There is little appetite, but excessive thirst.

Sloughing and ulceration of the mucous membrane of the mouth frequently follow, and if the mercurial doses have been excessive, the stomach and intestines are in a like manner affected, resulting in blood-stained vomits and sanguinary purging.

If suitable measures are not taken to check these effects, considerable irritative fever is established. Extreme debility follows, the hair falls off, the animal becomes rapidly emaciated, tremulous, and paralytic, and dies in convulsions or delirium. Not unfrequently the face is considerably swollen, and the joints are hot and tender. Mercurialism also gives rise to a species of eczema (*eczema mercuriale*). See " Skin Diseases."

Treatment.—The most effectual antidotes for poisoning by mercury are albuminous compounds, the white of eggs being perhaps the best, especially in the case of corrosive sublimate.

Christison, writing on the subject, observes: "It has already been hinted that albumen, in the form of white of eggs beat up with water, impairs or destroys the corrosive properties of bichloride of mercury, by decomposing it, and producing an insoluble mercurial compound. For this discovery, and the establishment of albumen as an antidote, medicine is indebted to Professor Orfila. He has related many satisfactory experiments in proof of its virtues. The following will serve as an example of the whole. Twelve grains of corrosive sublimate were given to a little dog, and allowed to act for eight minutes, so that its usual effects might fairly begin before the antidote was administered. White of eight eggs was then given; after several fits of vomiting the animal became apparently free from pain; and in five days it was quite well.* According to Peschier, the white of one egg is required to render four grains of the poison innocuous.† The experiments of the Parisian toxicologist have been repeated and confirmed by others, and particularly by Schloepfer; who found that when a dose was given to a rabbit sufficient to kill it in seven minutes if allowed to act uncontrolled, the administration of albumen, just as the signs of uneasiness appeared, prevented every serious

* Toxicologie Général, i. 313.
† Corvisart's Journal de Médicine, xxxviii. 77.

symptom. Dr. Samuel Wright has found that if the administration of albumen is followed up by giving some astringent decoction or infusion, the beneficial effects are more complete, because the compound formed is less soluble in an excess of albumen. Albumen is chiefly useful in the early stage of poisoning with corrosive sublimate, and is particularly called for when vomiting does not take place. But it further appears to be an excellent demulcent in the advanced stages."

Five or six parts of fresh gluten, in 50 parts of a solution of soft soap, has been found also a successful antidote, and where neither albumen nor gluten is at hand, milk is a convenient and useful substitute. Iron filings, the protosulphuret of iron, meconic acid, and charcoal have each been advocated as mercurial antidotes.

"The treatment of mercurial salivation consists in exposure to a cool pure air, nourishing diet, and purgatives, if the intestinal canal is not already irritated. In some of the inflammatory affections it induces, venesection is required, in others it is hurtful. In some complaints induced by mercury, as in iritis, the poison appears to be its own antidote, for nothing checks the inflammation so soon and so certainly as mercurial salivation.

"Dr. Finlay, of the United States, proposed to check mercurial salivation by small doses of tartar emetic frequently repeated, so as to act on the skin ;* and Mr. Daniel has recommended large doses of the acetate of lead as an effectual antidote for the same purpose.†

"Dr. Klose, a German physician, says he has found iodine to possess the property of arresting the effects of mercury on the mouth.‡ The iodide of potassium is generally acknowledged to be one of the best remedies for eradicating the constitutional infirmities left in many by severe courses of mercury."

* Edin. Med. and Surg. Journal, xxix. 218.
† Lond. Med. Repos. N. S., vi. 368.
‡ Lond. Med. Gazette, 1836-37, ii. 144.

CHAPTER IV.

DISEASES OF THE STOMACH.

INDIGESTION,	GASTRITIS,
VOMITING,	INVERSION,
WORMS,	CALCULI IN THE STOMACH,
HUSK,	FOREIGN BODIES.

INDIGESTION.

THE stomach of the dog is not so liable to disease as might be expected, considering the source from which at times he derives his sustenance (see "Feeding"), the morbid appetite that prompts him to devour strange and unnatural substances, the long fasts he frequently endures, and the "get what you can" rule of diet. Nevertheless he is subject, and some dogs more than others, to the diseases mentioned in this chapter, one of the most frequent of which is dyspepsia or indigestion, the causes operating in its production being much the same as in ourselves. Long fasts, innutritious and indigestible food, disease of the digestive organs, imperfect mastication, deficiency in the biliary, gastric, or salivary secretions, want of exercise, and suspension in the alvine evacuations.

Symptoms.—Flatulency, acrid eructations, constipation or diarrhœa, fulness of the abdomen, spasmodic pains, depression, loss of appetite, dry furred tongue, thirst, often increased salivary secretion, vomiting, and occasionally cough. (See "Husk.")

Treatment.—The system of feeding generally requires our first attention where the complaint is due to over-feeding, which is frequently the case with toy-dogs. Starvation for a day, followed by a spare diet, and an aperient draught will usually effect a cure. Or again, if the animal has been kept on one kind of food for a considerable period, given in excess, and that kind has been either too stimulating, or innutritious and indigestible, a correction and modification must be observed.

If owing to imperfect mastication, from the presence of loose, broken, or decayed teeth, their removal is indicated. Where we have reason to believe the ailment is due to deficiency in the biliary, gastric, or salivary secretion—which the stools, being of a clay colour, dry in consistency, and containing undigested matter, will denote, care should be taken that the meal is not excessive, the water not stinted, and the food plain and easy of digestion.

Constipation may be relieved in the first instance by a dose of castor-oil, followed, if necessary, with enemas. Diarrhœa generally proceeds from the presence of undigested matter in the intestinal tract, and castor oil is here also applicable. Acrid eructations and flatulency are best treated with small doses of bicarbonate of soda and charcoal, ten grains of the former and one scruple of the latter, given in a little water or made into a bolus, administered after meals.

Indigestion usually requires a moderate and plain diet: lime-water and milk, with simple buscuit or bread, form the most suitable, until the digestive organs have assumed a healthy tone. Fatty and, as a rule, vegetable matters should be for a time avoided. Exceptional cases are those arising from general debility. In such the food must be nourishing, and small doses of ferri and cod-liver oil will materially assist in restoring the animal to a healthy condition. Daily exercise should be insisted on.

VOMITING.

The stomach of the dog is peculiarly liable to reflex peristaltic action. Vomition in this animal is perhaps more easily excited than in any other of the lower species. We have abundant proof of this in the administration of medicines, and in common observance during exercise, when their instinct teaches them to seek what is termed "dog-grass," the effect of which after swallowing is quickly manifested.

Vomiting may be a symptom of disease, the result of an overloaded stomach, or the presence of irritating matters within it or applied to the fauces. or it may take place from œsophagal obstruction. Worms are a very frequent cause of vomition. (See "Worms.")

The vomit may consist of mucus, bile blood, or food mingled with other offending matters.

Vomiting is medicinally induced by agents termed "emetics," the favourite one being tartarised antimony— and a dangerous one it is when given injudiciously. Fortunately, however, the dog's stomach, as previously observed, quickly responds to its call, and it is for the most part thrown off; otherwise dogs would by quacks be killed by the score. If his more unfortunate companion, the horse, were equally capable of performing the same act, antimony would speedily cease to exist in the never-failing condition-powders of the groom and chemist. For all ordinary purposes, plain warm water or water in which (if immediate action be desired) a little salt and mustard is mixed, is sufficient; in fact, I have readily produced vomiting with the latter, when I have failed with antimony. The treatment of vomiting must be directed to the cause.

WORMS IN THE STOMACH.

Dogs are frequently troubled with worms in the stomach. Their presence gives rise to severe gastric disturbance, and is often productive of convulsions and death.

Symptoms.—Those usually presented are constant retching and vomiting, fœtid breath, a dry, husky cough, intestinal irregularity, pains resembling those of colic, large appetite, more or less emaciation. Occasionally cerebral symptoms are also manifest. (See " Epilepsy.")

The worms usually present are the *ascaris marginata*, or margined round worm.

For further particulars, see chapter on " Internal Parasites."

Treatment.—I have generally found ol. terebinth., from a teaspoonful upwards, in proportion to the size of the dog, mixed with plain or castor oil—if with the former, then followed by the latter—to be effective. The dose may be repeated in three days, if necessary.

HUSK.

Dogs are frequently affected with *gastric catarrh*, or what is commonly called *husk*. It is sometimes associated with distemper, but it more frequently exists as an independent affection, the result of severe indigestion or exposure to damp and cold.

Symptoms.—Like other catarrhal diseases, there is increased secretion of mucus, with more or less congestion of its membrane lining the stomach, attended with the usual febrile symptoms. Nose hot and dry; injection of the visible mucous membranes, particularly the conjunctiva; furred tongue; increased pulse and respiration; abdominal pain, with retching, vomiting, and constipation. A dry husky cough (hence the term) is usually present, and is accompanied, as the malady proceeds, by a frothy, tenacious expectoration, which the animal struggles to free itself from. Unless checked, the catarrh extends to the intestines, giving rise to a violent form of diarrhœa, followed by rapid emaciation and death.

Treatment.—The affection generally yields soonest to

tonics combined with opiates.* The following pill I have found most serviceable:

Opium .... 1 to 3 grains, in proportion to the dog's size.
Ferri Sulph.... 5 to 10 grains, ditto,
One to be given twice daily.

In protracted cases I prescribe the nux vomica, in combination with the iron, and find it attended with excellent results.

When the abdominal pain is severe, counter-irritation or hot linseed-meal poultices to the region of the stomach afford great relief.

Constipation is best removed with salad oil and enemas. Ordinary purgatives are injurious and dangerous.

The food should consist of mucilaginous liquids, owing to the sensitive condition of the stomach. Solid and indigestible matters are very prejudicial. Milk, rendered alkaline with lime-water, should be given the patient to lap, in lieu of plain water. Exposure to cold and damp must be avoided, and the return to ordinary food and life gradually introduced as convalescence advances.

When the intestines become involved and diarrhœa sets in, much care will be required to prevent a fatal termination. Astringents, combined with opiates, should be used:

Opium............................... $\Big\}$ aa 1 grain.
Tannic Acid ....

Administered every four hours in a little water, or, what is serviceable in some cases, brandy and water, with a few drops of chlorodyne.

Counter-irritation to the abdomen; starch and sedative enemas; and strengthening, mucilaginous food, are also important adjuncts in the treatment.

---

* Gamgee ("Our Domestic Animals") prescribes dilute hydrocyanic acid in doses from two to three drops given in water or a little wine; and he remarks, that in that stage of the disease when considerable prostration is observed, he has seen great good from the occasional administration of wine and spirits of nitric ether.

A common and apparently simple form of husk is frequently met with in dogs, particularly terriers, which I have generally attributed to the presence of worms in the stomach, and treatment accordingly has always removed it.

GASTRITIS.

Acute inflammation of the stomach is in the dog, comparatively speaking, of rare occurrence.

The mucous membrane lining the organ is generally alone involved in the inflammatory process, unless an exceptional cause arises, as the presence of some powerful irritant or corrosive matter. It will then be extended to the other coats.

Acute Gastritis quickly runs its course. The terminations are *resolution, suppuration, gangrene.*

Causes.—Sudden cold to the mucous membrane of the stomach, when the body is heated ; a continued course of stimulating food ; the presence of acrid matters or irritating poisons, as *arsenic, antimony, corrosive sublimate, croton oil, turpentine,* etc. ; mechanical injuries from sharp substances ; external violence, as kicks, blows, crushes, etc.; polypi, tumours, calculi.

Symptoms.—*Vomiting* is generally an early symptom in gastritis, and is prominent throughout the disease. The bowels are either obstinately constipated or relaxed. Considerable febrile disturbance is naturally present—the nose being hot and dry, breathing accelerated, pulse small and quick, mucous membranes injected, tongue hot and furred, and intense thirst.

The animal usually lies flat on his side, or stretched out full length on the belly, on the coldest spot he is able to find. A moan or pitiful whine is given utterance to from time to time, and the expression of the face is indicative of pain.

As the disease proceeds the countenance becomes exceedingly anxious, the moans more frequent, and the search for relief continuous. Severe rigors, cold extremities, sunken eye, a rapid and almost imperceptible pulse, sudden cessation of pain, denote that gangrene has set in, and the poor sufferer dies gradually and quietly, or in delirium.

A *post-mortem examination* reveals intense redness, either in patches or diffused, of the mucous membrane, with softening of its structure and sometimes sloughing. If the disease has been caused by the action of some corrosive agent, perforation of all the coats of the stomach, with extensive sloughing, will generally be found.

Treatment.—The less the patient is disturbed the better. In the early stages leeches may be applied over the region of the stomach. Cold water should be allowed *ad libitum*, for nothing is more grateful to the sufferer and so easily retained in the stomach, which, it must ever be borne in mind, is exceedingly sensitive under all conditions. Nourishment is best administered in the form of mucilaginous drinks, as barley-water, arrowroot, or broth thickened with isinglass or rice. Such matters, being bland, have the double effect of soothing and protecting the irritated mucous membrane, and giving to the patient at the same time the support required.*

With regard to medicinal agents, opium, from 3 to 10 grains, is the best agent for allaying an irritated or sensitive condition of the stomach, and also in checking diarrhœa.

---

* Ballard observes: " In prescribing *a diet in over-sensitive conditions of the stomach*, it must be recollected that the food which comes into contact with the interior of the organ is to be regarded much in the same light as a local application made to tender parts of the body ; and as we should avoid bringing in contact with the latter any but bland and unirritating dressings, so with the former a similar principle must guide us, and we must select such matters only, and in such quantities as, while they are fitted to sustain the body, would be unirritating if applied to an external sore, and which experience has shown may be used, introduced into the sensitive stomach without producing pain or distress.

" In inflammatory and ulcerative conditions of the stomach, where

Constipation is most safely overcome with tepid water enemas. The return to solid food should be gradual, and that which is given easy of digestion and plain.

Chronic or Sub-acute Gastritis is much more frequently met with in dogs than the former.

Causes.—Protracted dyspepsia, constipation, unwholesome and indigestible food, or it may be a sequel to acute gastritis.

Symptoms.—Tenderness over the region of the stomach, frequent eructations, vomiting after meals, furred tongue, bowels usually constipated, and often there is a dry cough.

Treatment.—Bicarbonate of soda and charcoal as advised in indigestion, an occasional aperient of aloes and rhubarb, with the same description of food named in the preceding form of the disease, are the measures to be adopted.

INVERSION OF THE STOMACH.

This is of rare occurrence in the dog, perhaps more so than might be expected, considering the frequency of and susceptibility to vomiting.

From the " Abstract of the Proceedings of the Veterinary Medical Association for 1838-9."

" Mr. Ainslie laid before the Association a singular specimen of inversion of the stomach in the dog. The

---

the tenderness of the stomach is more due to the extent and severity of these lesions than to the exalted impressibility of the nervous system, the diet must often be exceedingly rigid, being limited to some of the *most bland and soft or liquid articles of food,* such as milk, arrowroot, gruel or beef-tea, which can sometimes only be tolerated when given in the smallest quantities at a time, such as a tablespoonful or a teaspoonful. In cases in which acidity prevails, one-third part of lime-water is advantageously added. When these small quantities are given, they must be repeated every ten or twenty minutes with occasional longer intervals, and if insufficient to support the patient, injections of good beef-tea, in addition, be thrown into the rectum."

patient was three or four years old. He had for several months been subject to occasional vomiting, but this had of late become more frequent. He (Mr. Ainslie) attributed it to the treatment of the animal when under distemper The disease had assumed its severest form, and large doses of calomel had been administered. From that time he had had fits of vomiting, sometimes without any evident cause, and generally after a hearty meal, and always if he took exercise after a meal. There was also, to the great annoyance of the owner, a continual discharge of viscid saliva from the corners of the mouth, and more or less blood accompanied every act of vomiting. The owner did not seem to suspect the real origin of this nuisance.

"On the first of the month he appeared to be as well as usual. In the evening he cleanly picked a bone for his supper, and after that came a fit of vomiting. He lay quiet during the night, and in the morning began to vomit mucus mixed with blood. This continued during the day; the dog rapidly lost strength, and died in the evening. The blood retained its fluid state, mixed with mucus and saliva. When, on the following morning, he opened the dog, and began to feel for the stomach, no viscus of that kind was to be found in the abdomen. He then opened the thorax, and there he perceived a considerable enlargement of the œsophagus. At first sight it seemed to be a tumour attached to the parietes of that tube, but on closer examination the œsophagus was evidently dilated by some large soft body within it. He cut into it, and drew from it the stomach, inverted, and its mucous coat in the highest possible state of inflammation. The whole of the villous tunic was charged with congested blood. The dilatation of the œsophagus commenced even from the pharynx, and had probably existed for a considerable time. The food, or some portion of it, probably remained in this dilated portion of the œsophagus, and slowly passed into the stomach, and that might account for the frequent vomitings an hour or two after feeding, especially if the dog had taken any exercise."

CALCULI IN THE STOMACH.

These calculi are exceedingly rare in the dog. They differ but little in appearance and character from those found in other portions of the viscera, being chiefly composed of the phosphates of lime and magnesia intermixed with organic matter, and having a smooth glistening surface.

Medicinal treatment, particularly acids, would be more likely to have a direct influence on them, by coming in actual contact with them, than in renal or vesicular calculi.

FOREIGN BODIES.

The stomach of the dog is frequently the receptacle for strange substances, some interesting cases of which are recorded by Youatt.

The presence of hair, straw, wood, stones, dung, and such like, though usually found in rabies, are not to be taken always as an infallible sign of that disease.

The partaking of the latter (dung) is a frequent and disgusting habit with young dogs, apparently in perfect health. In unkennelled animals it is rarely seen, and would therefore appear to a great extent to depend upon the denial of sufficient liberty, and the contraction of morbid tastes through confinement and injudicious management. Hunger and filth play a prominent part in creating such tastes.

CHAPTER V.
DISEASES OF THE BOWELS.

CONSTIPATION,	COLIC,
DIARRHŒA,	ENTERITIS,
DYSENTERY,	PERITONITIS,
INTUS-SUSCEPTION,	PILES,
HERNIA,	PROLAPSUS ANI,
WORMS,	FISTULA IN ANO.

CONSTIPATION.

THE dog has a natural tendency to constipation, the evacuations being usually dry and solid, and attended with more or less straining; nevertheless, as Mr. Youatt correctly observes, "Costiveness is a disease when it becomes habitual," and to prevent such an occurrence due attention to the causes is requisite. Constipation is dependent to a great extent on the food, especially an over-supply of bones or other dry matter: confinement and denial of exercise have a like result, and the fear of a breach of cleanly habits with house-dogs has an equal tendency to produce it. Constipation may occur from a deficiency in the intestinal secretion, or impaired peristaltic action, as in chorea, paralysis, or tetanus or from piles and fistula.

Symptoms.—The symptoms of constipation are usually denoted by the character of the stool, and the difficulty and pain in evacuating it; where constipation is long and protracted, there are indigestion, retching, vomiting, and, from the long retention of the excrement, excessively foul breath. Ultimately, colicky pains come on, the animal increases his efforts to evacuate, and yells in the endeavour: the impaction at last becomes so considerable as to push out the anus, and give it the appearance of a tumour.

Treatment.—I agree with Mr. Youatt that "a dog should never be suffered to remain costive more than a couple of days," after the expiration of which we should first of all endeavour to remove the impaction with warm-water injection. If the fæcal matter is considerable and unusually hard, the finger, previously oiled, should be gently insinuated, and the mass therewith broken down, when, followed by the enema, evacuation will generally take place. A mild dose of castor-oil may be afterwards administered ; this, however, is not often called for, and the frequent use of purgatives has a tendency rather to produce than remove constipation.

Diet.—The recurrence of constipation may be avoided by judicious feeding. Dogs fed on oatmeal porridge occasionally mixed with paunch, potatoes, or green vegetables rarely suffer from it. Daily exercise, if only for a short time, is also essential.

DIARRHŒA,

Or the profuse evacuation of liquid fæces, is an alvine condition to which dogs of all ages, but more particularly puppies, are very liable.

Causes.—Pre-existing intestinal disease, putrid and indigestible food, undigested matter, acrid bile, worms, congestion or inflammation of the mucous membrane of the bowels ; abuse of purgatives, particularly aloes and calomel ; sudden change of diet, especially from plain to rich food ; excess of animal matter. Diarrhœa is frequently associated with distemper; for further information regarding this connection, see " Distemper." Badly drained kennels and accumulation of filth are also fruitful causes. Sucking puppies are often affected through the milk being too rich and stimulating, and creating acidity.

Treatment.—The treatment of diarrhœa in its early stage is exceedingly simple. A mild dose of castor-oil, to remove the irritant, and bland mucilaginous food without solids will generally effect a cure. Many people mistakenly rush to cordials and astringents at the onset, and thereby check, or attempt to do so, the very process nature is exercising to rid herself of the offending matter.

If there is reason to suspect worms as the cause, one of the remedies for their expulsion should be adopted. (See "Worms.") If from acrid bile, which vomiting and the character of the vomit will denote, a mild aloetic purge, succeeded, if not relieved, by the hyd. cum cretæ in 3 to 5 grain doses will be of the greatest service. Warm rice-water injections, in which, if there is much pain, a few drops of laudanum are mingled, will afford considerable relief. Where the complaint results from pre-existing intestinal disease, and the above remedies fail to check it, 1 grain of opium and 5 of sulphate of copper may be given twice or three times a day, and starch enemas should be had recourse to. Chlorodyne, 5 to 10 drops in a teaspoonful or two of brandy-and-water is also very efficacious.

Where the complaint occurs in unweaned puppies, it is usually due, as already named, to acidity, and is best treated through the mother, with carbonate of soda or lime-water.

The animal during the attack should be kept warm.

Diet.—This should consist of bland, mucilaginous food, as mutton broth, thickened with isinglass, or rice or barley-water, slightly chilled.

Cleanliness of the external parts should be strictly observed, and the bedding kept dry.

DYSENTERY,

Or inflammation of the intestinal mucous membrane, chiefly of the large bowels, succeeded by ulceration and hæmorrhage, is a much more serious complaint than the former. Dysentery differs from diarrhœa in that the discharge is unaccompanied by any fæcal matter, except, from time to time, small dark indurated lumps.

Causes.—Protracted and severe diarrhœa, putrid and unwholesome food, vitiated bile, intense heat, and foul smells.

Symptoms.—Dysentery may be ushered in with rigors, general febrile excitement, and offensive evacuation; or be preceded by flatulency, constipation, colicky pains, nausea, and vomiting. The anal discharge varies in appearance: sometimes it resembles pure mucus, at others blood mixed with mucus, while, not unfrequently, pure blood is voided. As the disease proceeds, and ulceration is developed, pus becomes mingled with the discharge, as well as membranous shred-like particles (the latter an ominous sign). Considerable prostration is attendant throughout; the pulse is weak and quick, the respiration increased, the eyes sunken, mucous membranes injected, the nose dry and hot, mouth slimy and breath offensive; with these there is loss of appetite, considerable thirst, and disinclination during the latter stages to move, the evacuations being involuntary and most disgusting.

Treatment.—The medicinal treatment of dysentery should be essentially anodyne and astringent. The sulphate of copper and opium stand pre-eminent, and may be given in the proportions named in the foregoing disease, three or if necessary four times per day. I am no advocate for blood-letting in this excessively reducing malady. As a local application I prefer a hot linseed-meal poultice to the abdomen. When the discharge is excessive, and mingled with blood, a tablespoonful of starch, with 10 drops of laudanum, may be injected, or 20 drops of tinct. ferri in a tablespoonful of iced water, and repeated if necessary.

Diet.—The same rules regarding the diet in diarrhœa will apply in dysentery, and warmth, cleanliness, and dryness are equally essential.

INTUS-SUSCEPTION.

This intestinal condition is commonly met with in the dog. When one portion of the tube "telescopes" or becomes invaginated, within the portion anterior or posterior to it, what is termed intus-susception is established.

The small intestines are those generally involved.

Intus-susception usually terminates fatally; adhesion, however, of the invaginated portion may take place, followed by suppuration and separation of that part.

In a recent *post-mortem* examination of a large mastiff dog I found death had resulted from stoppage and consequent inflammation, owing to constriction of the bowel immediately in front of an old intus-suscepted portion, in which adhesion was established, but the process of separation had not become complete.

In a still more recent one, of a fox-hound, I found acute inflammation of the bowels at and anterior and posterior to an invaginated portion of seven inches in length, in which adhesion had not commenced.

The following case was recorded by Jonathan Hutchinson, in 1876:

INTUS-SUSCEPTION OF THE ILEUM AND CÆCUM IN A DOG.

This specimen was taken from a dog about ten months old. The ileum and cæcum had passed into the colon for a distance of about eight inches, until the cæcum nearly presented at the anus. The layers were not in the least adherent, and it might have been reduced by traction from within the abdomen with great ease. Although the impacted parts were much congested, there was no tendency to gangrene, nor any trace of inflammatory effusion anywhere. It was chiefly in reference to its bearing on the feasibility of operations in these cases that the specimen was of interest. No treatment had been adopted during the life of the animal, because no diagnosis had been made. The dog was in perfect health until about eight days before his death, when, without any cause perceptible, he began to show signs of discomfort, and refused to hunt. He was never observed to be sick, nor did he pass blood. He took little or no food, and his belly became much retracted. For two days before his death he was intensely jaundiced. In reference to the non-occurrence of adhesions between the layers of impacted intestine, it must be borne in mind that experiments have established the fact that dogs are but little prone to peritonitis.—*Pathological Society's Transactions.*

Symptoms.—There are no special diagnostic symptoms of intus-susception in the dog. Those of colic are generally at the onset present, and are succeeded by enteritic ones. Frequent violent straining and vomiting are also invariably present. But the same may occur in strangulated hernia, and other intestinal affections.

Treatment.—A large dose of linseed or salad oil should first be administered for the purpose of mechanically facilitating the return of the invaginated portion, or inflation of the bowels with air might be adopted with good results, or the administration of quicksilver could be tried. The succeeding treatment should be as for colic and enteritis, or both combined.

WORMS.

Dogs are invariably, during some portion of their lives, troubled with worms, and the most common seat of these pests is in the intestinal canal. It is, perhaps, hardly necessary to observe that their presence causes their host much annoyance, and is frequently productive of disease.

Vomiting, paralysis, rectal irritation—denoted by the animal frequently licking the part, and dragging himself along in a sitting posture—purging, inordinate appetite, enlarged abdomen, harsh, staring coat, emaciation, and more or less febrile disturbance, are among the symptoms usually presented in such cases, while ocular demonstration of the fact is not frequently wanting.

For a fuller description of this subject and the treatment, see chapter on " Internal Parasites."

COLIC.

This disease in the dog is not of that frequency which might be expected from the strange circumstances unde which at times he exists, the exertions required of him the exposure he is subject to, and the bill of fare.

Causes.—Intestinal obstruction, calculi, intus-susception hernia, impaction of fæces, flatulency, worms, cold, or indi gestible food. A special form of colic is caused by lead poisoning.

Symptoms.—Colic comes on suddenly; the animal is t all appearance in perfect health, when he immediatel utters a sharp cry of pain, and, with his back arched an abdomen drawn up, he walks restlessly about, whimperin or moaning, and endeavouring vainly to find ease i various postures. Considerable tympany is often presen giving the animal a tense inflated appearance.

By careful inquiry the cause of the attack may be ofte ascertained: frequently it may be traced to the food; a unusual supply of bones may have been given, a great por tion of which may probably have been devoured in such form as to cause irritation, if not mechanical obstruction or from long submergence in water, which is frequently th case with swimming dogs, who no sooner approach th bank than another stick or stone is flung in, and away he i started again, and this repeated over and over again b thoughtless persons who never seem to dream of the exten to which they are taxing the good nature of the willin servant.

Constipation, flatulency, worms, are also causes equall easy of ascertainment, and by inquiry (in kennel dogs mor particularly) as to the source whence the water is supplie and the vehicle through which it flows or is drauk from, w may arrive at the conclusion the attack is caused from th action of lead. Intus-susception, calculi, or hernia, woul be indicated by the colicky pains being of greater frequenc and more protracted ; but usually, and especially to an unscientific person, these would be somewhat obscure.

With regard to medicinal treatment, an oleaginous aperient at the onset is generally advisable ; impaction of the rectum is best removed with a warm soap-sud enema. Flatulency may be relieved by aromatic cordials and antacids, as—

    Sodæ Carbonate .... 10—20 grains
    Essence of Peppermint......... 5—10 minims
        In a tablespoonful of warm water ;
            or,
    Spts. Ammon. Aromaticus ... 20—30 minims
    Zingib. .... 10 grains
        Administered the same way.

When the pain is severe 1—3 grains of opium may be given in a teaspoonful or two of equal parts of brandy and water, and repeated in an hour if not relieved ; or 6—12 minims of chlorodyne may be given in a teaspoonful of water, with the same directions.

Rubbing the abdomen affords ease, and in extreme cases mustard or ammonia embrocation may be applied.

Bitches in whelp are occasionally attacked with colic, owing to fœtal pressure on the bladder. In such cases we can only wait until the period of parturition arrives, and in the meantime not overload the stomach and bowels, and keep the latter gently relaxed ; urgent symptoms must, of course, be treated as above.

Puppies are said to be exceedingly liable to colic, but I have failed to find it so, except occasionally when they are sucking ; attention to the mother's diet will generally be found the most effectual means of preventing its recurrence, with a dose or two of carbonate of soda.

I question whether any but the most experienced would easily recognise a colicky puppy three or four weeks old, not to mention a more infantile age.

ENTERITIS,

Or inflammation of the bowels, is a disease to which dogs, from its ordinary causes, are fortunately not very subject. Enteritis is rarely confined to one tissue, both peritoneal, muscular, and mucous are generally involved in the inflammatory process. The latter is, however, in all instances, more particularly the seat of inflammation, and from the rapidity of its course seldom gives time for the others to be equally involved.

Causes.—Protracted colic, exposure to damp and cold, especially from lying on the earth or wet floor, intestinal obstruction from fæces, foreign bodies, strangulation, or intus-susception, local irritation, or irritant poisons.

Symptoms.—It is highly essential, in enteritis, that the practitioner should arrive at a correct diagnosis: in other words, that he should be able to distinguish it from other affections resembling it, more especially colic, with which it is most likely to be confounded. The usual cordials and stimulants given in the latter affection would be adding fuel to fire in enteritis, and speedily effect a fatal termination.

The pain in enteritis is continuous and extremely severe, and pressure to the abdomen greatly aggravates it. In colic the pain is intermittent, and pressure or friction to the abdomen affords considerable relief.

In enteritis the visible mucous membranes are highly injected, thermometrical insertion per rectum shows considerable increase of temperature, and the pulse is increased in frequency and small.

In colic there is no injection of the mucous membranes, no increase in temperature, and only slight acceleration of pulse and breathing during the spasm. Such may be considered the leading diagnostic distinctions between the two diseases.

The General Symptoms of enteritis are as follows: Its commencement is denoted by rigors, a dry hot nose, injected visible mucous membranes, pulse small, hard and frequent, considerable thirst is present, and usually obstinate constipation. The animal moves continually about, looks back at his flank and whines piteously ; he no sooner adopts the recumbent position than, with a sharp cry, up he starts again. As the disease proceeds these symptoms become greatly aggravated; the abdomen is hot and extremely tender, the breathing hurried and painful and entirely thoracic, pulse wiry and increased, mucous membranes deep red, urine scanty and high coloured ; the cries are more frequent and sharp, and if an attempt be made to pick the animal up he immediately resents it ; if the attendant is successful, a howl of pain is emitted. When the disease is due to irritant poisons or the presence of acrid bile, or associated with gastric derangement, incessant vomiting, often streaked with blood, accompany it, with frequent evcauations similar in character to the vomit.

Finally the mouth, ears, and limbs become cold and clammy, the abdomen it distended, an offensive cadaverous smell is emitted from the body generally, the breathing is difficult and irregular, pulse imperceptible, the heart can just be detected feebly beating, convulsions follow, and death closes the scene.

The terminations of enteritis are :—

Resolution.—A gradual diminution of the symptoms, and return to health.

Ulceration.—Frequent purulent evacuations, with rapid emaciation, and finally death.

Gangrene.—Sudden suspension of pain, suppression of secretions, cold, clammy condition of body, gums and inside of the lips livid, delirium, convulsions, and death.

Enteritis may assume a chronic form ; in such a case intermittent pains occur, the fæces are alternately watery and hard, the abdomen is tense, and flatulency and vomiting are more or less frequent.

Treatment.—I have already alluded to the importance of

diagnosing correctly between enteritis and colic, and from what I there mentioned it will be gathered that stimulants and cordials form no part of our treatment in this disease.

Our first duty is, if possible, to ascertain the cause. Purgatives usually, in enteritis, are not advisable. When however, the illness can be traced to local irritation from the impaction of fæces, worms, or foreign matter, a mild dose of castor-oil may be given at the onset with benefit.

Again, if the liver be associated with it, a small dose of aloes and calomel can also be administered with safety. If, on examination per rectum, impaction of hardened fæces are found, they should be gently broken down with the finger, and a simple warm-water enema thrown up to assist their expulsion. Drastic purgatives at any period of the disease are hurtful, and removal of the obstruction, if possible, by mechanical means is decidedly preferable. Salad oil is a valuable agent for this purpose; it effects its object by insinuation through the obstruction, supposing it to be the impaction of fæcal matter; it, at the same time, shields the mucous membrane, and if there is intus-susception it facilitates its removal.

To relieve the pain, from 1 to 3 grains of opium may be given in a teaspoonful or two of barley-water, and repeated in an hour if necessary. Opiate enemas can also be administered with the same view.

Counter-irritation to the abdomen is of great value, mustard plasters, hot linseed-meal poultices, bags of hot salt continually renewed, or hot fomentations may be used.

Bleeding is beneficial in the early stage only, and is best adopted locally, by means of leeches to the abdomen.

When the acute symptoms have subsided the counter-irritation may be discontinued, but the abdomen must be kept thoroughly warm and the patient quiet.

With regard to support during the illness, bland mucilaginous drinks should form the only diet, and should be continued for some considerable time after recovery takes place, owing to the sensitive condition of the intestinal mucous membrane.

Gastro-Enteritis is usually the result of irritant poisons. The symptoms are those of gastritis and enteritis combined. The treatment must consist, at the onset, in removing the cause, followed by that laid down for the two diseases respectively.

PERITONITIS.

Inflammation of the peritoneum is more frequent in bitches than dogs. The inflammation may be local or diffused, *i.e.*, it may be confined to one portion of the membrane, or extend to the whole. A general or diffused peritonitis is the form usually met with in canine practice.

Causes.—External violence, as kicks, blows, wounds (particularly punctured), parturition, hernia, constipation, exposure to damp and cold.

Symptoms.—Acute peritonitis is characterised by abdominal pain, which is considerably augmented by pressure. The animal exhibits great restlessness, continually moving about and endeavouring to obtain, if possible, a comfortable position, and this his broadside appears to afford him best. The pulse is small, hard, and wiry, conjunctival membrane injected, nose dry and hot, tongue white and slimy, breathing increased, and expirations hot.

As the disease advances the pain becomes most intense: the very countenance of the poor animal is expressive of the agony he is enduring. Sharp cries bespeak the torture produced by even the slightest pressure. Lying now in any posture affords not the slightest relief; and the patient stands, propped up, as it were, with his legs apart, breathing with difficulty, for this act is now performed independent of the abdominal muscles or diaphragm. The abdomen becomes distended the tongue dry and furred, thirst extreme, urine scanty and high-coloured, and there is obstinate constipation. In a short time the herald of death approaches, all pain ceases —*mortification* is the boon he grants before life leaves the suffering frame. The extremities become cold, the patient is comatose, and so passes quietly away; or, occasionally delirium closes the scene.

Post-mortem Appearances.—Intense inflammation of the peritoneal membrane, often extending through its whole thickness, and portions of it are not unfrequently found to be gangrenous. The membrane covering the intestines is frequently involved; livid patches are also to be observed on that portion of it covering the stomach and liver. The abdominal cavity contains more or less serous fluid; if the disease has existed long the quantity is considerable, of a bloody hue, and smells very offensive.

Treatment.—In the early stage of acute peritonitis, the bowels may be moved by an oleaginous aperient; but in the later stages—when, in all probability, the membrane covering the intestines is involved, together with the inability of the system to withstand depletion—purgatives are attended with great danger, and simple enemas alone should be relied on.

Hot fomentations, linseed-meal poultices, or bags of hot salt should constitute local treatment. At *the onset* leeches may be applied to the abdomen; but they are not admissible at a later period.

With regard to internal remedies, anodyne agents are indicated, and either of the following medicines may be given:—

Fleming's Tinct. of Aconite ... 1 to 3 minims,
in a teaspoonful of water every two hours;
or,
Opium .... 1 grain
Chloroform .... 5 minims,
in a teaspoonful or two of water every four hours;

Sedative enemas may also be used, and are attended for a time with much relief.

The same diet as for enteritis should be adopted.

Acute Peritonitis may terminate in recovery, ascites, or become chronic.

Chronic Peritonitis is generally the result of an acute attach.

Symptoms.—These are not so easily defined as in the previous form. The abdomen is hard, enlarged, and somewhat contracted at the sides. Uneasiness, or a kind of sub-acute pain appears frequently to be present, especially after feeding. There is also a degree of fever continually present. The nose is seldom moist or cool, and the pulse is low and fluctuating. The animal becomes gradually emaciated, the abdomen increases in size (vulgarly termed pot-bellied), the appetite fails, and death from exhaustion takes place. This form of peritonitis is generally associated with ascites.

Post-mortem Examination reveals a thickened condition of the peritoneal membrane, with frequently numerous granulations on its abdominal surface. The serous effusion is more abundant, and of a paler or more limpid colour than in acute peritonitis.

Treatment.—This consists in tonics, particularly the tincture or sulphate of iron, with fresh air, moderate exercise, and plain, nutritious food; if the debility is extreme, brandy, beef-tea, and cod-liver oil may be added.

PILES.

Dogs are frequently afflicted with this troublesome affection. Piles may be either external or internal, and assume either the form of vascular tumours around the margin of the anus, or within it.

External piles are composed of a congregation of varicose veins. Internal piles are usually similar in formation, but occasionally they are genuine pendulous tumours and so exceedingly vascular that the least pressure produces hæmorrhage (bleeding piles).

Causes.—Habitual constipation, abuse of purgatives, prolonged diarrhœa or dysentery, plethora, torpid liver, dyspepsia, over-stimulating food and confinement.

Symptoms.—A swollen and relaxed condition of the anus, with eversion and congestion of the mucous membrane. If the piles are external, the margin of the anus is tumefied and uneven. If internal, the tumours will frequently be observed to protrude in the act of defecation, which is attended with considerable pain, and the matter is often mingled with blood; occasionally also, an involuntary fœtid discharge takes place.

Considerable itching attends either form, and a dog so affected is continually licking the parts, or dragging himself in a sitting posture along the floor. To manipulation they are exceedingly sensitive, and the animal will avoid any interference as much as possible.

Piles, if neglected, give rise to the formation of abscess, extensive ulceration, fistula and tumour.

Treatment.—This consists, first, in attention to the diet and general health of the patient. The food should be plain, nutritious, easy of digestion, and laxative; daily exercise and occasionally cold baths are beneficial.

Medicinal agents will depend upon the cause of the affection. Under most circumstances, a mild oleaginous aperient is advisable. If the liver is inactive, the aloetic aperient with calomel is most suitable; while, if there is a relaxed system with dyspepsia, iron and cod-liver oil is indicated.

With regard to local treatment, iced water, or the direct application of ice affords considerable relief. If the piles are internal, and attended with hæmorrhage, recourse to astringents will be necessary, and I know of none better than alum, either in solution and injected, or the powder made into a paste with flour and water and gently inserted. A portion of ice may also, with benefit and ease to the patient, be introduced into the rectum and allowed to melt there.

When there is considerable pain without hæmorrhage, and the rectum is tumefied, leeches may be conveniently and advisedly applied to the parts. Pain, with internal hæmorrhage, is best relieved by the addition of a grain of opium to the astringent paste or injection.*

When obstinate constipation prevails, an enema of olive-oil is most suitable for facilitating the fæcal evacuation, and with less pain than with any other form of evacuation.

Tumours, external or internal, should be removed by ligature, *the animal being under the influence of chloroform*. The ultimate sore to be treated according to circumstances.

Fœtor may be counteracted by the application if external, or the injection if internal, of a weak solution of chloride of zinc.

PROLAPSUS ANI.

This condition of the rectum often occurs in aged dogs which are overfed, have but little exercise, and whose bowels are either continually constipated or relaxed. It is generally a protrusion or eversion of the mucous membrane of the rectum rather than the rectum itself.

Symptoms.—These need but little description—the eversion being in itself sufficiently diagnostic; at stool it is increased and considerably injected.

Treatment.—This consists in cleansing and returning the protruded portion, and afterwards in the application of cold and astringents. Tone will be given to the system, and constringement of the affected part effected by the administration of tinct. ferri, 10 to 15 minims, twice or three times a day in cold water.

Nutritious diet and a moderate allowance of exercise should be given.

---

* A drachm each of tannin and opium, with an ounce of lard, makes an excellent ointment for piles in dogs.—*Finlay Dun*.

Where these measures fail, an operation will be necessary; and this generally consists in removing one of the folds of the mucous membrane by knife or ligature, or the destruction of a portion of it by actual cautery. It is needless to remark that either operation should be performed under the influence of chloroform, and by a veterinary surgeon.

FISTULA IN ANO.

Fistula of the anus is frequently met with in dogs, particularly of the pampered house tribe, and is usually the result of neglected piles; it may occur from wounds, abscess, or ulceration of the rectum (the latter generally consequent on piles), or from impaction of hardened fæces.

The fistula may be external or internal, complete or partial, *i.e.*, external if the orifice of the wound is in the integument, or internal if within the rectum; complete, if the two orifices exist together, partial when there is but one orifice.

Symptoms.—The symptoms of fistula in the dog are continual irritation of the affected part; the animal will be observed continually licking the anus, and dragging himself along the floor with his fore-limbs. If the fistula be external it requires little diagnosis; if internal, and not complete, there is an offensive rectal discharge, and the fæces are often coated with matter and blood.

Treatment.—The treatment of fistula lies in laying open the sinus with a fine probe-pointed bistoury, and afterwards treating it in the first instance as a common wound, and subsequently with a solution of chloride of zinc. If considerable hæmorrhage follows, the part should be packed with lint or cotton-wool steeped in tinct. of iron, or a solution of tannic acid; or if it be from a divided artery, to tie the vessel if possible. The bowels should be properly regulated, and at no time constipation allowed to take place ; an injection of warm water twice or three times a day, after hæmorrhage is prevented, should be administered for the double purpose of facilitating the passage of fæces and removing the discharge.

CHAPTER VI.

DISEASES OF THE LIVER AND SPLEEN.

HEPATITIS,
JAUNDICE,
FATTY DEGENERATION OF THE LIVER
CANCEROUS DEPOSIT IN THE LIVER AND SPLEEN,
BILIARY CALCULI,
SPLENITIS.

HEPATITIS,

Or inflammation of the liver, may be acute or chronic.

ACUTE.

Predisposing Causes.—Overfeeding, with insufficient exercise, especially in pampered house pets.

Exciting Causes.—Exposure to damp and cold, intense heat, immoderate use of emetics, biliary concretions, acrid bile, external violence over the region of the liver, as blows, kicks, falls, or crushes.

Symptoms.—Pain on the right side, increased by pressure, quickened respiration, dry cough, pulse hard and fluctuating, rigors and vomiting. As the complaint proceeds, the skin and visible mucous membranes become yellow, the fæces pale, either relaxed or confined, urine scanty and of a deep orange tint; bile is mingled with the vomit, the tenderness on the right side is increased, and a considerable enlargement is observable in the region of the liver; the abdomen is more or less pendulous, the eyes dull, tongue coated with brown fur, gums congested, breath fœtid; and attendant on these symptoms we have great thirst, loss of appetite, flatulency, and rapid emaciation.

Acute hepatitis may terminate in resolution or abscess, or become chronic.

Treatment.—In the early stage local bleeding is exceedingly beneficial, the hair over the affected region should be shaved closely off and leeches applied, after which a hot linseed-meal poultice may be bound over the part.

With regard to medicinal agents—mild saline doses at the onset, as a drachm each of sulphate of magnesia and bicarbonate of soda, repeated for three days, and then followed by vegetable tonics, form the best internal treatment that I am aware of. Stimulants are rarely, if ever, admissible.

When the acute symptoms have abated, nourishing but unstimulating food may be allowed, with daily quiet exercise.

CHRONIC HEPATITIS

may, as I have observed, be a sequel of the former, or be associated with other diseases, or it may be created by some specific disease within its own structure.

It is, however, more generally brought about from long-continued injudicious feeding and denial of exercise, and is more frequently seen in the smaller breeds, particularly toy terriers.

Symptoms.—These are, to a considerable extent, a modified type of those existing in acute hepatitis. The size of the liver may be increased or decreased—more frequently the former, the enlargement being hard and more or less insensible to pain on pressure. The animal has an habitual jaundiced appearance, and is usually languid and dejected.

Treatment.—The treatment of chronic hepatitis may be more extended than when it is acute. Counter-irritation is decidedly indicated, and is certainly beneficial. I am of opinion that strong iodine liniment applied with a brush, after first removing the hair, is the best agent for this purpose, and more in accordance with the nature of a glandular disease. Calomel may also be administered with benefit in one-grain doses, combined with ten grains of rhubarb or a scruple of aloes every other day. Intermediate doses of dilute nitric acid, two to four drops twice a day, often assist recovery and keep a clean palate; or the iodide of potassium, in five to ten grain doses, may be tried. Plain unstimulating food and free exercise should be allowed, and a relaxed condition of the bowels maintained.

Chronic hepatitis, from interference in the portal circulation, often terminates in ascites, more particularly in old dogs. (See "Dropsy.")

JAUNDICE (ICTERUS).

This is an affection to which dogs are peculiarly liable. Greyhounds have been stated to be more generally the subject of it than other breeds. My experience of the disease, however, has been chiefly confined to the smaller breeds, especially pampered house-dogs.

Jaundice may exist alone, or be associated with other affections, particularly distemper, in which, by dog-men, it is usually separated from the malady giving rise to it, and treated independently as the "Yellows." (See "Distemper.")

Causes.—Suppression or retention of bile, more particularly the latter, which becomes re-absorbed into the system.*

---

* Sir Thomas Watson, in his lecture on this subject, says: "There can be no doubt that when the bile, after being formed in the liver, is detained there, or in the gall-bladder, in consequence of some impediment to its excretion, it is re-absorbed—both by the lymphatic vessels and by the veins—carried into the circulation, and so conveyed to the surface, and to the parts in which the change of colour is observed. In the beginning of the present century, Dr. Saunders, of Guy's Hospital, made, on this subject, some conclusive experiments, which have since been repeated by others with similar results. The hepatic duct of a dog having been tied, and the animal killed two hours afterwards, the numerous lymphatics in the walls of the bile-ducts were seen to be distended with a yellow fluid; the fluid in the thoracic duct also was yellow; and so were the intervening lymphatic glands. Again, two hours after the ligation of the hepatic duct, the serum of blood taken from the hepatic vein was found to contain much more of the colouring matter of the bile, than that of blood taken from the jugular vein in the neck. That bile is capable of being taken up by the absorbents is further apparent from the fact that when the cystic duct is permanently shut, the bile disappears gradually, but entirely, from the gall-bladder.

Biliary calculi in the gall-bladder or its duct, inspissated bile,* disease of the liver—as inflammation, enlargement, contraction, schirrous tumours, abscess—immoderate use of purgatives, especially aloes and calomel, repeated emetics, sudden chills after heat and fatigue, accumulation of fæces.

Symptoms.—General depression, inactivity, loss of appetite, bowels constipated and of a light drab or clay colour, or relaxed, the fæces being of a greenish tint mingled with mucus, and offensive; urine high-coloured, hot, occasionally turbid, and stains yellow; excessive vomition; pulse increased, contracted and hard; the skin is hot, and, if gathered up, remains stationary for some moments,—this is more particularly the case towards a fatal termination, It is also of a deep yellow tinge, especially on the thin parts. as over the abdomen, inside the thighs, forearms and ears. The same colour is present on the visible mucous membranes of the eye, conjunctiva, inside the lips, the gums and vagina. The mouth and nose are dry and hot, the tongue furred and breath offensive. There is pain on pressure over the region of the liver, with, sometimes, enlargement and hardness. There is also a great disposition to somnolence, and, during slumber, fitful starts with subdued whimpers will frequently be noted.

Convulsions, succeeded by a profound state of coma, usually precede death; a peculiar general offensive odour is also emitted.

In-whelp bitches occasionally become jaundiced from uterine pressure, which generally disappears after parturition.

Treatment.—If taken in hand early, and there is no struc-

---

* I have recently had two interesting cases of jaundice, one in a fox-terrier, the other in a Chinese pug, arising from inspissated bile. In both the disease was so far advanced, when placed under my charge, that all treatment proved useless. A *post-mortem* examination revealed the gall-ducts choked with inspissated bile.

tural disease of the liver, jaundice is not difficult to deal with. The cause, therefore, if possible, must be first ascertained. If it is the accumulation of fæces, an aloetic purge, assisted by enemas, will, in removing the cause, likewise dispel the effect.

If the disease proceeds from inspissated bile or gall-stone —in which case the urine is generally turbid and the pain more acute, with increased vomiting and difficulty in fæcal evacuation—a smart dose of aloes and calomel should be prescribed, followed by small doses of spirits of nitrous ether and laudanum, 2 parts of the former to 1 of the latter, in drachm doses, twice or three times a day. A hot bath will also afford considerable relief, and this may be followed by the application of a mustard or linseed poultice over the region of the liver.

When jaundice is due to the immoderate use of purgatives and emetics, an opposite line of treatment will be required: mucilaginous drinks, and alkalies with opium are indicated.

When diarrhœa is present, a mild dose of castor-oil may be first given, followed, if necessary, by small doses of opium. If the evacuations are excessive and attended with great straining, starch and opium enemas should be administered.

Bleeding in jaundice is of no earthly use: if the pain is acute, leeches may be applied to the side, but I must confess I am no advocate for the abstraction of blood in this disease in any form, and place far more confidence in counter-irritation or poultices.

The diet should be plain, unstimulating, and laxative. Moderate exercise may be allowed, but exposure to cold or damp must be strictly guarded against. Animals once affected with jaundice are peculiarly liable to a return of the complaint, and therefore need more than ordinary attention.

From the *Veterinarian*, May, 1870, I transcribe the following interesting paper :—

"JAUNDICE IN THE DOG AND ITS TREATMENT.
" BY M. WEBER, VETERINARY SURGEON, PARIS.

"The author believes he does not exaggerate in saying that, up to the present time, jaundice in the dog has been considered by veterinary practitioners as generally, if not always, mortal, and that therapeutics were powerless to combat it.

"The authors who have written on this disease, it must be acknowledged, were not well acquainted with it, and therefore not very competent. It is more particularly in the treatises on sport that we find any description or treatment of this malady, hence very different theories and treatments have been produced without resulting in any benefit, either to science or to the patient.

"Some veterinary authors, however, have treated the question, and have tried to connect it with a certain order of anatomical lesion; but in many cases these anatomical lesions are insufficient, at least, according to the results of my experience.

"Before proceeding, it is important to state what I understand by jaundice; it is not every malady in which the yellow icteric tint is often a symptom of a more serious organic lesion, and which it would be useless to attempt to cure, that should be considered as jaundice. The jaundice in the dog, such as I have often been able to observe, is, like the icterus, simple and grave in the human subject, and it is of this form only that I intend to treat; it corresponds to the malady in man, described by M. Ozanam as *Icterus essential character grave*, and which has also been designated as *Icterus malignus*. In a great number of cases the icteric tint is a symptom connected almost always with some serious lesions (such as rupture of the liver, abscesses and cyst in the same, scirrhous tumours, obstruction and ruptures of the gall-ducts, intestinal invaginations).

"The *Icterus benign*, so frequent in the human subject that it is considered of very little consequence, is very rare in the dog. On the other hand, the *Icterus grave* is nearly always fatal; but, notwithstanding, at the autopsy there are rarely found anatomical lesions sufficient to account for the death, or the gravity of the symptoms during life. Sex does not appear to have any influence in the production of the malady—male and female alike are subject to it, though the number of males that came under treatment might be greater. Neither has age any influence; the malady attacks both young, adult, and old, without distinction.

"Though it is often difficult to trace the cause of the affection, I believe I am not far out in saying that the most frequent causes of this malady are: (1) excessive action brought on by fatigue, (2) long journeys, (3) prolonged sport, (4) sudden chills, (5) external violence, blows, etc., (6) abuse of emetics and purgatives, (7) obstinate constipation. Thus the malady prevails among setters and pointers a few days after the opening of the shooting season; in hounds after a long run, and particularly in dogs which are not very fast, and are forced to keep up with the pack composed mostly of hounds of great speed; in dogs which follow carriages for long distances; and in retrievers which, after being heated, go into the water to recover the game.

"It also prevails among dogs which are left in the charge of keepers, and, as often happens, are subjected to strong drastic purgatives, or to emetics, with a view to cure the distemper; also in those animals which receive blows and kicks, too often in wanton thoughtlessness and cruelty, or accidental compression in the region of the liver. Finally, the obstinate constipation so frequent in dogs condemned to live in large towns seems to me to have a large share in the production of this malady. It is said that anger, combats amongst them, fright, etc., might cause jaundice.

"The first signs of the affection are variable, but most

frequently the following symptoms are observed: dulness, prostration, difficulty in locomotion, arched back, acceleration of the pulse, nose hot and dry, mucous membrane of a bright red colour, mouth dry and hot, staring coat, principally on the back, abdomen hard and tender in the region of the liver, and in a very short time seems as if adhering to the back. The animal soon refuses all food (liquid and solid), but there is an intense thirst, and the dog will not drink anything but pure water. Often the animal seems to be troubled with colic; soon supervenes a symptom which is rarely absent, that is bilious vomiting, which is very frequent and often mixed with blood; the urine becomes of a dark colour and bloody, constipation is frequently present, but sometimes there is diarrhœa, the excrements being bloody, and often the dog voids pure blood. At this stage the malady is easily recognised by an experienced eye, but soon there is no possibility of doubt, as the yellow tints set in—the mucous membranes are the first invaded by it, but soon the skin also shews the icteric tint. This tint varies sometimes from straw-colour to dark yellow.

"The pulse now becomes weaker and much slower, the urine has a more decided yellow tint; the animal becomes more and more feeble, gets up with difficulty, and exhales a peculiar disagreeable odour from the mouth; the weakness becomes extreme, the emaciation is visible, the extremities grow cold; the animal becomes now insensible to surrounding objects, and death terminates the scene. Sometimes the malady lasts only two days, but in general the duration varies from two to five days.

"In some cases a cough supervenes, with acceleration of the respiration, and an affection of the lungs complicates the malady (M. Leblanc). If the animal is bled in the course of the disease, the blood exhales a peculiar odour, and the serum is tinted with yellow. From the moment the yellow tint appears, the fæcal evacuations become often greyish white; at the commencement of the malady they are of ɩ blackish colour, and frequently mixed with blood.

"The termination of the malady, up to the present time has been most frequently mortal; some cases of cure have, however, been recorded, but so rare that they have been rather the exception, death being the rule. The pathological alterations, without being absolutely constant, are in the generality of cases as follows: all the tissues are coloured yellow, the mucous membrane of the intestine is sometimes the seat of pathological alterations, but at others is perfectly healthy. The liver in certain cases is enlarged, in others diminished in size; the colouration also varies in this organ, and it often shows no alteration, but one thing which I have always found at the autopsy of dogs who had died from the jaundice, is the accumulation of bile in the gall-bladder—this is of a yellowish-green colour and very thick. In the presence of these pathological lesions, it seems that jaundice in the dog is not an incurable malady; the only question to resolve is how to find therapeutic agents to combat the torpitude of the liver at the commencement of the malady.

"The author acknowledges that the microscopical investigations necessary to complete the study of the pathological lesions have completely failed.

"As often happens in maladies considered almost as incurable, the treatment of this disease in the dog has been most varied. Some have employed the antiphlogistic system, bleeding, and revulsives; others purgatives; others tonics. All these means have nearly always had the same success—that is, some patients have recovered by chance; notwithstanding all that could be done, however, the majority have died, sometimes of the malady, at others of the treatment. We will pass in review the remedies recommended by the different veterinary authors who have written on this malady.

" M. U. Leblanc, whose writing is the most complete on

the jaundice of the dog, recommends repeated bleedings at the commencement, manna, sulphate of magnesia, enemas, with the addition of starch and laudanum; if diarrhœa is present, disacordium, half a drachm. He insists on hygienic means; panades with the addition of butter, for which broth is to be substituted afterwards; clean, warm, dry quarters etc.

"Hurtrel d'Arboval, inspired by the writings of M. U. Leblanc, also recommends bleeding at the onset, mucilaginous drinks, with nitre, emollient enemas, etc.

"M. Prudhomme says that the treatment of jaundice in the dog does not often succeed, as it is one of the most fatal maladies of the canine species. He has, however, obtained some favourable results from small repeated bleedings, whey drinks, mucilage from decoction of linseed, or carrots and barley, to which were added a few grammes of cream of tartar, enemas, with starch and opium.

"Professor Hertwig, of Berlin, employs emetics, slight purges, as, for example, calomel with honey, or cream of tartar, friction on the abdomen, with ammoniacal liniment.

"M. C. Leblanc recommends baths with bran-water, leeches on the abdomen, emollient enemas, sulphate of soda (if constipated), mustard on the chest and feet. He adds that if an improvement does not speedily set in, death is certain.

"M. Lafosse advises the same means as those directed by M. C. Leblanc, the decoction of carrots and cream of tartar; if extreme debility sets in, to have recourse to quinine wine.

"The author says he has tried all the remedies suggested, and despairing of the results asks himself the question whether an agent could not be found which has a special action on the liver and the biliary system powerful enough to combat this terrible malady. Another question was whether the icteric colour depended really on bile being mixed with the blood in jaundice, as has been asserted, or whether it is owing to an incomplete separation of the elements which constitute the bile from the blood, in consequence of the liver not performing its proper function.

"'I am inclined,' the author says, ' to the latter supposition, seeing that the icteric colour supervenes principally when there is atrophy of the liver, and also in the adipose liver, and when the substance of this organ has been invaded by the tissue of foreign substance, such as cancerous tumours, it cannot be supposed that in these cases there can be a superabundant secretion of bile to mix with the blood ; it seems infinitely more simple to admit that the function of the gland is insufficient to separate the elements of the bile from the blood, and the liquids and solids are soon pervaded by the icteric tint.'

" This view, however, the author does not take credit for, as several physiologists have considered the bile as an excremental product. According to M. Colin the bile is thick, which is, moreover, the case also with other secretions. These physiological views seem to be completely borne out by pathological facts ; cons quent on these reflections I have thought it important to search for some remedy that was capable of restoring the function of the liver in jaundice of the dog. The author continues :—

" After several attempts I fixed on the chloride of mer cury (calomel), the purgative properties of which have been admitted ; but after having administered this drug in purgative doses without satisfactory result, I resorted to it in alterative doses, and the results obtained have been beyond my expectation, so that there is no case of true jaundice of the cure of which I despair at present.

"'Without, however, pretending to have cured every case, I can affirm that since I am in possession of this remedy the fatal termination of the malady has been very rare ; while before the cures were exceptional, and death the rule; but the method of administration is not a matter of indifference. The medicine must be given in small doses three or four times a day, without, however, carrying it to purging. As soon as that supervenes, the dose must be decreased, and stopped altogether for a time, if the purging is violent. The dose is from five to ten centigrammes, to be made up in pills, given from two to four times a day. This is to be continued for a few days, if purging does not set in; if, on the other hand, purging occurs, the dose must be reduced or suspended altogether, until it has stopped.

"'The administration of the calomel in the form of pills is preferable, as the agent is insoluble in water, and the suspension in other liquids is at best unsatisfactory and uncertain; enemas slightly charged with laudanum are to be given in accordance with the indications. If the dog is able to eat, he is to be allowed food, avoiding all salted substances. After four or five days of the administration of the medicine, an abundant salivation sets in, but I have not had this followed by inflammation of the stomach or gangrene of the mouth; in some cases, however, there is loosening of the teeth; this was the case particularly with a young terrier, which had taken the calomel for five days, in doses of five centigrammes three times a day. The animal lost five teeth, but recovered of the jaundice. The medicine may be given for the first four days at the rate of three pills a day, two on the fifth day, afterwards reduced to one, and discontinued altogether when the state of the patient admits of it.'

"The author gives several cases of jaundice in the dog successfully treated, but which would take up too much space."—*Recueil de Médecine Veterinaire.*

For the following translation I am indebted to Mr. Fleming :—

JAUNDICE, OR ICTERUS, IN THE DOG.

"Trasbot (*Archives Veterinaires*, 1876), in a very able paper on this malady, when alluding to its 'pathological physiology,' states that, after the anatomical study he has made of the disease, it appears to be sufficiently proved that it is not essentially an alteration of the liver; on the contrary, in the majority of cases this organ is perfectly healthy, and even less modified in its colour than many of the other tissues. It is sometimes found slightly congested and ecchymosed, but this is more rare, and always in a lesser degree than the lungs, kidneys, and lymphatic glands. When it exists it is only a secondary phenomenon, indicating a general alteration in the organism, which is marked by a tendency to the production of capillary hæmorrhage in different parts, and by no special lesion. The general condition of the animals, the increase in the respiration and circulation, as well as the elevation of temperature before the appearance of the yellow colour externally, indicate, as a primary and fundamental phenomenon, an acutely inflamed condition of some tissue. And, later, the prostration, insensibility, and low temperature prove the existence of intoxication by a poison; this poison evidently results from the accumulation of bile—or, at least, of some of its constituents—in the blood. So that icterus, at first of an inflammatory nature, is soon complicated by the incessant accumulation of bile in the blood, from the moment that its characteristic symptom—yellowness of the tissues—is manifested.

"Trasbot's observations go to demonstrate that the mucous membrane of the duodenum is *always* violently inflamed, and that this inflammation is also somewhat frequently noticed in the stomach, and sometimes to a certain extent in the small intestines. Exceptionally, circumscribed inflammatory centres are found in the lungs and kidneys, around hæmorrhagic points of recent date. But the inflammation is never absent in the duodenum, so that *duodenitis* should be considered as the primary condition and *sine quâ non* in the development of icterus. This localisation, however, is not absolute, as often there is simultaneously a very intense gastritis, or an enteritis which may extend to the cæcum. It therefore follows that icterus is primarily and essentially a duodenitis or gastro-duodenitis—or it might be designated a duodenal or gastro-duodenal catarrh.

"The existence of this condition explains in an absolutely satisfactory manner the development of all the symptoms; mucous and sanguinolent vomits, constipation, diarrhœa or dysentery, sensibility of the abdomen, dryness of the mouth, ardent thirst, etc., which are manifested from the commencement.

"Trasbot explains the mechanism of the biliary stasis as follows. The excretory ducts of the liver, not containing any *contractile elements* in their walls, cannot forcibly propel the bile passing through them, and this only passes into the intestine by the *vis-à-tergo* resulting from the secretion itself; the slightest obstruction, therefore, prevents its flow. This obstruction it finds in the swollen condition of the duodenal mucous membrane and its connective tissue, which compresses the biliary duct at its opening into that canal, and completely hinders the bile from passing into it.

"This obstruction is rendered all the greater when there is fibrinous exudate.

"Invagination of the intestine, so frequently met with in the *post-mortem* examination of dogs which have died of icterus, Trasbot is inclined to ascribe to the blood-poisoning. If worms produce the disease, it can only be by irritating the mucous membrane and inducing inflammation of it. With regard to treatment, Trasbot recommends calomel given in alterative, not purgative doses, as he has been very successful with it. At the commencement of the disease he gives tepid drinks which are slightly emollient— such as rice gruel—to which is added tartro-borate of potass, sulphate of soda, or calcined magnesia, administered five or six times a day. With the calcined magnesia he has seen recovery take place in four or five days. The animal must be kept warm and clean, and food easy of digestion, as milk, soup, etc., given. Emetics and powerful purgatives are to be avoided, as they are likely to increase the inflammation ; diuretics which do not irritate the intestinal mucous membrane may be advantageously administered—linseed tea and nitrate of potass fulfil this indication. A large blister should be applied to the epigastrium."

FATTY DEGENERATION OF THE LIVER.

This condition of the liver is not uncommon in dogs, though (probably from lack of scientific investigation) the instances on record are very few.

The following interesting case is taken from the *Veterinarian*, February, 1870 :—

"EXTRAORDINARY ENLARGEMENT OF THE LIVER OF A DOG FROM DEPOSIT OF FATTY MATTER.

"BY MESSRS. GOWING AND SON, M.R.C.V.S., CAMDEN TOWN.

"A few days ago the subject of the disease above referred to, a Skye terrier twelve years of age, was brought to the infirmary for treatment, in consequence of an irritable condition of stomach, which induced constant vomiting immediately after the animal swallowed any kind of fluid ; even cold water had this effect. It was ascertained that the bowels had not acted for some time, and there was great prostration present.

"To meet the urgent symptoms minimum doses of creosote were given, but still the vomiting continued, and the prostration became more extreme. In the next instance hydrocyanic acid was prescribed, in doses of one to two minims in water, in order to allay the irritation and sickness which prevented the effective administration of any food or medicine. Some amount of success attended the employment of the acid, and an attempt was made to support the animal by the exhibition of a little beef-tea with a small quantity of brandy; an enema was also given; but in spite of all treatment the dog become gradually worse, and on the next day it was evident that he was sinking; the owner then decided to have him destroyed.

"On making a *post-mortem* examination the liver was found to be excessively enlarged, pale in colour, having a granular surface when cut into. The intestines were in a healthy condition, and no obstruction was detected throughout the whole length of the tube. The lungs and kidneys were normal.

"The heart was empty and rather flabby, and the spleen was filled with black blood. No history of the case was obtained possessing any points of interest. The dog was exceedingly fat, as pet dogs commonly are, and appeared to have enjoyed an average good health.

"*Examination of the morbid parts.*—Messrs. Gowing & Son forwarded the liver, heart, and spleen of the dog referred to in the above record, for our inspection. Fatty deposits in the liver of fat animals are very common; but the organ in this instance might almost be said to have undergone fatty metamorphosis, if such a change is possible among pathological conditions. Estimating the bulk of the diseased organ roughly, we should say it was three or four times larger than the healthy gland; so large, indeed, that it must have encroached to a serious extent upon the other abdominal viscera. In texture the organ was granular, yellow in colour, and offered to the edge of the knife the resistance of a mass of lard.

"Under the microscope no healthy liver cells were detected; the entire structure was filled with fat globules, which not only occupied the interior of the cells, but existed everywhere in the tissue of the part. Large granular exudation cells, of the kind which is often seen in encephaloid growths, were numerous, but no other elements of cancer were observed.

"Fatty degeneration affected the fibres of the heart to a remarkable extent; in fact, from the state of the organ, it is certain that the circulation must have been extremely feeble. The spleen was congested, but not otherwise diseased."

Dr. Budd observes: "In our domestic animals, the fattening influence of fatty substances taken as food is far more constant. It was well exhibited in the experiments lately performed by Majendie, for the purpose of ascertaining the nutritive powers of different kinds of food. In one of these experiments, a dog was kept entirely on fresh butter, which it continued to eat, though not regularly, for sixty-eight days. It then died of inanition, although remarkably fat. All the while the experiment lasted, the animal smelt strongly of butyric acid; its hair was greasy, and its skin covered with a layer of fat. On dissection, all the organs and tissues were found infiltrated with fat. The liver, to use the common phrase, was *fatty;* and, on analysis, it was found to contain a very large quantity of stearine, but little or no oleine. *It had acted as a kind of filter for the butter.*"

Many other experiments of the same kind were made with hog's-lard and similar fatty substances, and with a like result. The dogs became loaded with fat, but their muscles wasted, and at length they died of inanition. In many of them, the cornea sloughed. In all, the liver was fatty. These experiments are interesting, as showing clearly that an animal may be loaded with fat, and yet die of inanition.

They place in a strong light the truth of the observation long ago made by practical physicians, that fat people are not so strong as they look, and, in general, ill bear loss of blood or other depletive measures. The muscles of fat people are small, and it is muscle which gives strength. These remarks will equally apply to the lower animals, the horse in particular.

CANCEROUS DEPOSIT IN THE LIVER AND SPLEEN IN THE DOG.

Veterinarian, Jan., 1870.

" We are indebted to Messrs. Gowing & Son for the particulars of two remarkable cases of cancer affecting the internal organs of the dog. In each case the animal was aged, and in a hopeless condition when first seen by Messrs Gowing, consequently no treatment was attempted.

" *Post-mortem* examination was made soon after death, and the appearances satisfactorily explained the condition of the dogs during life.

" In the first case, which was examined in the beginning of October, there was a large nodulated tumour, of a pale greyish-yellow colour at the root of the mesentery. Numerous deposits of a similar character were found all over the liver, both covering the surface and extending to the interior of the gland.

" Under the microscope the deposit was found to consist of cells of various forms, caudate, spindle and fibre-cells, with many others containing nuclei, and evidently multiplying by the endogenous process.

" A considerable quantity of fine fibrous stroma gave to the deposit a density and hardness characteristic of scirrhous growths. There was scarcely a trace of the milky juice which is an invariable constituent of encephaloid tumour.

" The second animal presented appearances in some respects more marked than those which have just been described. The subject of the disease was a Maltese dog, aged fourteen years, which was seen by Messrs. Gowing only a few hours before its death.

" On *post-mortem* examination the liver was found to be covered with yellowish spots, and a tumour of similar character was detected in the spleen.

" Microscopic examination of the morbid deposit resulted

in the detection of the same elements which had been observed in the former case.

"No history was obtained in either instance, but there can be no doubt that the primary deposit occurred in the mesentery in the first case, and in the spleen in the second, and that it was followed in both by cancerous infiltration into the structure of the liver."

BILIARY CALCULI.

These are not unfrequently met with in canine practice, and, as already stated, are one of the causes operating in the production of jaundice.

Symptoms.—The presence of biliary calculi is, as a rule, unattended with pain so long as their substance is small, and they can pass through the ducts without distending their walls; when, however, they become fixed, the pain is usually severe, and its seat denoted by the animal looking round towards the region of the liver, moaning and lying on the opposite side. Excessive vomiting and torpidity of the bowels, with flatulency and hiccup, attend this biliary impaction. When complete blocking of the duct takes place the bile is retained, and consequently re-absorbed—hence jaundice. The fæces are nearly white, the urine of a deep orange colour. The pain is of a colicky nature; there is no inflammatory fever, increased respiration, or disturbed pulse, and the passage of calculi once effected, a restoration to usual health follows.

Treatment.—This chiefly consists in relieving the pain during the passage of the calculi. Opium or aconite are the agents best adapted for this purpose; 1 to 2 grains of the former, or 1 to 3 minims of the latter, every three hours. With regard to the administration of solvent agents for biliary calculi, nitro-muriatic acid, sulphuric ether, and carbonate of soda are each advocated and may be tried, but there is no direct proof that in passing through the system they exert any solvent influence on the concretions. Small doses of calomel are more to be relied on, with attention to the bowels and regulation of the diet. If the animal is emaciated, has fared badly, and been continually confined, a new rule should be established, a plain but liberal diet allowed, with vegetable tonics, daily exercise, and strict attention to cleanliness.

SPLENITIS.

Diseases of the spleen have been but little recognised in canine pathology, save in *post-mortem* examinations. Splenitis usually occurs in connection with liver disease and intermittent fevers.

Youatt observes: "In the cases that I have seen, the earliest indications were frequent vomiting, and the discharge of a yellow, frothy mucus. The animal appeared uneasy, shivering, the ears cold, the eyes unnaturally protuberant, the nostrils dilated, the flanks agitated, the respiration accelerated, and the mucous membranes pale. The best treatment I know is the administration, twice in the day, of a ball composed of a grain of calomel and the same quantity of aloes, and 5 grains of ginger.

"The dog frequently cries out, both when he is moved and when he lies on his bed. In the course of three days the yellow mucus is generally disappearing, and the expression of pain is materially diminished.

"If the bowels are much constipated after two days have passed, 2 scruples of aloes may be given, and a grain of calomel; frequently injections may also be administered."

Enlargement of the spleen may occasionally be both felt and seen; there is more or less pain on pressure, and constipation and vomiting are generally present. The iodide of potassium and iron in scruple doses twice daily, with relaxation of the bowels by aloes, is the best treatment I am aware of.

CHAPTER VII.

DISEASES OF THE URINARY ORGANS.

NEPHRITIS,
HÆMATURIA,
RENAL CALCULI,
CYSTITIS,
CYSTIC CALCULI,

RETENTION OF URINE,
PARALYSIS OF THE
  BLADDER,
RUPTURE OF THE
  BLADDER.

NEPHRITIS.

INFLAMMATION of the kidney is a serious, but, fortunately, not a frequent malady in the dog.

Causes.—External violence, as blows or strain on the loins ; long exposure to wet, particularly in bathing ; renal calculi or abscess ; the indiscriminate use of diuretics, especially turpentine or cantharides—the former being a favourite vermifuge, and the latter being used as a blister, may get into the system through licking or absorption.

Symptoms.—The animal has a peculiar stiff gait, simulating lumbar rheumatism ; in bitches there is a straddling crouching gait as though about to urinate, pain on pressure to the loins, urine secreted and voided in small quantities, generally high coloured, and in severe cases mixed with blood. There is a considerable amount of sympathetic fever present, denoted by a quick, hard, wiry pulse, a dry hot nose, injected conjunctival membranes, and obstinate constipation.

Treatment.—This must be purely antiphlogistic.* Leeches

---

* Small doses of the potassio-tartrate of antimony are very useful (*Gamgee*).

to the loins at the onset are attended with considerable benefit. These may be followed by warm fomentations, linseed-meal or mustard poultices, and opiate enemas. Constipation should be relieved at the commencement with castor-oil. Frequent draughts of mucilaginous fluids should be given, as barley-water, solution of gum-arabic, or linseed-tea.

The patient must be kept perfectly quiet, and, except most moderate exercise, all exertion for some considerable time after recovery should be avoided.

HÆMATURIA,

Signifying bloody urine, is occasionally observed in canine practice.

Causes.—External violence across the loins, as falls, bruises, undue strain on the part or parts immediately connected with the kidneys; it also frequently occurs from calculi, either renal, cystic, or urethral, which, through impeding the flow of urine, set up inflammatory action, or by their irregular edges wound the inner coat of the part in which they may be located, and thus cause the discharge of blood.

Symptoms.—Pain in voiding urine, tenderness and heat in the renal region of the loins. Blood may be discharged without urination, during urination, or subsequent to it, each being dependent upon the seat of hæmorrhage.

Miller, in his "Practice of Surgery," observes: "The renal source of the hæmorrhage is known by the blood being diffused equally through the urine; by the expelled fluid containing cylindrical portions of fibrine, like small worms, the result of coagula in the ureter—sometimes colourless, sometimes of a pale pink hue; by the appearance of blood being preceded and accompanied by pain and heat in the loins, and other renal symptoms; and more especially when such symptoms are present on one side only."

"Vesical hæmorrhage may be so profuse as to furnish blood tolerably pure from the urethra. And in general this variety of hæmaturia may be known by the blood not being mixed with the urine; the latter fluid passes off first, tolerably pure; and the blood comes last, more or less changed by mixture with the residue of the urine. It is also known by the absence of renal symptoms, and by the presence of undoubted signs of stone in the bladder, or other disease of that viscus, or of affection of the prostate.

"*From the Urethra.*—In this case there is absence of both renal and vesical symptoms; the blood passes pure, irrespective of any desire to evacuate the bladder."

Treatment.—Hæmaturia demands prompt and active measures; nothing irritative must be administered, drastic purgatives, *and especially diuretics*, should be strictly avoided. The preparations of iron and barks are the most suitable agents for this disease. Mucilaginous drinks, as thick barley-water, solution of gum acacia, or beef-tea thickened with isinglass, can be given freely, together with the use of hot fomentations or linseed-meal poultices to the loins; or counter-irritants, as mustard or ammonia embrocations. Sedative enemas may also be administered where the irritation is considerable.

Bleeding, under all circumstances is unnecessary, and is strongly contra-indicated.

RENAL CALCULI.

Occasionally stones are found in the kidney of the dog, composed chiefly of uric acid, ammonia, or phosphate of lime, and containing as a nucleus some foreign matter. Renal calculi vary in shape, sometimes being oval and an exact cast of the pelvis of the kidney, at others irregular in shape and variously formed, according to the position they had occupied.

The presence of renal calculi creates more or less irritation of the kidney, and when, by their growing dimensions, pressure on the substance of the gland is produced, this irritation is considerably increased, inflammatory action arises, and suppuration follows.

Symptoms.—There is generally an irritable condition of the stomach, and the animal frequently vomits. In walking he moves with a stiff, straddling gait, and evinces tenderness on applying pressure to the lumbar region; the urine is generally voided with pain, in small quantities, and mingled at times with blood, mucus, or pus; considerable febrile disturbance is present, rapid emaciation ensues, and death sooner or later takes place from exhaustion, nephritis, or uremic poisoning.

When at first the calculi is small, oval, and smooth, it may descend by the ureter to the bladder without exciting any great disturbance, and be voided from thence again, or it may remain in the bladder, and in the course of time give rise to cystic irritation.

M. Latour records the following case of renal calculi in the dog: "Seized with pain, August 20, 1827. He barked and rolled himself on the ground almost every minute; he made frequent attempts to void his urine, which came from him drop by drop. When compelled to walk his hind and fore legs seemed to mingle together, and his loins were bent with a perfect curve; his flanks were drawn in; he could scarcely be induced to eat; and he evidently suffered much in voiding his fæces. Mild and demulcent liquids were his only food. Warm baths and injections were applied almost unceasingly, and in eight days he seemed to have perfectly gained his health. In March of the following year the symptoms returned with greater intensity. His hind-legs were drawn after him, he rapidly lost flesh, and his howlings were fearful and continuous. The same mode of treatment was adopted without any good effect." A calculus, weighing 126 grains, and composed of urate

PRIZE BULL TERRIER BITCH, NORA

of ammonia, and phosphate and oxalate of lime, was found in the pelvis of the kidney. The kidney itself was increased in size fourfold, the mucous membrane covered with ecchymoses, and the walls of the bladder thickened.—(*Moore.*)

A case of renal calculi, received from Mr. Clarke, of Islington, is mentioned in the *Veterinarian*, March, 1869. "No history of the case was given, but the morbid specimen is in itself of considerable interest. In both kidneys there are several small calculi, the largest of the size of a horse-bean, lodged in the pelvic cavities."

Treatment.—This consists chiefly in palliative measures. Opiates may be given when pain is present; the patient may also be placed in a hot bath, or counter-irritation applied to the loins. Mild diuretics and laxatives encourage the descent of the calculi, as also do mucilaginous drinks and sharp exercise.

CYSTITIS,

Or inflammation of the bladder, is occasionally met with in canine practice.

Causes.—Mechanical injuries, chronic inflammation of the kidneys, or stricture of the urethra, local irritation from the presence of calculi, worms, or the administration of cantharides or turpentine, blows, falls, or crushes on a distended bladder, etc.

Symptoms.—Considerable uneasiness, with symptoms of colic. The animal frequently looks towards the flanks which are exceedingly tender on both sides; the urine is voided sparingly and with great pain, it may be clear and high-coloured, clouded and thick, bloody, or mingled with mucus and pus. Considerable sympathetic fever is present, and frequently vomiting and obstinate constipation. There is intense thirst throughout.

Mr. Youatt, in writing on this subject, observes: "Inflammation of the bladder is of frequent occurrence in the dog; it is also occasionally observed in the horse and the ox. It sometimes appears as an epizootic. It is generally announced by anxiety, agitation, trembling of the hinder limbs, frequent attempts to urinate, vain efforts to accomplish it, the evacuation small in quantity, sometimes clear and aqueous, and at others mucous, laden with sediment, thick and bloody, escaping by jets, painfully and with great difficulty, and then suddenly rushing out in great quantity. To this list of symptoms colic may often be added. The animal drinks with avidity, but seldom eats much, unless at the commencement of the complaint. The skin is dry and hard, he looks at his flanks, and his back and flanks are tender when pressed upon."

"During the latter part of my connection with Mr. Blaine, this disease assumed an epidemic character. There was a very great drought through almost every part of the country. The disease was characterised by general uneasiness; continual shifting of the posture; a tucked-up appearance; an anxious countenance; a quick and noisy pulse; continued panting; the urine voided in small quantities, sometimes discharged drop by drop, or complete stoppage of it. The belly hot, swelled, and tender to the touch; the dog becoming strangely irritable, and ready to bite even his master.

"1st May, 1824.—Two dogs had been making ineffectual attempts to void their urine for nearly two days. The first was a terrier and the other a Newfoundland. The terrier was bled, placed in a warm bath, and an aloetic ball, with calomel, administered. He was bled a second time in the evening, and a few drops of water were discharged. On the following day the urine slowly passed involuntarily from him, but when he attempted to void any, his efforts were totally ineffectual. Balls composed of camphor, pulv. uva ursi, tinct. ferri mur., mass purg., and pulv. lini. et gum arab.

were administered, morning, noon, and night. On the 5th the urine still passed involuntarily. Cold lotions were employed, and tonic and astringent medicines administered, with castor-oil. He gradually got well, and no trace of the disease remained, until June 6th, when he again became thin and weak, and discharged much bloody urine, but apparently without pain. The uva ursi, oak bark, and powdered gum arabic were employed. On the 12th he had become much better, and so continued until the 1st of July when he again exhibited the same complaint more violently than before. He was exceedingly tender on the loins, and screamed when he was touched. He was bled, returned to his uva ursi and powdered gum, and recovered. I saw him two years after apparently well.

"The Newfoundland dog exhibited a similar complaint with nearly the same accompaniments.

"May 1st.—He was disinclined to move; his belly was hard and hot, and he was supposed to be costive. Gave an aloetic ball with iron.

"2nd.—He has endeavoured in vain several times to void his urine. He walks stiffly with his back bound. Subtract eight ounces of blood, give another physic-ball, and apply cold effusion to the loins.

"3rd.—He frequently attempts to stale, and passes a little urine at each time; he still walks and stands with his back bound. Syr. pav. et rhamni with tinct. ferri mur., a large spoonful being given morning and night.

"4th.—He again tries, ineffectually, to void his urine. Mist. et pulv.

"5th.—Unable to void a drop of urine; nose hot; tongue hangs down; pants considerably; will not eat; the countenance has an anxious character. Bleed to twelve ounces; apply cold effusion. Medicine as before, with cold effusion.

"6th.—Appears to be in very great pain; not a drop of water has passed from him. Medicine and other treatment as before. In the evening he lay down quietly.

"On the next morning he was found dead. All the viscera were sound except the bladder, which was ruptured; the abdomen contained two quarts of bloody fluid.' The mucous membrane of the bladder appeared to be in the highest state of inflammation. It was almost black with extravasated blood. On the neck of the bladder was an enlargement of the size of a goose's egg, and almost filling the cavity of the pelvis. On cutting into it more than two ounces of pus escaped.

"On June 29, 1833, a poodle was brought to me. He had not been observed to pass any urine for two days. He made frequent attempts to void it, and cried dreadfully. The bladder could be felt distended in the abdomen. I put him into a warm bath, and took from him a pound of blood; he seemed to be a little relieved. I did not leave him until after midnight, but was soon roused by his loud screams, and the dog was also retching violently; the cries and retching gradually abated, and he died. The bladder had burst and the parietes were in a fearful state of inflammation.

"A dog had laboured under incontinence of urine more than two months. The water was continually dropping from him. The servant told me that, three months before, he had been shut into a room two days and, being a cleanly animal, would not stale until he was liberated; soon after that the incontinence of urine was observed. I gave the usual tonic balls, with a small portion of opium, night and morning, and ordered cold water to be frequently dashed on the perinæum. A month afterwards he was quite well."

Treatment.—I cannot agree with Youatt in the adoption of depletive measures, especially when carried to such an extent in the abstraction of blood. In very acute cases moderate local venesection, by the application of leeches to the perinæum, is at times attended with benefit. More good, however, will be derived from hot loin baths—this, again, is opposed to his cold-water treatment. The latter I am at all times averse to in the primary stages of acute inflammations, for a little reflection will make it apparent that such applications aid in maintaining the very condition we are endeavouring to relieve, viz., the congested state of the affected part.

With regard to internal measures—diluent drinks, as barley-water, solution of gum arabic, milk and isinglass. and the like, are best adapted to the case. To relieve the pain and correct the acidity of the urine I prescribe the following pill :—

    Opium .... 1 grain.
    Sodæ Carb............................... 10 grains.

One, twice or three times a day.

Oleaginous aperients and emollient clysters may be administered if necessary. Perfect quietude is to be maintained, as much as it is possible to do so in so restless a patient.

The diet is partly supplied in the diluent drinks prescribed, beef-tea or mutton broth may be added if requisite.

When the animal is unable to urinate, and there is reason to believe distention of the bladder exists, the catheter should be passed without delay.

CHRONIC CYSTITIS

may be a sequel of the former, or depend upon some functional or organic derangement of the bladder or its adjacent parts. A mechanical impediment to the exit of urine may be produced by enlargement of the prostate, or from stricture at the neck of the bladder, or stone, resulting ultimately in the disease mentioned.

Symptoms.—The animal moves stiffly, with an arched back and straddling gait. The efforts to urinate are frequent and painful, the urine is mingled with mucus, and has an offensive odour: occasionally there is an admixture of pus and blood. There is always more or less constitutional disturbance, finally the kidneys become involved, and the animal wastes and dies a lingering death.

Treatment.—This consists, in the first place, in removing the cause. If there is stone, its removal is indicated—if stricture, passage of the catheter is required. Disease of prostate may be alleviated, but is rarely cured.

With regard to remedies for the disease, small doses of opium, combined with iron, form the best medicinal treatment.

  Opium .... $\frac{1}{2}$ grain.
  Ferri Sulp................................. 5 grains.

One dose, twice daily.

Alkalies are also useful, as the citrate of potash or carbonate of soda ; either will be readily lapped in milk. Mucilaginous drinks should be freely given, and the diet be much the same as in the acute form, only more generous. Painting the perinæum with iodine, or, in protracted cases, pencilling with nitrate of silver, is attended with considerable benefit. If there is much pain, thin gum mucilage to which a grain of opium is added, or a decoction of poppies, may be injected in the bladder.

CYSTIC CALCULI.

Stone in the bladder of the dog is probably more frequent than is suspected, though the records in canine literature are few.

Mr. Blaine mentions a case of a Newfoundland dog, in the bladder of which he found from forty to fifty calculi. (See p. 125.)

Mr. Youatt observes: "Of the nature and causes of urinary calculi in the bladder we know very little. We only know that some solid body finds its way, or is formed, there, gradually increases in size, and at length partially, or entirely, occupies the bladder. Boerhaave has given a singular and undeniable proof of this. He introduced a small round pebble into the bladder of a dog. The wound perfectly healed. A few months afterwards the animal was killed, and there was found a calculus of considerable size, of which the pebble was the nucleus."

The following interesting cases are recorded by Messrs. Gowing & Son, in the *Veterinarian*, March and August, 1869:

"NUMEROUS CALCULI IN THE BLADDER OF A DOG, FOURTEEN MONTHS OLD, PRODUCING DISTENSION AND CONGESTION OF THE ORGAN, AND DEATH.

"On Friday, February 12th, 1869, we were requested to visit a beautiful specimen of the King Charles breed, fourteen months old, which was reported to be unwell. The owner supposed him to be labouring under an impacted condition of the bowels; and, as a domestic remedy, he had administered a small dose of castor-oil, but this not having the desired effect, and the dog becoming worse and indicating much prostration of strength, the owner applied to us. Upon inquiry into the case we found that the dog had not passed any fæces for a day or two, neither had he urinated, although he had made frequent attempts. The first time he was observed to have any difficulty in urinating was about ten days previous to the application to us, when he passed from the bladder a considerable quantity of dark-coloured fluid. After that he made frequent attempts and was not able to pass any more. On Friday night, February 12th, the dog was in excessive pain, so much that the owner had to walk the room with him to tranquillise him. It appears that the dog could not rest, but was constantly crying out and moaning.

"The animal had been, we learned, fed upon luncheon-biscuits, with such meat as they partook of in the house; occasionally, also, he had a little liver and horse-flesh. He was frequently allowed a bone to play with, but never broke them up or ate them.

"Upon examination the bladder was found much

distended, so much so as to cause a bulging out of the perinæum.

"*Treatment.*—A mild purgative was administered, and stimulants were ordered to be given at intervals; gentle pressure was applied to the bladder by compressing on either side the walls of the abdominal cavity, but without producing the effect of emptying the viscus. An injection was also given, consisting of oil with soap and water; and the pain still continuing, hot flannels were applied to the abdomen frequently.

"The dog being a favourite, and the owner anxious, the treatment was pursued to meet his wishes, although it was considered that there was no hope of the animal's recovery. He died on Saturday morning, February 13th.

"*Post-mortem Examination.*—The abdomen was opened down to the pubis, and part of the pelvis was removed. The bladder and other parts of the urinary organs were dissected out entire.

"The bladder was observed to be dark in colour over the whole surface, from intense congestion. Upon making a section into the viscus, there escaped a quantity of deep, dark-coloured fluid, and also two calculi about the size of large peas, spherical in shape, and upon further examination intermingled with some mucus, there were seen numerous small ones of a seed-like character; one of a larger size was found to have passed into the urethral canal, and there, being perfectly impacted, had resisted all efforts of the animal or contraction of the bladder to overcome the obstruction. This appeared to be the immediate cause of death.

"The extensively distended condition of the bladder appeared also to interfere with the action of the rectum.

"*Examination of the Diseased Structures.*—The organs which Messrs. Gowing and Son sent for inspection were the generative organs, with the bladder, kidneys, liver, and intestines, all of which, excepting the bladder were normal. In the interior of this viscus, the morbid changes were very marked, the whole of the mucous membrane was intensely congested, and in many places patches of extravasated blood were firmly adherent to the surface. A quantity of dark-red fluid was taken from the bladder, and set aside for further examination. The most remarkable feature of the morbid changes was the existence of a large number of small calculi, varying in size from a pin's point to a large pea, principally clustered in the neck of the bladder, which was quite black in colour, on account of the quantity of effused blood in the sub-mucous tissues. In the urethral canal, which was cut open, the lining membrane was much congested, but there was no calculus, excepting the one to which Mr. Gowing alludes, and which was the direct cause of the fatal termination of the disease.

"*Microscopic Examination of the Urine and the Calculous Concretions.*—The dark-coloured fluid which was removed from the bladder contained a considerable quantity of blood; this was evident at once from the presence of large coagula; and under the microscope the blood-discs were very abundant; besides these there were epithelial cells, a quantity of amorphous matter, and some large crystals of triple phosphate. From the result of the microscopic examination of the urine there was good reason to conclude that the calculi were principally composed of the triple phosphates; but in order to determine the point some of them were submitted to examination. In form the bodies were spherical or polygonal, the colour nearly white or light yellow, the surface, to the unassisted eye, appeared smooth, but under a magnifying power of thirty diameters it was irregular, in consequence of numerous projecting angles of crystals, some of which had become rounded off from attrition. The calculi were unacted upon by water, and also by caustic potash, but dissolved readily in acetic acid, and in the mineral acids; the addition of a little ammonia to the acid solution caused an abundant white precipitate, which was found, under the microscope, to consist of phosphate of lime with stellate crystals of triple phosphate. It was therefore evident that the concretions consisted of this salt, in combination with phosphate of lime. The causes which led to the deposit are not apparent in the history of the case, but there is no doubt that the urine was highly charged with phosphatic matter, and, it may be, rendered alkaline, probably from mal-assimilation; and in such a state of the fluid the phosphate cannot be maintained in solution.

"Our limited literature on this subject does not permit us to refer to many instances of calculus in the urinary organs of the dog; but two cases occur to us, both possessing some points of interest. One instance of vesicular calculus is recorded by the late Professor Morton in his pamphlet on 'Calculous Concretions.' The animal affected with the disease was a very small spaniel; the calculus was so large as to nearly fill the bladder, and was felt easily through the walls of the abdomen. The next case was one of renal calculi,* forwarded to us by Mr. Clarke, of Islington. No history of the case was given, but the morbid specimen is in itself of considerable interest. In both kidneys there are several small calculi, the largest is of the size of a horse-bean, and is lodged in the pelvic cavities. In composition, all these concretions from the several dogs are closely allied."

"RETENTION OF URINE ASSOCIATED WITH CALCULI IN THE BLADDER OF A BITCH OF THE KING CHARLES BREED, AGED TEN YEARS.

"*By Messrs. Gowing & Son, M.R.C.V.S., Camden Town.*

"The bitch was observed to be dull and off her appetite for the last three or four days. Some time previously she had tried to urinate, passing a drop or two occasionally, but no effort could produce a full stream, and lately it was reported

---

* Already alluded to in "Renal Calculi."

that her endeavours were futile, none being passed. Upon examination of the parietes of the abdomen the bladder was found to be distended. Accordingly an attempt was made to pass a catheter, but without success. The animal was ordered a warm bath, and a small dose of castor-oil mixture. The stomach being irritable this was returned, and the dog getting no better was brought to the infirmary on Tuesday evening, July 6th. Upon examination, some calcareous matter was found adhering to the lower part of the vulva, and the bladder was distended with urine.

"It was now determined to attempt the passing of the catheter again—this time the operation was attended with success, after considerable difficulty. The catheter being passed into the bladder, the urine continued to flow through the instrument in a full stream, until six ounces of a somewhat dirty, pale-coloured, turbid, and alkaline fluid had been drawn off. The bitch seemed now much relieved; she was ordered beef-tea, and returned to her owner, an old lady upwards of seventy years of age, who was much gratified at the relief her pet had experienced. The owner was requested to report to me the following day the condition of the animal (no medicine was ordered). On the following morning, July 7th, her friend, Dr. George, called, and stated that the bitch was much prostrated, and that sickness was constant if anything was taken into the stomach. An hydrocyanic acid mixture was ordered, but this being objected to, a mixture of creosote in minimum doses was substituted. After two or three doses of the mixture the sickness subsided to some extent. Beef-tea and brandy were ordered as a support, and beef-tea injections, but the animal died the following morning.

"*Post-mortem.*—Upon removing the abdominal viscera the stomach was found slightly tinged with red; the intestines and spleen were healthy; the liver somewhat congested; the lungs were in a congested state, probably from gravitation of the blood; the right ventricle and auricle of the heart were full of dark, coagulated blood; the bladder was contracted, and contained no urine; its coats appeared thickened; and on making a section to examine the state of the mucous membrane two 'calculi' were observed possessing spines, or spiculated points; such an arrangement is very unusual. The concretions must have been a source of irritation to the organ, and would account for the pain and difficulty of urinating the bitch had experienced for nine months.

"From the results of many *post-mortem* examinations, we are led to conclude that cystic calculus in the dog is of much more frequent occurrence than has hitherto been supposed.

"[Messrs. Gowing & Son forwarded the morbid parts of the bitch for examination. The calculi were so peculiar in form that we deemed them worthy of an illustration. Chemically the concretions are composed of triple phosphate. Physically the prisms are arranged on very fine plates, and stellate masses, as shown in the drawing of one of the calculi, magnified five diameters and outlined with the camera.

FIG. 11.

CYSTIC CALCULUS (TRIPLE PHOSPHATE) FROM THE BLADDER OF A BITCH (MAGNIFIED FIVE DIAMETERS).

"A small quantity of the contents of the bladder, having the appearance of pus, was also sent ; the colour and consistency of the fluid, however, were found under the microscope to depend not upon purulent contamination, but entirely upon the presence of an abundant precipitate of ammonio-magnesian phosphate, the prismatic crystals of which were very large and well-defined. A quantity of the same deposit covered the lining membrane of the bladder, the walls of which were thickened. The pelvis of the right kidney was much dilated, but these organs were otherwise healthy.

"Messrs. Gowing's view of the frequency of calculous concretions in the dog is supported by the results of their own practice. We are indebted to them for several very interesting cases, but none more so than the one which is recorded in the present number of the journal.]"—*Veterinarian.**

RETENTION OF URINE.

This may proceed from paralysis of either the muscular coat of the bladder, the result of protracted distension, and though this is rare in dogs, who by habit are continually urinating, yet there are some who, from customary cleanliness, would, if confined, retain their urine to their own pain rather than misbehave themselves ; or it may occur from compression of the urethra by enlargement of the prostate gland, or bruises to the perinæum ; calculi in the urethra or bladder, urethritis, stricture, blood-clots, diseased penis, imperforate urethra, paralysis, may each severally act as causes of retained urine.

Mr. Blaine records a case of death in a Newfoundland dog, from the bladder of which he took forty or fifty caculi. He observes: "Death in this instance was occasioned by the obstruction to the passage of urine by means of these stones."

---

* In June, 1881, I performed the first recorded case in English literature of Canine Lithotomy on the St. Bernard bitch " Mab." (See "Accidents and Operations.")—J.W.H.

A short time since, I had an opportunity, during a professional call on the gentleman to whom this work is dedicated, of seeing what had been a case of retention of urine in a fox terrier puppy a few days old, due to an imperforate prepuce. This had been removed by his medical, attendant, W. Haslehurst, Esq., by slitting the prepuce along from its under surface to the end. The case did well, and the puppy was reared.

Symptoms.—The animal exhibits great restlessness, he is continually and vainly endeavouring to urinate ; he moves uneasily about, and with a straddling gait. When lying down he performs the act with extreme care, and moans or emits a sharp cry after the effort. The abdomen is enlarged, hot, and tense to the feel. As the case advances, the pain increases, there is repeated straining, with retching and vomiting ; the pulse becomes rapid and small ; the breathing hurried ; tongue dry and furred ; the poor animal looks piteously at its master, gazes from time to time at its flanks, finally reels about, becomes comatose, and dies.

Treatment.—If the bladder be emptied, immediate relief is afforded, but this is often only temporary, the urine is quickly secreted again, and often with the same result ; watchfulness is therefore necessary. If the patient be not thus relieved, the intense pressure on the bladder gives rise to acute inflammation or paralysis, decomposition of the urine takes place, sloughing of the coats of the bladder follows, ultimately they give way, and the contents are poured into the abdominal cavity.

The passage of the catheter is necessary in all cases where the retention occurs from mechanical impediment to the outward flow of urine.

When the retention results from urethritis, leeches, hot fomentations, loin baths, opiates, mucilaginous drinks and emollient clysters are the measures to be adopted.

The same treatment will apply to retention of urine, owing to bruises of the perinæum.

Imperforate urethra, or prepuce, requires immediate opening.

Retention from paralysis necessitates the use of the catheter, which should be repeated from time to time; but it is advisable not to withdraw the whole contents at first, otherwise collapse without contraction is likely to ensue; a small quantity of urine left in is more likely to stimulate the organ, and by its warmth aid in restoring it to a natural condition. Strychnine or nux vomica is in such cases, exceedingly useful.

When the retention takes place from disease of the penis, other than urethritis, as warty growths, an operation for the removal of the impediment is necessary. (See "Warts on the Penis.")

Youatt quotes a singular case of retention of urine, caused by the presence of a worm in the urethra.

M. Séon, veterinary surgeon of the Lancers of the Bodyguard, was requested to examine a dog who strained in vain to void his urine, often uttering dreadful cries, and then eagerly licking his penis. M. Séon, after having tried in vain to abate the irritation, endeavoured to pass an elastic bougie. He perceived a conical body, half an inch long, protruding from the urethra with each effort of the dog to void his urine, and immediately afterwards returning into the urethra. He crushed it with a pair of forceps, and drew it out. It proved to be a worm resembling a strongylus, four and a half inches long. It was living, and moving about. M. Séon could [not ascertain its species. The worm being extracted, the urine flowed, and the dog soon recovered.*

PARALYSIS OF THE BLADDER.

This cystic condition may occur from protracted distension of the bladder, owing to the retention of urine; or

---

* *Prat. Med. Vet.*, Fev. 1828.

from local or general paralysis, the result of spinal injury, or other and debilitating diseases.

Many dogs, from habits of cleanliness, will not urinate except out of doors, an illustration of which has already been given in the section on "Cystitis." The muscular coat of the bladder being thus overstretched, and the strain on it prolonged, it becomes paralysed. So that when liberty is accorded to the animal, the evacuation cannot take place, and unless speedy assistance is rendered, serious mischief will ensue.

Treatment.—This consists in frequently relieving the bladder with the catheter, but for reasons previously observed, in retention of urine the whole contents should not at first be removed. We must then endeavour to impart tone to the system by the administration of tonics. The best agents for the purpose are strychnine or nux vomica, alone or combined with iron. Counter-irritation to the perinæum is sometimes serviceable.

The diet should be chiefly liquid, nourishing and mucilaginous.

CHAPTER VIII.

DISEASES OF THE GENERATIVE ORGANS.

BALANITIS,
WARTS ON THE PENIS,
SCROTAL IRRITATIONS,
ENLARGED TESTICLE,
INVERSION OF THE VAGINA,
POLYPUS IN THE VAGINA,
INFLAMMATION OF THE UTERUS,
INVERSION OF THE UTERUS,
ULCERATION OF THE UTERUS,
HERNIA OF THE UTERUS,
DROPSY OF THE UTERUS,
FATTY DEGENERATION OF THE OVARIES.

BALANITIS,

Signifying inflammation of, and discharge of matter from the mucous membrane of the prepuce, is an affection which dogs are frequently troubled with.

Causes.—Balanitis is usually due to the secretion of acrid matter within the prepuce, and is more especially induced by a plethoric habit of body. It may also co-exist with a relaxed and anæmic condition of system.

Symptoms.—Considerable irritation of the part, denoted by the animal frequently licking it; a thick yellow discharge is continually present. On examination the part will be found red, swollen, and exceedingly sensitive. The prepuce is always more or less protruded, erections are frequent, and urination is performed at times with pain.

Treatment.—This consists in first bathing the parts with warm water until thoroughly cleansed, and then applying a weak solution of nitrate of silver, or acetate of lead.

If the animal is plethoric a dose of aperient medicine is advisable. If anæmic, tonics should be given, and a liberal but unstimulating diet allowed.

Occasionally the same condition exists in bitches, and may be removed by the same measures.

WARTS ON THE PENIS.

These are not unfrequent in the dog. They may be the result of the former complaint, or exist independently. There may be only a single growth, or several isolated, or they may be clustered together.

Treatment.—The seat of the affection having been exposed, the excrescences may be removed by excision or ligature, after which the parts should be slightly pencilled with lunar caustic. When there is an excessive congregation of warts, and a large amount of mucous membrane is involved, the repeated application of caustic or acetic acid will be the safest remedy. Occasionally warty adhesion exists between the sheath and the penis, which is of serious importance in stud dogs. In such a case a competent canine veterinary surgeon should be consulted, the necessary operation being too delicate for an amateur to attempt.

SCROTAL IRRITATION.

Dogs, especially aged ones, and those which have been freely used for stud purposes, are frequently troubled with irritation of the scrotum, which has been described by some authors (in my opinion, wrongly) as cancer.

Causes.—The irritation is due to a plethoric condition of the scrotum. The circulation of blood in the integument being excessive, an amount of congestion takes place, resulting in the irritation named, which Nature endeavours to relieve by a serous exudation in the form of pimples.

Symptoms.—The first indications are those usually found in all inflammatory processes—heat, redness, swelling, and soreness. In the course of a few days minute pimples appear; these soon break and give exit to a thin watery fluid, which becomes encrusted on the surface of the part, and is ultimately thrown off, exposing either a dry or moist and inflamed surface underneath, which is exceedingly sensitive. If not properly dealt with at this stage, ulceration frequently follows, the case becomes chronic, and when the soreness and rawness is removed a thickened cartilaginous condition of the scrotum remains behind.

Treatment.—When the earliest symptoms of the affection are noticed a smart dose of aperient medicine should be administered, and, if the pimples have not appeared, three or four leeches may be applied to the scrotum. If the animal is small, one or two will be sufficient. On the following day the parts may be frequently bathed with one part of vinegar to twenty parts of cold water; and when pimples have formed and broken, a weak solution of the acetate of lead, ten grains to the ounce of water, or the same quantity of glycerine, forms the best application, to be used twice or three times daily. If ulceration takes place, the application of lunar caustic, with alum or zinc ointment, are the measures indicated. A surgical operation is rarely necessary. The diet should be spare, unstimulating, and somewhat relaxing.

ENLARGED TESTICLES.

Occasionally the testicles become enlarged, and the enlargement may be associated with induration, with a considerable degree of insensibility, or, as is more frequently the case, full and exceedingly sensitive, giving to the touch a feeling of distension. The scrotum has a smooth, full, and shining appearance, and is usually hot.

Causes.—This condition may be either due to an excessive demand on these organs in stud purposes, or from denial of connection when brought in contact with the objects of desire; or it may result from injury, as blows, bruises, crushes, etc.

Treatment.—If the enlargement is due to the first-named cause, rest, tonics (particularly the iodide of iron and potassium), and nourishing food are indicated. If from the second-named cause, Nature should without question be allowed to follow her course, or relief by depletion from internal and local agents must be adopted. If it results from the latter-named causes, antiphlogistic measures must be had recourse to—aperient medicine, leeches, fomentations, and quietude. Castration is occasionally necessary in the last-named causes, but rarely if ever in the former.

INVERSION OF THE VAGINA.

This is very commonly seen in bitches who have had many litters of puppies, and who are of a relaxed and debilitated condition of system. It is frequently present during the period of œstrum, and as frequently disappears with the decline of that function. It has also arisen after connection when the animals have been suddenly or violently separated.

Symptoms.—The presence or protrusion of a red, soft, smooth body at the orifice of the vagina, easily returnable, but which is again, unless proper means be resorted to quickly re-inverted.* In chronic cases the tumour invariably remains persistent. Difficulty in micturition is more or less manifested, and febrile disturbance is occasionally present.

Long exposure to air gives the mucous membrane a somewhat leaden tint, and it becomes wrinkled and covered with epithelium of a leathery nature.

---

* In the bitch, inversion of the vagina has been sometimes mistaken for a condylomatous tumour; and cases are recorded in which tumours of this kind, protruding beyond the vulva, through insufficient examination have been mistaken for inversion. Inversion of the bladder has also been confounded with that of the vagina. The pyriform cysts which sometimes form in that canal, and contain a clear citron-coloured fluid, have likewise been sometimes confounded with inversion of the vagina.

To avoid errors which might have a serious tendency, a careful examination must be made, and nothing should be attempted in the way of operation until the state of affairs is exactly determined.

Treatment.—After the return, by pressure, of the inversion, which should be first thoroughly cleansed, the treatment consists in the frequent application of cold water to the parts, the injection of mild astringents (alum-water being the best), and the administration of agents that will give tone to the system, as the preparations of iron and bark. Where retention is difficult, a truss may be employed, or labial sutures ; but in the bitch the latter are not advisable. Lacerations* require strict attention, otherwise adhesions are liable to take place, and a permanent inversion be the result. The diet should be plain, unstimulating, and nutritious ; moderate exercise daily is beneficial, as the protrusion is not so liable to take place in the standing posture and during locomotion, as in the recumbent position. Constipation, or any of the causes which produce straining, must be avoided.

---

* When the submucous connective tissue of the vagina has been much lacerated, and abnormal adhesions have taken place, then a recurrence of the inversion is to be apprehended. This recurrence is, of course, most likely to take place in chronic inversion, and all the skill and patience of the veterinary surgeon will be required in dealing with such a case. At times the accident has proved so troublesome, and retention has so baffled every attempt after reduction was effected, that amputation of the protruded portion has been practised, and with success.

Rainard appears to have been the first to venture on this bold measure, and he practised the operation several times on bitches. He ligatured the entire inverted mass close to the vulva, in one case ; but as this gave rise to intense fever, and, when cured, the animal suffered from incontinence of urine, he adopted another procedure. Instead of including the whole of the tumour in one ligature, he divided the pedicle into three portions, which he tied separately, so that each ligature only enclosed one third of the mass. After tightening the ligatures the bitch was allowed to run at large, the only attention it received being the injection of emollient fluids into the vagina, and a smaller allowance of food. The pain was much less in intensity and duration than in the first case, and the tumour came away in five or six days, when recovery took place. Rainard, however, advises immediate excision of the portion of the mass beyond the ligatures, when these have been drawn tight.—Fleming's " Veterinary Obstetrics," p. 603.

A case is recorded of the Author's in the *Veterinary Journal*. May, 1884. Also see " Vaginotomy," Chapter xviii.

POLYPUS IN THE VAGINA.

Polypus is occasionally met with in the vagina of bitches. It consists in a pedicled tumour attached to some portion of the vaginal walls. It is generally situated some distance from the orifice, and is usually observed when the animal is in a lying posture. Sometimes it increases so much in size as to be continually protruded, and the act of urination causes it to be still more dependent.

Polypus may be confounded with uterine inversion; but a careful examination will at once remove this doubt, as its attachment can generally be felt.

Symptoms.—The tumour is usually pear-shaped, having a pedicle, or stalk, as its base. It is smooth, glistening, movable, and insensible when manipulated. It may be accompanied by a purulent discharge, but, as a rule, there is simply an increase in the secretion of mucus. It creates much inconvenience in the act of urination, and when of considerable size interferes with the evacuation of fæces.

Treatment.—Removal by excision or ligature, which is attended with but little danger or constitutional disturbance, and the injection afterwards of astringents, with occasional application of lunar caustic, if unhealthy action or fungus results.

INFLAMMATION OF THE UTERUS (METRITIS)

Bitches are not very frequently troubled with this affection. When it does happen, it is generally associated with parturition, particularly if the labour be protracted, and unskilful or rough usage has been had recourse to.

It may proceed from external violence, as blows or falls, or from the use of injudicious and excessive vaginal injections.

Symptoms.—Pain on pressure over the uterine region, and also on examination per vaginam ; in the latter, the *os uteri* will be found exceedingly sensitive and hot. Fulness of the abdomen, and general inflammatory fever. The animal is prostrate, but afraid to lie down. Vomiting is usually present, and sometimes a purulent discharge, which becomes fœtid as the disease proceeds, issues from the vagina, the labia of which are tumefied and hot, and the animal frequently endeavours to urinate. If metritis occurs at or after parturition, the secretion of milk is generally suspended. In such a case there is a considerable tendency for the inflammation to extend to the peritoneum (metroperitonitis), in which the pain is more diffused, and peritonitic symptoms are manifested.

Treatment.—The patient should be confined to a comfortable, soft bed; lying on hard, bare or cold floors is excessively injurious.

Opiates, containing 1 to 3 grains of the drug, with, if there is much prostration, brandy and water, and warm baths to the hind parts as far as the loins, or local fermentations, are the measures most advisable. A weak watery infusion of opium, *tepid*, may with benefit be injected in the uterus, but it is necessary to observe that extreme care should be used in inserting the end of the pipe within the mouth of the inflamed organ; indeed, when the inflammation is excessive, it is better to be content with *gentle* vaginal injection. Fœtor may be overcome by injections of a weak solution of carbolic acid or chloride of zinc.

In severe cases, counter-irritation to the loins and abdomen may also be adopted.

The bowels should be gently moved with castor-oil, aided by enemas.

The diet should consist of liquid, nourishing and mucilaginous food. Small doses of iron are serviceable when the acute symptoms have abated. Quinine is also useful.

INVERSION OF THE UTERUS.

This is not of very frequent occurrence, and is usually met with in bitches which have parturiated several times, and in which the organ is loose and flabby and the os uteri relaxed. It is usually connected with protracted parturition, where undue force or assistance has been used, or there has been violent straining.

Symptoms.—Inversion of the uterus is denoted by the protrusion of a round rough-surfaced body, which is easily compressible; the extent of the protrusion may be detected by examining with the finger between the tumour and walls of the vagina. If the inversion is protracted the organ becomes discoloured with a pus-like exudation on its exposed surface, and emits an offensive odour.

Treatment.—This consists in returning the uterus to its proper situation, which should be done without delay, otherwise its swollen and abnormal condition will render it next to impossible. The operation is best effected by gentle pressure on the centre of the fundus with a rod having the end padded; a little olive-oil or milk injected around and on the organ will facilitate its return.

The after-injection of a weak solution of alum or zinc, and the administration of an opiate, will assist in the retention of the organ.

When, owing to protracted inversion, the uterus has become enormously swollen, discoloured and cold, and return is impossible, excision will be necessary; and this may be performed either by a ligature round the neck of the organ, gradually tightened every day, or direct removal with the knife immediately before a tight ligature. The subsequent treatment should consist in warm water injections, with occasionally chloride of zinc, laxative diet, and quietude.

ULCERATION OF THE UTERUS

Is not very frequently met with in canine practice. The " Veterinary Record," vol. iii., gives the following :—

"Three weeks before the time of parturition a bitch fell

from a height of four feet. Four or five days after the animal became sleepy, and the belly pendulous and painful. At a later period the animal appeared very uneasy and made frequent shrill cries when the belly was pressed upon. At last four puppies, one dead, were born. Severe fits came on attended by protrusion of the eyeballs and unconscious wandering, and death supervened.

" On examination after death, the peritoneum was found inflamed, and there was dark-coloured effusion. There were two large unhealthy ulcers in one of the horns of the uterus, perforating all the coats of the uterus, and opening into the abdomen."—*Moore.*

Ulceration of the uterus may proceed from injuries, or the presence of foreign bodies, as the retention of a fœtus.

Symptoms.—A sanious discharge frequently accompanies it, there is frequent micturition, and the animal is occasionally observed straining; a desire for the male is also manifested. If the disease is extensive, considerable lassitude and emaciation ensues, with febrile disturbance.

Treatment.—Astringent injections, the administration of tonics (particularly the tinct. ferri), a liberal diet, exercise and cleanliness, are the measures chiefly to be observed.

Carbolic acid solutions, 1 to 40—50, are serviceable when the discharge is offensive and profuse.

HERNIA OF THE UTERUS.

Hernia of the uterus is of rare occurrence in the bitch. The following interesting case is recorded in the "Veterinarian," April, 1871, by Mr. T. Corby, M.R.C.V.S., Hackney :—

" About the middle of February, a small terrier bitch was brought to me, for the purpose of being destroyed, in consequence of the existence of a large tumour just posterior to the hindermost mammary gland, on the left side, the contents of which appeared to be irregularly solid and partly movable. The application of pressure caused considerable pain, besides which the bitch was constantly straining, as if apparently requiring to urinate; small quantities of urine, however, were only passed, mixed with some fœtid and brown-coloured matter from the vagina. She was an old animal, had lost all appetite, and was in an emaciated condition.

" The history given me of the case was that, about nine months ago, the bitch had a litter of pups, soon after which a swelling, about the size of a walnut, was noticed at the site of the present tumour. The enlargement continued almost unaltered in size until about four months ago, at which time she was missed from her house for a few days. Soon after her return the tumour began to increase in size, and the other symptoms now present to slowly develop themselves.

" By manipulation a round hard body could be felt, partly composing the tumour, which, considering the history of the case, the form of the enlargement, and the nature of the vaginal discharge, I came to the conclusion was the head of a fœtus.

" It having been determined to operate with a view if possible of still prolonging the animal's life, she was put under the influence of chloroform and the tumour opened. It was found to contain a considerable portion of the uterus, with one dead fœtus in it, having the head and fore parts entire. The hinder portion of the body was, however, broken up by decomposition, the parts remaining being very putrid and rotten. After removing the fœtus I endeavoured to return the uterus into the abdomen, but it was so swollen and thickened throughout that I could not do so, and as her owner did not wish her to suffer any further pain she was destroyed. On further examination the bladder was found not to be included in the hernia, but greatly distended by pressure of its neck between the brim of the pelvis and the anterior part of the vagina. Besides these lesions there was little else which requires special mention. Allied cases to this, in which hernia of the uterus exists at the base, as it were, of one of the mammary glands, are not uncommon, and are, I believe usually met with in old bitches. This is the first case coming under my notice in which the protruded portion of the uterus contained a fœtus."

DROPSY OF THE UTERUS.

This uterine condition is occasionally met with in bitches that have parturiated several times, are of gross habit, and in which the function of œstrum has become a rare occurrence.

Symptoms.—Dropsy of the uterus may be confounded with pregnancy, or other enlargement of the abdomen. Careful examination, however, will detect a notable difference between it and either of the latter; the absence of solid bodies, and the usual hard and tense feel in the former, together with its circumscribed shape and fluctuation, point out the improbabilty of pregnancy or other abdominal enlargements.

In the *Veterinarian* for January, 1871, Messrs. Gowing and Son record the following case :—

"DISTENSION OF THE UTERUS OF A BITCH WITH PSEUDO-PURULENT FLUID.

" On November 22nd our attention was called to the condition of a small, rough terrier bitch about ten years old. The animal presented some of the appearances characteristic of ascetes; the abdomen was enlarged, pendulous, and fluctuating. There was much prostration, the action of the heart was feeble, the breathing was accelerated, the appetite was impaired, but the desire for drink was constant. It was evident that the case was a hopeless one, and no attempt was made to apply any treatment. The dog died on November 29th.

The *post-mortem* examination did not reveal any lesion of the internal organs, except the uterus, which was distended with fluid; this viscus we have forwarded for your inspection.

"(As stated in Messrs. Gowing's report of the case, the uterus was distended with fluid; the horns and the body of the organ being about equally tense. When the walls of the viscus were opened, the contained fluid was found to present the ordinary characters of pus, being thick, yellowish-white in colour, and perfectly uniform in consistence. The lining membrane of the uterus was softened and somewhat pulpy but no ulceration or other morbid change was observed. Under the microscope the fluid was found to consist principally of epithelial scales, with small exudation corpuscles and blood-discs, but there were no pus-corpuscles. In the larger mammalian animals, collections of fluid in the uterus is not uncommon, and the condition is sometimes described as false conception; there is no reason, however, to conclude that this abnormal secretion is in any way connected with impregnation.)"

FATTY DEGENERATION OF THE OVARIES.

In aged bitches of an obese disposition, and those which have parturiated, there is a tendency to fatty degeneration in organs otherwise not usually adipose.

A short time since, when making a *post-mortem* examination of an aged Newfoundland bitch, belonging to the Rev. S. C. Adam, of Wolverhampton, I was struck, when investigating the generative organs, with the condition of the ovaries. All that remained of the one was a hard, gritty substance the size of a horse-bean, imbedded in a smooth, round tumour of fat, the dimensions of a large walnut, and, containing in the centre a cyst.

The other resembled a granular, fatty mass, with a full-developed ovum, ready to burst on the outside. The animal had borne whelps, and was supposed (erroneously) then to be pregnant.

CHAPTER IX.
FUNCTIONS OF THE GENERATIVE ORGANS.

ŒSTRUM. BREEDING. PARTURITION.

ŒSTRUM.

ŒSTRUM, or the period at which sexual desires commence is in the bitch an irregular function. Some animals only become so affected once or twice a year, while others do so much oftener. A mastiff-bitch belonging to myself, which up to a late period in life remained barren, would almost at any time allow connection.

The signs of œstrum are not long manifested before attention is attracted to the consequent change of condition and manners of the animal. The usually morose bitch of savage disposition suddenly becomes gentle and inclined to caresses. The presence of a strange dog, to which she has hitherto been noted for her antipathy, increases her wish to fraternise, no matter of how low degree the animal is; every tempting posture will be exhibited, and every means exerted to attract his notice and win his affections. The generative organs externally are full, vascular and hot, a glairy discharge issues from the vaginal orifice, which rapidly increases in quantity and gradually changes in character, becoming first blood-stained, and eventually blood itself under an altered condition. There is also frequent micturition. The duration of œstrum is usually from ten to twenty days.

During menstruation the animal is generally more or less feverish, and it is therefore advisable, particularly in high-bred bitches and those on which unusual care has been bestowed, that they should not unnecessarily be exposed to damp and cold. Seclusion, except during the visit of the male, is also prudent until the period has passed.

The food should be moderate, unstimulating, and if anything slightly relaxing.

The suspension of the discharge and return of the external genitals to their ordinary size and shape denote that the function is over.

BREEDING.

The subject of breeding is one requiring far more consideration in the canine world than has hitherto been given to it. In this work, wherein I have confined myself to narrow limits, I shall only suggest the following remarks as worthy of notice :—

1. The sexes should be as proportionate in size as is compatible with safe breeding. This for more than one reason is desirable. Like begets like. A large sire generally produces offspring which the female is unable to give birth to. Again, this incompatible mating is attended with danger to the animals at the time of connection. I have frequently had mastiff-bitches sent to my dogs, in which, from their deficiency in height, it was impossible for the dog to perform the act required of him without injury in various ways.

2. During the period of œstrum the bitch should be carefully secluded, for the canine race know no distinction, and ignore all propriety at this season. Again, mental impression is with them exceedingly strong; though I will not go so far as to say a passion formed for a dog of low degree will have its influence on offspring begat by other blood. But I do say, and I do so from experience, that connection with conception, particularly in maiden bitches, influences the marking and character of future litters.

I may give one instance as particularly illustrative of this fact. A pure-bred white English terrier, belonging to my brother, by mischance, had connection with a yellow-and-white mongrel, to which she conceived, and in each of her succeeding three litters, though put to stainless dogs purely white, the whelps were marked precisely like the first litter, *yellow and white!*

3. When the bitch has been served, she should again be secluded, for she will then be more likely to retain the impression of the dog she has been mated with, and not only so, but danger of a second conception will be avoided. This may appear contrary to the laws of nature, but it is nevertheless a fact that bitches will re-conceive.* Of this I have had ocular demonstration. One instance I will give. A full-sized black-and-tan terrier, belonging to a relative of mine at Abbots Bromley, had connection with a dog of the same species; within an hour afterwards I saw her connected with a curly half-bred black-and-white sheep-dog. When the period of parturition arrived, she gave birth to two whelps: one, to all appearance, a pure-bred black-and-tan, the other a rough-coated black-and-white whelp, double the size.

---

* In the bitch, many observers have assured themselves that super-fœtation is by no means unfrequent. Rainard, Blaine, and others speak of it. Blaine says: "I am disposed to think that bitches are capable of superfœtation; that is, they conceive more than once. If this is the case, a bitch may copulate to-day, and become impregnated, and in a day or two she may copulate again, and again become impregnated. This is not frequent, I believe; but it certainly does happen, or we could not account for the different periods at which the progeny sometimes appear. I have known a week, and in one case even ten days, intervene between the puppings; but one or two days is not at all uncommon. As a still more convincing proof, the whelps often appear of *different kinds*." (The italics are mine.—J. W. H.)

"It must be remembered that the bitch remains in 'heat' for three or four days, and will seek repeated intercourse with the male during that period. It must, therefore, either be concluded that the last intercourse was the successful one, or that one or more ova were impregnated at each copulation."—Fleming's "Veterinary Obstetrics," Anomalies in Gestation, p. 153.

4. Dogs of close relationship should not be mated. In-and-in breeding is strongly objectionable, and cannot fail to produce, whether it is observed or not, enfeebled intellect, deficiency in some organism, and lay the foundation for disease. What laws are brought to bear on animals existing in their natural state no one can say. It may be, and probably is, for Nature ordains all things well, that there is an innate principle with them in regard to this. Plain facts of this breach of Nature are continually in our own species brought to light; and in the canine race unaccountable outbreaks of rabies in kennels where the in-and-in system of breeding has been adopted, and other affections in park-deer, under similar circumstances, have not been few.

5. Breeding should not be allowed before either sex have arrived at maturity. Early fruition stunts the growth, and spoils the after symmetry of the animal. There are occasionally exceptions to this rule. Young weedy bitches have thickened out and improved after an early litter, but I must again observe that as a rule such a system is not advisable.

6. There is much diversity of opinion as to the number of visits necessary for the inducement of pregnancy. This is however, dependent to some extent on the length of time connection is continued. A bitch thoroughly lined, *i.e.*, a safe connection established for from ten to fifteen minutes, is generally sufficient for all purposes. There is nevertheless, no objection to a second visit on the following day. A third I consider superfluous.

7. Many and various are the opinions frequently volunteered as to whether the bitch is in whelp. If she is placed on her side or back after being fasted, and the region of the uterus manipulated, the presence of certain oval bodies, the third or fourth week after conception, can be pretty fairly distinguished by a scientific and practical man. In flatulent, gross dogs this is, however, not a very easy task, and the occasional presence of ovarian tumours may be mistaken

(and would be, in all probability, by the uninitiated) for whelps.

The presence of milk in the teats towards the last week of pregnancy is not to be depended upon by itself as a sign of approaching parturition, as its secretion frequently takes place after copulation, or œstrum without the latter, towards and at the period of what should have terminated pregnancy.

In the mastiff bitch, Duchess, already alluded to, this was always the case, so that eventually, when she did conceive, I was in some doubt as to the fact until she had nearly run the full time, when the alteration in her habits convinced me to the contrary. Some animals carry their young so close, *i.e.*, exhibit such slight signs of altered shape, as to render the case still more obscure. A fortnight before Duchess whelped I was most positively assured by numerous canine individuals, including one of vast and long experience, and who offered to bet five pounds on the event, that she was not with young, and, further, that the glairy discharge she evacuated was proof of the opinion. When the time arrived she gave birth to thirteen whelps.

When, therefore, there is any doubt about the matter, look to the habits of the bitch, and particularly towards the approaching period of parturition. A drowsy condition, a wish for seclusion, and in a place hitherto unnoticed, should arouse our suspicions that parturition is likely to take place.

PARTURITION.

I have now arrived at one of the most important subjects contained in this work, and one that I should handle with far more diffidence than I shall do, had my canine experience been limited only to the treatment of disease. There are, however, times at which Nature in the lower animals is compelled either to abandon her efforts to relieve, or accept artificial aid; and the act of parturition is one in which she frequently needs human assistance, and that assistance it has been my pleasure frequently to give.

Mr. Blaine remarks: " Great numbers of dogs die every year in bringing forth their young. A life of art has brought the human curse upon them, and they seem, in common with their female owners, to be doomed to bring forth in sorrow and pain."

Certainly, especially in breeds belonging to the pampered house class, this is frequently the case. The same propensity to fix their affections on animals considerably disproportionate to themselves in size, appears as predominant in the canine as in the human race, and life is oftentimes the forfeit paid for such injudicious choice.

The period of pregnancy is from sixty-two to sixty-four days. The first symptoms of approaching labour are denoted by frequent urination and fæcal evacuation, due to nervous sympathy; there is also extreme restlessness, the bitch seeks solitude, where she will be found continually moving her position. The external generative organs present a full and swollen appearance; from the vagina there issues a glairy, gelatinous discharge, mingled immediately before the pains commence with blood. At this period the animal should never be interfered with indeed, it is only when it is manifest by protracted straining and gradual prostration that there is an obstruction to natural parturition, that man should then use his power Many persons are oftentimes too hasty to exhibit their obstetrical skill, or at all events from a mistaken kindness they interfere far too soon. The time occupied in giving birth to a whelp is frequently very considerable, and the intervals between each one long. Were they not so, the prostration would be so great that before the last birth could take place death from syncope would result; but an all-wise and merciful Creator has ordained that even the lowest of His creatures shall not suffer unlimitedly.

The first throes are generally short and somewhat weak but as labour proceeds they become stronger, longer, and more frequent.

When we are satisfied the bitch is unable of herself to parturiate, an examination should be carefully made with the finger per vaginam. If a whelp is in the passage, with the head and fore-feet presented, traction should be made on both. If tail first, on the hind feet. If it is a breech-presentation, which rarely happens, the hind leg should be secured and held firmly, while the stern is pushed back. Delivery will usually easily follow.

In cases where the passage is small, and the parts powerfully contracted, the warm bath is an invaluable aid. Mr. Mayhew, in one of his poetic flights of fancy, strongly condemns this measure. He however appears to have forgotten, in his arguments against it, that the contractions of the uterus, under some circumstances, prove an obstacle to the removal of its contents. Uterine inflammation, which he mentions as a consequence of the warm bath, is far more likely to result from neglected and rough assistance than the application of warm water. The probability of the animal not surviving if retained in it for an unlimited period, might reasonably be expected, but with discretion on the part of the surgeon, no evil result need be feared. In fact, my own experience on this point is in exact opposition to the above authors. I select the following from my list in illustration. A small, rough toy terrier, several years old, was brought for my attention in parturition. She had been in labour since the previous day, and it was her first pregnancy. The passage was too small to insert more than the tip of the little finger; there were no pains, but the diagnostic fœtal smell was emitted. After administering a stimulant, I inserted a very small forceps, and succeeded in laying hold of one foot, and subsequently the other, but to no purpose—the whelp was fixed. I then placed the bitch in a warm bath, keeping my finger in the vagina. I soon detected a relaxation of its walls, and by gradual traction, encouraged only once by a feeble pain, I extracted the whelp, an unnaturally large one. A little brandy was given to the bitch, after which she was rubbed dry, placed in a basket, and made comfortable. In a short time a dose of ergot was administered, the pains returned, and the birth of three more whelps took place without mechanical assistance.

Mr. Mayhew exhibits a like prejudice to the ergot of rye in promoting uterine contraction, and in this opinion he is not alone. Again, however, I am at variance with him and his disciples. We have had abundant proofs of the value of this agent in parturition, and of the evils of it in pregnant cattle by procuring abortion which could be traced to no other cause, not to doubt its power; and independent of the evidence of eminent veterinarians and medical men as to its efficacy, I have that of my own tests, which in no single case have been attended with failure. In protracted labour, then, with weak throes, I strongly recommend the ergot with stimulants.

After parturition the bitch requires but little attention, quietude is generally all that need be observed; the custom of continually inspecting the offspring and removing the bed is injudicious, the natural instinct of the mother teaches her to do all that is necessary, and however kind our intentions may be, she is jealous of any interference and prefers to be left alone with her family. (See "Influence of Mental Emotion on Canine Lactation.")

In continuance of the subject, the means used to deliver bitches in unnatural parturition are various. From Mr. Fleming's able work on "Veterinary Obstetrics" I extract the following, and if more information on the subject is required, I refer my readers to the book in question.

"With regard to the smaller animals, such as the bitch, sow, sheep, and goat, in them we may often use the crochet, the ordinary forceps, or a small-sized model of the human forceps with advantage. Various patterns are in use, some of them fenestrated, others not; some resemble polypus-forceps, while others again are grooved, serrated, or toothed at the ends of the blades. An essential which should not be lost sight of in the forceps for such small animals as the bitch or cat, is that the blades should be sufficiently long to seize not only the head, but much, if not all of the body of the fœtus. If they are too short in the blades they cannot be made to grasp sufficient of the fœtus to remove it; while the joint being close to the vulva, or even within the vagina, is likely to pinch the mucous membrane and cause considerable pain.

" Hill, of Wolverhampton, who has had extensive experience in this direction, uses a small and slightly modified form of the human forceps for bitches; there is a spring between the branches of the handle. (Fig. 12).*

" Weber has proposed a forceps for these small animals, and it has been preferred by some authorities to the ordinary model. It is a modification of one for a long time employed by Leblanc, which again was fashioned after an instrument designed by Hunter. This is composed of an iron stalk, about ten inches in length, with a wooden handle at one end and two blades or bows at the other. On this stalk glides a long enveloping metal tube, which, near the handle, has a wide ferrule, or shield, that allows it to be pushed along by the thumb of the hand holding the instrument, and thus to bring the blades together. A nut, or female screw, running on a screwed portion of the stalk, near the handle,

---

* These forceps were made according to my directions for private use, as will be perceived from Fig. 12. There is a spring between the handles, consequently the instrument must be closed before it can be inserted. The handles are then relaxed in proportion to the requiremeets of the case, *i.e.*, to the vaginal distension necessary to pass the forceps on either side behind the head of the pup. In small bitches, where the passage is much contracted, and it is difficult to manipulate with the fingers, the instrument is useful in exerting a gradual strain on the wall of the vagina from the spring pressure between the handles.

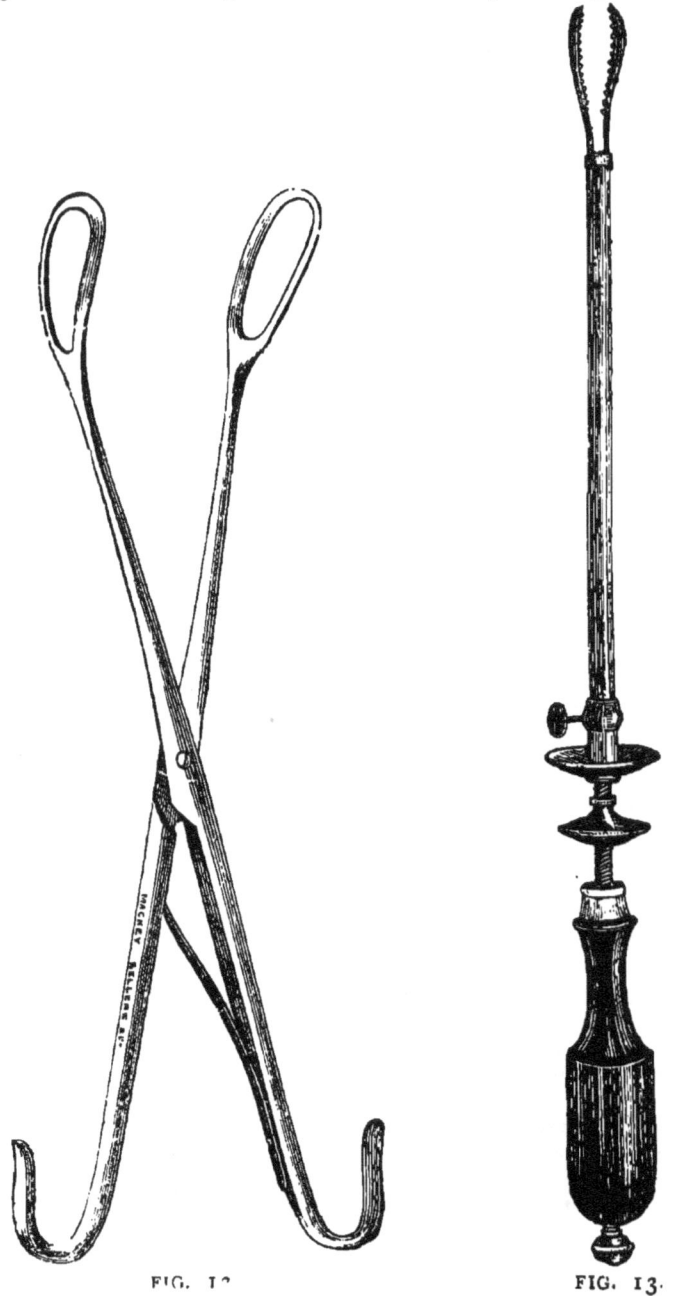

FIG. 12.
BITCH FORCEPS.

FIG. 13.
WEBER'S FORCEPS.

is intended to assist the pressure of the thumb when this is insufficient (Fig. 13). A finger of the other hand introduced into the vagina guides the instrument, and allows the part of the fœtus to be seized to be reached by the operator, either with the view of extracting the young creature or changing its position, according to the indications.

"Defays concludes that the forceps employed by veterinary surgeons in the accouchement of the smaller animals should not be merely a reduction in size of those employed in human practice, but ought to be something like that of Palfin. It is most difficult, he truly says, to apply an instrument in shape like that of the accoucheur's ordinary forceps, owing to the neck of the fœtus in carnivora being so thick, and the difference in volume between it and the head far less than in the human fœtus; so that, when the forceps is used, the ends of the blades press on the neck, slip under the throat, and the head escapes from them. To remedy this imperfection he has made forceps with the extremity of the blades notched or hollowed out (Fig. 14), while the head of one of the branches has a piece of metal with a slot in it, attached by a hinge, and which is intended to hold the blades together when the fœtus is seized.

"Though this forceps has sometimes proved of service, yet cases occur in which it is not so useful.

"When the bitch is large, or of moderate size, forceps may be employed with advantage, though they must be of various dimensions. But when the animal is very small, as is usually the case in difficult parturition in this species, the space occupied by the bows of the forceps—if they are ever so thin—so increases the volume of the mass which has to pass through the pelvic canal, that this instrument cannot be used.

"As we pointed out when studying the anatomy of the region, the pelvis is cylindrical in carnivora, and if we suppose its diameter to be three inches, and that of the

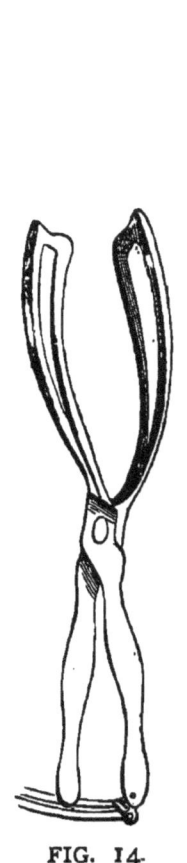

FIG. 14.
DEFAYS' FORCEPS.

FIG. 15.
DEFAYS' WIRE EXTRACTOR
WITH THE TORSION RODS.

head of the fœtus a trifle less, it will be seen that birth must necessarily be difficult ; and this difficulty will be increased if the vagina is narrow and rigid. When the forceps is used, the difficulty is further exaggerated ; for when the blades are passed on the head, the fœtus is then augmented in size by a quantity equal to their breadth, multiplied by their thickness, the whole constituting a mass greater than the pelvic cavity will permit to pass through it, so that delivery becomes impossible.

"Forceps, therefore, in small bitches, increase the difficulties of parturition, and those difficulties are all the more embarrassing as the animal is diminutive. Recourse to this instrument is consequently contra-indicated, and if delivery is to be effected, a means must be substituted which presents less inconvenience.

"As a rule, the loss of one or two puppies is not a matter of much moment, the principal object being to save the mother by bringing the act of parturition to a prompt termination. The *desideratum* is to apply an apparatus which will exert its force behind the head of the fœtus, as if the sum of expulsive efforts was directed from behind ; or as if a new force had been developed in the uterine cavity, which presses directly on the summit of the head.

"After much consideration, Defays finally produced an apparatus which fulfils these indications, and, besides its ingenuity, is very simple, and easily applied. It consists merely of two rather fine brass, or very pliable iron, wires which can be easily twisted, and are yet strong enough to withstand a moderate amount of strain. The wires should be at least sixteen inches in length, and looped in the middle, so as to be applied to the fœtus in the following manner : The first finger of the left hand being passed into the vagina, serves to guide one of the loops towards the summit of and behind the fœtal head, and it then conducts the loop of the other wire beneath the head behind the jaw. This done, the two wires on each side are twisted by a little machine (Fig. 15), composed of a thin iron rod in a handle, the other end of which is thickened and pierced by holes running nearly parallel to the stalk. Into these holes the two wires of one side are passed; the machine on each side is pulled up as close as possible to the head of the fœtus, and, each being turned round three or four times, the neck is enclosed in a kind of noose or collar formed by the two wires (Fig. 16).

"The rods are now withdrawn from the latter, and the fœtus can be extracted by exercising traction on the four ends of the wires outside the vulva. By this contrivance delivery is effected without injury to the bitch, and, unless

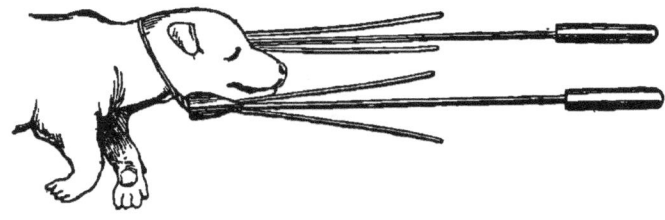

FIG. 16.

DEFAYS' WIRE EXTRACTOR APPLIED.

it is much decomposed, without separating the head of the fœtus.

"We have tried Defays' apparatus, and can speak highly of it; not unfrequently we have succeeded in extracting the puppy alive, and when the use of forceps would have been impossible.

"A much simpler, readier, and perhaps more successful apparatus (so far as our experience enables us to speak) is that devised by Breulet, of Marche, Belgium, which meets every requirement in the accouchement of small bitches, and might be successfully employed with sows, ewes, and goats.

This apparatus is the same in principle as Defays' wire extractor, but there is only one wire. The principal part of the invention is a noose-tube, consisting of a tubular piece of round wood, from four to six inches long, and half an inch thick. The wire may either be of copper, brass, or iron, about sixteen inches long (we have generally used a piece of catgut, and prefer it); this is doubled, passed

FIG 17.
BREULET'S TUBE AND NOOSE.

through the tube to a certain extent, so as to form a loop or noose at the end (Fig. 17).

"When it is to be used, the first finger of the left hand carries the loop into the vagina of the bitch, and slips it behind the occiput of the puppy; then the two ends of the wire are passed through the tube, and this is pushed into the vagina under the chin of the fœtus; the operator now tightens and secures the wire by giving it a turn round the first finger of the right hand, placing his thumb at the end of the tube (Fig. 18). A little traction then extracts the

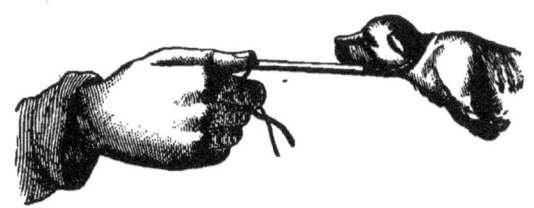

FIG. 18.
BREULET'S NOOSE FIXED ON THE FŒTUS.

fœtus, and without doing it or the bitch the least damage. We now employ no other instrument in canine obstetricy, and our success has always been complete, even with the tiniest toy terriers.

"When our assistance has been sought for in time, we have generally managed, expeditiously and easily, to extract the puppies alive. It will be seen that the noose is not unlike the 'fillet' used in human obstetrics."

FIG. 19.

THE CROTCHET.

The crotchet, or blunt hook, has been recommended by some authorities as an efficient obstetrical instrument. Mayhew observes with regard to its use:

"It has been long known to the human accoucheur, but by him is not employed save under certain conditions. A piece of stout steel wire constitutes its substance. The wire, about twelve inches long, is flattened at one extremity, and both ends crooked and made perfectly smooth or blunt, the flattened hook being the larger of the two. For the dog, the instrument must, of course, be proportioned to the passage into which it is to be introduced, and as the pup, in consequence of the weakness of the abdominal parietes in the bitch, often is felt lying below the level of the symphysis, a dip or lateral bend is given to the hooks.

"So simple is the crotchet, which ought to be highly polished, in order to secure its being perfectly smooth. It is first warmed and greased, then introduced with the index finger of one hand, while the other guides the instrument into the womb. The fœtus is to be first felt, and this is the more readily done if an assistant supports and compresses the abdomen. When the finger has ascertained that the pup is favourably placed, the hook (and I generally use the flattened extremity of the instrument) is to be pushed forward and then retracted, until the operator is aware that a firm hold has been obtained. The purchase

being secure, the finger is to be employed to keep the
fœtus from escaping, by pushing it against or towards the
point of the crotchet, and holding it there. Traction is
now made steadily, and in the proper direction; and the
assistant at the same time, by manipulating the belly,
facilitates the delivery of the bitch, which should be in a
standing position—not upon its back.

"The directions are not very complex, but they must
not on that account be disregarded. By introducing the
finger, and taking care that its extremity corresponds
with the point of the instrument, a great object is gained by
securing the pup more firmly; yet there are other advantages also obtained by this mode of operating. The head
of the fœtus is generally too large for the vagina, and hence
the difficulty of its expulsion; but by the employment of
an instrument which is simultaneously to pass, we appear
to be increasing the obstruction. However, by compressing
the head with the end of the finger, it is in some degree forced
to conform to the diameter of the passage, which the gelatinous development of the pup at the time of birth readily
enables it to do. Moreover, the hazard of injury being
done, if the instrument should lose its hold, is guarded
against; for, should the hook slip, the point would be
received upon the end of the finger before it could catch the
soft parts. However, the operator will feel the hold giving
way long before it is entirely lost, and will be enabled to
rectify the occurrence in the majority of cases before there
is a chance of accident. The finger, therefore, becomes a
sensible guide to the operator, and by its employment the
traction is rendered more firm and steady. But, above all,
care should be taken to have the instrument perfectly,
blunt, and the beaks of the hooks not too long. A
sharp point might, at the first glance, seem more likely to
answer the purpose in view; but its employment would be
attended with danger, and on being tested it would be
found more apt to tear away. In fact, the sharper the

point the less firm would be the hold, since the substance to be secured is somewhat of a pulpy nature; whereas, by using as broad and flat a point as possible, the force is exerted on a larger surface, and the grasp is proportionately the more likely to be retained; the object being not to rend the fœtus or tear it away, but to gently pull it through the vagina, using only so much violence as the judgment assures us is imperative for the accomplishment of the purpose."

A few weeks since, I was requested, whilst driving my round in the evening, to attend a fox-terrier bitch, which had given birth to a whelp early in the morning, and had continued throughout the day in labour. On my arrival I found the head of a large pup in the passage. I tried in vain to pass a loop over it, but it was too tightly wedged for me to do so. I then had recourse to a pair of silver sugar-tongs; but these were too soft for the purpose (otherwise, if electro, they are a capital substitute for forceps). I was loath to sacrifice the whelp, which was alive and close at hand; but having no instruments with me, and the owner being exceedingly fond of the bitch, which was becoming exhausted, I was compelled to do so. Having procured a small ordinary meat-skewer (Fig. 20), I bent the pointed end in the shape of a hook.

FIG. 20.

This, using my finger as a guide, I inserted between the branches of the lower jaw, and by gradual traction drew forth the head; then, seizing the whelp by the neck, I continued firm, steady pulling, in a few minutes extracting the whole, which proved to be almost double the size of the first-born. Considerable hæmorrhage followed. Some milk and brandy was administered to the bitch. No other birth took place, and she did well.

When it becomes apparent that delivery by ordinary means is altogether impossible, and it is desirable the offspring should be saved, the bitch either has to be killed, and the whelps extracted by what is termed the Cæsarean section ("Gastro-Hysterotomy"), or the latter may be performed during the mother's life, with the chance of hers also being saved. This operation English veterinarians have rarely practised.

The following is a case I recorded in the "Veterinary Journal," 1887:

"This morning (the 15th July), between ten and eleven o'clock, I was requested to attend an Irish setter bitch, which, I was informed, had yesterday afternoon given birth to one dead and three live puppies, and since eleven o'clock last night had been in severe labour with what the owner believed to be a 'cross-birth.'

"When I arrived the bitch was lying prostrate, with hurried respiration, rapid small pulse, eyes sunk, and extremities cold. On examination per vaginam, I found one fore-leg of a whelp presented, and the head doubled back within the womb. The leg in question had been so tugged at that it was dislocated, and almost severed from the shoulder; the vaginal parts were extremely inflamed, being of a deep purple tint and very swollen. After first administering a little brandy and milk to my patient, I placed a noose round the presented limb and returned it within the womb, and then endeavoured to bring the head into position, but without success. As the poor creature was now so extremely exhausted, in fact, too weak to stand, and the pains were very feeble and at long intervals, I suggested—as the only chance for the mother, and also because the offspring were valuable and several yet unborn—the *Cæsarean operation*, which the owner consented to.

"Placing her under chloroform, on a table, I made a section in the left iliac region, through the abdominal muscles and peritoneum; and then exposing the uterus, I incised it between four and five inches, and removed eight whelps—six alive and two dead.* I closed the uterine opening with continuous silk suture, the peritoneum and abdominal muscles with continuous gut suture, and the skin with interrupted linen-thread suture.

"The parts were then sponged with warm water; a little brandy and milk, with ten drops of laudanum, administered, and the patient placed on a rug over a thick bed of straw. Strict quietude was ordered, and a little brandy and milk only to be given in two hours.

"At six o'clock on the same evening I visited my patient, and, with much regret, learned she had just expired. I was informed she had not shown any symptoms of pain or uneasiness since the operation; that she had risen to her feet a few moments before she died, walked to her master and wagged her tail.

"In this case death resulted from sheer exhaustion. No support of any description had been given to the poor creature but what she chose herself to take, until I first arrived. She had been in severe labour for many hours; and only the following morning was any assistance rendered, and that, until my services were requested, had been rough, unpractical, and injurious.

"I feel convinced that had the operation been performed seven or eight hours earlier, the mother's life would have been saved; or that, in the first instance, proper assistance would have procured a natural birth of the abnormally presented one. The whelps that were alive are being reared by hand, and, so far, are doing well."

---

* The *uterus*, internally, was intensely inflamed—the *os* being perfectly black, and the whole membrane more or less livid. One portion of intestine, just observable, was also much inflamed. My prognosis from these appearances and other conditions of the bitch, was unfavourable

On the Continent some interesting cases of this operation are recorded. Among others, Mr. Fleming, in the obstetrical work alluded to, gives the following :—

"Brooks and Whitworth (Ibid., vol. xxxix., p. 33) relate the history of a bitch, which, while pregnant, had its pelvis injured by being run over by a carriage. When parturition had been going on fruitlessly for some time, an examination was made, and it was discovered that, owing to the fracture of the pelvis, just above symphysis pubis, the dimensions of the canal were greatly reduced and altered in form, so that the finger could scarcely be passed. Chloroform was administered; the hair removed from the skin in the right iliac region, where the incision was made. Two puppies were removed; the wound in the uterus closed by silver wire suture. In three weeks the bitch was well. The puppies, put to another bitch, also lived.

"Macorps ('Annales de Méd. Vétérinaire de Bruxelles,' 1862, p. 137) had under treatment a bitch which had in the right flank, towards the last mamma, a tumour the size of a fist, and which had appeared six weeks previously in a very gradual manner. It was neither hot nor painful to the touch, or on pressure.

"As it was supposed to be a mammary neoplasy, its excision was attempted. A large incision was made in the skin, and there immediately appeared a white saccular body, which was at once recognised as a *uterine hernia*. Instead of returning it to the abdomen, as this appeared to be both difficult and dangerous, it was decided to extract the entire uterine cornu, as far as the cervix uteri, apply a ligature round it there, and thus extirpate the organ. This was done; a few sutures firmly united the skin incision; the animal was kept quiet, the diet attended to, a few enemas administered, and in eighteen days after the operation, the bitch—of a sporting breed—was out in the field with its master.

"Saint-Cyr (Op. cit., p. 579) gave his attention to a bitch

which had been in labour since the previous evening. It had given birth to a puppy twelve hours before, but no more could be expelled. When Saint-Cyr first saw the bitch, the labour-pains had ceased; by vaginal exploration he could scarcely touch the foot of the most advanced puppy —which was not in the pelvis—with his finger; while the volume of the abdomen led him to believe that there were more than one in the uterus. The general condition of the animal was good; so it was decided to try the Cæsarean section, incising the right flank, where the fœtuses were most readily felt, by abdominal exploration. Three fœtuses were removed from the right cornu by a single incision; two of these were dead, but one was still alive. The operation being completed, the cornu was returned to the abdomen, but not sutured; and the abdominal incision closed by interrupted suture, a bandage being placed round the body. After the operation the bitch was very weak; it died in eighteen hours. The autopsy showed a moderate degree of metro-peritonitis.

"Feser ('Thierarztliche Mittheilungen der Munchener Schule,' part iii., p. 296) operated on a bitch which could not pup, making the opening in the left flank, against which the uterus lay; three puppies were extracted—one from each horn and one from towards the os uteri, the latter being dead, and from a deviation of its head it constituted the obstacle to birth. The heads of the other two puppies were likewise deviated. The uterus and Fallopian tubes—everything behind the cervix uteri—were extirpated by the ecraseur. The uterine and ovarian arteries were ligatured. The incisions were closed by suture, and ice applied to the left side of the abdomen. The animal lost about three ounces of blood. An hour after the operation it had a shivering fit, but this soon passed off; though it recurred three times a day for some time. In sixteen days the wound had healed and the bitch was quite recovered. The puppies were reared artificially.

"HAMPTON GORDON SUITE 'ROYLEIGH'"

"The same veterinarian (Ibid., p. 297) performed the 'sectio Cæsarean' on another bitch two years old. The animal had been in labour for two days, and was extremely weak; no puppies had been born. The section was made on the left side, and four dead puppies extracted. The uterus and ovaries were extirpated by the ecraseur, and the arteries ligatured. Frequent rigors appeared after the operation, In twenty-four hours death ensued, the fatal termination being apparently due to septikæmia.

"Feser (Ibid., p. 298) relates another instance in which he performed the operation, extracting four living puppies —two from each cornu; the incision was made in the left flank. The uterus and ovaries were also excised in this case, the animal loosing about five ounces of blood. Extreme' prostration ensued after the wounds were closed, but this was combated by stimulants, and sprinkling sweet spirits of nitre over the body. The appetite was good, and with the exception of traumatic fever, no unfavourable symptoms supervened. In eight days the bitch had recovered; two of the puppies were reared artificially.

"Adam ('Briefliche Mittheilung') performed the operation on a bitch, under chloroform, making the section at the linea alba, behind the umbilicus, and dividing the tissues with the scalpel, the peritoneum with scissors; the cornua were opened by incision. After removal of the fœtuses, the wound in the abdominal muscles was united by suture, then that in the skin. During the first day the animal was very depressed and feverish, but on the third day it was able to move about. The puppies, which were very large, were reared by hand. Eight months afterwards the bitch again became pregnant, and not being able to bring forth, died—no assistance having been rendered on this occasion, apparently."

CHAPTER X.

DISEASES IMMEDIATELY CONNECTED WITH PARTURITION.

PARTURIENT APOPLEXY, PARTURIENT ECLAMPSIA,
OR MILK FEVER, SEPTIKÆMIA
AGALACTIA. PUERPERALIS.

INFLUENCE OF MENTAL EMOTION ON CANINE LACTATION.

I NEED scarcely observe that during pregnancy and lactation, the mammary glands receive a greatly increased quantity of blood—in other words, they are more vascular and sensitive, and therefore more susceptible to take on inflammatory action. At the same period the mental condition is very active.

From a study and knowledge of mental emotional influence in human physiology, we may by close observation in canine practice, draw a reasonable simile. Just as tranquillity, irritability, anger, grief, anxiety, excitement, fear, and terror exercise their various actions upon the lacteal secretion in the human subject, and upon the infant, so undoubtedly do they in various degrees upon the canine subject.

The erroneous practice of continually interfering with and removing puppies, or creating jealous fear in the mother by allowing the approach of other dogs, or strangers, is fraught with much evil.

When we hear of a healthy litter born, and one after another quickly fading without any assignable reason, we should at once seek for the cause, which may frequently be discovered in those conditions I have named as influencing the human secretion.

A regular and healthy supply of milk is most desirable, and therefore comfort and proper management must be observed—in fact, it is most essential that due regard should be paid to the prevention of all emotional disturbance in connection with the nursing of the young. Of course the influence of habitual interference on the part of the master, or other members of the family, is not so deleterious as the advent of strange intrusion. Independently, however, of the modifying influence of external circumstances, I should still urge the wisdom of quietude and comfort.

The sensation of fear by the removing of a whelp is not always subdued on its restoration to the mother, but frequently continues to operate in the same direction, particularly with sensitive, timid bitches.

The first lacteal secretion, termed the "colostrum," which has a purgative effect on the offspring, and whose office is to cleanse the bowels of the meconium which is present at birth, is changed during the first week into milk proper, and therefore it will be readily seen that any action or influence which tends to this necessary alteration must have a serious influence on the condition of the young, for if the colostrum is retained, prolonged relaxation of the bowels must result, and under the effects of "scour" puppies rapidly decline.

The influence of a disturbing emotion on the intestinal canal or urinary apparatus, is well-known in the human subject, and precisely the same will apply to the lacteal organs. That a diminution of canine infantile mortality will result from due consideration of these remarks is my hope. Whether or not, it should always be remembered that a powerful instinctive desire is present in all animals, especially carnivora, to protect their young, and the less they are meddled with the better.

AGALACTIA (ABSENCE OF MILK).

Absence of milk in the mammary glands is occasionally met with in canine practice.

Causes.—Suspended breeding, plethora, general debility, exhausting disease, defective mammary development, acute or chronic disease of the mammary gland.

Treatment.—Good food, particularly of a leguminous kind. In debility, ammonia, bark, iron, cod-liver oil. In plethora, purgatives and plain diet. If from torpidity of the mammæ, friction to the glands, drawing the nipples, carminatives, and stimulating food.

PARTURIENT APOPLEXY, OR MILK FEVER.

This disease is rarely met with in canine practice. Probably the amount of hæmorrhage that frequently takes place in bringing forth the young, and the protracted labours of the bitch before the whole family is born, may to some extent account for its rarity.

A greyhound bitch, belonging to a gentlemen near Liverpool, gave birth to a numerous litter of whelps; the secretion of milk was very abundant. The family were all removed the following day, the bitch became ill the same evening, and the next morning succumbed to parturient apoplexy.

The pathology of the disease is much the same as in the cow and mare.

Causes.—Excessive plethora at the the time of parturition, the sudden removal of offspring, cold, extreme heat.

Symptoms.—Quick, full pulse, reeling gait, contracted pupils, nose hot and dry, tongue furred, extreme thirst, suppression of milk, constipation, ultimately coma, tympany, delirium and death.

Treatment.—Early venesection, counter-irritation at the back of the head and along the spine, stimulants and aperients. The head should be kept in an elevated position to prevent determination of blood as much as possible ; the urine and fæces are frequently retained, by reason of the progressive paralysis : in such cases the former should be drawn off with the catheter, and the latter removed as well by enemas as aperients. It is also advisable to repeatedly withdraw the milk, by natural means if possible, if not, by artificial aid.

PARTURIENT ECLAMPSIA.

A canine malady resembling the eclampsia of the human being has been observed by continental veterinarians ; but I fail to see that it bears any analogy to parturient apoplexy proper.

"Mauri (Fleming's 'Obstetrics,' p. 673) relates that a bitch, four years old, and which had been ill since the previous evening, was sent to the Toulouse Veterinary School. Fifteen days previously it had given birth to four puppies, which it suckled. That morning, about three o'clock, its owner was awoke by its plaintive cries and its restlessness. It was then anxious, its mouth was open, and it breathed as if it had been running fast on a hot day; it also appeared to be weak in its hind-parts. On its arrival at the school, it was found lying on its side in a large hamper, with its four puppies, which were at the teat ; the respiration was very hurried, short, irregular, and noisy; it was executed in a jerking, irregular manner ; the ribs appeared to be limited in their movements, as in a horse affected with tetanus. The mouth was halfopen, the tongue pendent, and the saliva flowing in a frothy, abundant stream. The animal convulsively closed its jaws, and withdrew its tongue from time to time, in order to swallow a portion of the saliva ; the buccal and conjunctival mucous membrane was greatly injected ; the physiognomy expressed great anxiety rather than pain ;

the eye was widely open, bright and animated, and the visual axis was not deviated. The limbs were kept extended and immovable, without tetanic rigidity. At intervals the animal attempted to get up, and managed to raise itself on its fore-limbs ; but the hind-legs moved in different directions, and automatically, so that the bitch could not co-ordinate them in a determinate manner. The joints could be easily flexed on each other by seizing the bones like the branches of a pair of compasses, but when left to themselves they immediately became extended. The pulse was strong and quick. The senses were unimpaired, and when its name was called the animal directed its eyes towards its master, and attempted to move its tail. This did not always happen, however, for the creature generally appeared to be completely absorbed by its condition—a circumstance which might have led to the belief that its general sensibility was diminished. There was no appetite, and the excretion of fæces and urine was completely suppressed since the commencement of the disease.

"Mauri, never having had an opportunity of witnessing such a malady, was much troubled to give a name to the collection of symptoms. As, however, paraplegia appeared to be imminent, he ordered sinapisms to the limbs and the spine, and enemas of tepid water. In the evening the symptoms were ameliorated ; the animal, instead of lying extended on its side, was curled round as in health, and when excited it got up, staggered, and fell on the litter ; a deep coma had given place to the excitement observed in the morning, and on some bread and milk being offered it slowly took a small quantity. Next day all the symptoms disappeared, and though the animal remained for five days in the hospital kennels, no relapse occurred.

"Mauri, in another instance (Ibid, p. 674)—that of a two-year old bitch, which had nursed two puppies for a month, and during that time seemed to be in perfect health, but which was suddenly seized with agitation and anxiety, appeared to be suffocated, could scarcely stand, and seemed to be paralysed in its hind-limbs—noted the following symptoms: General agitation of all the muscles, anxious physiognomy, and all the characteristic features described in the preceding case. The respiration was very laborious, though the ribs were immovable. The gait was unsteady, and the hind-quarters were feeble, as in confirmed rabies. The animal appeared to be impelled to move about incessantly, and if it stopped it fell; then the limbs became rigidly extended. In the midst of its convulsions it endeavoured to rise, but could not co-ordinate its movements—it turned itself on its back, so as to lie alternately on the right and left side. After numerous attempts it sometimes succeeded in getting up, and commenced to walk, but only to fall again; it could only stand on its rigid paws by resting against a wall or tree. An hour after its arrival at the school, it could not rise unaided. Its senses did not appear to be affected; the appetite was lost, and there was neither defecation nor micturition during the attack. The case in every respect appeared to be similar to the preceding. No treatment was adopted, and in the evening the bitch had almost completely recovered, though it was rather sleepy and dull. Next day it was taken away cured.

"The same authority (Ibid. p. 674) "records the case of a bitch brought to the Toulouse Veterinary School, and which caused anxiety about three hours previously by its agitation, breathlessness, and anxious look. It had fallen, was seized with contraction of the limbs, got up, and staggered about in all directions, until at last it became so weak that it could not stand. When Mauri saw it, it was lying on its side, the limbs extended, and agitated from time to time with clonic convulsions. The animal could not be induced to get up, the head only being raised towards the shoulder. The symptoms were altogether similar to those observed in the two preceding cases. No treatment was adopted, and next morning all the symptoms had disappeared.

"Lafitte (Ibid., p. 674) attended a bitch which, two days previously, had brought forth two puppies which it suckled. It appeared to be very weak and staggered in walking. Soon after, the feebleness of the hind-quarters was extreme and clonic convulsions affected all the muscles; the eyeballs pirouetted in their sockets, the jaws wer econtinually moved, and saliva ran from the mouth continually; hearing and seeing were unaffected. Two hours subsequently the animal could not rise. A belladonna draught was given, narcotic frictions were applied along the spine, and emetised enemata administered. In the evening the bitch was dull, weak and stupid. In the morning every trace of the malady had disappeared. Next day there was another eclamptic attack of shorter duration, and the fourth day another still briefer and weaker. The puppies were put to another bitch, and in about eight days they had attacks similar to those of the parent, though shorter and less intense. One, a female, had three attacks on successive days, and then died—the other, a male, had only two attacks.

"Lafitte (Ibid., p. 674) reports that a bitch, four days after pupping, had clonic convulsions in all its muscles; its jaws were agitated, it was much salivated, and respired with difficulty. Its expression was animated, but it could not stand, and was compelled to lie. During the night the convulsions ceased, and the animal, although a little somnolescent, appeared quite recovered; at ten o'clock next morning, however, it had another attack, and in the evening it died.

"The same veterinarian (Ibid, p. 674) alludes to the case of a bitch which, three days after pupping, had convulsions in the muscles of the trunk and limbs, and the hindlegs were so feeble that it could not stand. Its gaze was unsteady, and at times the eyes rolled about in the orbits.

The masseter muscles participated in the convulsive movements of the other muscles, so that there was a continual champing the jaws and an abundant salivation. The senses were not impaired, however. An antispasmodic treatment was adopted. The attack lasted four hours, when recovery took place.

"Mauri (Ibid., p. 675) reports another instance of this malady occurring in a bitch, eight years old, and very fat. It had pupped twelve days before, and suckled four puppies. When brought to the Veterinary School it was lying on its side, though it could raise itself on its sternum—it panted much, its mouth was wide open and much saliva flowed therefrom—the tongue was pendent. The respiratory movements were much quickened, but very shallow. The eyes were wide open and slightly squinted to the left. Violent convulsions, as if produced by electric discharges, agitated the limbs, and threw them into a state of forced extension; if a group of extensor muscles—such as the patellar—were seized in the hand, the energetic contractions, rapidly repeated, could be easily felt. Nothing of the kind could be distinguished in the flexor muscles. The senses were not affected. The urine did not offer any trace of albumen. In the course of the day the symptoms disappeared and the animal recovered.

"Mauri alludes to four additional cases of eclampsia—two in the cow and two in the bitch, all presenting similar symptoms to the foregoing."

SEPTIKÆMIA PUERPERALIS.

"Inflammation of the uterus and *septikæmia puerperalis* occur in all the domesticated animals. The latter would appear to be very frequent in the bitch."*

Parturient septikæmia may arise from the retention and putrefaction of a dead fœtus,† or the introduction of putrefying matter into the blood through inoculation.

Symptoms.—Increase of temperature, rigors, hurried respiration, small frequent pulse, nose dry, mouth hot and slimy, visible mucous membranes injected, extremities soon become cold, coma speedily sets it, frequently accompanied by delirium, and death quickly follows.

Post-mortem Examination.—In those cases in which death has taken place, and an examination of the body has been made, the local and essential lesions are found in the genital organs and peritoneum, and when puerperal septikæmia has been present, there are observed indications of general infection of the body. Decomposition sets in early, the tissues are dark-green and fœtid, and meteorism is largely developed.

"It is seldom, indeed, that the puerperal or septic inflammation is limited to the mucous membrane. Nearly always it extends to the submucous connective tissue (*metritis phlegmonosa*), which is infiltrated with an œdematous transudation; or it becomes the seat of acute

---

* Fleming's "Veterinary Obstetric," p. 632.

† "It is well known that bitches which retain the fœtus in the genital canal for any length of time (eighteen hours or therabouts), frequently perish from *septikæmia puerperalis*. This appears to be due to the fact that the puppy so retained quickly dies: owing to the shortness of the umbilical cord, the early separation of the placenta, and birth taking place in the amnion. The young creature also speedily putrefies, and the large raw surface formed by the maternal placenta is a ready inlet for the direct introduction of the septic material into the blood. Speedy death of the bitch is the consequence."—Fleming's "Veterinary Obstetrics," p. 639.

inflammatory œdema, in which the tissue swells, becomes tumid, and its interstices filled with fluid, small cells, and a gelatinous semi-solid material. The muscular tissue is swollen and softened, and a dark fluid flows from it."

Treatment.—In all cases of septic inflammation, prompt measures, both for the removal of the cause and effect, are demanded. The former consists in cleansing, by injections of warm water, those parts of the genitals upon which the infecting material is present, and also disinfection of wounds or abrasions.

Fleming observes: "The genital canal should be thoroughly cleansed by injections of warm water, and the wounds dressed with carbolic acid and olive-oil (1 to 10) applied by means of a brush or feather; or salicylic acid 1 part, spirits of wine 20 parts, warm water 24 parts.

"After the interior of the uterus has been cleansed by injections of warm water, an injection of carbolic acid solution (1 to 20—50) should be made every day, and the wounds, if accessible, must be dressed at the same time.

"Permanganate of potash (1 to 50 of water) may be employed to inject into the genital canal, when the disease is less acute.

"With regard to constitutional treatment, this must be directed towards neutralising the effects of the septic matter by the exhibition of antiseptic remedies, and reducing the high temperature; as a long continuation of this leads to rapid consumption of the tissues, and is fraught with danger to the system.

"There is no specific remedy with which to neutralise the action of the septic matters in the blood and tissues. The sulphites of soda and potash have been recommended, as well as sulphurous acid. These appear to have acted favourably in some cases. Carbonate of soda and permanganate of potash have also been well spoken of, as well as

---

* Ibid., pp. 635, 636.

large doses of quinine. Carbolic and salicylic acids are now most in repute, and are given in small but frequent doses.

"If there is a tendency to constipation, a purgative may be administered; indeed, unless special circumstances forbid it, a purgative may prove most serviceable in assisting in the removal of the septic matter through the intestinal canal. Dogs which have been poisoned by this matter often recover after profuse and fœtid diarrhœa; and a purgative generally reduces the temperature.

"In acute cases, in order to obtain the more prompt action of antiseptics, it has been proposed to introduce them directly into the circulation by intravenous injection. Solutions of carbolic acid and iodine have been employed successfully; and in woman a desperate case has recovered after the intravenous injection of liquor ammoniæ (1 to 3).

"As a last resource, and to substitute healthy for poisoned blood, transfusion had also been practised in woman, and with good results. The experiment is worth trying in the parturient fever of animals.

"With regard to the diminution of temperature, quinine has been highly lauded. Bleeding is certainly not to be recommended. If the temperature continuously remains very high, then the application of cold water to the surface of the body is indicated. The cold water may be applied to the larger animals by means of cold wet sheets, wrapped round the body, and kept cold for an hour or two at a time by pouring on water at intervals, by means of a small vessel. Smaller animals may be put in a gradually-cooled bath.

"The skin must be well-dried after the application of the cold water, and with the larger animals a dry blanket should be thrown over the body. The stable (or kennel) must be kept scrupulously clean and well ventilated. Tonics and good food must be allowed when recovery is taking place, and the *sequelæ* of the disease treated according to their indications."

CHAPTER XI.

DISEASES OF THE MAMMARY GLAND.

MAMMITIS, LACTEAL TUMOURS, CANCER.

MAMMITIS,

OR inflammation of the milk-gland, is by no means an uncommon complaint in canine practice.

Causes.—External injury, as blows, bruises, or wounds, exposure to cold or damp, retention of milk, etc.

Symptoms.—The part affected is red, hot, somewhat hard, and excessively tender; the lacteal secretion is changed in character, first having a curdled appearance, subsequently mingled with blood, and ultimately pus, the natural secretion becoming then totally arrested. Matter having formed may gradually approach the surface of the gland and point there, but it rarely becomes thus located, the whole gland generally being involved. Considerable febrile disturbance is present throughout.

Treatment.—In the early stage leeches may be applied to the part, and hot fomentations; a saline aperient should be administered, and perfect quietude on a soft bed enjoined. If the complaint results from retention of milk, owing to the removal or death of whelps, the sooner suckling is allowed the better—whether the secretion be altered or not, even to pus, its direction to the channel of the teat for evacuation is strongly advisable, and much preferable to permitting abscesses to form, and point at the surface, and thus destroy a considerable portion of the gland.

When matter has formed, and is approaching the surface, the sooner it is evacuated the better, otherwise sinuses are liable to form, and render the case tedious and difficult. For subsequent treatment see "Abscess."

Chronic mammitis is denoted by an indurated and enlarged condition of the gland, and may be the result of lingering subacute inflammation, or proceed from the acute form. It is attended with but little pain or constitutional disturbance; but, unless early measures are taken for its removal, it becomes a permanent induration, and may ultimately, if excited, assume a cancerous condition.

Treatment.—The daily application of iodine ointment, or the tincture, to the affected part, and the iodide of potassium in one or two scruples daily, are the most effectual agents in this complaint; repeated friction with the hand is also of service, and where the enlargement is considerable and weighty, it may be conveniently, and with benefit, suspended by means of a handkerchief tied over the back, or a net made for the purpose and fastened in the same way with tapes.

LACTEAL TUMOURS.

The milk ducts are liable to become obstructed when not sufficiently drained of their contents, or from some malformation. Any such obstruction to the outflow of milk is calculated to produce much mischief. Lacteal tumours, perhaps the least hurtful that can arise, are thus frequently caused.

Symptoms.—The mammary gland affected is knotty; the irregularities being even, movable, and painless: in the early stage these bodies have a fluctuating feel, which disappears as their period of existence lengthens.

Inflammatory action may be excited in them by injury, and suppuration result.

Treatment.—If still in milk, the daily withdrawal of the secretion should be observed—by natural means if possible.

Milk is frequently secreted, independent of the animal parturiating, more especially if connection has taken place. Its removal, if abundant, is advisable, which may be done with the fingers, or an ordinary female breast exhauster. A smart dose of aperient medicine, and for a few days short commons, is also of service in dispersing it.

Where the animal is comparatively or quite dry, and we have the tumours only to deal with, it becomes a question whether, so far as their direct treatment is concerned, we shall rely on external application, or a surgical operation. If the tumours are of recent date and fluctuating, they may be punctured with some amount of success: if hardened and of long existence, their removal with the knife can be adopted with safety and success.

Individually I should give the iodine a fair chance before resorting to either.

CANCER.

The so-called cancer of the mammary gland is chiefly confined to bitches which have parturiated. I say so-called, because it is rarely that the true cancer cell can be detected—the character is generally that of an indurated or scirrhous tumour. In chronic cases they frequently assume an osteoid form. I have removed numerous tumours so constituted—some with spiculæ of bone throughout their structure, others only ossified in the centre. If removed early, a sac containing pus or watery fluid will generally be found within them.

Causes.—External injury, cold, damp, retention of milk from not suckling, insufficient suckling, or obstruction, sudden withdrawal of whelps soon after parturition.

Symptoms.—These are usually slow in manifesting themselves. The primary ones are heat, redness, enlargement, and tenderness. These in time subside (with the exception of the enlargement, and this also is reduced as the condition becomes sub-acute), leaving behind a thickened, lumpy gland. This may remain *in statu quo* until the time of parturition again approaches, or at the period of œstrum. The gland will then assume the same acute symptoms as in the first instance, and pass away with much the same result, except an observable increase in the enlargement. And so this may go on for years, gradually increasing, until at last the whole gland, and not unfrequently its neighbour, becomes obliterated, and in its place is a large indurated tumour, or, it may be, cancer.

Treatment.—If the case is taken in hand during its acute stage, the early treatment laid down for mammitis—leeches, fomentation, saline aperients, rest, and removal from cold—should be adopted. When it occurs after parturition, the whelps should either be removed and the teats drawn, or watched when suckling, that they do not irritate the part. The scrambling and application of their needle-like claws only tends to bruise and irritate the inflamed gland. If it can be done without distressing the mother, it is advisable to remove the whole or a portion of the family until nourishment is again required.

In chronic cases, and when the gland is not wholly involved, and the enlargement not very considerable, the iodine ointment, or tincture, may be tried outwardly, and the iodide of potassium and iron inwardly, in the doses already prescribed. When the tumour becomes large, very pendulous and unsightly, or breaks, and gives vent to an offensive discharge, excision is decidedly indicated. The skin should be divided the whole length, or nearly so, of the tumour, the edges reflected, and the diseased mass, which is usually held by connective areolar tissue, is generally easily and quickly removed by dissection around it. Occasionally its base is attached by more vital structures, and hæmorrhage will follow its removal. In such a case, either the ligature may be adopted before severing the mass, or the vessels afterwards taken up and tied, or the actual cautery applied. The latter is sometimes used for separating a vascular base.

The superficial bleeding which occasionally takes place more or less all round it, when more closely connected to the skin, is usually harmless, and is readily stayed by the application of the tincture of iron.

The edges of the incised skin are to be brought in apposition, with interrupted silk sutures, steeped in a weak solution of carbolic acid. Healing generally takes place quickly, and the loose, hanging pouch of skin contracts to the level of the surrounding parts.

It is always advisable to wire-muzzle the patient after the operation; for the tongue, although a great healer, often does considerable mischief, and the teeth will speedily remove stitches and ligatures.

The after treatment consists in daily cleansing the wound from discharge, attention to the bowels, a plain, unstimulating diet, and tonics if there is much prostration.

CHAPTER XII.

DISEASES OF THE EYE.

OPHTHALMIA,
CATARACT,
AMAUROSIS,
IRITIS,
ENLARGEMENT OF THE HAW,
HYDROPHTHALMIA.
PROTRUSION OF THE EYE-BALL,
EXTIRPATION OF THE EYE,
HAIRY TUMOUR ON THE CORNEA.

OPHTHALMIA.

THE dog, though not liable to many of the diseases affecting the visual organs of the human being, is nevertheless frequently the subject of some of the more prominent ones. Ophthalmia, or inflammation of the mucous membrane lining the eyelids and covering the ball, is very commonly met with, especially in sporting dogs.

Causes.—External violence, as blows, bites, pricks from thorns, cat-scratches; or irritation from the presence of foreign bodies, as dust, grit, inverted lashes, accumulated pus, soap-suds, etc.; irritating vapours, particularly stable effluvia, or that of undrained and neglected kennels; damp and cold.

Ophthalmia may be sympathetic with other diseases, as distemper and disorders of the digestive organs.

Symptoms.—Simple ophthalmia commences with intolerance of light, deflux of tears, and repeated closing of the eyelids. If the latter are separated, the conjunctival membrane will be found highly injected, and the eye painfully susceptible to touch or exposure.

Unless the inflammation be checked it rapidly extends, other and deeper-seated structures become involved, and the vision dangerously impaired. The cornea is traversed with engorged vessels, the pupillary opening blocked by an opaque mass of exudation (lymph) ; and quickly upon this we get ulceration of the cornea, followed by fungoid granulations.

Treatment.—The lids should be carefully separated, and examination made for the presence of any foreign matter, which, should it exist, is to be gently removed. So long as inflammatory action is present, the avoidance of light, warm fomentations, and, at the onset, a mild dose of aperient medicine, is generally all that is requisite.

In cases where the disease will not yield to these simple measures, where the inflammation increases, and there is considerable distension of the corneal vessels, local bleeding is attended with much benefit; this may be produced by pricking the skin immediately under the lower lid, and applying a leech or two or puncturing the lachrymal vein with a lance, and placing the finger on the vessel beneath the opening. I shall probably be accused of being antiquated in advocating the latter measure (blood-letting), but experience in inflammatory eye diseases in the lower animals has taught me that, however old the doctrine, it still holds good in local inflammations, particularly in vascular parts, and in none more so than the eye. With regard to other measures--the avoidance of light, and warm fomentations, should still be maintained. Bathing the eye with an infusion of poppyheads is sedative to the inflamed part, and therefore useful. A low and unstimulating diet is absolutely necessary.

Chronic or constitutional ophthalmia is denoted by the eyes being always watery, but more so on exposure to light or cold; there is opacity of vision, and conjunctival congestion. The condition, however, is less irritable than in simple or acute ophthalmia.

Treatment.—Tonics; seton in the poll; painting the outside of the orbits with iodine; sponging the eyes with cold spring water; the application of zinc lotion, 2 grains to the ounce of water, or nitrate of silver 1 grain to the ounce, are the measures usually adopted and indicated. The seton is especially invaluable in these cases. If corneal ulceration exists, the application of the dry oxide of zinc has almost a specific effect, and may be repeated daily until the eye is perfectly clear.

CATARACT.

Cataract may be either lenticular, capsular, or capsulo-lenticular. It is lenticular when there is opacity of the crystalline lens, capsular when the opacity is confined to the capsule, and capsulo-lenticular when both lens and capsule are involved.

Though more frequently seen in old dogs, cataract may take place at any age.

Causes.—Inflammation of the eye-ball; diminished vitality, consequent on old age.

Symptoms.—The presence of an opaque body, which may be best seen from a posterior side view in a shaded light, or in a dark place by candle-light.

Treatment.—This consists entirely in the operation of extraction, and which only can be performed by an experienced oculist.

AMAUROSIS.

Amaurosis, commonly known as gutta serena, is an impairment of vision consequent on a disordered condition of the retina, optic nerve, or brain. This disordered condition may proceed from external violence, as blows or falls on the head, producing immediate paralysis, or giving rise to inflammatory action, extravasation of blood, the formation of tumour, and ultimate suspension of nerve force.

Extreme debility, either from disease, hæmorrhage, prolonged lactation or anæmia, may also be associated with amaurosis.

Symptoms.—The defect in vision may be gradual or sudden. Obstructions are not seen until the animal is close upon or touches them. The gait is peculiarly diagnostic of sight affection. An uncertain *feeling* action is observed in locomotion. The creature relies to a great extent upon the sense of smell, and snuffs the air as he moves about.

Eventually the function of sight becomes totally lost. The eye is clear (unnaturally so) and bright, hence the Arabic term "gutta serena"—*clear drops*. No irritability in the organ is observed, except occasionally at the commencement of the disease, but on the contrary, the brightest light is of no effect. The pupil is dilated, and the eye has a more or less vacant expression. One or both eyes may be affected, according to the seat and extent of the injury, or from sympathy, which is exercised to a great degree in eye affections, and in amaurotic ones generally in the end involves both.

Treatment is unfortunately of little avail, and can only be adopted with any degree of success in the early stage of the malady. An active seton in the poll, strong iodine liniment around the outside of the orbits, or blisters; and, internally, strychnia or nux vomica, are the measures indicated. The general health of the patient should be looked to, a liberal diet allowed, with moderate exercise.

IRITIS.

Inflammation of the iris, or colouring membrane of the eye, is not unfrequent in the dog. It may proceed from injury, or deep-seated ophthalmic inflammation.

Symptoms.—The iris is changed in colour, a deep reddish-brown tint, often extending beyond the edges of the cornea, may be plainly seen. The pupil becomes contracted, and to a great extent immovable to the stimulus of light. Excess in the lachrymal secretion, pain and intolerance of light, and cold, are the accompanying symptoms. As the disease proceeds the eye becomes, from the engorged condition of the vessels, generally bloodshot. Extravasation of blood occasionally takes place, resulting in the formation of pus, and the total destruction of vision.

Treatment.—Here the local abstraction of blood is strongly indicated, together with absolute darkness. Warm fomentations, and free movement of the bowels.

When the acute symptoms have passed away, the administration of tonics, and small doses of the iodide of potassium, and, if protracted, a seton in the poll, will materially assist in restoring the eye to its natural condition.

The light should be subdued so long as inflammatory symptoms are present, and gradually increased as these disappear.

ENLARGEMENT OF THE HAW.

The haw (membrana nictitans), or fold of membrane placed at the inner corner of the eye, is for the purpose of removing foreign bodies or irritants from the globe. Occasionally, from external violence, irritation or constitutional disease, it becomes enlarged, prominent, and obstructive to vision and closure of the eyelids. In such cases the part presents a red and highly inflamed appearance, is exceedingly sensitive to touch, causes the animal considerable pain, and gives rise to profuse lachrymation.

Treatment.—The primary treatment consists in scarifying and warm fomentations. Should the enlargement persist it may be gradually reduced with the scalpel or scissor and caustic, or the whole substance drawn out and snipped off.

Astringent lotions are useful, and in many cases sufficient.

PROTRUSION OF THE EYEBALL.

Occasionally in fighting the eye-ball is displaced from its socket. If the accident is of recent date and the appendages are not torn asunder, the return of the organ is not difficult. In the case of a toy dog, not long since brought for my inspection, I had the eye and surrounding parts well fomented for a quarter of an hour with warm milk and water; a few drops of olive oil were then poured over the ball, the upper lid drawn forward with blunt forceps, and gentle pressure exercised, when it returned easily to its natural situation, but when pressure was removed it again protruded: once more returning it, I placed a small pad of wet lint over the organ, and closed the lids over it with silk sutures. The case did well, and no evil results followed.

When the ball is completely torn from its attachments, excision at once is advisable.

EXTIRPATION OF THE EYE.

This, from unsightly blindness, disease, or protracted protrusion, is sometimes rendered necessary. The ball being drawn forward and held firmly, the muscles and optic nerve are divided with a bistoury or scalpel. A pledget of cotton wool steeped in iron should then be placed in the vacant socket, and a couple of stitches inserted through the upper and lower lid. These and the pledget may be removed in forty-eight hours, and the socket daily dressed with the following liniment

Glycerine.............................. 1 ounce.
Acid Carbolic........................ 5 minims.

It is occasionally necessary, where there is fungoid disease, with adhesion, to dilate the canthus. This should be done from the outer one.

It is advisable to keep the patient in a dark place after the operation, until all symptoms of inflammatory action have subsided, and on moderate diet. It is almost needless to add that this operation ought always to be performed under chloroform.

HAIRY TUMOUR ON THE CORNEA.

An instance of this exceedingly rare occurrence is recorded by Mr. J. M. Parker, M.R.C.V.S., Birmingham, in the *Veterinary Journal* for April, 1877:

"In June, 1875, a setter puppy, three months old, was brought to me for advice about one eye—the left—which was discharging a considerable quantity of muco-purulent matter. On washing the eyelids, and carefully examining the eye, I found that the whole of the eye-ball was covered with long black and white hairs (the puppy was black and white) spread out like a fan.

"With some trouble, I fixed the eyelid, and found that the hairs grew from a warty substance as large as half a pea on the cornea, at the posterior part of the eye, near the eyelid, but not connected with it.

"I plucked out thirty hairs with the forceps, and sent some lotion containing laudanum and zinc sulph.

"In about a fortnight I saw the patient again, and he was reported as having improved considerably. This I found to be the case; and I removed a few more hairs—twelve or fourteen, perhaps. He was not brought to me afterwards, but I heard from his owner that all pain and discharge had ceased. Having occasion to pass the owner's house in September, 1875, I called to see the pup; and found that the eye was much inflamed, and a fresh crop of hairs had grown.

I then determined to pare off the 'wart '—for such it seemed to be; but how to do it without chloroform or proper instruments was the question.

"I decided to transfix the base of the wart with a needle, and cut it clean off the cornea with a scalpel. Making a hook with a silver probe to steady the lid, which was held by an assistant, I was able, after a little trouble, to pass a strong sewing-needle, armed with a stout thread, through the base, and, pulling it away from the cornea, I dissected the growth very carefully from its attachment, and effectually eradicated it. No more hairs made their appearance, and the wound speedily healed. There was, unfortunately, a considerable deposit of lymph in the eye from long-continued irritation, which, perhaps, might have been prevented had I excised the portion at first. I may add, in conclusion, that it was horny to the touch, and not like transplanted skin, which the presence of coloured hairs would appear to indicate."

In the following number for May, Mr. W. A. Taylor, F.R.C.V.S., records a similar instance in a fox-terrier puppy, fourteen weeks old:

"My attention was recently directed to the dog's eye by my brother, whose property the puppy is. He had noticed the existence of the tumour soon after the usual nine days blindness of puppy life.

"An examination of the eye (in this instance the left) reveals to the beholder what at first appears to be 'something white' in the dog's eye. On a more careful inspection, the white object is discovered to be a fixed tumour, circular in outline, of a pinky-white tint, and having a diameter of three-sixteenths of an inch; it is slightly raised above the level of the eye, and from it grow some white hairs, in number about fifteen, resembling those of the eyelashes. Two-thirds of the tumour are attached to the sclerotic coat, the remaining third to the cornea, and it receives a covering of conjunctiva.

"In appearance and structure this *lusus naturæ* bears a close resemblance to the mole on the human skin.

"The presence of the tumour does not apparently cause any inconvenience to the puppy beyond a slight increase in the flow of the lachrymal fluid.

"Are these hairy tumours hereditary? If so, it would be unadvisable to breed from animals possessing them. The eyes of both parents of the puppy above alluded to are perfectly normal."

Since the above records, similar cases have come under the Author's notice.

HYDROPHTHALMIA.

The abnormal accumulation of fluid in the chambers of the eye, which gives rise to what, in ophthalmic surgery, is termed "Hydrophthalmia," is a disease to which attention was first drawn by the author in 1884, through the *Veterinary Journal*, under the heading of "Special Notes on Canine Diseases." Hitherto the subject had passed unnoticed in the literature of canine patholgy, probably owing to its non-recognition.

The disease is usually confined to one eye, unless congenital predisposition exists, when both eyes may be involved.

Causes.—A cachectic state of the constitution is favourable to hydrophthalmia, but it may more frequently be traced to injury, particularly violent concussion to the eyeball from a blow.

Symptoms.—A hydrophthalmic eye is protruded from the socket, and looks as if it were about to burst; the eye-ball is hard and tense to the touch, usually of a dull opaque colour over the cornea, and the pupil is stationary.

In dogs, hydrophthalmia generally involves both the anterior and posterior chambers of the eye. The distension caused by the dropsy produces considerable discomfort to the patient, vision is obviously impaired, and total blindness is a common sequel.

Treatment.—Tapping through the sclerotica, followed by continuous pressure, secondary infiltration may occur, and tapping may be again resorted to. This treatment has been successfully adopted by the author on two occasions, the eye being punctured immediately behind the outer margin of the cornea. In one operation a drachm of clear watery fluid was removed; in the other, half-an-ounce of a deep amber-coloured fluid, approaching red. After each evacuation the eye assumed its natural size and position; a cold wet sponge was placed over it, and maintained *in situ* by a head cap. The sponge was re-applied daily for a week; and then one drop of a weak solution of iodine was each morning placed on the eye-ball for the removal of the opacity, and the result proved satisfactory. In persistent cases the application of iodine round the eye, and atropine injections, are sometimes beneficial.

Congenital dropsy of the aqueous chambers is not unfrequently present in *in-bred* dogs, especially toys.

CHAPTER XIII.

DISEASES OF THE EAR.

CANKER (External), POLYPUS,
CANKER (Internal), DEAFNESS,
SEROUS ABSCESS, SCURFY EARS.

CANKER (External).

THERE are few diseases which cause more trouble and annoyance, alike to owner and subject, than the one known as "canker." All dogs are liable to this malady; but long-haired ones, and especially water-dogs, are those usually affected.

The disease is generally divided into external and internal canker. External canker is that which attacks the edge or margin of the ear-flap.

Internal is usually confined to the passage leading to the ear proper.

Both forms are the same in character, and may co-exist or arise independently of each other.

Causes.—Canker may be produced by external violence, gross feeding, over-heating food, plethora, uncleanliness. It is frequently associated with mange and eczema.

Symptoms.—The first generally observed is repeated shaking of the head and flapping of the ears. Examination reveals the integument covering those organs red, puffy, and hot, and this condition is aggravated by the animal continually scratching them. If this is left unchecked, the amount of irritation produced on the inflamed part gives rise to a serous exudation along the margin of the flap, and ulceration quickly follows, leaving a thickened irregular crusted edge.

Treatment.—Immediately symptoms of canker are observed, a dose of aperient medicine should be administered, and warm fomentations applied to the part. Where exudation has taken place, all extraneous matter should be gently removed with warm water, and mild astringents applied to the sore surface. The following is a useful lotion :—

Alum	5 grains.
Vinegar	1 drachm.
Aqua	1 ounce.

To be applied twice or three times a day. Or a drachm of oxide of zinc to an ounce of vaseline may be used with benefit.

When the case will not yield to this treatment, and when ulcers have formed, and show a tendency to spread, I find occasionally touching the parts with nitrate of silver after washing is of great service; and when the eschar is detached either of the following lotions may be applied with a camel-hair brush :—

Tinct. Myrrh Co.
Tinct. Arnica
} equal parts.

or,

Tinct. Ferri Mur.	1 drachm.
Acid Carbolic	5 minims.
Aqua.	1 ounce.

In obstinate cases, when the cartilage becomes diseased, and remains, in spite of all that can be done, persistently so, it will be advisable to remove that portion of the flap beyond the line of disease; but only in an extreme case should this be done. If simply thickened, painting with iodine will suffice.

CANKER (INTERNAL).

Internal canker is most generally seen in water dogs. Youatt observes: "When the whole of the body, except the head and ears, is surrounded by cold water, there will be an unusual determination of blood to those parts, and consequent distension of the vessels, and a predisposition to inflammation." With this author I quite agree.

Again, water being continually lodged in the ear, and remaining there, is in itself a source of irritation, and calculated to produce canker. Allowing dirty suds to remain after washing, is an especially fruitful cause both of canker and deafness.

Internal canker, if neglected, is very much more disastrous than the external form. The disease will extend to the internal bones of the ear, and cause the most maddening pain; or it may, and often does, without these ravages, result in deafness, in which case treatment for the latter is generally hopeless.

Symptoms.—The membrane lining the passage, as far as can be seen, is red and inflamed, and the root of the flap hot and tender. There is the same disposition to shake the head and scratch the ears as in the external canker. The patient is depressed, often disinclined to feed, probably owing to the increase of pain through the movement of the jaws in mastication. As the disease proceeds, an offensive, dark-coloured discharge issues from the passage of the ear, the itching becomes intolerable, and the animal in his misery rolls about, rubs his ears along the ground, frantically scratches at them, and utters pitiful cries. Occasionally the cervical glands are swollen, and the sides of the face considerably tumefied.

Treatment.—This is of the same character as that prescribed for the former, only differing in its mode of application. The ear should be syringed (not too powerfully) with warm water, and whatever lotions are used must be poured into the ear, applied with a feather, or some cotton wool saturated with it and packed gently in. For internal canker, the zinc lotion, 5 grains to the ounce of water, applied three or four times a day, I find usually answers better than anything else. If raw spots or ulcerations are noted, the parts should be mopped with a solution of nitrate of silver, and this may be repeated every other day. In many cases after syringing with carbolised warm water (1—40), the parts may with benefit be dusted with the dry oxide of zinc. Equal parts of balsam of Peru and ox-gall, daily dropped into the ear, has also been found successful. When the disease extends to the bones of the ear, humanity dictates an end to the creature's sufferings.

In all cases of canker, whether external or internal, it is absolutely necessary, in order to ensure success and rapidity of cure, that the animal should be prevented as much as possible from flapping, scratching, or rubbing the ears. For this purpose a cap of wash-leather or stout calico (the latter is coolest) should be placed over the animal's head and tied under the throat (Fig. 21). It should be similar

FIG. 21.
DOG WITH CANKER CAP.

in shape (with the exception of the ear portion) to a horse's hood, and is kept much easier in position than the usual three-cornered one.

o

With regard to the further treatment of canker, I quote the following from the "Veterinary Journal," Sept., 1875, p. 216:

TREATMENT OF ULCERATION IN THE EARS OF A DOG BY COCULET.

"The disease vulgarly known as 'canker' in the dog is frequently most troublesome and unsatisfactory to treat, for several reasons. In the 'Recueil de Méd. Vétérinaire,' Coculet recommends, as a very successful method of dealing with these auricular chancres, the application of some blistering ointment or liquid over the external surface of the ear. The preparation he employed was tincture of cantharides forty-five grammes, tincture of oak galls ten grammes. This was applied once every two days, and by its influence the intolerable itching which accompanies the disease was allayed, and a smart but inconvenient pain substituted. The animal no longer shakes its head, nor scratches the ears with its paws, and the chancres soon disappear."

SEROUS ABSCESS.

It not unfrequently happens from the violence applied in canker to the inflamed organ by the dog himself, or independent of canker existing, from blows or bruises, that an infusion of serum takes place between the integument on the inside of the ear and the cartilage underneath, giving the organ a peculiar, dropsical, baggy appearance. In such a case it is best to open the sac at its most dependent part with a lance, making a free incision, and evacuating the contents. In a short time the wound will heal, and the ear assume its natural condition. There is no necessity to induce suppuration; if nature establishes it, well and good, and it must then be treated as a suppurating sore.

POLYPUS.

The formation of polypus on the lining membrane of the external meatus is not uncommon in the dog. The tumour usually assumes one of two forms: the soft and vascular situated in the anterior half of the meatus, or the full and fleshy (sometimes fibro-cartilaginous), in the lower half of the meatus.

Causes.—Protracted, irritation or chronic inflammation of the lining membrane of the meatus, or of that covering the tympanum.

These tumours, when small and quiescent, are not attended with any great inconvenience; but when they become irritable, and the animal, in his attempts to rid himself of the offending body, increases the irritability, they rapidly increase in size, and give rise to deafness, pain, giddiness, and other untoward results.

Symptoms.—In describing the symptoms of this affection, I cannot do better than follow the example of other authors, in transcribing a portion of Dr. Mercer's paper in the "Veterinarian" for 1834, on this subject:

" Polypi produced from the tissues of the meatus may be divided into two kinds:

"First, the soft vascular and bleeding polypus, usually produced from the fibro-cartilaginous structure of the outerhalf of the tube; and, secondly, the hard and cartilaginous polypus or excrescence produced from the lining membrane of its inner half.

"As to the first of these forms of polypi, the hæmatoid, that arise from the external soft structure of the tube, they may be situated in any part of its parietes, but most commonly at its superior and posterior surface. In form they are generally pedunculated; their surface is rough, irregular, and glistening, in consequence of being covered with a thin layer of mucus, which is often tinged with blood, especially when any degree of violence has been applied to the external ear, and which has also been exerted upon the tumour. When the tumour becomes protruded externally, it has a blood-red and pulpy appearance, and its sensibility is so great that any manipulation of the concha, so as to investigate the condition of the external meatus, is attended with great pain, and is also often followed with considerable hæmorrhage.

"The second variety of polypus growth, the chondromatous, is that which is produced from the lining membrane of the inner half of the tube, the dermo-periosteum, and in its structure differs somewhat from the former; it is more dense, and almost cartilaginous, and usually having a broad and more sessile base, occupies a greater extent of the parietes of the tube. Its surface is comparatively smooth, pale, and almost insensible to the touch; but according to the extent of the ulcerative process behind and within it, so will the nature and properties of the discharge be with which it is accompanied.

"Both these species of polypus of the meatus, the hæmatoid and chondromatous, are most commonly connected with, and accompanied by, ulceration of the softer tissues, or caries of the auditory process. These excrescences are usually situated externally to the seat of ulceration, being produced from the vascular margin of the ulcer; and so long as they are permitted to remain, the latter morbid condition, the canker of the ear, will be kept up for an indefinite period; hence, should the animal be of any value, it becomes a matter of considerable importance to arrive at an accurate diagnosis of the actual condition of the diseased parts. The symptoms, therefore, which attend the existence of polypoid growths of the external meatus are very similar to those that indicate the chronic form of internal canker of the ear. These are also preceded by those of general pyrexia, which usher in the local disease, such as general languor and lassitude, loss of appetite, considerable thirst, turning out of the coat, and balling of the fæces. As these constitutional and general symptoms diminish in severity, then those characteristic of the local disease become gradually and more manifestly evinced. The animal has a dull, heavy, and rather a watery eye; he moans or whines at intervals; and if his master be present he feels a pleasure, a confidence, and a relief in pressing and rubbing his aching ear against any part of his master's body. Under other circumstances he presses and harrows it against the ground, so as to obtain a slight relief, and then with an instinctive feeling he flaps his ears and shakes his head rapidly and repeatedly, so as to keep up the pleasurable relief he thus obtains. Should the symptoms be not so severe as those which I have now mentioned, the animal may still be suspected, at a glance, to be labouring under acute disease of the ear, by his running about with little intermission, his mouth open, and tongue protruded, and panting, and with a stupid sensibility shaking his head, and pointing the affected ear to the ground. These symptoms are, however, most commonly allowed to pass unheeded, and in a few days a partial relief is obtained to the animal by the sudden and profuse discharge of a quantity of fœtid pus. From this time the general and constitutional symptoms disappear, and those indicative of the local affection are alone predominant. The local discharge of pus, or pus and blood, becomes daily more and more fœtid, in consequence of the extension of the disease to the body tissue of the meatus, and the poor animal is thrust aside as an object of loathing and disgust.

"Should the dog, in the earlier stage of the disease, be muzzled and cast, and an inspection of the meatus be had recourse to, then there will either be found a phlegmonous abscess of the cellulo-fibrous structure of the meatus, circumscribed dermo-periostitis of the inner part of the tube, with caries of the osseous portion, or internal muco-tympanitis, with perforation of the membrana tympani, and evacuation of the matter along the external canal.

"In that form of the disease to which I specially refer—where a polypoid excrescence follows and accompanies the uluceration of caries—if a period of three weeks or a month be allowed to elapse between the first exhibition of the discharge and the examination of the meatus, it may be found that the vegetation has attained a considerable size, and the discharge has become more and more profuse and bloody. The extent of bloody discharge and its fœtidity, will much depend on the nature of the tumour, and the original tissue of the meatus that may be affected. If there is much blood mixed up with the discharge, then in all likelihood there will exist a soft and vascular polypus, produced from the more vital fibro-cartilaginous structures of the meatus; and should the smell be great, and the discharge little tinged with blood, then the original disease will be found to exist in the osseous portion of the tube, and the polypus, if it does exist, will be of the chondromatous or cartilaginous kind."

Treatment.—This should consist, if the growth is in the outer half of the meatus, and within reach, in removal by torsion, ligature, or excision, and the subsequent application of caustic. If near to the tympanum, such an operation would be attended with danger, and the potassa cum calce, as recommended in human surgery, is best adapted to the case. The injection of mild astringents should, in the course of a few days, follow either measure.

DEAFNESS.

Deafness in dogs may be congenital,* or result from obstruction in the auditory passage, caused by disease, injury, the lodgment of water, or it may result from

---

* I recently examined a white terrier, belonging to a clergyman, in which the sense of hearing had never been recognised—being, in fact, congenital, and the animal was destroyed in consequence.

paralysis of the auditory nerve from severe shock. Youatt observes, with regard to cropping: " Deafness is occasionally produced by it in some dogs, and constantly in others. The frequent deafness of the pug is solely attributable to the outrageous, as well as absurd, rounding of his ears. The almost invariable deafness of the white, wire-haired terrier is to be traced to this cause."

Treatment.—If deafness proceed from congenital causes, it is needless to remark that a cure is hopeless. Where it is due to morbid growths, resulting from canker, polypus, or other diseases, the removal of such obstruction is indicated. If from paralysis, counter-irritation behind the ears, by blisters or seton, and the administration of strychnine or nux vomica, are the measures to be adopted.

SCURFY EARS.

Scurfy ears are frequently met with in long-haired dogs, and may either be associated with mange, or the result of an over-heated, plethoric habit of body—more frequently the latter. If neglected, this condition is apt to run on to canker.

Treatment.—An aperient, followed by drachm doses of sulphur in a bolus daily, and a spare, unstimulating diet, usually removes the affection. An ointment composed of sulphur and whale-oil may, in obstinate cases, be applied with success to the ears.

CHAPTER XIV.

DISEASES OF THE SKIN.—EXTERNAL PARASITES.

MANGE (Sarcoptic),　　ALOPECIA.
MANGE (Follicular),　　WARTS,
ECZEMA,　　　　　　　　FLEAS
ERYTHEMA,　　　　　　　LICE,
RINGWORM (Proper),　　TICKS.
RINGWORM (Honeycomb),

MANGE (Sarcoptic).

The term "mange" is generally used by those people who dabble in canine matters without the knowledge necessary to diagnose correctly, to denote any affection of the skin which results in eruption, irritation, or the detachment of hair.

The true mange of the dog is analogous to the itch of man, and the riff of the horse. It is due to the presence of a small acarus (*Sarcoptes canis*)—Fig. 22. Another species, termed *Follicular mange*, is also very frequently met with in dogs. This likewise is due to the presence of an acarus (*Acarus folliculorum* or *Demodex caninus*)—Fig. 23.

Mange, of whichever species, can only be propagated by the migration, directly or indirectly, of the parasite giving rise to it. Filth and neglect favour parasitic development, but do not of themselves produce the disease.

Symptoms.—Ordinary or sarcoptic mange is characterised, at its earliest period, by intense itching. If the skin of the affected part is examined, there will be observed small red points like flea-bites. These eventually become pustular, and break, exuding a serous fluid, which produces thick, dark crusts, which are ultimately cast off, leaving the part denuded of hair, and of a bleached appearance.

The violent scratching attendant on the affection throughout, creates extreme soreness, and frequently open wounds. The hair about the affected region becomes matted together, and the animal is rendered an object of disgust and pity.

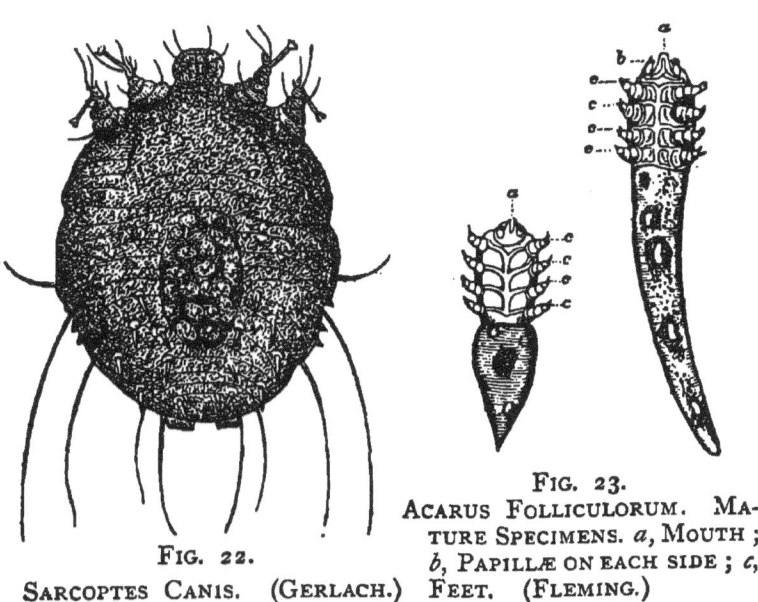

FIG. 22.
SARCOPTES CANIS. (GERLACH.)

FIG. 23.
ACARUS FOLLICULORUM. MATURE SPECIMENS. *a*, MOUTH; *b*, PAPILLÆ ON EACH SIDE; *c*, FEET. (FLEMING.)

The disease, if not checked early, rapidly extends to the

whole body. In such a case the poor animal knows no peace, and the debility is extreme.

Treatment.—The treatment of mange is a matter of no great difficulty, if properly adopted. The recipes are various, and most of them good ; and failure is dependent, as a rule, on the mode of applying them, and in neglecting those sanitary measures so necessary in diseases of this description.

A dog suffering from mange requires either shaving to ascertain the extent of the affection, or else to be thoroughly dressed all over. The necessity of this will be apparent when we bear in mind that a single acarus will produce in a fortnight upwards of twenty young.

For the same reason all the litter should be destroyed, and the habitation thoroughly cleansed each day—if in the kennel—with boiling water, slightly impregnated with ammonia or carbolic acid. Old mats, particularly wool ones, should never be allowed for repose in mange ; plain straw or shavings, where litter is required, are the most suitable agents.

Before the application of any dressing, the animal should be well washed with warm water and soft soap. The ointment I find most successful in mange is,

Sulphur Sub.	8 ounces.
Whale-oil	8 ounces.
Oil of Tar	$\frac{1}{2}$ ounce.
Ung. Hydrarg	$\frac{1}{2}$ ounce.

To be well blended, and applied as indicated. Wash off and repeat in three days, and again after the same interval if necessary.

For mild cases the ordinary sulphur ointment, made with sublimed sulphur and soft soap, whale-oil, or lard frequently suffices ; or half an ounce of ol. terebinth to six ounces of whale-oil is a useful application.

Benzine and paraffin have of late been commonly and

successfully used, and I have no fault to find with those agents, save that they usually require frequent repetition.

Tobacco-water is a popular remedy with some persons, but from its narcotic effects, through absorption, it is not an advisable one.

Carbolic acid is another, and in the use of this drug still greater caution is required; its strength should never be less than 1—50 of soap-suds or whale-oil.

Mr. Fleming* observes: "The remedies proposed for scabies in the dog are exceedingly numerous; and it would be altogether beyond our object to attempt an enumeration of even a tithe of them. They consist of baths, liniments, and ointments. Among the former may be mentioned the sulphuret of potassium—one part to five of rain-water; also corrosive sublimate, one part to fifty of water; carbolic acid, in the proportions of one to forty of soap-suds or glycerine, is also a good remedy, but requires care. The liniments, are, perhaps, better applications than either the baths or ointments. A very good preparation is the following: Oil of tar one ounce; sulphur, one ounce; common oil, one pint. To be allowed to stand, in the sun or near a fire, for some time, and frequently shaken. Prangé recommends the subacetate of lead (liquid) and olive-oil, of each thirty parts; sulphur, fifteen parts.

"With regard to ointments, the Helmeric pomade already mentioned is very efficacious. Mercurial ointment, and different compounds of mercury, are much resorted to; but these are readily absorbed by the skin. Dressings of tobacco have the same disadvantage. It is generally a good plan to wash the animal well with soft-soap or carbonate of potass, in warm water, before applying the parasiticide. The latter should be washed off the skin after it has been applied three or four days. If the skin is covered with long, thick hair, it is advisable to have this cut off.

---

* "Veterinary Sanitary Science," vol. ii. p. 458.

" The success of the remedy depends very much on the care with which it is applied to every part of the skin.

" For house dogs, and especially those with fine skins and smooth hair, a very excellent and safe remedy is the balsam of Peru, dissolved in alcohol (one of balsam to four of alcohol). This is an effective acaricide, and has not an unpleasant odour."

FOLLICULAR MANGE.

This species of mange, from the acari being buried in the sebaceous and hair follicles, and their migration to a great extent thus hindered, is not so contagious as the sarcoptic form. "Indeed, an affected dog may cohabit with others for some time without extending the disease.* The animal whose case is described by Weiss, lived for from eight to fifteen days with other dogs, which remained unaffected. This feature in follicular scabies is accounted for by the situation and habits of the parasite, and its conformation. Burrowing deeply into the follicle, it only leaves its habitation, in all probability, when carried from it by the fluid thrown out in the follicle, for its limbs are very short, and are not furnished with suckers, so that it is not well adapted for travelling, differing in this respect from the ordinary acarus. Nevertheless, in some instances, the slightest accidental contact will suffice for its transference from a diseased to a healthy dog ; and, when conveyed experimentally to the skin of the latter, it propagates it in a remarkable manner. Haubner deposited several, with a view to elucidate the contagiousness of the affection, and he found that, in about twenty-four hours, there was a slight

---

* This fact will serve to explain why the contagiousness of scabies has been denied and affirmed by different authorities in this country, where only one kind of parasitic " mange " has been hitherto recognised in the dog.

tumefaction of the skin where they had been placed ; in forty-eight hours the follicles contained a purulent fluid, in which young and adult acari and ova could be perceived. The eruption extended; but eventually the parasites disappeared, and a spontaneous cure took place."*

Symptoms.—These likewise are not so easy of distinction as in sarcoptic mange. At first, circumscribed tumefactions of the skin take place: these tumefactions are hot, and usually blotchy, or patched with red. In a very short time small pimples make their appearance, which rapidly become pustular, break, and exude serum, or, in severe cases, pus. The matter thus exuded forms scabs, or crusts —the skin is thickened and chapped as in common mange.

The itching attendant on follicular mange is not excessive nor continuous. The disease usually commences on the head, and from thence extends to the body ; it is of long duration, and very obstinately yields to treatment.

Detached hair is rarely replaced, owing to the destruction of the hair follicle.

Treatment.—The difficulty experienced in reaching the acari renders curative measures somewhat troublesome and unsatisfactory. Mercurial agents are, perhaps, the most useful. White precipitate, combined with sulphur and whale-oil, is a very excellent formula.

The following ointment (my own prescription) has been in my practice attended with the best results in cases of follicular mange.

Acid, Acetic .... }	aa 2 drachms.
Ol. Terebinth .... }	
Ol. Tar	½ ounce.
Ung. Hydrarg.	1 "
Sulphur	8 ounces.
Whale-oil	10 "

---

* Fleming's "Veterinary Sanitary Science," vol. ii. p. 457.

The whole to be well mixed, and rubbed on the affected parts for five minutes. Wash off in forty-eight hours with soft-soap and warm water, and when the skin is dry apply to the surface whale-oil ; and the following day, without washing, repeat as before the ointment-dressing. Allow a week to elapse before another dressing of the same, if necessary, is applied. In recent cases a third application is not often required. After each dressing, the kennel should be thoroughly cleansed and disinfected before the dog is suffered to inhabit it. All wood and iron-work should be well scoured with boiling water and soda, and to any brickwork, after first brushing, limewash with carbolic acid should be applied.

Mr. Hunting, after a series of unsuccessful experiments, made conjointly with Professor Duguid, in the treatment of follicular mange, observes :

"It occurred to Mr. Duguid that, as the parasites were situated so deeply in the skin, it might assist the action of any dressing if we could soften and break up the cuticular layer of the skin. With this object in view we employed a solution of caustic potass, in addition to a creosote dressing, and with marked benefit. To facilitate the action of the dressing still further we adopt the plan of frequent washings of soap and warm water, gently removing at the same time any scabs, and rupturing any pustules. The following," says Mr. Hunting, "is the formula I advise : olive-oil, seven parts, and creosote one part, well shaken together, then add two parts of strong solution of caustic potass. This is to be applied every third or fourth day, to all diseased spots, with a piece of rag, and the dog should be washed a few hours before each dressing. To prevent the spread of the disease when limited to small or single spots, it is well to shave off the hair for about an inch around each diseased part, and in cases where most of the body is affected, we shave the whole animal. This operation deprives the parasite of all protection afforded by the hair, and is not unnecessarily severe, as, without shaving, the loss of hair is certain to be very great, and much hair hides from view the first symptom of new centres of disease.

"Considering the damage done to the roots of the hair, we should expect but a very partial reproduction of the coat. It is, then, satisfactory to be able to state that it is thoroughly and completely restored when the parasite is got rid of, save on any small spot where the skin was so damaged as to be repaired by cicatrisation.

"The proper recognition of this disease is the most important part, because many dogs will not pay for three or four months' treatment, and because this dressing is unnecessarily severe for ordinary mange, and decidedly injurious to those cases of skin disease due merely to constitutional disturbance. Very young or very small dogs must be treated carefully, as the dressing is apt to affect them injuriously. If lessened in strength it is not certain to destroy the parasite."*

"Zürn asserts that he has frequently succeeded with an ointment composed of one part of benzine to four of lard. Weiss recommends the inunction of essence of juniper. Zundel states that the balsam of Peru has often yielded good results when the malady has not been of too long duration. He has employed it, dissolved in alcohol (one to thirty); he has likewise used the green iodide of mercury with success, as well as the nitrate of silver ointment. Hoper speaks highly of an ointment composed of carbolic acid; and Vogel prescribes a solution of caustic potash."†

ECZEMA.

This disease, which is commonly known as "blotch" or "red mange," is a frequent and troublesome affection with

---

* Hunting, "Diseases of Dogs," "Live Stock Journal and Fancier's Gazette," February 11th, 1876.
† Fleming's "Veterinary Sanitary Science," vol. i. p. 459.

dogs. It is analogous to the eczema, crusta lactea, humid tetter, or scald, so often seen in infants and young children.

Eczema may be either acute or chronic, and local or general. The two forms usually seen are: 1. That which attacks the head, and along the back. 2. That in which the integument generally is red, more particularly visible between the thighs, underneath the arms, and on the abdomen, and which is the form called "red mange."

Eczema* is a non-contagious affection of the skin, characterised by the eruption of minute vesicles in great numbers, and frequently confluent, upon a surface of irregular form, and usually of considerable extent. The vesicles are so closely aggregated in some situations, as to give rise to one continuous vesicle of great breadth. These larger vesicles, when laid open, appear to be cellular in their structure; the cellular disposition obviously depending on the juxtaposition of the numerous small vesicles of which they are composed. The vesicles of eczema terminate by absorption of the fluid which they contain, or by rupture and moist excoriations succeeded by thin crusts, and by furfuraceous desquamation. The eruption is generally successive, and variable in duration; it sometimes extends to the mucous membrane, and is often developed on the scalp and hair-bearing parts of the body.†

All dogs are liable to become eczematous, but those used for sporting purposes more particularly so. One attack predisposes the animal to another, and the latter frequently establishes chronic eczema.

Causes.—Insufficient exercise and injudicious feeding are the two chief causes of eczema in dogs. A too stimulating diet, an excessive supply of animal food, a denial of the exercise necessary in such cases to balance the effect of

---

* From ἐκζεῖν, *effervere*, to boil out.

† Wilson's "Diseases of the Skin," p. 164.

these measures, result in an over-charged and over-heated system, and Nature, to avoid worse consequences, endeavours to get rid of this pressure by means of serous outpouring or exudation.

Treatment.—Saline aperients are in the first instance advisable; when the irritation is extreme and considerable constitutional disturbance is manifested, a grain each of opium and calomel may be administered with benefit.

With regard to local applications, the skin should never be washed or rubbed, in the dressing with agents, more than is absolutely necessary. The benzoated oxide of zinc ointment smeared over once or twice a day is a very effectual remedy. Another exceedingly useful one is:

> Oxide of Zinc .... ⎫ $aa \frac{1}{2}$ ounce.
> Olive-oil .... ⎭
> Arnica Tinct.................. 2 drachms.
> Rose-water .... 7 ounces.

To be applied three or four times a day.

Where there is much wetness of surface and irritation, the parts may with benefit be dusted from time to time with plain flour, or 1 part of powdered alum to 6 of flour. Debility and wasting is overcome with mineral tonics and cod-liver oil. The diet should be plain, nutritious, but not stimulating. Daily exercise should also be allowed.

Chronic Eczema, though not accompanied by the same amount of irritation and constitutional disturbance as the former, is nevertheless a troublesome, and oftentimes a tedious affection.

" In chronic eczema other topical remedies are required, one while to relieve prurities, and another while to exert a discutient action on the affected part. The juniper-tar ointment, considerably diluted, is an excellent anti-pruritic remedy; while stronger, or of its full strength, it is powerfully discutient. Among the best of the discutient remedies are the ointments of the nitric and hydrochloric salts of mercury, variously diluted ; for example, the nitric oxide of mercury, unguentum hydrargyri nitratis, and unguentum hydrargyri ammonio-chloridi. In some forms of chronic eczema one or other of these ointments is specific; for example, the unguentum hydrargyri, nitrico-oxydi diluted to the extent of one part in four, in pityriasis capitis ; the unguentum hydrargyri nitratis, one part in eight, in psoriasis palpebrarum, etc. Sometimes eczema rubrum and eczema impetiginoedes, when of long continuance, or when the water-dressings or poultice have been unduly prolonged, become excessively tender, so tender in fact, as to be irritated by the mildest application. I have such a case in remembrance, wherein the disease of the skin was rendered most distressing by its associations with a kind of cutaneous neuralgia ; and I have since seen several cases of a similar kind. In this morbidly sensitive state of the skin and of the eruption, I have found no remedy act so well as a solution of nitrate of silver in distilled water, in the proportion of one grain to the ounce."*

In such cases, constitutional treatment is not to be overlooked. Small doses of arsenicum or calomel are attended with considerable benefit, iron and quinine also are of service. The animal should be kept dry, and the bedding clean. Exercise and nutritious feeding must likewise be observed.

A species of eczema is not unfrequently produced through the incautious use of mercury (*eczema mercuriale* or *hydrargyria*). " An eruption occurs, characterised by round irritable patches of skin from which a secretion oozes, and which are denuded of hair. The skin is at first red, swollen and afterwards rough and hard. In dogs the eruption occurs chiefly on the limbs and scrotum. The general symptoms are loss of appetite, salivation, closure of the

---

* Wilson's " Diseases of the Skin," p. 191.

eyelids, great dulness, offensive exhalations from the skin, and sometimes death. Recoveries occur slowly.*

ERYTHEMA.

Dogs are occasionally affected with superficial inflammation of the skin, which chiefly takes place on the face, especially about the mouth and the extremities. The inflammation occurs in patches, which are throughout attended with but little heat or irritation, except in the latter stages of the affection, when the skin on the portions attacked peels off, leaving the surface underneath red and sensitive; then more or less febrile disturbance is apt to take place. When the pad of the foot is involved, the animal walks with reluctance and evident soreness. Young dogs, particularly when teething, are those usually attacked. The disease is non-contagious, and readily yields to treatment.

Treatment.—Mild saline aperients in the first instance, followed by tonics, form the most effectual medicinal treatment.

With regard to local applications, the oxide of zinc ointment or lotion is most suitable. Sponging with cold vinegar and water or a weak solution of alum is likewise beneficial. The diet should be plain and unstimulating.

RINGWORM (PROPER).

This disease is occasionally met with in the dog. It is due to the presence of a minute vegetable parasite or fungus (*Tricophyton tonsurans, Malmsten,* or *Achorion Lebertii*).

Ringworm is exceedingly contagious, communicable from man to the lower animals, and *vice versa.*

---

* Gamgee's "Our Domestic Animals in Health and Disease," vol. ii. p. 133.

Causes.—Cold, wet seasons; badly drained, dirty, and uncomfortable kennels; insufficient and nutritious food; inattention to the cleanliness of the skin, are each conducive to the presence of ringworm.

Symptoms.—The most prominent symptom is the characteristic circular patch, with silver scaly crusts, whilst the presence of the fungus at once removes any doubt that may exist. The hair has a dry, harsh appearance, is exceedingly brittle, and easily detached. As the disease advances, the hair breaks of itself close to the crust, and when the latter is removed, the hairs are exhibited in short, bristle-like pieces, surrounded with the spores of the fungus.

From the animal biting, rubbing, or scratching itself, the characteristic shape is sometimes obliterated.

The period of incubation is from eight to fourteen days.

Treatment.—Mild mercurial and iodine ointments are generally effectual in the treatment of ringworm. The following is also a very useful application:—

Whale-oil	6 ounces.
Terebinth	2 ounces.
Oil of Tar	1 drachm.
Acetic Acid	1 drachm.

To be applied to the parts after first thoroughly washing the skin with soft-soap and warm water, and repeated in two days and so on, as may be necessary.

*Attention to hygiene is the principal object. Good food and cleanliness must be insisted upon. Recovery will be greatly accelerated by topical remedies. The scales should be removed by washing the parts with soap and water, or hyposulphite of soda lotion; or, if the crusts are very adherent dressing them with oil and afterwards washing. The diseased places may then be treated with a weak solution of corrosive sublimate, carbolic acid, tincture of cantharides, or iodine, oil of tar, chloride of zinc, paraffine; or mercurial iodine, or oxide of zinc ointment. This cures the disease very speedily, and promptly checks its extension.

"If there is any emaciation, tonics may be necessary."*

RINGWORM (HONEYCOMB).

But little is known of this species of ringworm as affecting the dog. The disease, like the former, is due to the presence of a fungus, the *Achorion Schonleinii*, or *Favus Tinea favosa*. The parasite is situated in the hair follicle, external to the layer of epithelium which covers the root of the hair. It has a peculiar mousy odour, or, according to others, that resembling cat's urine.

The causes giving rise to this affection are supposed to be uncleanliness, neglect in hygiene, and certain peculiar and humid conditions of the skin.

Symptoms.—Fleming observes: "The disease may appear in any part of the body of animals, according to the point of infection. It affects mice generally; but cats which are infected from them usually have it first at the base of the claws of the fore-feet. In the dog it has been seen on the head, and it usually affects the head in the human species. In the rabbits I saw diseased the parasite was at first on the nose and face, but gradually extended towards the shoulders.

"The disease commences with an increased proliferation of epidermic cells, and soon after a little white sub-epidermic speck becomes visible, which quickly develops into a favus-cup—the developed fungus. As the elements of the latter grow, they collect about the hair-follicle, each favus-cup being pierced near its centre by a hair. At first the *favi* are merely yellow specks.

"When the malady is of some duration, it is characterised by one or more masses of irregular crusts, more or less fissured, of a pitchy consistency, offering, when broken, a

---

* Fleming's "Veterinary Sanitary Science," vol. ii. p. 471.

fine granular structure, and having a bright yellow colour like sulphur. They affect a remarkable disposition; their contour, sometimes very circular, at other times more or less notched, forms a slight prominence that rises a little above the surrounding skin; their centre is, on the contrary, to a greater or less degree concave: the conformation that gives the crust the aspect of a cup.

"These capsules, or *favi*, are more or less numerous, and more or less extensive. At the free surface of the crusts there are often found dry, bristly hairs that appear to pass through the entire thickness of the favus mass, and are easily pulled out. At a later period, these hairs are shed from the follicles—not broken off, or sharply cut away close to the crusts, as in *Tinea tonsurans*.

"If the crusts are carefully removed, the skin beneath is observed to be thin and depressed, and looking as if atrophied by compression; but smooth, not ulcerated, and either quite dry and moist from serous exudation; sometimes it is pale and anæmic; but more frequently red, irritated, and sufficiently transparent to show some very fine bloodvessels. Around the margin of the crust the skin is sensibly inflamed, red, thickened, and rises into a somewhat salient prominence. In the dog there is much pruritis: a symptom which is rarely noticeable in the cat; otherwise, it does not appear to exercise any prejudicial effect on the general health.

"Another form is that in which the plant is found in depressions on the surface of the skin, forming the yellow honeycomb-like masses which gave the name 'favus' to the disease, and which, from their being frequently bucklershaped, suggested the term 'scutulata.' A cuticular elevation is seen, beneath which is a small favus. Generally there is no pus or fluid of any kind; the fungus grows, and the cuticle above it, supposing it to have become forcibly detached, finally separates, leaving the favus exposed."*

---

* Fleming's "Veterinary Sanitary Science," vol. ii. pp. 474, 475.

Treatment.—With regard to curative measures the same able writer observes: "The crusts should be removed by alkaline washes—hyposulphite of soda, or raising them by means of a spatula or the blunt extremity of curved scissors, taking care not to make the part bleed. When the skin has been cleansed in this manner as much as possible, a concentrated solution of corrosive sublimate (one to five of the sublimate to fifty of distilled water) should be applied every day. After the first application, the favus crusts sometimes have a tendency to be reproduced, and the cryptogamic elements to multiply. In such a case, it is necessary again to remove the crusts, as at first. Five or six dressings are usually sufficient. At times, however, and especially when the disease is seated at the base of the claw (as in the cat), they must be continued for a longer period. Under the influence of this treatment, the skin, which is depressed on its surface, is not long before it regains its normal vitality and thickness. During the first two or three days a new crust forms; but this has not the sulphur-yellow colour of the primary crust, and if examined with the microscope, there are no longer to be found traces of the parasite, but only numerous epithelial elements. Finally this kind of crust falls off, leaving the skin hairless, but everywhere level, smooth, and supple. Then the hair begins to grow, and in a variable period—generally about three months—it is difficult to discover the part that has been affected.

"An ointment composed of one part nitrate of silver to 100 parts of lard, has also been successfully employed.

"Mercurial ointment, tar ointment, and sulphate of mercury ointment have also been beneficially used. In some cases it may be necessary to remove the hair."*

ALOPECIA (BALDNESS).

This condition, which is most prevalent amongst foxes

---

* Fleming's "Veterinary Sanitary Science," vol. ii., pp. 480, 481.

is sometimes seen in smooth-coated toy dogs, especially black and tans. This baldness, which is chiefly confined to the crown of the head and the ears, is caused by deficient nutritive functions, general debility; and the pernicious system of in-and-in breeding.

Treatment.—Nourishing food; vegetable and mineral tonics; bald parts to be well brushed; cantharidine applications.

WARTS.

The dog, though not perhaps so frequently as the horse, is nevertheless very subject to warts. The eyelids, ears, mouth, and lips are the situations most favourable to their growth; not unfrequently they are seen on the penis.

"A wart is a state of hypertrophy of the papillæ of the derma, attended with an increased production of epidermis. Warts are usually of small size, and of a rounded figure, *verruca simplex*; sometimes, however, they appear in the form of bands several lines in breadth, and of variable length. They are generally insensible, rough to the touch, and their medium projection from the surface is about a line."

"When warts have grown to some length, their extremity becomes rough, and their fibrous structure is distinctly apparent; it not unfrequently happens that warts of long standing split and break up in the direction of these vertical fibres, *verruca lobosa.*"

"Warts are generally known as isolated growths, or dispersed in scanty groups on different parts of the body; but they are sometimes met with so numerously as to constitute an *eruption of warts.*"*

Treatment.—Excision, ligature, or caustic. In isolated warts the two former are most advisable, and the occasional application of caustic afterwards may follow. Of caustics,

---

* Wilson's "Diseases of the Skin," pp. 546, 547.

potassa fusa, nitric acid, acetic acid, and nitrate of silver are those generally used. I have found the oxide of mercury made into a paste with sulphuric acid, and a thin layer applied to the surface of the wart, more effectual than anything else. Of course the latter treatment is chiefly adapted to external warts.

FLEAS.

Fleas are one of the common pests of dog life. Not only are they a perpetual annoyance, but an indirect cause of much mischief, from the remedies sometimes adopted for their destruction. As more or less in all parasitic associations, uncleanliness favours their presence. In hot weather they are more abundant, and increase very rapidly.

Treatment.—Among the popular remedies for the destruction of fleas may be mentioned: Persian insect powder, various dog-soaps, paraffine, benzoline, tobacco-water, carbolic acid solutions, etc,

I usually, and with success, prescribe the following:

Spts. Camph............ 1 drachm.
Ol. Terebinth............ ½ drachm.
Acid Carbolic............ 10 minims.

A tablespoonful, in half a pint of chilled water, to be rubbed into the skin with a piece of flannel. Wash off in twenty-four hours with soft-soap and warm water, and repeat in three days, if necessary.

Gamgee observes: "The best remedy that I have used for fleas is oil of aniseed in common oil. The dog or cat must be well smeared, and a few hours afterwards is to be washed with soap and water. It is essential to attend to cleanliness, and to destroy all fleas or their larvæ wherever dogs are accustomed to sleep, such as in kennels," etc.

Fresh fine shavings, or sawdust, on which turpentine may be slightly sprinkled, forms a protective bedding from fleas.

LICE.

These insects, though not giving rise to the same amount of irritability as the former, are, nevertheless, troublesome, and perhaps more annoying from the fact that they are usually an indication of uncleanliness. They are generally found in greater abundance about the back and posterior parts. They are hatched from eggs or nits attached to the hair. The dog-louse produces no irritation on the human skin.

Treatment.—The white precipitate powder, brushed into the coat, or the ointment rubbed in the skin, and removed in the course of five or six hours, forms the most effectual treatment for their destruction and removal.

TICKS.

The dog-tick (*Ixodes ricinus*) is uncommon compared with the two preceding parasites. The creature causes considerable irritation to its host, and, from feeding on the blood by suction, gives rise, where they exist in any number, to debility.

Treatment.—Forcible removal, and dressing with mercurial preparations.

CHAPTER XV.

INTERNAL PARASITES (ENTOZOA).

ENTOZOA.

OF all the domesticated animals, the dog appears most subject to being infected with internal parasites.

Thanks to Dr. Cobbold, this matter has of late years been made a prominent and distinct study at the Royal Veterinary College, London. From his interesting and able work on "The Internal Parasites of our Domesticated

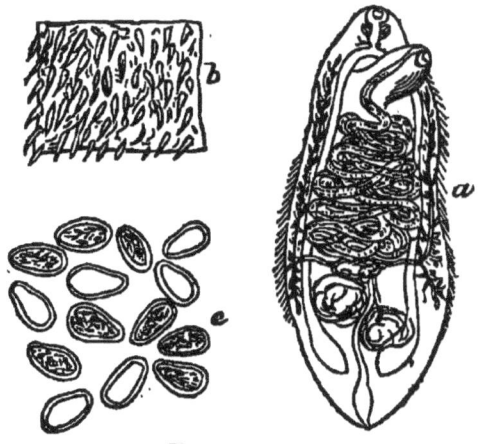

FIG. 24.

THE LIVER FLUKE OF THE DOG. (LEWIS.)

Animals"—to which for a fuller description I refer my

readers—I transcribe some of his remarks referring to the dog, with the accompanying illustrations:

"It is surprising what a number of entozoa infest the dog: and it is still more remarkable to observe what a number of creatures, including man himself, are destined to play the *rôle* of intermediary bearer of the canine parasites in their juvenile stages of development. It is this consideration which, to my mind, renders the dog, in the matter of parasitism, far more important than any other domesticated animal that can be named."

The following are the specimens mentioned by Dr. Cobbold: *Distoma conjunctum* (Fig. 24), obtained originally by Dr. Cobbold from the liver-ducts of an American red fox, and spoken to by Dr. Lewis as "not unfrequently met with in the bile-ducts" of the pariah dogs of India.

Holostoma alatum, another fluke, (the winged), which, Dr. Cobbold observes, may be readily taken for the above, is occasionally found in the stomach and intestines of the dog, but more commonly in the alimentary canal of the fox.

"When people speak of 'worms' in the dog, they commonly refer to round and tapeworms; and in place of recognising, as they might, fully a score or more of internal parasites, they are content to roll the entire series into three or four species only. It is the function of the helminthologist to correct this error. Thus, of the so-called lumbricoid and filariform worms, we have no less than eight or nine distinct forms, and of these the most common species is the margined round worm."

This lumbricoid of the dog (*Ascaris marginata*) is probably identical with the moustached worm of the cat (*Ascaris mystax*). It is sometimes described as the long round worm. The males acquire a length of from two to nearly three inches, whilst the females measure four, five, or even six inches from head to tail. To afford some notion of its prevalence, I may state that it was found at

Vienna in 104 out of 144 dogs dissected for that purpose; and Dr. Krabbe obtained it at Copenhagen in 122 instances from the *post-mortem* examinations of 500 dogs.

According to my own experiences, it occurs in English dogs at the rate of about seventy per cent. Occupying principally the small intestines, but often wandering into the stomach, and occasionally also making its way into the throat and nostril, this parasite is a frequent source of severe intestinal disturbance, sometimes producing even death itself. Cats and dogs alike are constantly throwing them up, and it is a great relief to the host when they are thus dislodged. Their occasional passage by the ordinary outlet is also a matter of common observation ; but it is not so very generally understood that these modes of egress are often the result of a voluntary wandering on the part of the guest. This is practically of some moment, because it accounts for the circumstance of their being sometimes found in the nasal passages, and in other unusual situations.

The formidable nature of the symptoms which may thus be superinduced have been fully indicated in a letter of mine which appeared in the *Field* for December 21, 1872. Under ordinary circumstances, the symptoms in the dog are those of irregular intestinal action, accompanied with nausea and spasmodic colic, irritation, a voracious appetite, and more or less loss of flesh. In addition, there may be fœtor of the breath, accompanied by a short husky cough, and an impoverished state of the coat ; and, either with or without any of these symptoms, there may be more or less paralysis. I may here make mention of an interesting case of paralysis in puppies brought under my notice by Mr. Lewis (*Field*, December 7, 1872), in which it was instructive to notice how complete a cure followed the administration of a simple aperient drug. Quite recently also a correspondent, writing from Ceylon under the signature of "Veddah," gave a suggestive instance where paralysis in dogs seemed to be entirely due to worms (*Field*, March 15, p. 238).

A great variety of anthelmintics have been recommended; but for this particular worm there is probably nothing better than castor-oil and santonine. As with the lumbricoids of man, so with those of the cat and dog; in either case they seem powerless to resist the action of this remedy. In the human subject I have known a grain of santonine sufficient to expel a lumbricoid as large as a lob-worm; and in the dog or cat similar experiences have followed the employment of from three to five grain doses. Several of my pupils have adopted this mode of treatment with success.

The employment of more powerful vermifuges is rarely necessary; and even the areca-nut powder should generally be reserved for tapeworm. Areca-nut powder is unquestionably a good vermifuge, as I can testify from personal experience; and I observe that it is strongly recommended by "Stonehenge," in his admirable memoir, "On the Management of Dogs." It is, however, rather as a tæniafuge than as a lumbricifuge that the merits of areca-nut powder stand out most conspicuously. The powder may be given in half-drachm or one-drachm doses, followed by castor-oil, and repeated twice or thrice in the day. In bad cases turpentine may be cautiously resorted to, and, when given, should be combined with twice as much either of castor or linseed oil. The dose of turpentine should be rarely more than one drachm, and in no case should it exceed two drachms in the very largest dog. Three drachms of turpentine have been known to occasion violent convulsions in the full-grown dog; and in the case of young puppies such a dose would probably prove fatal. Calomel, in one to three grain doses, is a favourite remedy with some; but, considering its varied action, it should only be resorted to when other remedies have failed. The mechanical irritants such as powered tin and glass, or even cowhage, should in all cases be eschewed, because they are liable to cause much suffering without entailing any adequate result.

It is also worthy of remark that, after the expulsion of the worms, everything tending to support the system should be employed in view of restoring the animal to perfect health; and lastly, as a hygienic or prophylactic measure, I would advise the frequent application either of carbolic acid solutions, or of salt and water, to the flooring of kennels. Furthermore, I would strongly recommend the occasional throwing down of bucketfuls of boiling hot water, since the performance of this very simple act could not fail to be productive of good results in ways too numerous to be particularised.

The Cruel Thread-worm (*Filaria immitis*) inhabits the heart of the dog. Dr. Cobbold observes: "If a female *Filaria immitis* be removed from the heart of a dog, and be examined with a microscope, the oviducts will be found to swarm with eggs and embryos, in all stages of development." Dr. Jones Lamprey, writing from China, July, 1865, says: "The hearts of native and foreign dogs at Shanghai are *invariably* found to contain these entozoa," and he suggests that the animals may have obtained their parasites from ova of ascarides passed by man. He also remarks that human excrements constitute "the principal food of the native dog," and he asserts that the fæces are "not disliked by the foreign dogs, however well fed."

Dr. Cobbold continues: "The symptoms of the disease are extremely variable; some of the dogs dying suddenly in a fit, whilst others linger and betray evidences of excruciating pain. As to treatment, it is obvious that nothing can be done when the parasites have once got possession of so vital an organ as the heart. Nevertheless, further researches may enable us to suggest prophylactic measures, by which the epizootic may be checked. There is one important point that ought not to remain long unverified. We want to know for certain whether the blood of these dogs contains free embryonic filariæ, and whether such immature worms, if found, correspond or not with the embryos found in the oviducts of the full-grown worms. It is probable that they do, for Dr. Krabbe, in his admirable *resumé* already referred to, states that the worm reproduces viviparously, and that the young are carried along in the circulation.*

"*Estrongylus gigas* (Fig. 25), or giant strongle, infests the kidneys of various animals; but it is rarely met with in the dog. The males seldom exceed ten inches in length, but the females have been known to exceed a yard in measurement from head to tail, whilst their thickness equals that of the little finger. The accompanying figure of a female specimen, from Blanchard, is reduced to one-third of the natural size.

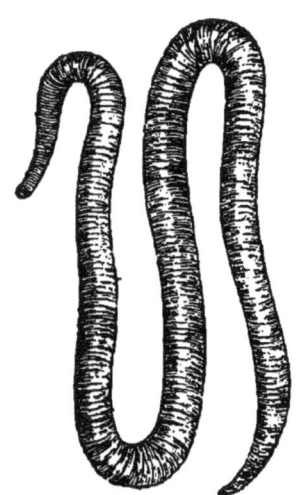

FIG. 25.
THE GIANT STRONGLE. (BLANCHARD.)

"The remaining round worms of the dog are *Spiroptera*

* In the *Veterinary Journal* for February, 1878, extracted from the *Customs Gazette* there is an exhaustive and most interesting paper "On Chinese Hæmatozoa," by Patrick Manson, M.D

sanguinolenta—the blood-red species—which usually occupies small tumours in the mucous lining of the stomach.

"The three-corner-headed strongle (*Dochmius trigonocephalus*) infests the intestinal canal. The wrinkled threadworm (*Trichosoma plica*) gains access to the bladder. The whip-worm of the dog (*Tricocephalus depressiusculus*) inhabits the cæcum. The spiral flesh worm (*Trichina spiralis*) has frequently been reared both in the intestines and muscles by experiment.

"The blood-infesting thread-worm of Grube and Delafond (*Filaria hæmatica*) is probably a distinct species; and the same may possibly be said of Gescheidt's small nematode (*Filaria trispinulosa*), discovered in the eye. There are also the small thread-worms (*Filaria hepatica*) found by Mr. T. Mather, V.S., in the liver-ducts and substance of the gland, as well as in cysts within the walls of the intestines.

"Lastly, there is another canine hæmatozoon, the males, females, and embryos of which, according to Professor Leisering, occur in the venous blood of certain parts of the body of the dog (*Hæmatozoon subulatum*)."

Another, one of the most difficult to eradicate, and perhaps, as Youatt observes, "the most injurious of the intestinal worms," is the *tænia*, or *tapeworm*. With regard to this species, Dr. Cobbold remarks : "Although the lumbricoid worms of the dog constitute an important section of the canine parasites, the practical interest attaching to them is scarcely so great as that which appertains to the tapeworms. If, on the one hand, it be allowed that the canine cestodes are not so numerous as the nematodes, it must, on the other hand, be admitted that (as regards public health,* and the propagation of parasitic diseases

---

* In the first report of the medical officer of the Privy Counc l, Mr Gamgee observes : " There is no doubt that eggs of the tapeworm, developed from *Cysticercus tenuicollis* in the intestines of the dog, will produce the hydatid in the mesentery and liver of human beings, as it

amongst animals) the part these tapeworms are destined to play in the economy of life is not merely remarkable, but altogether unique."

The first he notices is the cucumerine tapeworm (*Tænia cucumerina*): "It is a delicate and almost transparent tapeworm, measuring from ten to twenty inches in length."

This parasite is very common in English dogs, and, according to Krabbe, infests 48 per cent. of the dogs in Denmark, and 57 per cent. of the dogs in Iceland. The animals infect themselves in a singular manner. The joints of the worm, having escaped *per anum*, readily crawl, as semi-independent creatures on the coat of the dog, chiefly on the back and side. The eggs thus distributed are readily swallowed by the louse of the dog (*Trichodectes latus*).

In the body of the louse the six-hooked embryo, hitherto contained in the egg of the tapeworm, escapes the shell and becomes transformed into a minute cysticercus or louse-measle. When the dog is irritated by the lice, it attacks, bites, and frequently swallows the offending external parasite. In this way the louse-measle is transferred to the dog's intestinal canal, where, in course of time, it develops into the sexually mature cucumerine tapeworm.

Thus the mange-mite, or scab insect (as it is rather incorrectly termed), serves as the intermediary bearer of larval tapeworm, and forms an essential factor in the production of this particular species of cestode parasite.

---

loes, according to the experiments of Luschka, Leuckart, and others, in the organs of the domestic quadrupeds.

"It is of the greatest importance that careful and extended inquiries should be made as to the prevalence of these cysticerci in animals. It is evident from the observations of Küchenmeister and others that many individuals of these species, forming extensive cystic tumours, are to be found in pigs, and not unfrequently there has been a confusion between cysticerci and echinococchi. Thus, in Ireland, the endemic cystic disease appears to be due to both these hydatids."

Internal Parasites.

The Gid Tapeworm (*Tænia cœnurus*). This parasite Dr. Cobbold observes, probably does not occur in more, than 5 per cent. of our dogs. In the native dogs of Iceland, according to Dr. Krabbe, it occurs in 18 per cent.

In order, says Dr. Cobbold, to understand how the dog obtains this tapeworm, it must be observed that gid-hydatids, or *cœnuri*, each represent a sort of colony of larval parasites. When, therefore, the dog eats a sheep's brain containing a single hydatid, he swallows a colony of larvæ, each of the latter being destined to become transformed into a tapeworm in the bowel. Thus Fig. 26 represents two hydatids, one being viewed from without, and the other from within. At A the young tapeworm heads are seen projecting from the exterior surface of the hydatid; whilst at B they are seen retracted within the interior of the bladder-worm. There may be from three to five hundred of these heads projecting from the surface of a single gid-hydatid.

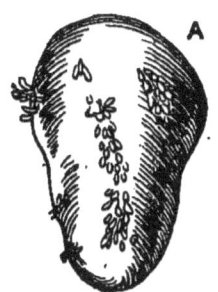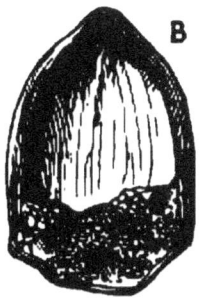

FIG. 26.

LARVÆ OF THE GID TAPEWORM. (NEWMAN.)

If a small fragment of the gid-hydatid with its characteristic processes be magnified about eighty diameters, all the more essential structures will be brought into view.

As in the accompanying drawing (Fig. 27), such a demonstration may display a bunch of young tapeworm heads, one or all of them showing the crown of hooks (*a*), the

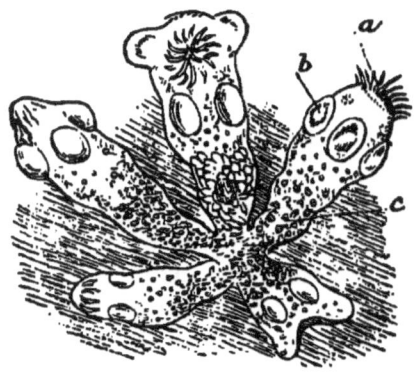

FIG. 27.
TAPEWORM-LIKE HEADS OF THE GID-HYDATID. (NEWMAN.)

four suckers (*b*), and a multitude of minute oval calcareous particles (*c*), which the old naturalists formerly supposed to be eggs. The common bladder vesicle, from which the heads project, exhibits cellular markings.

The above figures are copied from Newman's treatise, and I can testify to their perfect accuracy of detail. In one remarkable instance, recorded by Eichler, as many as 2000 heads were displayed by a single *cœnurus*.

Dr. Cobbold proceeds to speak of the measures to be taken in such cases, and advocates the destruction of the tapeworms in their ova. He points out the necessity of the sheep-owner and grazier seeing that no dog, either belonging to himself or his neighbours, is permitted to go about the land distributing the eggs of tapeworms with every act of defæcation, as well as by dropping the ova off its coat.* If a dog harbouring tapeworms be allowed to

---

* Easier to advocate than adopt. To prevent dogs trespassing on some portion of land would necessitate a staff of watchers far beyond the ordinary number of farm servants.

plunge into an ordinary field pond to wash himself, such an act conveys numerous eggs into the water; and the next herbivorous animal that comes to slake its thirst will be liable to drink in one or more of the parasites' eggs. If thus the hogget or a calf swallow the eggs of a gid-tapeworm, "turnside" will be the consequence; but if the herbivore swallows the eggs of the hydatid tapeworm, properly so-called, hydatids will be the result. And so on with other creatures which happen to ingest the ova of different and appropriate parasites.

To hares and rabbits the dog thus communicates another bladder-worm disease; and we ourselves are also liable to become infested with hydatids from the same source.

Another parasite of this class is described as follows by Dr. Cobbold: "The largest tapeworm liable to reside in the dog is a parasite chiefly derived from the sheep; that is to say, the sheep acts as the principal intermediary bearer of the larval cestode, which latter acquires tapeworm maturity when it is taken into the stomach and intestines of the dog along with flesh food. The entozoon in question is the margined tapeworm. This worm (*Tænia marginata*) reaches a length of from five to eight feet. It is an abundant species, occurring, probably, in fully 25 per cent. of English dogs that are not less than one year old. In

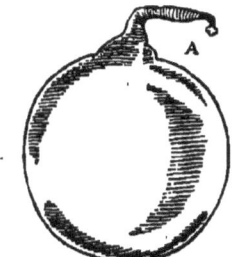
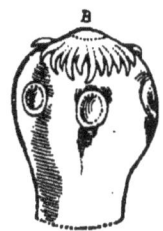

FIG. 28.

LARVA OF THE MARGINED TAPEWORM. (GOEZE.)

Denmark it occurs in 14 per cent.; and in Iceland, according to Krabbe, in no less than 75 per cent. of the native dogs. I have elsewhere characterised the larva of this parasite as the slender-necked hydatid (*Field*, Feb. 22, 1873). The accompanying illustration, from the learned Pastor Goeze's work, shows the hydatid (*Cysticercus tennuicollis*) of the natural size at A, Fig. 28; whilst the letter B represents a magnified view of the head, displaying the suckers and double crown of hooks."

The Hydatid Tapeworm.—" Of all the entozoa infesting mankind and animals, the little *Tænia enhinococcus* is one of the most remarkable. The larvæ form the common hydatids, or bladder worms, of veterinarians (*Echinococcus veterinorum*).

"As in the dog the full-grown tapeworm only reaches the third of an inch in length, it is difficult for the non-professional man to realise the fact that the same entozoon

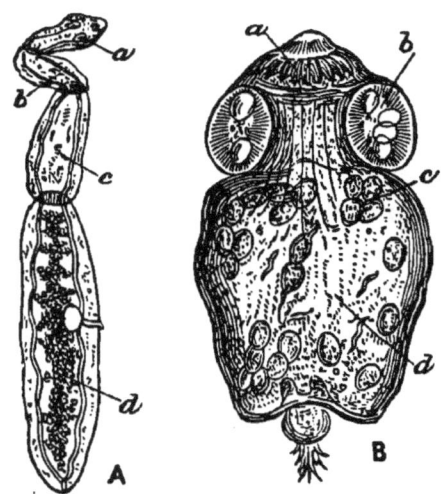

FIG. 29.

HYDATID TAPEWORM AND ECHINOCOCCUS HEAD. (COBBOLD.)

in its larval or vesicular state attains a size many thousand times exceeding that of the parasite in its adult condition. Harmless when full-grown, it is fearfully destructive to life in the juvenile stages of growth. To be sure, its bad effects are chiefly witnessed in the human subject; but cattle, sheep, horses, and swine occasionally perish from the presence of the lavræ within their vital organs.

"The herbivorous animals and ourselves get the echinococcus disease by swallowing the eggs of the hydatid tapeworm.

"Fig. 29, A, is a representation of the parasite. It exhibits the head-segment with its four suckers, and crown of hooks (*a*), and three ordinary segments (*b, c, d*), the lowermost of which is sexually mature, displaying numerous eggs internally. Water-vessels traverse the entire length of the worm.

One of the strangest points connected with this entozoon is the extraordinary provision made for its propagation. In ordinary cases one tapeworm only results from the growth of the products of a single egg; but here we may have thousands of tapeworms all resulting from a solitary germ."

He thus explains it:

"Eggs escape from the dog *per anum*. One swallowed by any herbivorous animal, say a sheep, will (by a lengthened process of development, the details of which I need not give) eventuate in the formation of hydatids. These hydatids, under favourable circumstances, will by internal budding produce innumerable heads or scolices (Fig. 29, B), each of which display the tænia-like crown of hooks (*a*), the suckers (*b*), the calcareous particles (*c*), and a vesicular body (*a*).

"When, therefore, a dog is fed on the viscera of a sheep containing perfect hydatids of this description, all the numerous heads become developed into tapeworms in the animal's intestines. This has been proved over and over again by experiment.

"Most of the heads are developed in delicate sacs, termed brood-capsules, one of which is here represented in the collapsed or broken-up state (Fig. 30). It will be further seen that the seven attached heads have their respective crowns of hooks inverted and concealed with the visicular

FIG. 30.
GROUP OF ECHINOCOCCUS HEADS. (COBBOLD.)

body; and their appearance in this condition strikingly contrasts with that displayed by the single echinococcus

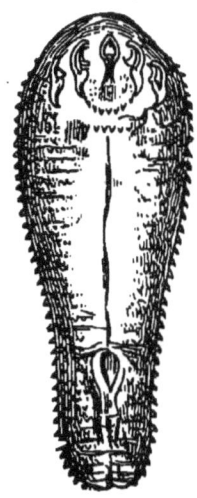

FIG. 31.
LARVAL PENTASTOME. (KUCHENMEISTER.)

head figured above. These illustrations are reduced

copies from figures given in my general treatise on entozoa.

"It is a fortunate circumstance that this destructive little tapeworm is comparatively rare in England. It is the smallest cestode infesting the dog, and the one most likely to be overlooked.

"Every year, notwithstanding its rarity, this little canine entozoon, by means of its larvæ, claims the lives of scores, or it may be hundreds of persons in this country; but, with all England's wealth, I do not suppose a dozen people could be found who would be prepared to sacrifice a few pounds each for the purpose of promoting an investigation, the results of which would be eminently conducive to public health, and most certainly help to diminish our annual mortality. At the same time such a research would inevitably tend to lessen the amount of, if it did not altogether put an end to, at least one frequent form of parasitism affecting our domesticated animals.

"Sportsmen who care for the welfare of their dogs should never allow these animals to devour the entrails of hares captured in the field. In the county of Norfolk I have myself witnessed this piece of carelessness on the part of keepers and have ventured to remonstrate accordingly.

"Almost every hare (and the same may be said of full-grown rabbits) harbours within its abdominal cavity a larval parasite (*Cysticercus pisiformis*), which, when swallowed by the dog, becomes transformed into a tapeworm, varying from two to three feet in length (*Tænia serrata*.) In harriers and greyhounds the serrated tapeworm is very abundant; but in other dogs it is comparatively rare.

"Of the remaining internal parasites infesting the dog I need only allude to several species and varieties of pit-headed tapeworm (*Bothriocephalus latus, B. cordatus, B. fuscus, B. reticulatus* and *B. dubius*), since so far as I am aware only the first-named has been recognised as a canine entozoon in England.

"I must not omit to mention the arachnidan parasite

(*Pentastoma tæmoides*), which, as already stated, is the adult representative of the *Pentastoma denticulatum*, residing in the viscera of the horse, as well as in the internal organs of ruminants. (Fig. 31.) The illustration is from Küchenmeister.

" In the full-grown state this creature dwells in the nasal and frontal sinuses, our dogs commonly obtaining the worm by frequenting butchers' stalls and slaughter-houses, where portions of the fresh viscera are apt to be inconsiderately flung to hungry animals."

Professor Dick records a case of suspected poisoning in the " Veterinarian " for 1840, in which he found death had resulted from the presence of three of these pentastomes—one in the larynx, one in the trachea, and a third in the left bronchus. With regard to this case Dr. Cobbold observes : "As these singular parasites appreciate warmth, I have no doubt that the cold air of the winter's morning (on which the dog was taken out by the keeper) caused the downward migration of the pentastomes, thereby also producing the fatal suffocation."

Respecting what Dr. Cobbold terms the "misnamed maw-worms," so frequently seen on the fæces of dogs, "they are," he remarks, " merely the semi-independent segments, or proglottides of two of the larger species of tapeworm which infest the dog, namely, *Tænia marginata* and *Tænia serrata*.

" It follows, therefore, that the treatment for this common kennel-worm is the same as that for the tapeworm, seeing that it is only a cast-off portion of the self-same entozoon.

" Areca-nut powder is the best remedy ; but male fern may be sometimes substituted with advantage.

" I may add, that when santonine is employed for any of the round worms, it should always be combined with a purgative, if it is to prove effective. For this purpose nothing is ordinarily better than castor-oil ; but 20 or 30 grains of aloes may be employed instead of the oil in obstinate cases. In the latter case, a few grains of ginger should be added, to prevent griping."

By those interested in canine matters, and especially parasitism, I shall be excused for quoting at such length, and all the more so as my quotations are taken from our most able writer on the subject: a gentleman from whose works I have learnt much myself, and to which with sincere pleasure I refer my readers.

With regard to the treatment of worms, various remedies are advocated by different authors. I have already given the treatment recommended by Dr. Cobbold.

The usual anthelmintics in canine practice are:

Turpentine....................	20—60 minims.
Santonine	1— 3 grains.
Areca-nut	30—60 grains.
Pomegranate Bark	1— 3 drachms.
Oil of Male Fern	10—20 minims.
Calomel	1— 3 grains.
Stinking Hellebore ...	5—10 grains.
Indian or Carolina Pink Infusion	1— 2 tablespoonfuls.
Kousso (Abyssinian) ...	2— 4 drachms.
Kamala (Indian)	2— 4 drachms
Wormwood	10—30 grains.
Powdered Glass	half a thimbleful, mixed
Tin or Iron Filings.........	with treacle or butter.

The three first named are the most effectual remedies in canine practice. The two last, from the irritation produced on the intestinal mucous membrane, should be at all times condemned. All worm medicines require to be given fasting, to produce a successful and speedy result.

Finlay Dun prescribes 20 drops of the oil of male shield fern, 30 drops of oil of turpentine, and 60 of ether, beat up with an egg, and given in soup or broth. The dog should be kept on sound, good, cooked food, and have daily, for at least a week, a pill containing 5 grains each of gentian quassia, and sulphate of iron, and made up with conserve of red roses or treacle.

According to Pavesi, a combination of santonine and sodium bicarbonate, with soluble albumen, forms a good vermifuge (in human practice). The preparation is made by heating together one part of santonine, four parts of sodium bicarbonate, and two parts of dried soluble albumen with sufficient water at 60° or 70° C., until the whole is dissolved, and the solution evaporated with a gentle heat to dryness. The "albuminate of santonine and soda" forms white shining scales, soluble in water. Mineral acids precipitate the santonine and albumen, with disengagement of carbonic acid. Pavesi states that the use of this preparation is not followed by coloured vision, as is the case where santonine is used alone.—" L'Union Pharmaceutique," May.

PARASITIC MEASLES.

The *Cysticercus cellulosus*, commonly known as "Pigmeasle," or leprosy, has been observed in the dog.

The veterinary professor Dupuy, according to Davaine, found a large number on the surface of a dog's brain. Gurlt has also discovered a great many in the muscles of a dog. The preparations containing these are shown at the Berlin Veterinary School.—See "Magazin f. d. Gesammete Thierheilkunde," 28 Jahr., 34 Jahr.

Roloff, veterinary professor in the University of Halle in 1869, found the cysticerci in the lungs and liver (greatly enlarged) of a dog, where they formed numerous vesicles the size of a pea, and around them were tubercles varying in size from a grain of millet to that of a hazel-nut. Leblanc, a Parisian veterinary surgeon, has described the symptoms produced by the parasite in the dog. In October, 1872, a medium-sized "griffon," aged fifteen months, was brought to him in consequence of its sufferings from attacks

---

* "Veterinarian," December, 1876.

of epilepsy. Most frequently very quiet, and even dull, it was seized, whenever it went out of doors, with convulsive movements, and lay for some minutes before it got up again. It was treated for cerebral congestion, with commencing ventricula effusion, which is not uncommon in young dogs affected with convulsions.

Notwithstanding the treatment the symptoms became aggravated, and were as follows : Convulsions without any assignable cause, grinding of the teeth and champing of the jaws, foaming at the mouth, and struggling when lying on the ground. There was a marked and increasing tendency to turn to the left ; the coma became more urgent, and the animal appeared quite torpid, though its appetite was undiminished. It was kept until December, when, its recovery appearing hopeless it was killed. A necroscopical examination showed that all the abdominal organs were healthy, with the exception of the liver and pancreas, on the surface of which were observed transparent vesicles similar to those of the pig-measle. The liver had two of these on its right lobe ; they were about the size of a large pea, lay beneath the peritoneum, and had made a depression in the organ. Those on the pancreas were five in number ; they were on its upper border, but had not affected the structure of the gland. The thoracic organs were healthy. On opening the cranium the meningeal membranes were found to be very congested ; in the upper and lateral parts of the right lobe of the cerebrum were four elevations, corresponding to four hydatid cysts, covered by the arachnoid, and lying in depressions in the cerebral tissue ; in the left lobe only one was discovered. The hydatids were carefully examined by M. Mégnin, a veterinary surgeon who has made helminthology a special study, and they proved to be identical with those of the pig-measle.

The dog had doubtless obtained the ova from eating human excrement, as this animal is sometimes apt to do.

Siedamgrotzky, of the Dresden Veterinary School, in the

report of that establishment for 1871, cites an analagous case. "A large-sized dog, always apparently in good health, was suddenly seized with cramp and convulsions, especially of the jaws. In a short time it was unable to stand ; the pulse and respiration were much quickened, the head hot, and the conjunctivæ injected : considerable prostration was present. By starts it would jump up spontaneously, run forward until it met some obstacle, push hard against it, and bark for half an hour at a time ; then it would lie down, convulsively champ with its mouth, from which saliva would flow, and remain in a state of coma. It died on the evening of the day on which it showed these symptoms. On examination the brain, and more especially its envelopes, were found greatly congested. In the superficial part of the two hemispheres of the cerebrum were found twenty-three cysticerci, each about the size of a pea; they were enveloped in a thin white cyst of connective tissue, around which the proper texture of the brain appeared redder than usual, and a little softened. Nothing abnormal was observed in the other organs."*

---

* Fleming's " Veterinary Sanitary Science," vol. ii. pp. 525, 526.

CHAPTER XVI.

DISEASES OF THE NERVOUS SYSTEM.

RABIES,
EPILEPSY,
APOPLEXY,
VERTIGO,
CHOREA,
PARALYSIS,
CONCUSSION OF
THE BRAIN,
COMPRESSION OF THE
BRAIN,
HYDROCEPHALUS,
TURNSIDE,
MENINGITIS,
DEMENTIA,
NOSTOMANIA,
NEURALGIA.'

RABIES.

THIS disease may be truly designated the scourge of the canine race; horrible in its nature, alike terribly fatal to man and beast. As such it was recognised centuries ago, and the alarm engendered appears to have been as great then as in the present day. Among the ancient Greeks recipes both for the bite of a rabid dog and the flesh of one affected with rabies, were numerous and singular.

Much, but far from enough, has been written of late years concerning this disease; much that is sensible, and no small proportion that is calculated to do harm. Rewards have been offered for the discovery of a cure, but the probability of their ever being claimed is extremely dubious—especially so long as spurious hydrophobia and various phases of hysteria are indiscriminately mixed up and mistaken for the real malady.

Pasteur's alleged prophylactic still remains a controversial question; many unfortunate calamities have resulted from his system, and the necrological record is anything but encouraging.

Fortunately, however, compared with other canine maladies, rabies is of rare occurrence, and it would almost appear to derive its importance from periodical scares. The year 1887 will be memorable for the intense public excitement on the question, and especially for the extraordinary manner in which morbid minds magnified the complaint, and painted harmless affections in hideous colours. These morbid minds being suffered to run riot, worked an almost irreparable injury to our ordained companions and most devoted friends. An absurd hysterical scare promoted an equally absurd, and in my opinion, ungrounded hydrophobic alarm. The outcome of this panic, and the arbitrary administration of the police regulations, were the formation of "The Dog Owners' Protection Association," the preliminary meeting for its promotion, over which I had the honour to preside, being held at the Hyde Park Hotel, on the 30th August, 1887. Subsequently Lord Mount Temple became president. Following this, but holding adverse views, "The Society for the Prevention of Hydrophobia" sprang into existence. Then Lord Mount Temple's Registration Bill was introduced, and referred to a select committee of the House of Lords, at which I was summoned to give evidence.

It is a fact worthy of note that the sudden withdrawal of the Police Regulations and Muzzle in London, which took place the day before my address at the first public meeting of "The Dog Owners' Protection Association" in the Kensington Town Hall, produced *no increase of rabies*.

Before going into the nature and symptoms of the malady, a few words regarding the terms applied to it are, I think, necessary.

Hydrophobia, signifying *fear of water*, is in canine pathology a misnomer, and probably has had much to do with the erroneous idea that this symptom is present in dogs. To this

I give, as I did many years ago in "Land and Water," a most emphatic denial. *The rabid dog never in any stage of the disease exhibits a dread of water, neither will the sight or sound of it produce spasms.* On the contrary, *thirst* is present throughout.

The inability so swallow fluids, when it does happen, is dependent entirely on either the inflammatory condition of the throat, or from paralysis of the muscles of the lower jaw and deglutition.

Rabies, signifying *madness*, is a far more appropriate term, but even this is not sufficiently distinctive as to the particular class of madness it is intended to designate.

The true nature of rabies is still involved in mystery. We know that a specific virus is the active agent in its production, but in what this virus consists, or how it is developed, we know not. That the saliva is the vehicle of the poison is clear, the why or wherefore is equally mysterious. Post-mortem and microscopic examinations afford little clue. The nerve centres in which, from the character of the disease, we should expect to find the greatest lesions, are in many instances but slightly affected, while the throat and digestive organs often exhibit the greatest alterations.

Causes.—In almost every instance rabies is due to inoculation; the disease, however, may, and is at times unquestionably spontaneously generated, and if this is so, wherein lies the value of the vexatious and absurd police regulations? I am very much inclined to think that the pernicious system of breeding in-and-in encourages its development, for it undoubtedly predisposes the next generation to weakened intellect, if not absolute lunacy. We know that intermarriage materially helps to fill our lunatic asylums; and although it may be observed that the madness produced by consanguinity is not hydrophobic, yet any agency acting deleteriously on the nerve centres, weakening their stamina, and diminishing the intellectual faculties, will render, or may be reasonably supposed to render the mind susceptible to morbid impressions.

Again, individual idiosyncrasies are present in the canine, as they are in the human race; and this fact should not be lost sight of when investigating the cause of nervous disorders.

It is a well-recognised fact that, since the improvement (query) of breeds, the fashion of dog breeding, and the growth of canine exhibitions, rabies, or what has been alleged to be rabies, has correspondingly increased.

It is true, advance in scientific knowledge and research may have made more acute diagnostic talent, but it must not be forgotten that nature abused will result in abnormality of some kind. Of this we have palpable evidence in those specimens of the Toy breed, with prominent foreheads, protruding vacant eyes, and hairless skulls, which creatures, to use a common expression, have been "bred to death."

Probably, as a veterinarian, and having made canine pathology a *specialism*, I have had as wide an experience in rabies as any member of my profession now living; and I can say, without the least hesitation, that in those dogs proved to have been inbred, rabies and other nervous disorders have been more prevalent than in natural breeds.

That dogs, especially of the female sex, are subject to hysteria, there is no doubt, whilst the tendency to such a condition amongst the female portion of our own species is beyond all question.

And we have it on the authority of one of the greatest physiologists of our time, that "many forms of that protean malady, *hysteria*, are attended with a similar irritability of the nervous centres" as occurs in hydrophobia; further, that the latter disease "is nearly allied to that of traumatic tetanus."

This evidently is an hysterical age, and persons of highly nervous temperament and excitable dispositions are prone to manifest certain symptoms indicative of hydrophobia, should they have the misfortune to be bitten by one of our longsuffering canine friends.

Those who have had much to do with dogs, and have carefully studied their various dispositions, cannot have failed to note those same peculiar hysterical tendencies in highly-bred specimens—nervous and violently excited at an angry word or sudden sound. Shrieking at a trivial injury, convulsed with fear at an upraised hand—not rabidly inclined, I don't say that, although it has been positively asserted that the bite of an angry dog is as dangerous as that inflicted by a rabid one, and equally capable of producing hydrophobia; an opinion, however, which I do not at all agree with. But I cannot see why the nervous system of a physically weak and excitable dog should not be acted upon much in the same manner as in a physically weak and nervous human being, and in such a way as to excite symptoms strongly representative of rabies.

I have already spoken of the saliva as the vehicle of the rabid poison, and of the mystery as to its development. It is known that certain conditions of the nervous system exert an influence on the secreting process of the salivary glands, and we know that in canine rabies there is an abundance of such secretion abnormally altered. In fact, it may be said that all the secretions are more or less influenced by the condition of the mind; so much so that in certain instances they become poisonous from chemical change, and lose entirely their individual characters. May not this be so with the canine secretions?

Although I grant that canine rabies is most frequently due to inoculation, I do not lose sight of those causes favourable to spontaneity, of which there is far greater weight of practical evidence than that built up on theoretical bases. Nor do I forget that every disease has had a beginning, and canine rabies (which is now being dealt with as though it were a modern invasion) was well recognised by the ancient Greeks and Romans, and if we are to believe history, the prophylactic value of the hot-bath and accompanying sweat for bitten persons was well understood by Celsus.

Further information on this point may be obtained from the Blue Book containing the evidence of the various witnesses who attended the select committee on rabies in the House of Lords, 1887.

The influence of climate, season, or sex, would appear to have little bearing on the subject.* The so-called dog-days no more act in the production of rabies than does cold. In the hottest season of the hottest years, statistics show fewer cases, while in tropical countries, Australia to wit, it has as yet been unrecognised. Heat is more likely to generate brain affections other than rabies.

With regard to sex, male and female are alike disposed to it, and various conditions of system in the latter, as catamenia, pregnancy, or suckling, have no influence on the disease, though they may produce symptoms of other cerebral aberrations.

---

* "Professor Guiseppe Canettoli ('Lo Sperimentale,' June, 1875) summaries his studies and researches in hydrophobia in the following propositions:

"1. Hydrophobia is a disease of all climates and seasons.

"2. Extreme climates yield the smallest contingent of cases, and are therefore, it may be said, privileged.

"3. The disease is spontaneous in the dog, and communicable to other animals and to mankind.

"4. Nothing has been discovered of the nature of the malady or autopsies.

"5. The disease may be prevented by having recourse to timely cauterisation—the best means being the galvano-caustic.

"6. Finally, to explain the duration of incubation, Canettoli supposes that the saliva of the rabid dog is not in itself a poison, but that it becomes so through prolonged retention in the living tissues into which it has been inoculated."—" Veterinary Journal," Oct., 1876.

Anger and pain are alike uninfluential in the origin of rabies.*

Pain may produce frenzy, but not rabies. A dog may be driven frantic with torture or furious with rage, but his bite is harmless, so far as production of rabies is concerned.

---

* In reply to this theory, advanced by Dr. Verity in the *Manchester Courier*, 1876, and his assertion of possessing a cure for the malady, I wrote the following:—

"That the bite of a dog or cat is rendered poisonous from anger at the time of its infliction is as absurd as it is false.

"That *rabies* is a specific disease usually produced by inoculation, but that it may, as I stated in 'Land and Water,' some four years since, and unquestionably does, arise spontaneously. Certain peculiar changes in the system, possibly due to atmospherical influence, or some cause not fully understood, act in producing it. I have always had a strong opinion that *breeding in-and-in* tends to do so.

"That if once the virus enters the system through inoculation, no amount of treatment, however scientific, will in my opinion prevent the awful result that must sooner or later take place.

"That when such result is established, there are as yet no positive means of preventing death.

"That the only means of preventing its introduction into the system are in immediate excision or suction, if possible, of the part, and the application of nitric acid or lunar caustic.

"That many diseases have been mistaken by persons having a smattering of a dog knowledge for hydophobia (*rabies canina*), particularly epilepsy.

"That I have no doubt a person whose nervous system is highly sensitive may, from the excitement consequent on the bite of a dog (especially a ferocious one), exhibit symptoms resembling hydrophobia, and that it is probably from such cases as these that Dr. Verity has derived his imagination of a cure.

"That individuals ever have true hydrophobia, from pure fright, I do not for a moment believe.

"That in all supposed cases of hydrophobia, the public may rest assured that either the inoculation was not hydrophobic, or that the saliva was wiped off when the teeth passed through the garments.

"That in all instances where the animal which has inflicted the wound is suspected of rabies, he should be confined, and not slaughtered until a sufficiently long period has elapsed to prove the suspicion correct or otherwise. This, if it were adopted, would soon test the truth of enumerated cures and the value of marvellous specifics."

Were it not so, what a fearful result must follow! Where we have one case of the disease, we should have hundreds Indeed, they would be daily occurring, and no individua who possessed a dog would be secure.

No one distinct breed is more liable to it than another.

Mongrels (particularly homeless ones) are perhaps more frequently affected than other classes, and this is more likely from the manner of their roving from place to place, coming into contact with strange dogs, and usually those of thei own kind; added to which, they are reared in filth, and live by scavenging.

How often, after an outbreak of rabies, do we hear that a strange dog has been seen in the neighbourhood, belonging to nobody knows who, and generally described as a mongrel?

Dogs are especially inclined to fraternise, or, at all events to inspect one another; and this, as with human paupers is particularly the case with mongrels and curs. A stranger is immediately gathered round, sniffed over, followed some distance, and perhaps hustled; the stranger resents it, or ever if not thus interfered with, snaps at the one obstructing him and passes on his way. The same thing happens over and over again in his course: and I need hardly say (presuming him to be rabid) the horrible result is multiplied indifinitely in a like manner by his victims.

INCUBATION.—The incubative period of rabies is extremely uncertain. My experience, with a few exceptions has been from two to five weeks.

" In the dog, Lafosse states that the shortest authenticated period that occurred in his experience was seven days, and the longest one hundred and fifty-five days. Roll gives for the same animal, from three to six, and rarely from seven to ten weeks. Blaine asserts that the majority of cases occur between the third and seventh week, though some are protracted to three, four, or even a greater number of months. A week was the shortest period he had noted.

Youatt has known instances in which the first symptoms have only become manifest after from five to seven months, and he never knew of a case occurring before seventeen days intervening. Other authorities have related cases in which the disease was developed within from three to ten days after contamination. Of nine cases which Peuch could rely upon, the symptoms appeared after the bite, in each, at an interval of 95, 88, 35, 26, 24, 22, 18, 15, and 10 days, respectively."

"In 1863, Renault reported that of 68 dogs inoculated experimentally or bitten, the malady was developed in:

1	from the	5th	to the	10th day.	7	from the	45th	to the	50th day.
4	„	10th	„	15th „	2	„	50th	„	55th „
6	„	15th	„	20th „	2	„	55th	„	60th „
5	„	20th	„	25th „	4	„	60th	„	65th „
9	„	25th	„	30th „	1	„	65th	„	70th „
10	„	3toh	„	35th „	4	„	70th	„	75th „
2	„	35th	„	40th „	2	„	80th	„	90th „
8	„	40th	„	45th „	1	„	100th	„	118th „

"In Saint Cyr's 87 cases of confirmed rabies in 1865, there were only 26 the date of whose inoculation could be positively ascertained. In these the latent period was:

CASES.	DAYS.	CASES.	DAYS.
1	16	1	36
1	18	1	38
3	21	1	41
2	24	2	50
1	30	2	60
1	31	1	62
2	32	1	86
1	33	2	90 to 100
1	35	2	105 to 115

"Bouley has known instances in which the latent period was twelve days and seven months, though they were rare; it was usually from six to twelve weeks.

"According to Haubner, in 200 cases the appearance of the disease within two months was 83 per cent.; three months, 16 per cent.; four months, 1 per cent. He mentions an instance in which the incubatory period was from seven to eight months, and another in which it was fourteen months. He gives an average of three months.*

With such variations in the incubative period, it is little to be wondered at that persons, after being bitten, and under what condition of the animal they know not, should be filled with dread, and exhibit, especially those of nervous temperament, great mental excitement.

What takes place during this incubatory or latent period we know not; but it may be confidently asserted that in no other malady is this interregnum more variable and uncertain; indeed, if we are to credit some reports, the duration of the latent stage is indefinite. The capriciousness of the virus of rabies in this respect is certainly very remarkable and unaccountable. The wounds produced by rabid animals generally heal up readily, and leave but slight trace, and to all appearances those who have been injured appear to be as well as usual. True, in some rare instances in the human subject, pain has been experienced in the region of the wound for a considerable time after the receipt of the injury, and still more rarely a quickened pulse and slight fever have been present from this time until the disease became manifest. In other exceptional cases silent changes seemed to be taking place in the constitution, evidenced by general debility, a quick, weak, and easily excited pulse, sallow looks, and sunken eyes. But, as a rule, the health remains to all appearance the same as before the inoculation; and so subtle is the poison that, according to Van Swieten, persons who afterwards die of hydrophobia may, in the incubatory stage, contract diseases of various kinds, even virulent diseases, such as variola, without the course of the rabies being thereby modified in the least, or its evolution retarded.

"What occult influence is at work, what changes may be

---

* Fleming's "Rabies nad Hydrophobia," pp. 178—180.

taking place previous to the manifestation of the first symptoms, is a matter of pure hypothesis. The venom of the cobra, hydrocyanic acid, strychnine, and other poisons, produce effects more or less prompt and decided, according to the amount introduced into the body of any animal, and we can exactly prognosticate not only the result, but the time about which it should occur. The virus of contagious diseases, and more particularly hydrophobia, differs from these, inasmach as a minute quantity is as potent in inducing its particular malady, in a certain time, as a large quantity; and in the special disease now under consideration it may lie in a latent condition for a long period without affording the slightest indication of its presence."*

Duration.—The duration of rabies is rarely long—from one to ten days may be taken as the two extremes. A few cases have been noted over the latter period; but they are very exceptional instances, and attended with some degree of doubt. Those in my own experience have been from four to five days; most of them have died on the fifth.

Fleming observes: "The progress of rabies in the dog is always very rapid, and the termination, it may well be said, invariably fatal."

Its duration in no case appears to have exceeded ten days; and in the majority of instances death takes place about the fourth, fifth, or sixth day after the appearance of the first morbid symptoms. Of course, it also occurs much earlier. Out of several tables we will only refer to those of Professors Saint-Cyr and Peuch, of the Lyons School, as they afford a fair idea of the duration of the disease in a number of cases. In 1864, fifty-four rabid dogs were reported. Death took place at the following periods:

---

* Fleming's "Rabies and Hydrophobia," pp. 165, 166.

Two days	4 instances.
Three	5 ,,
Four	10 ,,
Five	8 ,,
Six	7 ,,
Seven	8 ,,
Eight	2 ,,
Twelve	1 instance.
Thirteen	1 ,,

The last case recovered spontaneously. The duration of the remaining eight cases could not be satisfactorily determined.

In the sixty-eight dogs that were rabid at the school in 1865, the duration of the disease was:

Two days	1 instance.
Three	6 instances.
Four	15 ,,
Five	20 ,,
Six	12 ,,
Seven	8 ,,
Eight	4 ,,
Nine	2 ,,

In 1868, in seventeen cases at the same school, it was:

Two days	2 instances.
Four	8 ,,
Five	4 ,,
Six	1 instance.
Seven	2 instances.

Symptoms.—Rabies assume *two* forms: *the furious* and *the tranquil or dumb.*

I shall commence first with furious rabies.

The earliest symptoms usually observed are a change in the dog's natural manner and habits: he becomes all at once sullen, or, as it were, melancholy; retires into obscure corners and dark places; when called, instead of obeying with his usual alacrity, he languidly and apparently with unwillingness approaches, and as suddenly slinks off again. Companionship renders him uneasy; in fact, throughout there is an unmistakable desire for solitude. If the eyes at this period are closely observed, a vacant expression will be seen in them; and immediately they meet the gaze of the observer they are dropped in a weary, sleepy manner.

As the disease proceeds, other and more marked symptoms become developed. A tendency to mischief is suddenly manifested. Boots, slippers, hearth-rug, carpet, chair-legs, and what not, are worried. If the animal is in the kennel, the straw is mangled and scattered about, the brick-work scratched, flooring torn up, and the whole place, more or less, shows signs of destruction.

The eyes assume a still more vacant expression; the gaze appears to be fixed on some distant object. Then a change takes place: the animal proceeds to examine most minutely every crevice and brick round his kennel; this done, he retires again into obscurity, and in a few minutes repeats the operation. Or the eyes are directed with earnest attention to some imaginary moving object, as a beetle or spider, which they appear to be tracing in its course. Suddenly he jumps forward with a snap at the supposed offender; and then, as if ashamed at the hallucination, he crouches down, crawls away and hides himself.

A flow of tenacious salvia is now present. The animal champs his teeth, and smacks his lips. As its tenacity becomes greater and its secretion more rapid, he strives to free his mouth of it with his paws, and this latter act has sealed the fate of more than one individual by being mistaken for a bone fixed in the teeth or throat.*

---

* Last year I was requested to visit a small toy terrier, belonging to a lady of title. The messenger informed me the animal was supposed to have a bone in its throat. On my arrival, which was between 9 and 10 p.m., I found the subject, which the keeper's wife was nursing, sitting with mouth slightly open. On removing my hand, after closing the

The voice at this time becomes strangely altered. It is hardly possible to describe it, though when once heard, it can never be forgotten. It is a kind of blending between a bark and a howl, having a croupy sound, and most frequently is heard at night.

A thoroughly savage and morose disposition becomes at this period firmly established. Any article presented will be seized and ferociously mangled. The poor creature, in its paroxysms is regardless of pain ; the lips are wounded, and even the teeth broken, in its frantic efforts to avenge some imagined injury or offence.*

---

jaws, the lower one again dropped half an inch. External manipulation about the throat produced no indications of pain or irritability. I then—not suspecting anything serious or unusual from the information I had received, proceeded, with the aid of a candle-light, to examine the posterior part of the mouth. This was discovered to be inflamed, but no bone could be detected. I then passed my two fore-fingers down, with the same result. Thinking it possible the bone had passed on, and probably left some laceration behind, with paralysis from its long retention in a fixed position, I ordered a hot linseed-meal or mustard-poultice to the throat, and a little warm beef-tea or broth to be given, promising to call the following day. This I was prevented from doing, and an assistant was sent instead. I, however, omitted to tell him the nature of the case, but he came back with the idea probably from being also told the same tale, viz: that the dog had "swallowed a bone." The following day I again visited the patient, when, upon opening the door of the room, the animal, without barking made a rush at me. Pulling the door to quickly, I waited a minute or so, and then cautiously looked in. He was crouching in a corner with his eyes half-closed, and his head nodding in a drowsy manner. He gave a start, or, as it were, awoke suddenly, changed his position, and fell off again in the same drowsy state; the lower jaw still remained dropped. I immediately became impressed with the belief that it was a case of dumb rabies, but, to make the matter more certain, I ordered the animal to be placed in security, and carefully watched. Next morning, unmistakeable symptoms of rabies manifested themselves, and the dog was shot. Another animal, a companion, sickened in like manner, and was also destroyed. Fortunately, I had no abrasions on my hands, or I might have shared a similar fate.

I mention this case as illustrative of the great care and suspicion with which such cases and their history should be received

* These fits of fury are not always attendant on rabies, if the animal

During and immediately after the paroxysm, the breathing is short and painful, and the animal looks an exhausted object, as if suffering from the effects of a hard-fought sanguinary battle.

As the malady proceeds towards its last stage, the head frequently becomes swollen, particularly about the eyes, which assume a brilliant lustrous appearance, and the conjunctival membrane is deeply injected. An anxious haggard countenance is present throughout.

The animal may gradually sink into a state of stupor, or die in a paroxysm of rage. Paralysis is sometimes associated with the disease from its commencement, and is rarely absent towards its termination. Emaciation is rapid under all circumstances.

One marked symptom in rabies, as opposed to all other nervous affections, is the magical influence of voices the animal is accustomed to. Even in moments of frenzy the call of one the poor sufferer knows is instantly recognised, and for a brief period produces an appearance of sanity.

It has been stated by a professed authority, Grantley F. Berkeley, that "Dogs become utterly *insane* through distemper, and are for the time *mad* to all intents and purposes." "If you prevent distemper in dogs 'by vaccination' (?) well performed, you decrease the *madness* in dogs, which in numberless cases arises from the effects of the 'common distemper,' but which is often vulgarly termed 'hydrophobia.'"* (I presume *rabies canina* is meant.)

Any such marked insanity in distemper it has never yet been the lot of the author to observe, nor, as far as he can gather, has it been noted by any other veterinarian. Rabies and distemper are, in fact, as widely different in character and pathology as it is possible for two canine maladies to

---

be left to itself; but nervous excitability appears to be predominant more or less throughout the disease.

* From letter in the *Morning Post*, dated Sept. 11th, 1887. The italics are mine.

be. Those nervous symptoms which are frequently present in the subacute stages of distemper do not bear the slightest analogy to "rabid insanity," and only those inexperienced in the latter disease could mistake them.

An unusual affection has been described as another symptom, and whether the unfortunate creature being aware of its hopeless condition accounts for it, is only surmise. Certain it is such a manifestation is, especially in the earlier stages, very frequent.

Another symptom worthy of note and exceedingly characteristic, is the *appetite*. This invariably assumes a morbid character. Portions of wood, stones, earth, hair, excrement, and other filth are devoured, whilst the ordinary meal remains untouched.*

The vomiting of blood in the early stage of the malady, described by some authors, is not by any means an invariable symptom of rabies. The sanguinary tinge of the vomit more frequently proceeds from wounds of the tongue or mouth, than from any morbid condition of the stomach.

Lastly, when a dog unconfined becomes rabid, there is much that is characteristic in his mode of travelling. His gait may be termed as rambling, or jog-trot. The head is carried low, the tongue protrudes from the side of the mouth, or hangs pendent in front, swollen and covered with

---

* Devouring the excrement has wrongly been described as an infallible sign of rabies. I say wrongly because dogs in robust health will occasionally contract this disgusting habit, *puppies in particular*. Therefore it is only to be taken cognizance of in connection with the other symptoms. Again, morbid appetites are often associated with some peculiar condition of the sympathetic nervous system, independent of rabies. This is especially to be observed in pregnancy. Strange and impossible gratification of fancies and desires fill the human mind, and the same idiosyncrasy exists in the lower animals. In-calf cows often devour leather, linen, and other strange substances. Looking at it from another point of view, rabies coming under the class of nervous diseases, we should not be surprised at similar morbid appetites being present.

dirt. It is rare he turns from his path to attack anything (unless it be an animal of the same species, to which they invariably show the greatest animosity), but woe betide anyone who attempts to stay his onward course. This pace is continued with little intermission until exhaustion overtakes him, or it may be a fit, when he creeps into an obscure place, and lies in a fatigued or comatose state for hours.

Such then as I have endeavoured clearly to desribe them, are the leading symptoms of this horrible malady.

Tranquil or Dumb Madness.—The general symptoms in this form of rabies are much the same as in the preceding, with the exception of absence of voice, modification of nervous excitability, and paralysis of the muscles of the lower jaw. The latter is a curious and characteristic feature in this type of the malady. As I observed in *Land and Water* with regard to the Albrighton hounds, " No particular period can be given at which this symptom is observed. One at feeding time had refused its food, and in three hours after its jaw had dropped ; another apparently well at night was found similarly affected the following morning, and, in fact, in many of them this paralysis was noticed before any other symptom."

Frequently in packs of hounds the two forms of rabies exhibit themselves simultaneously, and as inoculation from glanders produces farcy, and *vice versâ*, so ferocious madness may give rise to the dumb or furious form.

Maternal affection is not interfered with.*

---

* "The maternal affection for its young remains as strong in the rabid as it is in the healthy dog. M. Defays, a professor at the Brussels Veterinary School, gives an instance of a bitch that had three puppies, and two days afterwards suddenly exhibited all the symptoms of rabies. Notwithstanding the severe attacks of the malady, the poor creature continued to suckle its young, and ran anxiously to them when they emitted the slightest cry; not being able to swallow any fluid, however, the secretion of milk was suspended, and the puppies died.

" But this event did not alter its desire to be near, and to fondle them, and to cover them over with straw, as if to hide them ; it was

Post-mortem Appearances.—These differ considerably: two in all particulars scarcely ever being alike. Indeed, the pathological anatomy of rabies appears to be as varied as it is obscure. The following may be taken as some of the chief conditions usually seen, but rarely combined.

Congestion of the brain, occasionally extending to the spinal cord.

Serous effusion within the membranes of both.

Hæmorrhage into the substance of the brain.

Inflammation of the fauces, glottis, upper portion of the trachea and glands of the throat, with enlargement of the latter. These structures are more particularly implicated in dumb madness.

Lungs frequently gorged with blood, especially if the animal has died from asphyxia.

Foreign matters in the posterior part of the mouth, in the stomach and intestines, as hair, straw, wood, earth, etc.

Or the absence of either, and the presence of blood, mucus or brown coffee-coloured fluid in the stomach.

Patches of inflamation in the lining membrane of the stomach and bowels.

Enlargement and inflammation of the mesenteric glands.

Enlargement and engorgement of the spleen and liver.

The appearances in the brain, throat, and digestive organs form the most confirmatory evidence of rabies.

From the excellent and valuable annual report of the cases brought for observation on treatment, to the Vienna Imperial Veterinary Institute, and published in the ' Œsterreichische Vierteljahresschrift fur Wissenschaftliche Veterinarkunde," for 1875* we observe that in the session of 1873–4, there were no fewer than 125 dogs admitted as rabid, or suspected of being affected with rabies. Though

---

only when complete paralysis had supervened that the unfortunate animal ceased to occupy itself with its dead offspring."—"Annales de Méd. Vétérinaire," Brussels, October, 1871. (Fleming.)

From the " Veterinary Journal," October, 1876.

PRIZE BULL STEER "HADDOCK."

some of the pathological alterations were so frequent that they could be accurately grouped, yet others were so inconstant that there could not be said to be any certain indication of the presence of the disease. In some were found alterations in the brain; in others, changes in the blood, lymphatic glands, and kidneys; and in others, morbid manifestations in the digestive organs were met with. The malady prevailed as an epizooty, and animals of both sexes, various ages and breeds, when or whether bitten often unknown, were at different times brought to the Institute. Frequently little could be learned with regard to the animals which were brought dead, and even their condition previous to death could rarely be ascertained. With regard to the value of some pathological alterations in forming a judgment as to the presence of the disease, the following epitome is given of the result of the necroscopical examinations made of these animals:

a. Alterations in the brain. 1. Hæmorrhage into the subcutaneous tissue of the cranium of a suspected dog. 2. Hæmorrhage into the *dura mater* of two rabid and one suspected animals. 3. Injection of the *pia mater* and *plexus chorides* in 28 rabid and 2 suspected. 4. Hyperæmia of the brain in 2 rabid. 5. Softening of the brain in various degrees—from mere shining softness (*glazend und weicher sein*) to complete pulpy liquefaction—in 35 rabid and 2 suspected animals (of these the whole brain was generally involved in 3 rabid cases; the cerebellum in 3 rabid, and 2 suspected; the upper surface and base of the brain in 1 rabid animal. 6. Distension of the lateral ventricles, through a collection of serum therein, in 10 rabid animals, 1 of which had the right ventricle unusually dilated, while the left was normal.

b. Alterations in the circulatory apparatus and the blood. 1. Pericarditis in 1 suspected dog. 2. Capillary hæmorrhage into the pericardium in 2 rabid cases. 3. Hæmorrhage beneath the endocardium in 1 rabid case. 4. Alterations in the blood alone in 83 rabid, and 28 suspected animals. The blood was of a light-red colour in 13 rabid and 1 suspected; fluid in the heart in 2 rabid, slightly coagulated in 5 rabid, and with a dense whitish fibrinous clot in 6 rabid and 1 suspected dogs. The blood was dark-red to black-red (*schwarzroth*) in 70 rabid and 27 suspected. (*a*) In the heart it was quite fluid in 11 rabid and 4 suspected. (*b*) Slightly coagulated in 21 rabid and 11 suspected. (*c*) With a soft fibrinous clot in 9 rabid; and (*d*) it had a dense grey clot in 29 rabid and 7 suspected animals. Bacteria (*Stäbchen*) in the blood were in some cases numerous, in others few; in none were they very abundant. Anæmia was present in 4 rabid animals.

c. Alterations in the spleen and mesenteric glands were noted in 68 rabid and 11 suspected animals. 1. Lymphatic nodules in the spleen alone in 1 rabid creature. 2. Enlargement of the spleen alone in 25 rabid and 3 suspected. 3. Tumefaction of the mesenteric glands alone in 21 rabid and 6 suspected. 4. Enlargement of the spleen and mesenteric glands in 21 rabid and 2 suspected dogs.

d. Alterations in the respiratory apparatus in 86 rabid and 16 suspected animals. 1. Marked pallor of the mucous membrane of the larynx and trachea in 2 rabid and 1 suspected animals. 2. Intense injection of the same in 51 rabid and 8 suspected creatures. 3. General dark discoloration of the pharyngeal, laryngeal, and partially of the respiratory mucous membrane in 2 rabid and 1 suspected animals. 4. Capillary hæmorrhage at the entrance to the larynx in 1 rabid. 5. Capillary hæmorrhage in the laryngeal mucous membrane in 1 rabid. 6. Capillary hæmorrhage in the *pleura pulmonalis* in 1 suspected. 7. Bronchial catarrh in 3 rabid. 8. Pulmonary œdema in 11 rabid and 4 suspected. 9. Pneumonia at the border of some lobules—seldom involving entire lobes; and 10. Hæmorrhage into the thoracic cavity from gunshot wounds, in 2 suspected cases.

e. Alterations in the digestive organs. 1. Injuries to the tongue in one rabid dog. 2. Foreign bodies in the mouth and throat of 1 rabid and 1 suspected. 3. Stomach empty in 19 rabid and 1 suspected. 4. Foreign matter in the stomach—hair, wood, straw, grass, leaves, soil, cherrystones (and in one case a living horse-fly attached to the mucous membrane)—in 56 rabid and 21 suspected. 5. Foreign matter besides hair in intestines in 6 rabid and 3 suspected. 6. Blood in the stomach in 2 rabid. 7. Injection of the serous membrane of the stomach only in 43 rabid and 2 suspected. 8. Injection of serous membrane of the stomach and intestines in 3 rabid and 3 suspected. 9. Pallor of the gastric mucous membrane in 1 rabid. 10. General redness of the same in 6 rabid. 11. Patchy redness of the same in 2 rabid. 12. Hæmorrhagic erosions and ulcers in the same in 40 rabid. 13. Marked yellowness of the intestinal mucous membrane and contents of same, in 4 rabid. 14. General redness, with tumefaction of the intestinal mucous membrane and tape-worm, in 58 rabid and 17 suspected. 15. Patchy redness of the mucous membrane of the small intestines, particularly involving Peyer's patches, in 27 rabid and 9 suspected. 16. Diverticular formations in 1 rabid animal.

f. Alterations in the urinary and generative organs. 1. Nephritis in one rabid and 1 suspected ; 2. Cystitis and nephritis in 1 rabid ; 3. Pregnancy, about three weeks, in a rabid bitch.

g. Alterations in the locomotory apparatus probably due to injury to the head, were discovered in 3 rabid and 13 suspected dogs.

In the "Bericht über den Veterinärwesen in Sachsen," for 1874, Professor Siedamgrotzky has a paper on the pathological anatomy of rabies.* He remarks that the peculiar expression of the rabid dog's physio-

---

* From the "Veterinary Journal," October, 1876.

gnomy has long been recognised as an essential part of the diagnosis, and that this characteristic indication is largely due to the dull heavy eyes, which are so commonly partially covered by the membrana nictitans in rabies. Besides, the malady has a tendency to be accompanied by catarrh of the conjunctivæ, indicated by a collection of mucus in the inner canthus of the eye. Beyond this, there sometimes suddenly appear circumscribed opacities of the cornea, with breaking up of its texture in the centre of these, and so leading to the formation of ulcers. This ulceration progresses so rapidly, that in some cases the substance of the cornea is perforated within two days. These corneal ulcerations are not, however, very common: Siedamgrotzky had only observed them in six cases, in which two or three ulcers appeared in both eyes. They are not an accompaniment of only one form of rabies, but appear in both—dumb as well as furious. On a *post-mortem* examination, it is found that the ulcer has penetrated the cornea, in a conical manner, and that nothing but a thin layer of fibrin, or a blood coagulum in the anterior chamber, has prevented the escape of the entire contents of the organ. Examined microscopically, the corneal ulcer offers no essential difference from that witnessed in distemper: moderate cell-heaping in the vicinity of the ulcer, fatty degeneration of the corneal elements, and opening out of the interstitial substance; but nothing otherwise characteristic.

Siedamgrotzky at first believed that the alteration was produced by mechanical causes, but from close observation he is satisfied that it may appear in the quietest animals whose eyes have not been exposed to external injury. It is therefore not unlikely that an interruption in the nutrition is the cause; though not a general alteration in the nutritive function, but perhaps rather due originally to an alteration in the trophic nerves of the eye.

This explanation, of course, cannot be experimentally

proved; but that it has some foundation in fact may be deduced by reference to the extensive derangement in the other nerve regions, particularly in the branch of the fifth pair supplying the lower jaw.

Alterations in the ophthalmic branch are likewise few when those of the maxillary are so—proving, apparently, that the lesion is central.

According to Professor Benedikt ("Wiener Med. Presse," No. 74)* the disease is a special acute exudative inflammation of the brain, resulting in various forms of hyaloid degeneration, which is particularly observed in the neighbourhood of the lenticular nucleus of the anterior lobe— often in this alone. Siedamgrotzky states that he has, in his examinations, been particularly careful to inquire into the correctness of this; and in some cases of "dumb madness" there was certainly a marked inflammatory condition of a portion of the brain about the fissure of Sylvius.

In the "Giornale di Anatomia," etc., edited by the veterinary professors at the University of Pisa, Rivolta gives the description of a careful examination he made of the brains of seven dogs which had perished from furious rabies transmitted to them by inoculation. The result goes to show that the pathological alterations in that organ consist mainly in more or less marked hyperæmia of the pia mater in the cerebral fissures, but especially at the base of the brain, and this hyperæmia is never absent from the cerebral plexus choroides; that softening of the cerebral substance is not frequent, though, on the contrary, the grey substance is constantly higher coloured; and that perivascular infiltration of a fatty nature cannot be recognised as characteristic of this disease, as Rivolta has noticed it in other maladies.†

In the "Centralblatt für die Medicin-Wissenschaften,"

---

*From the "Veterinary Journal," October, 1876
† Ibid. ‡ Ibid.

Kolesemkoff reports the results of the examination of ten mad dogs made in Rudneff's pathological laboratory at St. Petersburg. The parts examined were the *cerebral hemispheres*, the *corpora striata, thalami optici, cornua ammonis, cerebellum, medulla oblongata, medulla spinalis*, and the sympathetic and spinal ganglia. The changes were always most marked in the ganglia, and were as follows:
1. The vessels were much distended and filled with red corpuscles. Here and there along their course were seen groups of red corpuscles, and round indifferent elements (probably emigrated white corpuscles) scattered in the perivascular spaces. The walls of the vessels were spotted with hyaloid masses of various forms, sometimes extending and obstructing the lumen of the vessel-like thrombi. Not far from these were collections of white and red corpuscles.
2. There was found to be a collection of round, indifferent elements in general around the nerve-cells, sometimes penetrating into the protoplasm of the cells to the number of five or eight; sometimes in such number as quite to displace the cell-protoplasm. he number of migrated cells produced various changes in the form of the nerve-elements. The nuclei of the cells were sometimes pushed forwards towards the periphery by the intrusive elements. In other cases the nerve-cells seemed entirely replaced by masses of round indifferent corpuscles. These changes were seen even in isolated nerve-cells. The author points out the analogy of these changes to those described by Popoff in enteric fever and injuries.

With regard to the innocuousness of the milk derived from rabid animals, there is a conflict of opinion. Cases, however, are on record both of human beings and the offspring of animals becoming affected through partaking of milk secreted by hydrophobic and rabid subjects; but many of these cases, it must be confessed, are involved in doubt.

Mr. Fleming, in his work on "Rabies and Hydrophobia,"

observes: "The influence of the *milk* obtained from animals supposed to be infected with rabies has received much attention, and, as in the case of the flesh, the facts relating to its virulence are negative and positive. Among the negative facts, however, those must be distinguished which have reference to the milk derived from animals only bitten by mad dogs, and those really affected with the disease.

"Andray reports that peasants have used, for more than a month, the milk of a cow which was wounded by a mad dog, without experiencing any inconvenience.*

"An infant fed on the milk of a goat until the day the animal became mad, remained in perfect health. And, what is more striking, another child drank the warm milk drawn from a rabid cow, and no ill effects followed. The veterinarian, Gellé, has stated that he was commissioned by the Préfet of the Haute-Garonne to inquire into an occurrence reported from the commune of Gagnac, near Toulouse, in which several persons had drunk the milk of a rabid cow every day from the commencement until the fatal termination of the disease. Though some of them were plunged into the greatest terror, none were affected with the disease.

"The experiments made by Baumgarten and Valentin concord with the observations made by Gellé; they are also confirmed by the researches instituted by Baudot, who, a great number of times, noted that neither the milk nor butter obtained from rabid cows produced unpleasant effects on whole families who had consumed these articles of food.†

"At the Alfort Veterinary School a ewe which had been wounded by a rabid dog was soon after delivered of twin lambs, which of course it suckled. Twenty-one days after the infliction of the bite the ewe became rabid, and died, but the lambs did not manifest any signs of the disease.

---

* "Recherches sur la Rage," Paris, 1781.
† "Mémoires de la Soc. Royale de Médecine," vol. ii. p. 911.

"The only positive statements I can meet with as to the milk of a mad dog producing rabies, are the following: Soranus of Ephesus, the most distinguished disciple of the Methodic School of Medicine, averred that infants at the breast are sometimes attacked with hydrophobia.* Balthazar Timæus speaks of a peasant, with his wife and children, as well as several other persons, becoming rabid through drinking the milk of an affected cow. Eleven of these died; but the peasant and his eldest child were restored by medical treatment—a circumstance which might tend to throw some doubt on the occurrence. Faber mentions instances in which the milk has proved injurious. An observation made by M. Dussort, and quoted by Roucher, offers a very probable instance of transmission by the milk of a hydrophobic patient. This was the case of a negress in Algeria, whose child died presenting symptoms similar to those of the mother before she perished. In the same country, however, M. Hugo relates the case of a rabid bitch, whose puppies were suckled by her, and remained in good health. But, again, an instance is given in 'Cassell's Magazine' for July, 1871, in which the puppies suckled by a mad bitch also became rabid."†

Treatment.—After what I have already said, it is almost needless to add that I believe treatment, according to past

---

* Cæl. Aurelianus, Op. cit., lib. iii. cap. 2,

† "A friend of mine once owned a favourite terrier, which had recently littered five puppies, and as she was kept constantly in his garden, she could not possibly have been bitten for some considerable time. But she suddenly displayed unmistakable symptoms of madness, and ran up and down the garden, with the saliva flying from her jaws, and her head twitching from side to side, as the heads of all mad dogs do. . . . But, even in her frenzy, her maternal instinct was too strong, and she ran back to her kennel, and began suckling her puppies. . . . Here is the strangest part of the story, and to me it seems very pathetic: all her little puppies were raving mad too, and the foam hung in flakes about their mouths, and their poor little heads twitched, just as the mother's had done. They had sucked in madness with the milk, for she had not bitten any of them. This was, in my experience at least, a new feature in the history of hydrophobia."

and so far as present experiments have gone, to be of no earthly use; and no man having any regard for his life, however valuable that of his dogs may be, would, I imagine, risk it in administering all the talked-of remedies that have from time to time cropped up.

Prevention is at all times better than cure, and when rabies makes its appearance in a kennel, isolation of the apparently healthy or unbitten ones I strongly recommend, until a sufficient period has elapsed to prove they have escaped inoculation. With regard to ourselves, all dog-bites, as a precautionary measure, should be treated as if they were inflicted by a rabid animal—*i.e.*, by immediate suction, followed by the application of the actual cautery nitric acid, or pure carbolic acid. When rabies is suspected, the suction should be directly followed by complete excision of the wound, performed as quickly as possible; after which, without loss of time, the cautery or acid should be freely used. Compression above the wound, especially in the first instance, is also valuable.

Failing the adoption of these measures or even accompanying them, the Russian or Turkish bath should, if possible, be immediately had recourse to, and in the absence of such measure, free and intense perspiration should be promoted by other means, such being the most efficacious treatment at present known. Whatever contrary opinions may be expressed, the remedy, if considered useless, is harmless, *i.e.*, the bath cannot produce hydrophobia or rabbit paralysis, whereas Pasteur's system of inoculation can and unfortunately has done.

I also advise a powerful stimulant before taking the bath, and subsequently full doses of chlorate of potash and iron.

The same measures, excepting the baths, and the suction, which might be done with a *cupping*-glass, will apply to a dog bitten under suspicious circumstances.

An antiquated idea, which unfortunately still prevails, is, that the danger arising from the bite of a dog *supposed* to be mad, can only be averted by the death of the animal. This is an egregious mistake. A dog must be infected with rabies before it can produce "Hydrophobia." Again if a dog after biting a person is at once destroyed before being examined by a qualified canine veterinary surgeon, the mind of the wounded individual may be in a state of continual disquietude, from the oft-recurring thought that the dog may have been mad, and this painful and haunting uncertainty acting upon a highly nervous temperament is not unfrequently productive of a fatal issue from Hysteria and nervous exhaustion, so often wrongly reported as "Hydrophobia." My advice has always been to let a dog which has been guilty of biting, be fully secured until the maximum period of incubation has passed—then if he is in perfect health, or free from rabid symptoms, the mind of the injured person will be relieved, and the animal, if still desired, can then be destroyed—not with the policeman's truncheon, but with *chloroform*. In a few instances when I have appeared in court to plead this arrangement, and even volunteered to take personal charge of the dog, I have met with opposition, and unnecessary terror and anxiety to the bitten individual has been the consequence, but a sensible magistrate will always see the wisdom and humanity of granting such an application, and even advocating it to the injured person.

There is no such disorder as "epileptic rabies," which was alleged, during the recent London scare, to exist. Such an allegation is not only misleading, but purely imaginary on the part of the originator. Canine rabies is a specific disease and has no concomitant malady.

EPILEPSY.

Dogs of all breeds are very liable to fits, and the epileptic is the form most frequently met with. To say that epilepsy has been confounded over and over again with rabies, would be stating what is correct. A mistake, unfortunately, for the poor dog; but which, I am happy to say, is usually made, not by veterinarians, but by misguided policemen, with the usual mob to back them up. I remember reading, some few years since, in a leading paper, of madness in dogs, in which article the writer, if he had been a professional man, could not have more faithfully described the leading symptoms of epilepsy. Sudden reeling, falling over, foaming at the mouth, and convulsions are not diagnostic of rabies. Hence, it is from the mistake these symptoms engender, from not being understood, that a panic is, from time to time, created in otherwise peaceful districts by such newspaper headings as "A mad dog at large," "Outbreak of rabies, exciting scene," and such like.

Not long ago I was walking to town with a young mastiff-dog. Soon after starting he vomited a quantity of worms; half a mile farther on an epileptic fit seized him, and being on a main road, innumerable suggestions of rabies were offered, with kind offers of destruction. However, the animal was secured by his chain to a post, a cold water douche given, and shortly afterwards a gig conveyed him safely home.

Epilepsy may take place at any age; but youth and old age are the two most susceptible periods.

Predisposing Causes.—Hereditary disposition, nervous irritability, general debility, suckling large families.

Exciting Causes.—Worms, dentition, suppression of natural secretions and evacuations, sudden fear or excitement, over-exertion after feeding, rapid exertion in obese condition, and too much flesh meat—especially in young dogs.

Symptoms.—Epilepsy, as a rule, is not ushered in by any premonitory warning. The animal, apparently in perfect health, is in a moment seized with a fit, and this generally occurs during locomotion. He suddenly reels, as though intoxicated; falls on his side; and violent convulsive spasms attack the voluntary muscles, especially of the limbs, which keep up a continuous kicking motion. Frequently a sharp cry escapes the animal when he falls, and these are at times succeeded by others of a whimpering nature. During the attack the urine and fæces are often voided. The tongue is sometimes severely bitten, the gums are of a leaden or livid hue, the mouth filled with frothy saliva, and the eyes unnaturally prominent.

Epilepsy passes through its course with marvellous, rapidity; five minutes from the seizure the animal may regain its legs, and appear in its usual health. There are, however, cases in which, after the foregoing symptoms have passed away, the creature lies motionless and utterly unconscious, as if it were sound asleep; and this state may continue for half an hour or more.

The dog recovering from epilepsy usually has a peculiar, bewildered look. Immediately he regains his feet he either makes off with himself as fast as his legs can carry him, or viciously rushes at those about him. This latter is one of the most unpleasant phases of the disease, for the animal is indisposed alike to friends and strangers; and this is another of the inducements for a verdict of madness.

One fit is often the forerunner of others, which continue in rapid succession for a considerable time. In such instances the prognosis is unfavourable.

Epilepsy frequently ushers in distemper, and also more frequently terminates it.

Treatment.—Immediately a dog at large is seized with epilepsy, care should be taken to secure him, for the double purpose of preventing him biting, and also running away. The collar should not be tighter than is absolutely necessary, or dangerous results will follow from pressure on the vessels of the neck, and consequent obstruction to the return of blood from the head.

Cold water is certainly the best ready-at-hand application; this may be dashed freely in the face, or what is better, if within reach, a tap turned on the animal's head.

Bleeding as a rule is unnecessary and injudicious.

Epilepsy generally arises from debility and nervous irritation; therefore in the after treatment it is our duty to seek for and remove the causes giving rise to this condition. If it be worms the speedier they are removed the better. If dentition, a proper attention to that process, and the regularity of natural functions is to be observed. If from the suppression of natural secretions and evacuations, a restoration of suspended function must be induced. If from sudden excitement, as music, steam-engine whistles, and the like, such noises should be avoided, or we should by degrees get the animal accustomed to them. If from suckling, withdrawal of whelps and a more liberal diet, with tonics. If from over-exertion after feeding the cause must not be repeated. If from rapid exertion in obese condition, reduce the latter and regulate the former. If from flesh-meat, an alteration in the quantity should be made, or suspended for a time altogether.

When coma succeeds the attack, ammonia should be applied to the nostrils, and the gums rubbed with brandy. The back of the head may also in protracted cases, be stimulated with mustard or turpentine embrocation.

The bromides of ammonium and potassium are very useful in recurrent epilepsy.

APOPLEXY.

Apoplexy, or congestion of the vessels of the brain, is generally met with in aged gross dogs, irregularly exercised.

Predisposing Causes.—Plethora, obesity, especially in pugs and bull-dogs.

Exciting Causes.—Violent exercise, intense heat, pressure on the vessels of the neck from tight collars or dragging at the chain, derangement of the digestive organs, violent straining, especially in parturition narcotics.

Symptoms.—Partial or entire insensibility; heavy stertorous breathing; fixed bloodshot eyes; slow pulse.

Treatment.—Blood should be abstracted from the jugular, if possible, or the hair shaved off the back of the head, and leeches applied. Ammonia should be placed to the nostrils, brandy rubbed on the gums, and counter-irritation along the spine.

VERTIGO.

Dogs are occasionally seized with a kind of dizziness or vertigo. They suddenly fall, remain unconscious for a minute or two, and motionless; and then almost as suddenly regain their legs, and with the exception of appearing a little bewildered, seem as though nothing unusual had happened.

Such seizures are generally due to brain pressure, most frequently from some retarding influence in the return of blood from the head, as a tight collar, glandular enlargements, bronchocele, etc. A disordered condition of stomach is likewise a predisposing cause, and the susceptibility to an attack of vertigo is greater after a full meal, and particularly if any of the above-named obstructions to the circulation also exist.

Treatment.—This consists in removal of the cause; neck pressure as far as possible should be avoided; a healthy state of the digestive organs maintained, with proper observance of hygienics.

CHOREA.

Chorea, or St. Vitus's dance, is a purely nervous affection, and is the result generally of an irritable and impaired condition of the nervous system. It may be general or local. The limbs are frequently first observed affected, ultimately the body, face, and jaws may be involved, the latter exhibiting tetanic symptoms.*

Symptoms.—Chorea is denoted by a peculiar snatching or twitching of the part affected. If the brain is involved,

---

* I have at the time of writing this, under treatment, a pug dog extensively afflicted with chorea; the jaw can only be opened half an inch, and goes to again with a sharp snap. The lips are convulsed.

the head is in continual spasmodic tremulous motion, and may best be described as a fac-simile of an aged palsied person. It has been known in human practice to arise from sympathy and imitation. I am not aware of any instance in which a dog has so contracted it.

Treatment.—With regard to medicinal agents, the one most applicable to this affection is undoubtedly strychnia or nux vomica. I do not recollect a single case of chorea, taken in its early stages, in which I have failed to effect a cure with this drug. Great caution is, however, required in its administration. It should always be given at a stated time, and after a meal; this is especially necessary where the doses have been gradually increased, otherwise a fatal result is likely to ensue.

I could mention more than one instance in which death has occurred from neglecting this caution. In each the patient had been under a long course of strychnia, and the dose had been increased to more than treble the original quantity: by some mischance the drug was omitted for a day, and when next given it produced convulsions and death.

The dose of strychnia is $\frac{1}{30}$ to $\frac{1}{10}$ of a grain; the nux vomica from 1 to 2 grains. It is best, however, to commence below either of the minimums mentioned, and after the first three days gradually increase it. It should be given twice daily in the form of a pill. If there is any difficulty in administering it, the liquor strychnia may be substituted, which contains half a grain to the drachm, and may be proportionately divided.

Local remedies in chorea are sometimes beneficial. I have found setons exceedingly valuable. If the convulsive movements are confined to the hind parts, the seton should be inserted across the loins; if general, at the back of the head and loins. Counter-irritation along the spine is also serviceable. Mercurial ointment in chronic cases.

Though in principle the hot-bath, from its relaxing tendency, may appear wrong, it is nevertheless in chorea occasionally attended with considerable benefit. It certainly affords relief in those cases where the convulsive movements are excessive, and so far I have found no after evil from its use.

The less the patient is disturbed the better; particular attention should be paid to the bed being dry and the bowels regular—two great essentials in paralytic affections. When abatement of the twitchings with returning strength is observed, a favourable issue may be expected; but the medicine should not be discontinued so long as any nervous affection remains, and it should be gradually, not suddenly, suspended. When the patient is able to walk, a short exercise each day may be given with benefit. The fresh air acts as a tonic, new scenery diverts the mind, and exercise encourages the natural habits and functions of the animal.

Tinct. ferri and cod-liver oil is advisable after discontinuing the strychnia, until recovery is complete.

The diet throughout must be nourishing and digestible, and forcibly administered if the patient refuses to take it.

Constipation is generally present in chorea, and is best relieved with enemas.

Occasionally rheumatism becomes associated with chorea and then the heart is frequently complicated. (See "Heart Diseases.") In such cases a cure is hopeless, but under judicious treatment and careful nursing the rheumatic and chorea symptoms may be considerably modified, and the animal's life thereby prolonged.

PARALYSIS.

Paralysis may be general or partial; *i.e.* the whole muscular system may be involved, or certain branches of it.

Paralysis generally is due to pressure on the brain or spinal cord, or it may arise from injury, disease, or pressure of the nerve itself.

When it arises from the brain the whole of the body is usually affected. If only one side of the brain is injured, then the reverse side of the body is most frequently paralysed

When the spinal cord is injured the paralysis is confined to those parts behind the seat of injury.

Paralysis also follows certain conditions of the body, independent of actual disease of the brain or other nerve centres, as in protracted constipation, distended bladder, chorea, distemper, old age, and general debility.

Paralysis of the hind-quarters is the form commonly seen in canine practice, and this is frequently associated with distempter or chorea.

Paralysis of the lower jaw, unless it arises from direct injury to the nerves in that part, is a marked symptom of *dumb madness.*

Symptoms.—Loss of power, weakness, and muscular twitchings are the early symptoms of paralysis. The affection may come on gradually or suddenly; if of long duration atrophy of the muscles and emaciation take place, the effect of inaction through lack of nerve stimulation.

Treatment.—In the treatment of paralysis, it is necessary that we should first ascertain the cause. If, for instance, it arises from injury to the brain from a depressed portion of the skull, an operation is at once indicated for the removal of that pressure. If from constipation or distended bladder, means used for the relief of both are to be afforded; if from debility, a restoration to vigour by liberal diet exercise, and tonics is necessary. The same will apply in chorea and distemper. In old age, when the nerve force is as a nutural result weak, no treatment beyond attention to the secretory and excretory functions is of service.

The medicinal agent most effectual in paralysis is undoubtedly strychnia or nux vomica, and this, in chronic cases, may be advantageously combined with iron, quinine, or both. Nux vomica, which is perhaps the most convenient form of administering strychnia, is prescribed in from 1 to 2 grains twice daily, and may be gradually increased after the third or fourth day, in proportion to the requirements of the case.* The dose of iron (sulphate) is 5 to 10 grains, quinine 1 to 2 grains.

Local measures are of often serviceable in paralytic affections, as counter-irritations, setons, and galvanism.

When walking, if only imperfectly performed, is within the power of the animal, it should be daily but not tiringly insisted on.

The diet should be nourishing, easy of digestion, and slightly relaxing.

In all cases of paralysis particular attention to the material of which the bed is composed, and its dryness, is most essential. Straw, dried fern, or heather, form the most suitable materials. Whichever is used should be on a perforated boarded floor, and as far removed from the ground as may be necessary to health. (See " Kennel Arrangements.")

When the affection is established in such a manner as to render the animal helpless, the patient should not be allowed to lie too long in one position, otherwise troublesome sores are apt to arise. In cases where they do, fuller's earth, alum and flour—one part of the former to three of the latter, or the oxide of zinc ointment or lotion, are the most suitable applications.

In confirmed and chronic paralysis, complete recovery

---

* It may be well, perhaps, to observe that in the administration of this drug extreme care is required, particularly in the increase of the dose and the times at which it is given. When any alteration is made in the quantity, it should be very gradual. The best time for the patient to have it is shortly after feeding, and the hour should always be the same. Neglect in these matters has caused many fatal issues in what might otherwise have been satisfactory cases. It is advisable, also, in leaving the medicine off, to gradually and not suddenly suspend it.

is rarely witnessed ; some lingering effect, as twitching or tremor of a part, being observable throughout life. In such instances, undue exposure to cold and damp should be avoided.

CONCUSSION OF THE BRAIN.

The brain of the dog, though strongly protected in comparison with that of the human being and some of the lower animals, is nevertheless at times subjected to severe shocks from external violence, as falls, blows, etc.

Symptoms.—The patient lies insensible or (in common parlance) stunned and motionless. The respiration is slow and feeble, the pulse quick and small, the pupils are generally contracted and insensible to light.

As the senses gradually return, vomiting usually takes place ; when in locomotion, the head is carried low, the eyes have a vacant dreamy expression, and the gait is reeling and unsteady, the animal blunders forward and butts against various objects in its way.

Treatment.—The attention of the surgeon should first be directed to the head, which should be carefully examined to ascertain if there be any injury or fracture of the skull. If the latter exists, and there is depression of the broken parts, their elevation is at once indicated. If there is an external wound, it should be carefully attended to, and hæmorrhage, if any, arrested.

With regard to further treatment, ammonia may be applied to the nostrils, and the gums and lips rubbed with brandy ; and, so soon as the patient is able to swallow, a little of the latter may be poured down the throat.

When inflammatory symptoms succeed the coma, local bleeding by means of leeches to the temples and back of the head, followed by counter-irritation, is advisable. The bowels at the same time should be kept freely opened.

Strict quietude should be observed throughout. The food should be plain and not excessive in quantity.

The effects of concussion are often apparent for some considerable time afterwards, being usually exhibited in a wild unnatural stare of the eyes, with, from time to time, particularly after feeding, a reeling gait.

In such cases I recommend the insertion of a seton at the back of the head, small doses of aperient medicine pretty frequently, and the daily administration of nux vomica.

COMPRESSION OF THE BRAIN.

Compression of the brain may arise from extravasated blood within the cranium, morbid growths in connection with the latter or its contents, the formation of pus or accumulation of serum within the cranial cavity or substance of the brain or by mere distension of the blood-vessels (congestion); but probably it more frequently occurs from fracture of the skull, with depression of the broken parts.[*]

Symptoms.—Partial or complete coma, depending upon the seat and extent of compression. The breathing is slow, laboured, and generally stertorous, pulse slow and sometimes intermittent, eyes fixed, pupils dilated and insensible to light; the limbs are relaxed and motionless, the fæces and urine are frequently passed involuntarily.

Treatment.—To remove, if possible, the cause. If it arises from congestion of the brain—from mere distension of the bloodvessels—full local bleeding, and the after administration of stimulants, with aperient medicine, are the measures indicated. If from depression resulting from fracture, elevation of the broken parts will be necessary; or, if from formation of pus or accumulation of serum, trephining may be attempted as a *dernier ressort*. But whatever may be the cause, it is very important in the treatment adopted, to

---

[*] See " Fractures."

guard as much as possible against secondary or inflammatory symptoms, which, should they arise, are to be treated as previously described.

HYDROCEPHALUS.

Hydrocephalus, or water on the brain, is by no means an unfrequent canine affection. It is invariably congenital, and is more particularly seen in high-bred dogs, and especially where the in-and-in system of breeding has been adopted. Several instances have come under my own observation, attributable, in my opinion, to the latter cause. In one or two cases absolute idiotcy existed: the animals performing absurd motions, and alike regardless of petting or scolding. They were diminutive black-and-tan toys, and, if I may be allowed the expression, were "*bred to death;*" destitute of hair on the ears and skull, the latter unsightly large; the eyes painfully prominent and expressionless; the body deficient in symmetry, and the limbs distorted. And some of the defects named were considered by the creatures' owners as indications of the purity of the strain; and animals of this type are kept, regardless of entreaties to destroy such insults to nature, for purposes of breeding. Fortunately, however, nature rarely sanctions issue from such parents.

Symptoms.—In addition to those I have named, paralysis is very frequently present, usually in the hind-limbs, which, in locomotion, are dragged after the animal. There is also often a great disposition to sleep; but it is generally disturbed by fitful starts and suppressed moans, and the eyelids during that period are only partially closed.

Treatment.—I have no remarks to offer on the treatment of canine hydrocephalus, beyond observing that the measures adopted in human practice—compression, puncturing, and the various medical agents—might be tried, and possibly with success, in those cases where exceptional reasons for saving animal life and removing the unnatural effects of the disease existed.

TURNSIDE.

This condition, commonly known in sheep as "Gid," is sometimes met with in the dog; but in the latter it is not so frequently due to the presence of hydatids as to other causes. The symptoms are not unlike those mentioned in the preceding disease, so far as the inclination to move in one direction and the paralytic associations are concerned. Youatt describes them as follows:

"He becomes listless, dull, off his food, and scarcely recognises any surrounding object. He has no fit; but he wanders about the room for several hours at a time, generally or almost invariably in the same direction, and with his head on one side. At first he carefully avoids the objects that are in his way; but by degrees his mental faculties become impaired; his sense of vision is confused or lost, and he blunders against everything. In fact, if uninterrupted, he would continue his strange perambulation incessantly, until he was fairly worn out and died in convulsions."

With regard to *post-mortem* examinations, he observes:

"In some cases I have found spicula projecting from the inner plate of the skull, and pressing upon or even penetrating the dura mater. I know not why the dog should be more subject to these irregularities of cranial surface than any of our other patients, but decidedly he is so; and where they have pressed upon the brain, there has been injection of the membranes. and sometimes effusion between them.

"In some cases I have found effusion without this external pressure; and in some cases, but comparatively few there has not been any perceptible lesion. Hydatids have been found in the different passages leading to the cranium, but they have not penetrated " (?).

MENINGITIS.

Meningitis, or inflammation of the coverings (meninges) of the brain, in which those enveloping the spinal cord generally become involved, is occasionally seen in the dog. It is usually associated with epilepsy, especially if the seizures are frequent and protracted. At the present time I have a well marked case under treatment, the subject being an aged colley sheep-dog.

The following were the symptoms presented on my first seeing him : eyes deficient in lustre and somewhat vacant lids frequently closed, head drooped, clonic spasm of the muscles of the lower jaw, the latter repeatedly closing with a sudden click. The animal always lay on the left side; when walking he inclined the same way; hurried, reeling locomotion, tongue loaded with fur, nose dry, hot and stuffy, excessive drowsiness with occasional spasmodic twitchings, pulse frequent and small, appetite moderately good, with a preference for liquids.

I inserted a seton at the back of the head, ordered milk diet, and prescribed

        Nux Vomica............................. ½ grain.
        Quinine Sulph. .... 1 grain.
        Ferri Sulph. .... 5 grians.

This was given in a dessert-spoonful of sherry, three times a day. The patient is slightly but daily improving under this treatment, and I have hopes of a recovery. He has now been three weeks ill, and a fortnight under treatment. A slight increase was made in the nux vomica recently.

M. Leblanc records the following case of meningitis in the " Veterinarian," 1843 :

"A dog, aged three years, was very subject to epileptic fits. After a considerable period the fits would cease. I have often seen these fits cease with the complete evolution of the adult teeth. The last fit was a very strong one, and was followed by peculiar symptoms—the animal became dispirited, the eyes lost their usual lively appearance, and the eyelids were often closed. The dog became very drowsy, and during sleep there were observed, from time to time, spasmodic movements, principally of the muscles of the head and chest. He always lay down on the left side. When he walked he had a marked propensity to turn to the left. The animal was placed under my care. I employed purgatives, a seton in the back part of the neck, and the application of the cautery to the left side of the forehead ; but nothing would stop the progress of the disease, and the dog died in the course of two months after the last epileptic fit.

"During his abode in my establishment, he had the run of the garden when it was fine weather. From the drowsiness that he manifested when he was shut up, he nearly always recovered himself when he had his liberty, and especially while his strength remained. He was constantly in motion, and perpetually walking up and down from right to left. This terminated by falling from mere weariness ; but he presently rose again and recommenced his travels, and always with a quick pace. Latterly he began to take a circular course instead of following that of the walks, which were rectangular : he then traversed the squares, totally regardless of, or not seeing, the obstacles that were in his way.

"When he was stopped by some obstacle, he at first endeavoured to make it give way ; but if it resisted his efforts in a circular direction he turned aside, but always to the left. The nearer he approached his end the smaller were the circles that he took, and, in the latter period of his existence, he did little more than turn, as he would on a pivot. When the time arrived that he could walk no more, he used to lay himself down on his left side, or, if we put him on the right side, he turned his head always to the left. During the whole of the case I did not observe any very evident signs of palsy. For a considerable period he had eaten with appetite; but nevertheless he grew thin from day to day, although he was too well fed by the owners, who continually crammed him with food, notwithstanding my efforts to prevent it.

At the *post-mortem* examination I found a remarkable thickening of the meninges on almost the whole of the left lobe of the brain.

The dura mater, the two layers of the arachnoid membrane, and the pia mater, did not constitute more than one membrane of the usual thickness, and presented a somewhat yellow covering. The cerebral substance of the left lobe appeared to be a little firmer than that of the right lobe.

"The fissures of the cerebral circumvolutions were here much less deep than those of the other side. The blood-vessels which ran in the fissures were of smaller size, and in some places could scarcely be discovered."

The following interesting case, recorded by Messrs. Gowing and Son, in the "Veterinarian" for May, 1870, may be classed under the head of meningeal disease :

"On the 2nd inst., our attendance was requested at Brook Street, Grosvenor Square, in respect of a white terrier dog, eighteen months old. The history of the case is as follows :

"The owner stated that the dog had been brought from Oxford, and that he had recently lost his vision. On examination it was found that the pupils of both eyes were somewhat dilated, and there was no power of recognising objects; the other special senses did not appear to be interfered with, as the dog recognised his master's voice, and would come to him when called; this he would do slowly and carefully, apparently using his sense of smell as his guide. The owner was asked if the animal had ever received a blow upon the head, and in reply he stated that he had reason to believe he had met with some injury in the stable, he thought from one of the horses. The owner had had the dog examined at Oxford, and afterwards brought him to London for our opinion. After the examination we felt satisfied that the dog was suffering from some diseased condition of the brain, and that his loss of vision was due to this cause. It was noticed that the dog was steady and cautious in his movements, turning neither to the right nor to the left, yet he seemed perfectly obedient to his master's call. For the purpose of treatment the dog was removed to our infirmary, and general depletive measures were used at first; mild doses of aperient medicine were given occasionally, and some improvement appeared to be produced, as the animal could, after a time, see with the left eye; he recognised his feeder, and ran after a cat that accidentally got into his box. This was so far satisfactory, as indicating that his sight had partially returned; he ate his food, and took fluids freely, but on the 15th inst., after his meal, he vomited, and seemed much prostrated. The attendant desired us to look at him, as he thought he was considerably worse; he was found lying on his left side, with the head protruded and the nose pointing upwards. There was a rigid condition of the muscles of the neck, the pulsation of the heart was feeble, and it was apparent that the animal's end was approaching. He died at five o'clock p.m."

Post-mortem Examination.—On removing the calvarium it was apparent that effusion had taken place into that part of the arachnoid sac which is reflected over the left hemisphere; a slight puncture, made by the saw while the bone was being removed, was followed by the forcible expulsion of pus-like fluid. The dura mater was dark-red in colour, and came way from the bone very easily; the inner surface of the portion under which the effusion had occurred was covered with a soft pulpy mass of pus and recently-exuded fibrin, which also was spread over the surface of the hemisphere. This portion of the brain was somewhat diminished in bulk, but no morbid appearances were observed in its structure; in the centre of the left corpus striatum a recent hæmorrhagic clot was found.

"Under the microscope the exudation was found to consist of ordinary inflammatory products, numerous pus corpuscles, large exudation corpuscles, fat granules, and fine white fibres."

DEMENTIA.

In April, 1883, a remarkable case of canine dementia came under the author's notice, which originated in the first sexual connection. The subject was a young well-bred Scotch colley dog, belonging to Mr. Charnock, of Wolverhampton, which the owner desired to mate with a maiden female of the same breed. The following day, after being together, cerebral disturbance was noticed in the dog, indicated by much the same symptoms as when the brain is involved in chorea. The pupils of the eyes were remarkably contracted. Ultimately the patient became perfectly blind, deaf, and dumb, and possessed very little feeling. The evacuations intestinal and urinal were involuntary. From a quick, intelligent, and lively dog, he speedily became a poor demented creature.

Almost immediately symptoms of cerebral mischief were observed, his method of locomotion altered, and he persisted in a slow shambling walk, with the back arched and the head down, round and round the loose box which he inhabited, in much the same manner as a tiger or hyæna, to the latter of which he was frequently likened by spectators. This he would do for hours at a stretch, sometimes to the right, sometimes to the left, but always never swerving from the beaten track, and always keeping close to the wall. When exhausted, he would fall on his side in an apparently comatose state, and after this had passed away the perambulations were recommenced, or if lifted up, he would start off again in a circle to the right or left as headed.

When fed, his nose had to be thrust into the food to induce him to eat, which he did in a lethargic mechanical kind of way without relish, or any corresponding good result, as he gradually became emaciated.

Seton's behind the ears, blisters, bromide of potassium, nux vomica, galvanism, and a variety of other measures were adopted in the treatment, but all in vain.

An eleven months' existence under the above conditions was nearly terminated by the dog himself, who was discovered one day breathless and apparently lifeless, with his head in a vessel of porridge, in the eating of which he had evidently fallen asleep. Artificial respiration and galvanism brought back vitality, but after this he lived only a few hours. Throughout the case the patient was visited by many members of the Medical and Veterinary Profession, and others interested in the matter.

After death I sent the head and spine to the Royal Veterinary College, without any examination of the brain or cord on my part, but extreme atrophy of the former (the organ being little larger than a walnut) was the chief report I received, nothing being assigned as the original cause of dementia or abeyance of the mental faculties.

That some severe shock or lesion occurred during coitus or immediately after is evident. I thought it possible an embolism or some obstruction in a cerebral artery might have been found.

As a singular coincidence, the bitch he had connection with proved barren, but at the period when parturition should have occurred, had conception taken place, she suddenly died, and a post-mortem examination revealed ovarian disease and metritis.

NOSTOMANIA.

Nostomania, or home sickness, is frequently demonstrated in dogs (especially those which have been much petted, and of toy breeds), when illness, accident, or other circumstances compel their removal to strange quarters and new guardians. Under such conditions they may become melancholic, refusing food, continually whining, restless, sleepless, and rapidly losing flesh.

Thorough kindness, tempting food, daily exercise if practicable, amusement, and constant companionship are the measures indicated in such a case. These failing, the patient should be returned home or to individuals it knows and likes.

It is the height of cruelty to place a tenderly reared dog, of affectionate disposition, and high nervous sensibility with a number of strange animals in a sick hospital.

There are dogs and dogs ; but pet dogs enjoy a peculiar distinction in the canine world. The lines of a pet dog usually fall in pleasant places : he is indulged (not always wisely) beyond his fellows ; and being, in the majority of instance, under the protection of a lady, he may be looked upon as an exceptionally lucky dog. No expense is spared, no time or trouble grudged, to make his short life pleasant ; and in the hour of sickness, care and attention, as that bestowed on a member of the human family (possibly more) is freely and affectionately exercised. Unfortunately, however, cases occur in which the removal of the animal to another sphere becomes necessary, and it is under such circumstances that nostomania is developed, the new and unpalatable surroundings having much to do with it. The treatment therefore of a pet dog thus removed should first be directed to a strict observance, so far as possible, of his usual comforts.

A kennel to a drawing-room dog is as a cell to a human being, under analogous conditions ; and the approach of an ordinary kennel attendant as that of a jailer. All indoor pet dogs should be received indoors, and not stacked away in the kennel, above kennel, or menagerie style, in close proximity to dogs of all degree, and tortured or excited by their continual snarls, yelpings, or whines.

Secondly, to treat a pet dog, especially with a disposition to nostomaniacal melancholia, real affection for the canine species is necessary; assumed affection will not answer. No animal so readily detects and appreciates kindness in man as the dog, or as quickly discovers his assumed affection. A piece of sugar to a spoilt child is not the bait to quiet and assure a timid and sensitive dog. The clean sawdust or cushion on the day of visiting will not atone for the lack of improvement in health, or diminish the wild delight of the patient on seeing his mistress.

Thirdly, a tenderly handled dog requires tenderly handling, and doubly so when invalid. A caressed dog invites caressing; and, under pain, soothing words and gentle treatment are more appreciated than, perhaps, any measures the attendant can adopt. Finally, to go thoroughly into the treatment of pet dogs, the attendant must go thoroughly into the usual home life of the animal, its disposition and peculiarities, and enter into the feelings of its owner. Everything must be ascertained that is likely to add to its comfort or discomfort, its pain or alleviation; and no one but a genuine dog-lover can do this. The same argument will apply to the nurse: see "General Management," Chap. I.

NEURALGIA.

Mr. Fleming has kindly given me the following particulars of an interesting case which came under his care:

"An Irish setter, three or four years old, very fond of the water, which she went into all seasons, summer and winter, was sent to me for my opinion. Her master complained that at night, and even during the day, she was seized with fits of howling and screaming, and appeared to be suffering most acute pain. I examined the mouth carefully for decayed teeth, the ears for canker, etc., but nothing could be found the matter with her in these respects. When being led away she suddenly gave a piercing howl, bent her head round to the right side, as if suffering from earache or toothache. She gradually rose up on her hindlegs, fell backwards, and lay howling for a considerable time. Another examination was made, but nothing could be discovered to account for the peculiar symptoms. The animal was perfectly conscious throughout.

"Surmising the case to be one of tic-douloureux or neuralgia, I had a blister applied from the root of the ear along the right side of the face, and a dose of castor-oil administered. The symptoms continued for two or three days. Twice a day a little extract of belladonna was rubbed on the blistered surface. In about a week the animal was quite well, and there has since been no return of the symptoms."

CHAPTER XVII.

GENERAL DISEASES.

ABSCESS,	RICKETS,
TUMOURS,	OSTITIS,
CANCER,	PERIOSTITIS,
BRONCHOCELE,	SCROFULA,
DIPHTHERIA,	GLANDERS,
DISTEMPER,	SMALL-POX,
MALIGNANT DISTEMPER,	MEASLES,
DROPSY,	TETANUS,
LEUKÆMIA,	CRAMP,
ANÆMIA,	HEART DISEASES,
MARASMUS,	PERICARDITIS,
PLETHORA,	EMBOLISM,
OBESITY,	EMPHYSEMA.
RHEUMATISM,	

ABSCESS.

AN *abscess* signifies an encysted collection of pus, *i. e.*, a quantity of matter enclosed in a newly-formed cyst or capsule.

An abscess may be external or internal, acute or chronic.

External abscess may exist on any portion of the body, and be superficial or deep-seated.

Internal abscesses are frequently associated with a phthisical or scrofulous diathesis, hence *pneumonic*, *hepatic*, and *mesenteric* abscess.

Or they may exist independently of such diatheses, and arise from acute inflammatory diseases, blood-poisoning, wounds, and the like, and any of the internal organs become the seat of their formation.

Glandular structures are especially liable to abscess, and from the complexity of blood-vessels surrounding them, this is not to be wondered at.

Symptoms.—The early symptoms of external abscess are pain, heat, redness, and swelling. As the formation proceeds, the enlargement becomes more or less œdematous on its surface, from the exudation of serum external to, and surrounding the cyst, and this causes it to pit on pressure.

The abscess enlarges as it develops, the pain increases, and throbbing or "jumping" is felt on placing the fingers on the part. As the pus approaches the surface, fluctuation is perceived, the surrounding parts become glazed and discoloured, while the point to which the matter is tending for exit becomes thin and colourless.

Treatment.—The primary treatment of abscess consists in encouraging a speedy formation of pus, and this is usually effected by the application of poultices, hot fomentations, or stimulating liniments.

When the abscess has arrived at what is vulgarly termed "a head," which may be known by the symptoms alluded to in its latter stage of development, evacuation by incision should at once take place. A poultice may afterwards be applied, or the sac syringed out with tepid water.

The customary practice of squeezing is strongly objectionable; it increases the inflammatory condition of the part, and inflicts additional and unnecessary torture on the patient.

It is advisable, to prevent secondary abscess, that the incision be kept open for a few days by the insertion of a tent of lint or tow, or the injection of a little stimulating liniment.

Usually, more or less febrile disturbance accompanies the formation of acute abscess, and it is advisable, therefore, at the onset, to administer a mild aperient. Again, it must be borne in mind that abscesses, especially if they are of any magnitude, or diffused, are exceedingly debilitating—full support in the shape of nourishing food and tonics (iron) are thus indicated.

Chronic Abscess is comparatively slow in development, and is usually seen in old animals, and those of feeble or weak constitution.

Such abscesses are generally large and deep-seated, and considerable emaciation usually accompanies them.

Treatment.—Evacuation by incision, as in the acute form, is, if practicable, decidedly advisable. Where, however, the situation renders opening dangerous, and the abscess is small, discussion should be attempted by the application of a stimulant to absorption over the part, and the administration of a similar agent internally. The tincture of iodine for the former, and the iodide of potassium for the latter, are the agents most frequently and beneficially used.

Attention to the general condition of the system, especially to the secretions, is also necessary. The food should be plain, wholesome and nutritious.

Internal Abscess can rarely be treated by surgical means. The symptoms are usually discovered, if in the lungs, by auscultation, nasal discharge, and the nature of the expectoration; if in the uterus, by the discharge of pus per vaginam; if in the kidney, by heat and pain over the loins and difficulty in voiding urine, which is at times mingled with pus.

The symptoms of hepatic abscess are extremely obscure—the usual indications of deranged liver are invariably present, and there is excessive pain on pressure to the right side, which the animal avoids lying on.

TUMOURS.

These may be divided into *fatty, fibrous, calcareous, osseous,* and *melanotic.*

Fatty Tumours are of common occurrence in dogs,

especially of the spaniel breed. Their situation is generally subcutaneous; I have removed them from the cheek, back, side, thigh, and axilla.

They possess a very low organisation unless injured, when they will become inflamed—though this is a very rare occurrence in the dog.

Their growth is usually slow, and dependent, to a great extent, on the condition of the patient; in other words, these tumours being composed of adipose tissue, they increase in proportion to the obesity or development of this tissue in other parts of the animal.

Diagnosis is generally simple. The substance is smooth, movable, and unattached, and pressure produces no pain.

Treatment.—Excision, which in all cases may be safely and successfully adopted. One long incision, nearly the length of the substance, is made, the skin reflected back, and there being nothing but areolar tissue to divide, the tumour is easily and quickly removed from its bed. The lips of the incision are then drawn together with silk sutures, and the part afterwards may be treated as a common wound.

Fibrous Tumours.—These occasionally come under the notice of the canine surgeon. They usually proceed from injuries, and are chiefly found in connection with the jaws or limbs.

Diagnosis.—They have a firm attachment, are irregular in surface, hard, and insensible to pressure.

Treatment.—Excision is most advisable; but from the tumour frequently being adherent to the integument, it is not so easily accomplished as in the previous kind.

On examination after removal the tumour will generally be found to be composed of a cyst (Fibro-cystic),* filled

---

* In the *Veterinary* for January, 1871, Messrs. Gowing & Son record a case of cystic tumour in the lumbar region of an aged spaniel dog, which they removed by excision. "The tumour presented several peculiar features; its walls were principally composed of white fibrous

with serous fluid; and it sometimes happens during life, from inflammation being created in the substance of the tumour, that this cystic fluid becomes purulent, the sac ruptures, and degenerates into a common, unhealthy, sub-acute abscess. Excision is, even under the circumstances, still advisable; for even if we get it healed, and the tumour still remains, absorption is out of the question. Fibro-cystic tumour is usually present in "capped elbows." Removal by excision is simple, and is followed by no ill effects. When they occur in connection with the hocks it is more advisable to use outward applications. I have found iodine the best agent.

Calcareous Tumour.—This description of tumour is most frequently found in the vicinity of glands. In the dog, it is generally seen in connection with the fibrous tumour of the mammary gland. In long-existing cases, the latter is often entirely supplanted by the former.

Treatment.—As in the two former, excision is the only

---

tissue, intermixed with a few fibres of yellow elastic tissue. Besides the cyst which Mr. Gowing punctured, there was another of equal size which contained about four ounces of fluid, having the appearance of pus slightly tinged with blood. This fluid, under the microscope, was found to contain a large quantity of cholesterine, with exudation—corpuscles and blood-discs. In the interior of the cyst which was last opened, there was a small detached tumour of the size of a chestnut, smooth on the surface, and quite firm in texture. To the interior of the walls of the two cysts were attached small tumours, varying in size from a pea to a hazel-nut, and on the surface of the lining of the cysts a quantity of flocculent white matter was deposited."

Three accompanying microscopic illustrations are given, to convey an idea of the structure of the morbid growths, which were all composed of the same elements. It is further observed: "It is obvious that the morbid growth originated in disease of the structures of the true skin, probably the result of an injury."

I recently removed a fibro-cystic tumour the size of a hazel-nut from a fore-toe of a small black-and-tan terrier. Placing a ligature round close to its attachment, I drew it sufficiently tight to sever it at once; the hæmorrhage, which was excessive for the situation, I stayed with cautery.

advisable treatment, except when the deposit takes place in situations other than the mammary gland, and where it would be impossible, with safety, to use the knife. Counter-irritation, or the daily application of iodine, would then be indicated, but absorption in such cases is hopeless.

Osseous Tumours.—These are of comparatively rare occurrence in the dog. When seen, they are usually found in connection with the limbs, more especially about the hocks and knees,* and are generally associated with the disease called "rickets," for the treatment of which see "Rickets."

Melanotic Tumour.—Melanosis is, I believe, an unrecorded, if not almost an unknown, disease in the dog. To Mr. Fleming I am indebted for the following particulars of an interesting case which came under his own notice:

"A large, black, well-bred setter was brought to me for advice, with regard to a swelling on the back part of his fore-leg. The skin was very much thickened from the elbow to near the carpus, and destitute of hair. The en-

---

* At the present time I have a patient, a mastiff, under my care, with an enormous osseous tumour of honeycomb or cancelled structure, surrounding the lower end of the radius. Though the knee-joint is not involved, yet the foot is comparatively useless, being greatly swollen, benumbed, and dangling, owing to the pressure by the tumour on the structures above. The friction of, or injury by, the chain, is supposed to have been the original cause of the disease. Prior to my advice being sought, it had been under the treatment of other veterinary surgeons, without any successful results. For the first ten days I had applied, externally, absorbents and hot fomentations; in the softest portions I lanced it, and there was discharged from the two openings made, a thin bloody fluid, not offensive, and containing no pus. The probe came in contact everywhere with rough, spongy bone. The fomentations are continued, with an occasional injection of a strong solution of nitrate of silver. Iron and iodine are administered twice daily, and the food is of a substantial nature. The poor creature is much emaciated, but is now slightly improving, and the pain and swelling have abated. An entire removal of the deposit is, of course, out of the question, but I have good hopes of prolonging the animal's life, and rendering him useful.

largement was movable and soft. As it was too extensive to remove without blemishing the dog considerably, and as it did not cause any pain or inconvenience, I deemed it advisable to let it alone. In a week or ten days afterwards, my farrier-major brought me a portion of a dog's lung, which he said was obtained from this setter, it having suddenly died the day before. The surface of the lung was covered with round, soft, globular masses, as black as ink, varying in size from a millet-seed to a large pea. He had opened the dog, and stated that he found the swelling on the leg full of black matter. The liver, heart, other portions of the lungs, and beneath the skin over the body, were all in the same condition as the portion of lung which he brought to me. Examination of the latter proved that the deposits were of a melanotic nature, and no doubt had been the cause of death."

I have at the present time, 1888, a melanotic subject under treatment, a young black retriever. The tumour, which is mulberry-like, has continually for some time past broken out, the discharge being like thick tarry ink. The deposit is situated on the withers between the shoulders. I purpose removing it by excision.*

CANCER.

The same varieties of cancer exist in the dog as occur in the human being. Scirrhous and encephaloid are the most prominent forms met with in canine practice. I have met, however, with cases of melanoid, osteoid, and gum cancer.

Cancer of the mammary gland has already been mentioned in chapter xi., though the majority of such so-called cases are spurious. I have, since writing that section, had several decided illustrations of true cancer growth in connection with the mammæ. Amongst the cases I have recorded, there will be found an interesting one in the

---

* This I have since accomplished successfully.

Veterinary Journal for February, 1880, the subject being the deerhound bitch "Teilda." On making a section of the growth I removed, which weighed over half-a-pound, the scirrhous type of cancer, in both stages, *hard and soft*, was found to be well marked—the former in the centre, the latter towards its circumference. The external appearance of the cancerous gland, before operation, was glazed, tense, and of a varied livid hue. In several places it was puckered, and the nipple retracted. There were three fistulous wounds, from which a thin offensive discharge issued. In 1886 I operated on two very typical cases from Hastings and Battle, but, in both instances, secondary growths elsewhere took place.

Cancer frequently invades the canine liver. A case (encephaloid) involving the liver and spleen of a retriever dog, nine years old, is recorded by the author in the *Veterinary Journal* for June, 1880. Also another very remarkable case in the *Live Stock Journal* for July 13th, 1883 ; the subject being a pointer, nine years old, in which death occurred from embolism of the posterior vena cava. A post-mortem examination revealed, amongst other complications, large deposits of medullary cancer in the liver. In making this autopsy, I had the misfortune to become inoculated on the forefinger of the right hand, and had a narrow escape from death.

Two cases of melanoid cancer will be found under the heading of " Melanosis."

Osteoid cancer (osteo sarcoma) is most frequently met with in the bones of the fore-arm. I have had two well-marked cases in my hospital practice, the one subject being a mastiff dog, bred by myself, the other a St. Bernard bitch. In both instances the radius, ulna, and carpal bones were involved, an enormous mass of honeycomb-like osseous deposit being especially thrown out on the radius. These cases, with full particulars, are recorded in the *Veterinary Journal*. Amputation might successfully have been adopted, in either subject, at an earlier period; but, when admitted to my hospital, the disease was too far advanced, and secondary deposits had occurred elsewhere.

Gum cancer is somewhat exceptional in the canine race; and, when it occurs, is generally associated with alveolar disease, bad teeth, or necrosis of the jaw.

BRONCHOCELE.

Bronchocele, Thyrocele, or goitre, an enlargement of the thyroid glands on one or both sides, is commonly met with in every breed of dogs. The cause of this glandular enlargement is somewhat doubtful. Animals in a debilitated condition appear most liable to it, while, on the other hand, those in robust health will become affected.

The anatomical formation of the neck and throat would seem to have some predisposing influence ; for short, thick-necked, throaty dogs are those, according to my experience, most frequently the subject of this disease.

Symptoms.—Bronchocele may come on insidiously or suddenly; hence we hear of dogs, to use a common expression, with " kernels" in the throat, which have been observed there for some time, but become no larger. Others are discovered to have an immense swelling at the throat, which was undetectable the previous day.

In cases where the thyroid enlargement is considerable, difficulty in breathing will be one of the prominent symptoms: this arises from pressure by these enlarged glands on the trachea, which also cause much inconvenience to the neighbouring structures, as the throat and vessels of the neck, creating obstructed circulation and difficulty in swallowing.

Treatment.—Our object in the treatment of bronchocele is to arrest growth and promote absorption. Iodine, externally and internally, is the most powerful remedy for this purpose. In the former, after first shaving off the hair, the liniment or tincture should be painted on with a brush daily. In the latter it is best combined with iron (ferri iodidum) in 5 to 10 grain doses daily.

When suppuration takes place, which in the dog is not unfrequent, the ordinary treatment for abscess is indicated.

Extirpation of the thyroid gland or the insertion of setons are dangerous operations, and only warranted in extreme cases.

The following interesting case may be useful :—On the 24th September, 1885, I received a telegram to attend a Dandie Dinmont Dog, at Chetwynd Park, Newport, Salop, the property of Sidney Burton Borough, Esq., which upon my arrival I found to be suffering severely from double bronchocele; the pressure of the enlargement, which involved both sides of the neck, being so great as to have almost prevented respiration: indeed, suffocation was so imminent that only by prompt, active, and persistent measures was relief afforded. I applied hot linseed-meal poultices every hour throughout the night, supporting my patient in the meantime with frequent small quantities of beef-tea and brandy, cautiously administered on account of the difficulty of deglutition. At 8 a.m. I detected a little softening on the right side, and, as it was evident the dog could not survive the ordinary process of maturity in the abscess, I inserted the needle of a sub-cutaneous injection syringe, and drew out nearly an ounce of dirty-coloured, partially formed pus. This gave considerable relief, and the breathing became freer. I then enlarged the opening, and ordered the poultices continued, with strengthening diet, including stimulants, cod-liver oil, and Parish's chemical food. By request I paid a second visit on the 29th, when I found the wound still discharging, but with considerable glandular enlargement, and surrounding hardness. I advised painting with iodine, and previous treatment to be continued, watching my patient carefully throughout the night.

A note of anxiety called me again to Chetwynd Park on the 5th of October, but, beyond enlargement of the lymphatics down the neck, and some remaining induration of the tumour, with external soreness due to the poultices and iodine, I found no immediate cause for alarm. Zinc ointment was applied on lint and iodide of potassium prescribed. On the 10th I received a most anxious letter from the owner, in which he abandoned all hope of saving the dog—a relapse having occurred—attributed to a chill on going out of doors in damp grass for the first time. I telegraphed treatment, and advised his admission to my hospital, which was promptly obeyed, and on the 12th his owner brought him to Hastings; the wound was still suppurating, and considerable lymphatic enlargements existed, with throbbing of the vessels. The surface of the skin was weeping, and extremely sensitive. Zinc ointment was applied for a few days, and subsequently iodine, and under careful regime, with exercise on the sea front, the patient made a perfect recovery, and left me in good health and spirits on the 18th November, to the delight of his master, who came for him,—and my own satisfaction. In these glandular diseases I am persuaded the sea coast is most beneficial, whilst severe cases of rheumatism and eczema have left my hospital here in a far shorter space of time than when I resided in the Midlands.

In the early treatment of bronchocele, the arrestment of growth and promotion of absorption is very important. Unfortunately, however, the case just described had been wrongly diagnosed, by the previous attendant, as having arisen from a blow: hence the aggravation and complications which had followed, and so nearly proved fatal. Few, indeed, would have gone to the trouble, expense, and exercised the patience of the humane owner of this dog "Sandy;" in fact it is worthy of note that for three weeks he sat up himself nightly with his favourite, and performed personally all the offices necessary: giving another example of the value of good nursing in disease.

DIPHTHERIA.

Among the laryngeal diseases affecting the dog diphtheria (so-called) finds a place. As I have not seen any throat malady that could be correctly termed such, myself, I transcribe from the *Veterinary Journal* for August, 1875, some interesting cases recorded by Mr. W. Robertson, M.R.C.V.S., Kelso ; subsequently Principal of the Royal Veterinary College.

"In the outbreak of diphtheria amongst the dogs, a certain amount of variation or modification, as respects the phenomena exhibited during the course of the development of the disease, was observed in several of the individuals.

"The dogs amongst which this outbreak occurred formed part of a kennel of high-bred greyhounds. The kennel was in two divisions ; the exercise-yard of the one division running to within two yards of the door of the dormitory of the other, which had originally been a stable, and where all the cases of the disease occurred. The inmates of this kennel were a mixed lot as regarded age ; one half were puppies about twelve months old, the other half consisted in greater part of dogs between eighteen and twenty-four months, with a few aged animals. There had been no importation of animals for some time, and no illness, not even distemper, amongst the residents. The disease first made its appearance amongst the puppies, and nearly the whole, if not the whole, of these were dead before any of the others were seized. Many of the puppies had died before alarm was taken, the kennel-man imagining that they were suffering from distemper ; at last suspicion was aroused, and, as usual when any considerable mortality occurs amongst animals, which is rather puzzling to those engaged in their management, poison administered maliciously, or obtained accidentally, was credited with the mortality. An analysis, however, of the viscera of two animals negatived this idea. The average duration of the disease in those fatal cases was a little over two days; many died earlier, and none survived beyond the fourth day.

"With the exception of the glands of the throat and cervical region, the structural alterations observable in all cases may be said to have been confined to the fauces and the air passages anterior to the glottis. The urine, in all the instances where this secretion was examined, was opaque, increased in density, and charged with albumen.

" In some cases, from the outset, the fever was high, the local inflammatory action markedly acute, the mucous membrane over the fauces, tonsils and palate became of a dark-red colour, tense, smooth, and glistening in appearance, apparently from distension from infiltration of the submucous tissue. In these also the whole gland-structures of the mouth and throat were more or less swollen and tender, with deglutition from the first extremely difficult or altogether impossible. The earliest stages were marked by exaltation of temperature, accelerated pulse and respirations, together with slight restlessness, if not actually giving evidence of pain; very shortly, however, these signs of increased functional activity disappeared, there was marked depression, listlessness, and want of muscular energy; emesis and diarrhœa might also be present.

"The majority of the cases were of this type, and they were also those which succumbed the quickest, death in them seeming to result as much from the extension of the local diseased action into the larynx as from the virulence of the septikæmia.

"*Post-mortem* examination of these cases showed that,

only when the animals had survived more than twenty-four hours was there observable anything in the form of the peculiar and characteristic grey coagulated exudation; this being sometimes in spots, and at others in considerable stripes, but always adherent to the mucous membrane.

"More frequently the exudation, which was always present, was a glossy, tenacious, soft, structureless, or granular material, more thickly deposited on some parts than others.

"Another form or type in which the disease manifested itself was that where the febrile disturbance seemed scarcely so severe, the extension of the local diseased action less rapid, and the power of swallowing never entirely gone ; but where the glands of the throat and cervical region were early swollen, and increased in size rapidly, together with extensive infiltration of the connective tissue in which these gland-structures are embedded. In such there was from the first marked stiffness of the neck and greater restlessness until coma supervened.

"A third class, again, exhibited what may most fitly be termed the 'nasal type.' After a certain amount of dulness, and fever of a lower character than was met with in either of the other forms mentioned, there would appear evident sore throat, with a discharge of a sanious material from the nostrils. On examining the mouth, material of a similar nature, but more watery from mingling with the saliva, might be seen bubbling over the tongue from the fauces. Cases of this form survived longest ; and in them only did we find sordes on the teeth and lips, the breath becoming fœtid and the lymphatic glands much swollen. The after-death examination of these showed that the disease had extended—whether from continuity or separate centres was impossible to say—into the posterior nasal channels.

"The infiltration, however, of the submucous tissue and exudate, in connection with the membrane, was always most distinctive in the pharynx and at the pillars of the soft palate. Of the few affected animals which survived, one, while recovering, became blind of both eyes, with, at first, no appreciable structural alteration of the organs, although in a few days the cornea of both became opaque, apparently from infiltration of the intimate structures of the membrane; ultimately, sight was restored.

"Another, about a fortnight after the obvious symptoms of the disease had disappeared, became affected with clonic spasms, or twitching of the muscles of the face and cervical region, followed in a few days by paraplegia. After a tedious convalescence, this animal also regained full nervous power.

, "Being satisfied regarding the nature of the disease, we counselled the removal of all those dogs housed in the kennel as yet uncontaminated; and the shifting of such as were still, to appearance, healthy from the kennel where the disease had arisen to this one, vacated by the unaffected. Immediately following this, the drains of the place were ordered to be examined, as the sanitary condition was the opposite of satisfactory. On being laid open, these were found all but completely choked with filth, the more fluid portions of the sewage having for some time been percolating into the soil beneath the flooring of the kennel, rather than discharged in the natural or proper manner.

"The principal drain, I may mention, had a communication with the dormitory portion of the kennel, by means of an ordinary perforated grating. This kennel had no communication by means of its drains with the other, which, as already mentioned, was in close proximity, and where the dogs continued healthy.

"The dogs removed from the uncontaminated kennel were placed in a stable a mile distant, and continued healthy.

"Among those taken from the kennel where the disease originated, and located in the other, three fresh cases occurred after their removal, one of which died.

"After removing the flooring and opening the drains, it was deemed advisable, considering the condition of the walls of the house, not to repair it, but to build another on a different site. After a considerable time, both the new kennel and the one which remained, and into which the dogs from the old one had been removed, were again occupied; and with no bad results, the disease having ceased a few days after the kennel where it first appeared had been vacated.

"I have purposely refrained from commenting upon, or drawing any conclusions from these facts; or attempting to enter upon the question of the etiology of diphtheria: whether we are in all cases to regard it as the result of the reception into the animal body of contagion, living, particulate, and specific—a true '*mycosis*,'—or, in many cases, to revert to our knowledge of chemistry and chemical laws for an explanation of the different phenomena.

"Circumstances which have occurred, and conditions which have been observed, have been stated, in the hope that possibly some inquirer in this particular path of research may find these facts, when collated with others, helpful in shedding a light over what at the present, in some of its aspects, is rather obscure."

In a leading article in the same journal, on "The Transmissibility of Diphtheria from Man to the Lower Animals," it is remarked: "We have no strong proof that croup or diphtheria is contagious in animals, except the first-named disease, which is so in poultry.

"The relations of diphtheria in animals to the same disease in mankind have only been recently definitely established; while the transmission of the malady from one species to another has been satisfactorily demonstrated. There are certainly no proofs that any relationship exists between the malady termed 'distemper' in the dog and diphtheria, though on occasions they may have prevailed coincidently in a district.

"Thus, in 1851 or 1852, a severe outbreak of the latter disease occurred in Tasmania, which swept off two or three members in every family; at the same time, according to the report of the Australian Royal Commission on Diphtheria, all the dogs died of distemper. There may have been some morbid influence at work which favoured the genesis and extension while it added to the virulency of both scourges; but beyond this we cannot at present go, for if we remember aright, dogs perished about the same time in great numbers from distemper in New Zealand and Australia—even the dingoes, or native wild dogs, being found dead in multitudes in the scrub; and yet we cannot ascertain that diphtheria was at all prevalent, or even present, in these countries at that period.

"To our knowledge, there is only one instance of a case in which accidental transmission of the disease from man to an inferior animal appears likely to have occurred, and this is alluded to by Dr. Sir J. Rose Cormack, in the *Lancet* for April 24th of the present year. It is related by Professor Bossi in the 'Giornale di Medicina Veterinaria Pratica d'Agricoltura,' and is to the following effect: 'A friend who had lost a child by diphtheria, after a few days' illness, requested me to visit a very beautiful small-breed greyhound about one year old, which had become unwell a few days after swallowing some of the child's excreta, and some remains of food which had been served to him. On making a careful examination of the dog, Bossi found it in a state of great prostration; languid look, lachrymant eyes, and open mouth copiously discharging a viscid fluid; quick sibilant breathing, hoarse voice, full, hard, rapid pulse; the neck so stretched as to be almost rigid; and difficulty in deglutition. By digital examination, the throat was discovered to be œdematous, and the seat of severe pain. On opening the mouth—a difficult operation—the mucous membrane of the fauces was seen to be red and swollen, and two ulcers were on the veil of the

VILLAGE GOSSIPS.

palate and right tonsil ; that on the latter was of some size and depth, and had an elevated border.' The symptoms and appearances in this case led Bossi to conclude that the animal was suffering from diphtheria, or perhaps more correctly speaking, from laryngo-pharyngeal angina of pseudo-membranous or croupal character. The dog died on the third day, from suffocation, after having had some convulsive movements. At the necropsy, the mucous membrane of the fauces was found in a pulpy condition and denuded of epithelium. Here and there the membranous exudation presented the appearance of compact thick, adherent excrescences. The ulcerations were blackish and very deep. The inflammation extended to the mucous membrane of the pharynx and larynx. The heart and lungs, which presented a blackish, flabby appearance, contained pitch-like blood and several fibro-albuminous concretions.

"This is a remarkable case, and one well worth remembering by members of the veterinary profession, many of whom have a great deal of practice among dogs ; animals which, from their intimate association with mankind, and from their habits and tastes, would be the most likely to receive the contagion, if it be really transmissible.

" Experimental evidence as to the transmissibility of diphtheria from man to animals is not very abundant, but it appears to be sufficiently clear to enable careful pathologists to come to a decision ; as several have concluded, from the results of their attempts to produce the disease in animals, that the morbid process generated in these by inoculating portions of diphtheritic concretion is not simply what has been designated a 'mycosis,' but is, in reality, the specific malady itself. In his report on the ' Pathology of the Infective Processes,' just published in that of the Medical Officer of the Privy Council, Dr. Burdon Sanderson gives a *résumé* of the experiments made by the principal of these pathologists.

x

"Of these observers, Dr. Sanderson points out that Dr. Letzerich,* of Braunfels (Nassau), and Dr. Oertel,† of Munich, are most important. The former is the author of several papers on diphtheria, the titles of which are given in a note. These papers contain various observations relating to diphtheria as it presents itself clinically, and serve to illustrate the intimate association of the development of microzymes in the affected parts with the morbid process; the author also records numerous experiments showing that when the disease is communicated by inoculation, its characteristics reappear in the infected animal, even those which belong to its more remote complications.

" Dr. Letzerich's facts lose much of their value, according to Sanderson, from their not being set down with that simplicity which ought to characterise all scientific writings. His papers, moreover, contain a great deal of questionable mycology, in which the patient reader is apt to lose himself in his search after objective facts.

" The Mémoire of Dr. Oertel, published three years ago, also embodies anatomical and experimental investigations relating to the effect of inoculating animals with material derived from the larynx in cases of diphtheritic laryngitis in children. Like Letzerich, the author found that a disease having well-defined pathological characteristics, and in particular, associated with nephritis, could be produced by such inoculation; and further, that it could be communicated from one animal to another without losing any of its distinctive features. He further showed that the disease in question, whatever were the local peculiarities given to it by the tissue in which it was ingrafted, was always a mycosis; in other words, that all the 'localisations' of the

---

* Letzerich, " Beiträge zur Kenutnisf der Diphtheritis," " Virchow's Archiv.," vols. xlv. p. 327; xlvi. p. 229; xlvii. p. 516. "Monographie der Diphtherie," Berlin, 1872. "Die Entwickelung des Diphtheriepilzes," " Virchow's Archiv.," vol. lviii. p. 303 (1873).

† Oertel, " Experimentelle Untersuchungen über Diphtherie;" "Deutsches Archiv. für Klin. Med.," vol. viii. pp. 242—354.

disease were associated with the presence in the affected part of innumerable microzymes. As regards the agents of infection, he concluded that their presence was the only constant characteristic of the contagion, for he found that the disease could be produced by the transference to the tissues of a healthy animal of even the smallest fragment of any diseased tissue, and that all diseased tissues contained microzymes in greater or less numbers."

After giving a short account of a series of experiments, in which the disease was transmitted through five successions of animals, the first inoculative material being taken from a child twelve hours after death, the article proceeds to observe :

"In 'Virchow's Archiv.' for April of the present year (p. 178), Letzerich relates an interesting case, in which diphtheria was transmitted to a child through the medium of vaccine lymph ; and he also gives the details of an important test experiment, in which a dog was inoculated with vaccine matter that had been mixed with a small proportion of matter from a diphtheritic mass removed from the tonsils of a child that had died of the disease ; this was supposed to contain the active organisms of the affection *(Diptherie organismus)*. The dog was inoculated on the left side of the body, near the spine, by eleven points, and three punctures, and four wounds. On the third day a soft swelling was observed, and the skin was red and hot ; the wounds were gaping, indurated, and covered with a whitish, doughy-looking exudate. The swelling, it may be mentioned, continued until the dog died. The inoculation points were also somewhat gaping, and in the same condition as the wounds and punctures. From the third day the dog lost its appetite, and there was noted an important and considerable periodical increase of temperature. From the seventh day it would eat nothing ; the pulse was small and exceedingly quick, and the respiration hurried ; the animal lay on its side, and in this condition died.

" On an examination of the body, it was discovered that in the swollen baggy part of the skin where the inoculations had been made, there was fibrous infiltration of the subcutaneous connective tissue, with hæmorrhagic patches of a bluish-black or dirty light-red colour, that passed deep into the muscles of the back. In the abdominal muscles attached to the spine, as well as in the peritoneum, there were also a few isolated patches, generally running into each other in an irregular manner. In the connective tissue of this region were many marked hæmorrhagic patches, and they were all related more or less to others in the connective tissue surrounding the left kidney. This organ exhibited on the infero-external portion, which was in contact with the lumbar region, a circular, eroded, hæmorrhagic spot, about the size of a rather large pea. The liver was reddish-brown in colour, and very much enlarged and indurated. The spleen was also enlarged, very full of blood, and its parenchyma softened. The heart was softened, and its texture very light-coloured. The lungs were healthy, but the stomach and intestines were somewhat swollen; the stomach was empty, and the small intestines nearly so; the large intestines contained a quantity of fluid fæces, but no scybala. The right lumbar region was normal, and the right kidney large and light-coloured. The bladder contained a small quantity of muddy urine.

" A colleague of Dr. Letzerich made a most careful and interesting histological examination of the body, and found at the seat of inoculation, in the wedge-shaped exudate formed at the punctures and wounds, bacteria and plasma-globules (*plasma-kugeln*) closely agglomerated, the latter being in a finely granular condition. In a prepared section of the skin it was noted that the sheaths of the hair in various parts were full of bacteria, micrococci vesicles, and plasma-globules. In the texture of the skin itself were numerous masses of bacteria and plasma-globules, as well as clusters of micrococci. In the vicinity of those muscles which were stained by hæmorrhagic patches, the capillaries were distended, and contained the same abnormal elements; these were also seen in the connective tissue of these parts, as well as between the nerve-bundles and muscular fibres. In the interior of the capillaries of the hæmorrhagic patches themselves, between the masses of red blood-globules, were immense colonies of micrococci; the same condition was observed in the peritoneum and its connective tissue. The muscular fibrillæ were scarcely distinguishable in these patches, and their meshes were enormously distended by escaped red blood-globules and an extraordinary number of colonies of micrococci, with an exuberance of plasma-globules.

"In the round hæmorrhagic spot on the left kidney, and for some depth in its substance, were masses of red blood-globules and clustering rows of wandering micrococci. All the tubules of the gland were filled with exudate, in which bacteria and plasma-globules were seen in great quantities. In the right kidney the migratory vegetable organisms (*wandering pilzen*) were observed to be in their first stage of development. Not a part of the liver that was examined but contained the retrograde vegetable formations; all the cells were filled with them. Between the fibres of the heart were only discovered layers of plasma-globules and bacteria; but many of the smaller veins were filled with colonies of micrococci which adhered to their walls. The spleen was in the same condition as the liver; indeed, the reporter states that it was only an emulsion of cells, cell-debris (*trümmern*), nuclei, bacteria, small micrococci, and a diversity of large plasma-globules. The pulmonary blood-vessels contained the characteristic diphtheria organisms (*diphtheriepilzes*); in one portion of the parenchyma of the lungs was found a small micrococci ecchymosis.

"All these alterations are well illustrated by coloured drawings.

"From the case of accidental transmission of diphtheria

through vaccination, and this experimental conveyance of the malady to a dog, Letzerich draws the following conclusions. 1. Vaccine matter which has passed through a diphtheritic subject, and become tainted, will not produce a vaccine pustule at the place where it was inserted. 2. That lymph so tainted, when introduced by inoculation, speedily gives rise to general diphtheria. From the obvious results of the experimental case in particular, it may be concluded : (1.) That inoculation with lymph which has not been tainted with diphtheritic organisms will, in a given time, and in a normal manner, give rise to the well-known pustules ; and (2.) On the contrary, that the local diphtheria of an inoculation wound is followed by general diphtheria, as a secondary process.

"Whether the diphtheria of the lower animals is intertransmissible, or whether it may be communicable to the human species, we have no evidence to base even a supposition upon ; but there can scarcely be any reason for hesitation in accepting the fact that another malady is added to the list of those which are at least capable of being conveyed from man to creatures lower in the scale of creation. This new addition furnishes another proof of the value of comparative pathology, and the close relations which exist between animal and human medicine."

DISTEMPER.

Probably no disease to which our canine friends are subject has received less attention *scientifically*, or caused greater diversity of opinion when it has received that attention, than the one termed " Distemper." Every gamekeeper, dog-breaker, or kennel-man has his particular recipe ; most druggists possess some wonderful prescription ; while sporting and other papers abound in advertisements of specifics and nostrums.

In discussing this subject, it is not my intention to lay down any fixed rule of treatment adapted to every case, but only for those in which the disease assumes the forms herein described, and from which I have derived the greatest benefit.

Nature, in many instances, works her own cure; while numerous methods of treatment produce mischief, and result in death.

Distemper may be described as a catarrhal fever, generally affecting the mucous membranes of the head, air-passages and alimentary tract, in which the nervous system frequently becomes involved—hence distemper fits, and local or general paralysis. It is a highly contagious disease, though oftentimes it is undoubtedly self-generated. Age is no preventive; at any period of life dogs are liable to become infected. But Mr. Fleming correctly observes, "It is more particularly a disease of youth, and is much more frequent and fatal among highly-bred, pampered animals, than those which live in a less artificial manner, and whose constitution is less modified by breeding and rearing."* Neither does one attack render a dog secure from a second; but in the latter it is contracted, I believe, invariably by contagion alone.

Distemper is not, as many persons suppose, a necessary disease, as numbers of dogs pass through life without ever becoming the subjects of it. The fact of the malady being unknown in this country prior to the seventeenth century (?) strongly supports this view, as dogs then were probably as numerous as now, though not perhaps so mixed in breed.

In all cases it is ushered in with catarrhal symptoms, and these, as the malady proceeds, may become complicated with pneumonia, jaundice, enteric disease, epilepsy, chorea, or paralysis: though the two latter are, as a rule, sequels, I have occasionally seen them exist in conjunction with distemper.

Causes.—These may be enumerated under the following

---

* "Veterinary Sanitary Science and Police," vol. ii. p. 294.

heads:—Contagion, badly-drained and ill-ventilated kennels (which in young dogs are especially fruitful causes of distemper), exposure to damp and cold, insufficient feeding, and poor food, over-feeding (particularly with flesh), and too little exercise.

Worms have been mentioned by some authors as another cause, and certainly they are frequently present in this disease; yet it must be borne in mind that they are equally so in dogs that are over, or have never had, distemper. That their presence bodes no good to the animal while under the influence of the infection (or indeed at any time) can be readily understood, but especially, I should say, during the existence of distemper; because the mucous membranes are then in an irritable condition, and these pests are not likely to reduce, but to increase that irritation, and produce—what is to be dreaded at all times, but doubly so in distemper—a fit. The condition of the patient then justifying it (I qualify it thus, because there are circumstances under which it would be unwise to administer the drugs usually given for this purpose), the sooner the worms are expelled the better. As a vermifuge, the areca nut is least harmful; turpentine, at other times most valuable, must be used with great caution here.

Teething has been affirmed as another cause of this disease, but here again the assumption has probably taken place from dogs at that period of their lives being most liable to distemper. An irritability of system and a degree of inflammatory fever is undoubtedly established at that crisis; and such a condition may render the subject more liable to contract the disease, if brought in contact with it; but certainly not otherwise, any more than the same process can produce in human beings measles, chicken pox, or scarlet fever.

The period of incubation is usually from one to three weeks, and the duration of the malady may be a week, or two or three months.

Symptoms.—The premonitory ones are: A heavy, sleepy look about the face, nose hot and dry, a disinclination for food, shivering, arched back, and more or less lassitude. In from two or three days a watery discharge takes place from eyes and nose, the animal frequently sneezes, and this is followed by coughing, retching, and vomiting. The discharge from the eyes and nose soon becomes purulent, the eyelids are inflamed and swollen, the breathing is accelerated, the inclination for warmth more evident, and the prostration greater.

Treatment.—Prompt and judicious treatment, in a case of this kind, will generally be attended with success. Immediately the first of the foregoing symptoms are observed, the patient should be placed in a dry, but not too warm, atmosphere, and the habitation—if in the kennel—well drained and disinfected.

With regard to medicinal agents, a mild emetic is at the onset advisable, as—

    Antim. Tart............................1–3 grains.

                     Or,

    Antim. Tart. ⎫   *aa* 1 grain.
    Calomel   ⎭

                     Or,

A good household emetic is a teaspoonful each of mustard and salt in a little warm water; its action is speedy and safe, and it fulfils all the purposes required.

The favourite draught of syrup of buckthorn and castor oil is not always commendable; but in the majority of cases of this kind it is beneficial, and should follow the emetic within a short time. When the catarrhal symptoms advance, and coughing takes place, I recommend the insertion of a small seton in front of the chest; this is to be daily dressed with mild digestive ointment, and not removed so long as bronchial irritation is present. Stimulants, combined with tonics, are also required at this period. Either of the following forms may be used:

Spts. Æther Nit. .... 4 drachms.
Tinct. Gentian Co. .... 4 „
Aqua Menth. .... 1½ ounce.

A teaspoonful three times a day for a terrier; double the quantity for a large dog, in the same quantity of linseed tea;

Or,

Port Wine .... 1 teaspoonful.
Quinine Sulph. .... 1 grain.

With the same directions.

The food should be light and nutritious—as milk, mutton broth, or beef-tea deprived of its fat. If the patient refuses to take anything, meat nearly raw, chopped small and made into balls and administered, will afford the best means of support. When the catarrhal symptoms have subsided and recovery commences, cod-liver oil and iron materially assists in hastening the process. The dose is a teaspoonful of the former and five minims of the latter for a small dog, double the quantity for a large one, twice a day. The natural diet to be gradually introduced as strength returns. I must not omit to observe that it is highly important that the discharge from the eyes and nose should be frequently and carefully removed, especially from the former; otherwise, ulceration of the eyelids, conjunctiva, and even the eye itself, is apt to take place, and not unfrequently results in total loss of vision. A daily application of some mild astringent—as five grains of alum to one ounce of water—will assist in preventing ulceration, by counteracting the relaxed condition of the mucous membrane and secretory glands.

If, however, ulcers have already formed, warm fomentations with milk and water, the avoidance of glare (as the sympathetic inflammation is often very great, and the parts peculiarly sensitive to light), and the use of either of the following lotions may with benefit be adopted:

1. Tinct. Myrrh Sim..................... 20 drops.
   Sol. Alumen .... 1 ounce.
   Aqua Distil .... 10 ounces.
                        Or,
2. Zinc Sulph. or Plumbi Acetat...... 1 scruple
   Aqua Distil. .... 10 ounces.
                        Or,
3. Nitrate of Silver .... 4 grains
   Aqua Distil. .... 1 ounce.

The second and third forms are more applicable when fungoid growths succeed the ulcerative process.

When the eyes remain weak after recovery from distemper, with opacity of vision, a seton inserted at the back of the ears, and daily smeared with stimulating ointment, is of great benefit. The time for its removal is to be regulated according to the condition of the eyes: here the third form of lotion is useful. Frequently small circular depressions present themselves on the cornea, which, if neglected, assume an ulcerated condition, and extend to the anterior chamber of the eye. In such cases I have found a little calomel or oxide of zinc daily blown on the surface of the eye attended with the greatest success.

I will now proceed to speak of distemper in some of its more complicated forms.

It not unfrequently happens, particularly in house pets, whose diminutive bodies are foolishly and unnaturally clothed in miniature horse apparel, from their susceptibility to cold, or from not being observed in time, that the catarrhal symptoms increase suddenly in intensity, bronchitis sets in, and pneumonia speedily supervenes. The hot, rapid, gasping breath, and unmistakable mucous rattle of the former, with, on auscultation, the rasping crepitating *rale* in the latter, the sunken eye, jerking and increased heart-beats, haggard face, dilated nostrils, and mouth drawn back at the angles, soon inform the practical man where the mischief is located.

A seton, if not already inserted, should be placed immediately in front of the chest, and its action excited as quickly as possible. Turpentine is, I think, the best agent for this purpose.

Hot linseed-meal poultices, applied to the sides, are exceedingly beneficial. They should be covered by a handkerchief brought under the girth, and tied over the back, *but not too tightly, so as to compress the walls of the chest.* These should be repeatedly renewed, and followed, if the animal is not relieved in six hours, by mustard plasters.

With regard to internal remedies, diffusible stimulants are best adapted to such cases. I recommend the administration, to a small dog, of a teaspoonful of brandy and water (equal parts of each), with two to four drops of chlorodyne every hour; double the quantity for a full-sized terrier, treble for a large dog.

Beef-tea, mutton-broth, or milk in which plain biscuit or bread has been soaked and broken down, should be given with a spoon, unless voluntarily taken, two or three times during the day.

If there appears danger of suffocation, emetics may be administered until vomiting is induced. The ipecacuanha wine in some cases answers well—dose from fifteen to thirty drops in a little warm water.

When the acute symptoms have subsided,—which the breathing becoming laboured and panting, the heart's action steadier, pulse less frequent and softer, and an occasional deep-drawn sigh will denote, the brandy may be given at longer intervals, the chlorodyne suspended, and the tincture of iron substituted in five, ten, or fifteen drops, in proportion to the size of the dog. The body must be kept warm, but fresh air is throughout absolutely necessary; therefore ample ventilation, without draught, should be allowed. This is a point on which I am most particular Often and often again have I found my little patient, through the mistaken kindness of its fair owner, smothered in shawls before a hot fire, and almost totally deprived of one of the great essentials to recovery—the inhalation of fresh and cool air. As veterinarians, we are by this time all thoroughly aware of the importance of this great principle in the treatment of catarrhal diseases in the lower animals; and in proportion to that knowledge, so has our success in treatment been greater; so that diseases of this type are now few and far between, whereas they were once rife and fatal.

As the symptoms continue to abate, the nourishment of the diet can be increased, and cod-liver oil may be given as previously described.

When distemper becomes associated with jaundice, it is commonly called the "yellows," and treated by kennel-men and quacks as a distinct disease; though I need hardly say that it is but the result of general derangement of the system, consequent on improperly treated or neglected distemper.

The symptoms are a yellow tinge of the eyes, visible mucous membranes, and thin parts of the integument—as inside the thighs, forearms, and ears, and that covering the abdomen; pain on pressure over the region of the liver, and sometimes enlargement, with hardness; the fæces pale and hard, or soft and greenish, and mingled with mucus; the urine high-coloured, hot, and occasionally turbid.

The patient may or may not exhibit catarrhal symptoms, with jaundice. In distemper it most frequently follows the former.

A mild dose of aloes and calomel is generally at first advisable, but in the administration of this we must be guided by the other symptoms. If the catarrh is still present, or the bowels irritable, aloes must certainly be avoided. Five-grain doses of hydrarg. cum creta may be given daily to a medium-sized dog; and if this is found to be unattended with benefit, sulphurous acid—from three to ten drops in a little cold water—may be tried, as it is frequently given with success. The addition of quinine is often useful.

A mustard poultice applied over the region of the liver in severe cases, affords considerable relief, and at the onset is of especial service.

The diet should be plain and light ; milk, with one-third its quantity of lime-water, is most suitable until an improvement in the symptoms is observed.

When the disease extends to the bowels—which, in neglected cases of distemper, or even in those most assiduously attended, it frequently does—a violent form of diarrhœa or dysentery sets in. The fæces are dark, streaked with blood, and offensive ; the patient rapidly wastes, has a sickening odour, and speedily dies, often, under even the most energetic and judicious treatment. A mild dose of oil (linseed or salad) is generally at first advisable, and in three hours this is best followed up with antacids and astringents :

1. Sodæ Bicarb .... 10 grains
   Catechu Pulv. 10   „   } 1 Pill or Powder.
   Opii Pulv. 2   „

2. Cupri Sulph. ...... 5 to 10 grains } Do.
   Opii Pulv. 2   „

3. Tannic Acid ...... 3 to 5   „
   Opii Pulv. 2   „   } Do.
   Zingib. 10   „

In severe cases, the last prescription (No. 3) is the most effectual. Should the purging continue, and symptons of pain be manifested, hot linseed-meal poultices applied to the abdomen afford relief, and materially assist in checking enteritis. Starch enemas are likewise serviceable

The diet should consist of strong beef-tea, in which isinglass or gum arabic has been dissolved in proportions to make it sufficiently mucilaginous to shield the living membrane of the stomach and intestines.

With regard to the so-called "distemper fits," it is

almost needless to remark that they are always a dangerous sign, being seldom limited to one attack. Sometimes they appear as the forerunner of distemper, but more frequently as an accompaniment, and when the patient is low and wasted.

Immediately symptoms of cerebral disturbance are observed, a seton should be inserted in the occipital region, and action excited as quick as possible. Let the animal freely breathe fresh air, and administer brandy and water; and if diarrhœa is still present, suspend the opium, but continue the antacids and astringents, and give the brandy with beaten egg or other mucilage. During the seizure, neat brandy may be rubbed on the gums, and ammonia applied to the nostrils. The food should be nutritious, and all other means adopted which are calculated to impart tone to the system.

In protracted cases of distemper, when the system, as it were, has been taxed to the utmost, and the patient reduced almost to the lowest ebb of existence, a cuticular eruption makes its appearance. This generally, in the first instance, assumes a pustular form, and these pustules in the course of a few days break, and leave by their exudation a crust or scab. Either the whole or a portion of the body only may be involved. I have seen a dog literally naked, with the exception of the head, ears, and feet.

This condition is not unfrequently mistaken by the would-be "knowing ones" for mange, and treated as such.*

---

* I well remember a case in point which came under my own observation—the subject being a Skye terrier. The case, when first brought to me, was one of distemper, associated with pneumonia (the animal being thought consumptive); later on dysentery set in. Several times the animal was on the verge of death, and it was only by my persuasion that he was allowed to continue under treatment. Ultimately he took a turn for the better, and almost simultaneously the eruption described broke out; the stench emitted after it made

There is, however, no analogy between the two. The distemper eruption and loss of coat is simply owing to suspension of the secretions necessary to the growth and support of the hair ; or if not actual suspension of these secretions, then from such an exceedingly low state of vitality of the surface of the body, that life ànd health in the appendages of certain parts cannot be maintained.

Occasionally this eruptive stage is the forerunner of a return to health, but much more frequently it is the precursor of a fatal issue.

At this period of the disease, tonics are especially indicated, and everything in the shape of diet, exercise, cleanliness, etc., calculated to promote vigour.

When chorea or paralysis co-exist with distemper, remedies specially adapted to either must be used in addition to, or in conjunction with, the distemper treatment. Strychnia or nux vomica is undoubtedly the most effectual restorative agent in such cases.

It would be superfluous on my part, so far as scientific

---

its appearance was simply abominable. In a few days every vestige of hair, with the exception of that on the head, ears, and lower part of the legs, came off. He continued in this state for several weeks, the skin being perfectly clean, and whole, but very glazed. In every other respect he improved daily and gained flesh. The owner and another gentleman maintained that the dog had contracted mange ; nor could I convince them to the contrary. In vain I argued the difference of symptoms, and that as the system gained tone so would the patient regain his coat. But no: the dog was removed, and placed out to nurse in the hands of a dog-breaker—he also being of opinion it was mange; and this worthy individual, according to his own account, brought away that which the patient never in my possession possessed —*a hatful of worms*. Some time afterwards I met the gentleman to whom the animal belonged, and was asked if I recognised the dog he had with him. Certainly, as my old patient, which he proved to be, I did not ; for he was clothed in an entirely new coat, and of an entirely different colour—dark, nearly black, stubbly hair having taken the place of the original silver-grey—the result, in all probability of the dressing applied to the sensitive and weak skin. In this instance the breaker claimed the cure which nature had wrought.

persons are concerned, were I to hint at the care required in the administration of this drug. I will merely observe, for the benefit of non-professional persons, that cases have fallen under my notice in which death had resulted from irregularity in the time of giving such medicine, and more particularly where the dose had been for some time gradually increased until it had reached more than treble the primary quantity. Forgotten for some hours, or it may be a day, and then given perhaps fasting, a fatal issue is pretty nearly certain to follow.

When there is any difficulty in administering the medicine in the form of pills, the liquor strychnia may be conveniently substituted.

Local remedies in chorea and paralysis are often very beneficial. I have found setons exceedingly valuable. If the convulsive movements of the former, or the numbness of the latter, are confined to the hind parts, the seton requires inserting across the loins; if general, at the back of the head and across the loins. Counter-irritation along the spine is also serviceable, and galvanism is occasionally useful.

Though, in principle, the hot bath, from its relaxing properties, may appear wrong, it is nevertheless, in chorea, sometimes attended with good results. It certainly affords relief when the convulsive twitchings are excessive, and so far I have observed no after-evil from its use. I should not advise its adoption when distemper also existed. Quietude, except when the patient is necessarily disturbed, is very essential; and attention to the bed being dry, and the excretions regular, are also matters of importance in chorea and paralytic affections.

When abatement of the twitchings, with returning strength, is observed, a favourable issue may be expected; but it is advisable not to discontinue the medicine so long as any nervous complication remains; afterwards it should be gradually, not suddenly, suspended.

Y

As soon as the patient is able to walk, a short exercise each day may be given with benefit. The fresh air acts as a tonic, new scenery and objects divert the mind, while exercise encourages the natural habits and functions of the animal.

Tincture of iron and cod-liver oil are advisable after the disuse of the strychnia, until recovery is complete. The diet throughout should be nourishing and digestible, and forcibly administered if the patient refuses to take it. Constipation, which is frequently present in chorea and paralysis, is best relieved by enemas.

With regard to preventive measures for distemper, I have only to observe that due attention to hygienics is one of the most important considerations. Vaccination has been extolled and condemned—condemned justly, inasmuch as there is not a shadow of analogy between canine distemper and small-pox. The introduction of equine lymph has also been tried, and in like manner extolled, but where, again, is the resemblance between the disease known as "grease" in the horse, from which the lymph is supplied, and canine distemper? There is not the least similarity in the character of one and the other. Good management—the dog not being brought in contact with the infective agents, or it may possibly be from possessing a degree of insusceptibility that the malady is not easily contracted—has far more to do with immunity from distemper than the imaginary power of vaccination, be the lymph what it may.

Inoculation with distemper-virus on the system I have practised for many years, and discovered, by myself, is undoubtedly a protection against distemper, and, even where by some peculiar idiosyncrasy the disease is contracted, it still reduces the risk of death to a minimum. The value of this simple and inexpensive operation is now widely acknowledged at home and abroad. *The Fox Terrier Chronicle,* in commenting upon it in 1883, said: "The many recent deaths of valuable puppies from distemper will doubtless induce breeders to give Professor Woodroffe Hill's principle of inoculation an extended trial. We are able to say, from cases under our own observation, and from information received from various owners, that up to the present the operation has been attended with uniform success."

Lately, efforts have been made, though unsuccessfully, to establish an identity between distemper and human typhoid fever: for, as Professor Axe pertinently remarks, "Did distemper in the dog possess the property of communicating typhoid fever to man, it is difficult to understand how myself and others have so long escaped infection. During the past twelve years I have examined large numbers of distempered dogs immediately after death, and thus exposed myself to the emanations from every secretion and excretion of the body; but in no case have I suffered the least constitutional disturbance. This illustration, it may be argued, is worthless in itself, and is capable of explanation on the ground of insusceptibility; but the same remarks apply to scores of others who have been exposed from time to time in a similar manner." In regard to the propagation of the typhoid contagium, Dr. Budd says: "If the poison from which typhoid fever springs were capable of being bred elsewhere than in the human body, it would surely be in the bodies of animals which are made of flesh and blood like ourselves, and from whose substance we draw sustenance for our own. And yet it appears to be almost certain that this is not the case. In the most virulent outbreaks of typhoid fever, there is no evidence that the domestic animals which gather round the fever-stricken dwellings ever take the disease. At Cheffcombe, while nearly all the human inmates of the infected homestead were laid low by the poison, the dogs and cats which belonged to the house, and the poultry, pigs, horses, and cattle which thronged the yard, continued to enjoy perfect health. Yet the pond from which the latter drank was being continually polluted by a drain which received the whole bulk of the intestinal discharges from the fever patients!* The statement of 'H. H.' that the symptoms of distemper in the dog and typhoid fever in man are 'alike,' is true only so far as refers to the febrile state. The specific phenomena of the latter most surely find no counterpart in the symptomatology of the former. It is only in the continued type of the fever that any identity can really be said to exist. If we examine the main features of the two affections, we find at once a broad and unmistakable difference in their clinical and pathological equivalents.

"Typhoid fever is an eruptive disease. Its course and duration are definite, and the lesions resulting from the fever process are localised and specific. In distemper of the dog not one of these essential characters can be applied. The pathological changes of the latter have no specific form or seat. Universal congestion more or less intense, local inflammation, blood extravasations, and serous exudation of varying extent, constitute the principal *post-mortem* phenomena."†

MALIGNANT DISTEMPER.

In 1881 and 1882 I had occasion to investigate the causes and nature of a malignant outbreak of disease in various parts of England. I received many dogs, alive and dead, for examination and advice, the victims of this malady, which proved to be a severe form of distemper associated with diphtheria and rash. The symptoms usually presented were as follows:—

---

* This is strong evidence: sufficiently so to be conclusive.—J.W.H.
† From the *Veterinarian*, Feb., 1867.

1st. General catarrhal fever, denoted by red and watery eyes, dry nose, hot mouth, tongue furred and red at the edges, high-coloured urine passed in small quantities, frequent sneezing, a short husky cough and depression, impaired appetite, and unusual thirst.

2nd. Purulent discharge from the eyes and nose, an elevated irregular line of red abraded mucous membrane immediately inside the top lip ; posterior part of the mouth inflamed, troublesome cough, short breathing, irritable bowels, turbid urine, prostration greater, no appetite, intense thirst.

3rd. Mucous membrane inside the lips broken, vesicular formation above the eyes, round the orbital arch ; throat livid, expectoration, laboured breathing, difficulty in swallowing, diarrhœa.

4th. Broken sores above the eyes, at the angles of the mouth, pustular eruption all over the abdomen, throat clogged with tenacious fluid, and the external region swollen and painful, thick sibilant breathing, hoarse croupy voice, hard rapid pulse, and general distress.

5th. General aggravation of all the symptoms, head stretched out, tongue frequently protruded, fauces swollen and purple, reeling delirium, and suffocation. Emaciation rapid throughout.

Post-mortem appearances.—Tonsils and adjacent structures swollen and nearly black, covered by an adherent membranous exudation, and, in some cases, deeply ulcerated ; mucous membrane lining the larynx and trachea intensely inflamed and coated with exudation, films or casts of lymph found in the bronchi ; the lungs more or less congested, often intensely inflamed, and sometimes adherent to the walls of the chest ; occasionally suppuration in the lung tissue is present. Pericarditis is also met with. The liver, spleen, and kidneys present a variable appearance of congestion.

The terminal portion of the intestines is usually inflamed,

and the anus protruded and deeply injected, due to the continual diarrhœa and straining.

Causes.—Of these I have invariably traced the leading one to defective sanitary arrangements, notably the drainage; dampness of the walls and floors through clogged drains produces a condition of atmosphere favourable to catarrhal symptoms, while the collection of effete matter, particularly where the drains are untrapped, poisons the atmosphere, and acts as a pyœmic agent on the inhabitants. No more patent illustration of the value of a strict regard to hygiene could be offered to canine fanciers than the outbreaks I have alluded to. Too often the disease is treated, and its founder neglected, to the disappointment of employer and employed. The site of kennels and their drainage are matters of vital importance.

Treatment.—Concerning the treatment of this malignant type of disease, no hard-and-fast line can be laid down; generally speaking, the most valuable measures consist in the inhalation of acid vapour, the administration of mineral tonics and diffusible stimulants, a nutritive and mucilaginous diet, counter-irritation to the throat (and the sides in chest complication), antiseptics and disinfectants, complete isolation, with warmth and dryness. Diphtheritic conditions must be treated under that head; the throat may be mopped with warm carbolised water, and the tonsils painted daily with tannic acid and glycerine, tincture of perchloride of iron and glycerine, a weak solution of liquor chlorinated soda, or nitrate of silver. Subsequently cod-liver oil, nux vomica, quinine and steel, may be given. For the skin rash nothing excels the oxide of zinc ointment prepared with vaseline and sanitas oil. In all such cases the owner of the animal will best consult his own interests, and that of his dog, by calling in the aid of an experienced canine pathologist.

DROPSY.

Dogs, especially old ones, frequently, and from constitutional disease, become what is termed "*dropsical*," *i.e.*, a serous exudation takes place in some portion of the organism. The usual forms met with in canine practice are, *hydrothorax*, viz., when the exudation is within the cavity of the chest; *hydrops-pericardium*, when within the pericardial sac or membrane covering the heart; *hydrometra*, when within the uterus; *hydrocephalus*, when within the head; *ascites*, when within the peritoneal sac or abdomen; *anasarca*, when within the areolar tissue of the body generally.

I shall here commence with the form known as *ascites*, placing the others in their respective classes.

Ascites, or abdominal dropsy, may be the result of inflammatory action or of chronic disease of the circulating system, hence it is either *active* or *passive*.

The active form is usually met with in young dogs, and is caused by exposure to damp and cold, especially after being heated. The natural exhalation from the skin being suddenly checked, the water is retained in the blood vessels, and seeks an outpour elsewhere; and this either takes place in the areolar tissue—producing anasarca—or in some of the serous cavities of the body, frequently the peritoneal, and giving rise to ascites.

The analogy with human dropsy being very close, a brief extract from Sir Thos. Watson's instructive lecture on this subject will not be out of place:—" To comprehend this rapid change from a state of health to a state of dangerous disease, we must again have recourse to the findings of physiology.

" Besides the constant exhalation which takes place from the inner faces of the shut serous cavities, a large amount of watery fluid is continually thrown out of the system by all those services that communicate with the air by the skin, the lungs, the bowels, the kidneys.

"Now it is well ascertained that when the excretion of aqueous fluid of one such surface is checked, the exhalation from some other surface becomes more copious.

"It is probable that the aggregate quantity of water thus expelled from the system in a given time, cannot vary *much*, in either direction, without deranging the whole economy. But we are sure that the amount furnished by any excreting surface may vary and oscillate within certain limits consistent with health, provided that the defect or excess be compensated by an increase or diminution of the ordinary expenditure of watery liquid through some other channel. Sound health admits and requires this shifting and counterpoise of work between the organs destined to remove aqueous fluid from the body. This supplemental or compensating relation is more conspicuous in regard to some parts than to others. The reciprocal but inverse accommodation of function that subsists between the skin and the kidneys affords the strongest and the most familiar example.

"In the warm weather of summer, when the perspiration is abundant, the urine is proportionately concentrated and scanty. On the other hand, during winter, when the cutaneous transpiration is checked by the agency of external cold, the flow of dilute water from the kidneys is strikingly augmented.* All this is well known to be com patible with the maintenance of the most perfect health. But supposing the exhalation from one of these surfaces to be much diminished, or to cease, without a corresponding increase of function in the exterior, then dropsy, in some form or degree, is very apt to arise. The aqueous liquid thus detained in the blood-vessels seeks, and at length finds, some unnatural and inward vent, and is poured forth into the areolar tissue, or into the cavities bounded by the serous membranes.

---

* This is especially noticeable after bathing.

"If water be injected in some quantity into the blood-vessels of a living animal, the animal soon perishes—dying generally by coma, or by suffocation; and when the carcass is examined the lungs are found to be charged with serous liquid; or water is discovered in the areolar tissue of some other part, or in the shut serous membrane. If, however, the animal be first bled and then a quantity of water injected equal to the quantity of blood abstracted, the injection is followed by no serious consequences.

"Facts like these throw, as it seems to me, a strong light on a confessedly obscure part of pathology. It appears that under various circumstances the blood-vessels may receive a considerable and unwonted accession of watery fluid, and that they are very prone to get rid of the redundance. When they empty themselves through some free surface, their preternatural distention is relieved by a flux. If, on the other hand, the surface be that of a shut sac, in discharging their superfluity they cause a dropsy. Why sometimes this organ and sometimes that is selected as the channel by which the superabundant water shall be thrown out of the vessels, we can seldom tell."

Chronic or Passive Ascites is more commonly seen in old dogs, and is usually associated with some old-standing disease, either connected with the heart or large venous trunks, in which some obstruction to the proper return of blood is present, often originating in some morbid condition of the liver, spleen, lungs, or kidneys. In the dog it is *never* the result of chronic peritoneal inflammation.

"Active and passive dropsy," Watson observes, "resemble each other in the result; namely, in the collection of serous liquid in the circumscribed cavities and vacuities of the body. They differ in the rate at which the collection augments.

"In the well-marked acute dropsies, the liquid is rapidly effused in quantity much beyond the natural amount of exhalation. In the well-marked passive dropsies the exhalation goes on as usual, but the fluid exhaled is not taken back again into the circulating vessels with sufficient facility. In one case the circulation is disturbed and tumultuous; in the other, it remains tranquil.

"Although all dropsical transudations probably take place through the walls of the capillary vessels, there would seem to be, in the more acute forms of dropsy, an increased flow of blood in the arterial channels ; while in the completely chronic forms there is a defect of absorption by the veins. Active dropsies are sometimes spoken of as belonging to the left side of the heart, passive dropsies to the right.

"What connects all these forms of dropsy is a preternatural fulness in some part, or the whole of the hydraulic machine. And this seems to be the grand key to the entire pathology, as well as to the remedial management, of the disease."

Symptoms.—The first symptom generally observed is an enlargement of the abdomen, but as this may arise from causes other than ascites—to wit, *pregnancy, tumours obesity, or ovarian dropsy*—it is necessary to obtain, by examination more confirmatory evidence. The abovementioned writer remarks :

"In ascites the enlargement is uniform and symmetrical, in respect of the two sides of the body. When the patient lies on her back the flanks bulge outwards, or sway over from the weight and lateral pressure of the augmenting fluid. This increased *breadth* of the trunk is not observable in the case of an ovarian tumour ; nor, I may add, in pregnancy."

Blaine says : " Dropsy of the belly may be distinguished from fat, by the particular tumour that the belly forms, which, in dropsy, hangs down, while the backbone sticks up, and the hips appear prominent through the skin ; the hair stares also, and the coat is peculiarly harsh. It may be distinguished from being in pup by the teats, which always enlarge as the belly enlarges in pregnancy; but more particularly it may be distinguished by the undulation of the water in the belly, whereas in pregnancy there is no undulation. The impregnated belly, however full, has not that tight tense feel nor shining appearance observed in dropsy. There may be also inequalities distinguished in it, which are the puppies, and, when pregnancy is at all advanced, the young may be felt to move. The most unequivocal mode, however, of detecting the presence of water is by the touch. If the right hand is laid on one side of the belly, and with the left hand the other side is tapped, an undulating motion will be perceived, exactly similar to what would be felt by placing one hand on a bladder of water, and striking it with the other."

Youatt observes : " The dog is peculiarly subject to *ascites* or *dropsy of the belly*, and the quantity of fluid contained in the abdomen is sometimes almost incredible. It is usually accompanied or characterised by a weak, unequal, small, and frequent pulse—paleness of the lips, tongue and gums—flaccidity of the muscles, hurried breathing on the least exertion, feebleness of the joints, swellings of the lower limbs, effusion of fluid into the integuments, or among the muscles, before there is any considerable effusion into the thorax or the abdomen, and an unhealthy appearance of the cutaneous surface. The urine seldom coagulates. This form of dropsy is usually seated on the abdomen or cellular tissue."

In addition to this principal and what may be termed abdominal symptom, there is loss of happiness and spirits, dryness of the nose, thirst, constipation, scanty urine, quick feeble pulse, and increased respiration, the latter chiefly thoracic. As the accumulation increases, the breathing becomes more difficult. The poor animal, to avoid suffocation by pressure of the fluid on the breathing space, either assumes a continual standing position, sits on its haunches, or lies on its side. The enemy, however, continues to advance, and suffocation terminates the case. Towards the latter stage infiltration into the areolar tissue usually takes place (anasarca).

Treatment.—The treatment of ascites is far from satisfactory. Bleeding, as advocated by some, for the purpose of unloading the veins, in which the circulation is impeded and the vessels thereby congested, from compression by the dropsy, is rarely admissible in so lowering a disease; where it is practised, the administration of a stimulant should immediately follow.

Tapping is of little use in the lower animals, and is only warranted in extreme cases. The secretion is more rapidly renewed after the operation, and a second withdrawal may be, but a third is rarely, allowed by Nature.

I have far greater faith in medicinal agents, and recommend diuretics alternately with mineral tonics.

Iodine, as advocated by Mr. Youatt, may be tried, and in some cases, for a time, is apparently beneficial; but, when given for a long period, it is apt to produce atrophy of the glands, and considerable constitutional debility. To avoid this, it is better combined with iron, and when any such symptoms occur it should be withheld.

The food should be of the most nourishing kind, and every other measure adopted which is calculated to strengthen the system, and prevent a return of the malady.

LEUKÆMIA.

Leukæmia, or Leucocythæmia, is a term used to denote " *white-cell blood*," or *white blood*. It is a condition in which there is a preponderance or increase in the number of these bodies in the blood, and is usually associated in the human being with diseases of the spleen, liver, and lymphatic glands.

In the *Veterinary Journal* for July, 1875, the following instance in the canine subject is recorded:

"Mastronardi Innorenza, of the Naples Veterinary School, in the 'Giornale delle razze degli animali utili e di Médicina Vétérinaria,' after giving some general indications as to the nature, &c., of leukæmia, describes an instance of this disease in a dog. The symptoms were those of combined lienal and lymphatic leukæmia. The animal died. Innorenza was inclined to attribute the development of the malady to the alterations due to the disease of young dogs commonly known as 'distemper,' the manifestations of which had preceded those of leukæmia in this case."*

ANÆMIA.

Badly cared-for dogs, and especially those of weakly constitution, are, like human beings, subject to poverty or deficiency in the quality of the blood. In other words, they become anæmic. Puppies are more likely to be so affected than adult animals, and this is due to the method of rearing, or, at all events, to neglect in avoiding causes which I shall mention as giving rise to this condition of the circulation.

Over-crowding, defective ventilation, stinted light, bad drainage, innutritious food are each productive of anæmia. Observe the pallid countenance and languid step of an individual who is confined in a crowded, ill-ventilated workshop throughout the day, as contrasted with one whose occupation gives him every chance of imbibing pure, or at any rate, fresh air, and you have a true and daily illustration of the effect of these sanitary arrangements, which may be with equal force applied to the canine race.

Indeed, fresh air and light are as essential to dogs, for the formation of good blood, as to man. Air must, to maintain health, *be renewed, not re-used.* It is the oxygen

---

* "Leukæmia in the Dog," by Innorenza; "Annales de Méd. Vétérinaire."

which gives colour to the blood. Stint the supply of this necessary element, and though externally not so perceptible in dogs, you withdraw the colouring matter, and obtain the same pallid condition. Again, good nutritious food is just as necessary for the production of pure blood and healthy muscle. We may as well try to build a strong substantial house out of bad material, as expect that blood derived from such a source, and under the circumstances enumerated, will make sound strong muscle.

Symptoms.—Anæmic animals generally exhibit considerable muscular prostration, with depression of spirits; the mucous membranes are pallid, particularly on the gums, and inside the lips, the tongue is also unusually white and dry, the extremities are cold, and the limbs not unfrequently swollen, and the secretions and excretions scanty.

M. D'Arboa relates the following cases :

"Two dogs were sent into the hospital of the Veterinary School at Lyons. They did not appear to suffer any considerable pain. Their skin and the mucous membranes that were visible had a peculiar appearance. They had also comparatively little power over their limbs: so little, indeed, that they rested continually on one side, without the ability to change their posture. When they were placed on their feet their limbs gave way, and they fell the moment they were quitted. Notwithstanding the care that was taken of them, they died on the second day.

"Incisions were made through the skin, but in opening them no blood flowed. The venæ cavæ themselves did not contain any—there were only two clots of blood in the cavities of their hearts. One of them, of the size of a small nutmeg, occupied the left ventricle; the other, which was still smaller, was found at the base of the right ventricle. The chest of one of them contained a small quantity of serosity ; a similar fluid was between the dura mater and the arachnoid membrane, and the same was the case in the larger ventricles of the encephalon. The other viscera did not offer anything remarkable, except the paleness and flacidity of their tissue. The great fatigues of the chase, and the immersion of these animals in water at the time when they were very much heated, appeared to have been the causes of this singular disease. In the 'Report of the Clinique of the School of Alfort,' in the year 1825, the same anæmia was remarked in two dogs that died there ; one of them had lately undergone a considerable hæmorrhage, and in the other anæmia had developed itself spontaneously.

"It is, in fact, among dogs that this extreme anæmia has been principally observed, and it is ordinarily fatal.

"This disease, according to M. Vatel, is generally the symptom of a chronic malady, or the instantaneous effect of an excessive hæmorrhage. It is rarely primary. The extreme discoloration of the tissues, and of the mucous membrane more particularly; the disappearance of the subcutaneous blood-vessels ; and the great feebleness of the animal, are the principal symptoms. There also often exists considerable swelling of the limbs."[*]

Treatment.—This, in the first instance, should consist in removing the cause; and, secondly, in assisting nature to restore the deficiency in the colour and quality of the blood by those agents which form the necessary constituents of healthy blood. For the former, a nutritious diet, with a free allowance of fresh air, sunlight, and exercise, should be ordered. Vegetable and mineral tonics especially the preparations of iron, and, if there be much emaciation, cod-liver oil, should be prescribed for the latter. Salt-water baths are also beneficial.

---

[*] Youatt on "The Dog."

MARASMUS.

This condition is frequently dependent on mesenteric disease. The term marasmus is used to signify leanness or emaciation. Dogs apparently healthy in themselves, *i.e.*, so far as feeding well, performing their duties, etc., are concerned, nevertheless do not thrive, or, to use a common expression, they are "*out of condition.*" Hence the frequent inquiry addressed to the canine surgeon is, "Can you give me something to get my dogs in condition?" This leanness, however, is not necessarily a result of disease: in many animals it is a natural and hereditary condition; in others it may result from neglect of hygiene.

Symptoms.—Such animals have usually large appetites, and an unkind and unthrifty appearance. The bowels are generally constipated, and attacks of colic are not unfrequent.

When it proceeds from mesenteric disease, the abdomen is pendulous and large, the coat is particularly harsh and dry, the mucous membranes are pale, the eyes watery, and the nose often dry and hot; the appetite is not so extreme as the thirst, the fæces are offensive, and the bowels are either relaxed or costive, and the excretions coated with mucus. In the latter stage the pulse is weak and accelerated, and the animal exhibits considerable indisposition for exertion; the thirst increases, and the bowels are continually relaxed.

Treatment.—Fresh air, daily exercise, nourishing food, and, in the case of disease, cod-liver oil, and the preparations of iron, are the measures chiefly indicated.

PLETHORA.

Dogs highly fed and allowed but little exercise are those generally subject to excess of blood, or what is generally termed full habit of body (plethoric). Fits frequently occur from this condition, and are more particularly induced by the injudicious adoption of rapid or violent exercise after long confinement.

Symptoms.—A general full, bloated appearance of the body, mucous membranes injected, redness and heat of the skin. The pulse is usually full and bounding; bowels to frequently constipated; drowsiness and indisposition exertion.

Treatment.—Depletion by medicinal agents, as occasional aperients. Reduction in the quantity of food and its feeding qualities. Regular exercise.

OBESITY.

Dogs, and some breeds more so than others, under certain circumstances, become inordinately fat, in other words, obese. The immense accumulation of adipose tissue undoubtedly constitutes disease. At all events, such a condition is abnormal. Fat takes the place of muscle; hence what is termed fatty degeneration is a disease of serious import when occurring in vital organs. Some parts of the body are more prone to depositions of fat than others—such as around the kidneys, within the mesentery, and the heart, the latter being frequently a cause of sudden death.

Close confinement, and injudicious and excessive feeding, are among the causes of obesity. Some animals, as I have observed, are more predisposed to fatten than others, and among this class may be mentioned spaniels, pugs, and a few of the long-haired toy dogs. The first-named appear to increase in obesity with their years; no matter how plain the food, fat is accumulated, and with it they become lazy, useless (so far as accompanying the sportsman is concerned,) and unsightly.

Treatment.—This consists in avoiding, as much as possible those causes which predispose or give rise to obesity. The food should be less fattening, and more sparingly given. Daily and somewhat vigorous exercise should be allowed. Where the deposition has a tendency to increase in spite of these observances, small doses of iodine may be given with benefit, along with an occasional aperient.

RHEUMATISM.

Dogs are frequently affected with this "human misery.' It may locate itself in the joints (articular rheumatism) or in the muscles, chiefly their tendinous portions, producing lumbago and "chest-founder."

Causes. — Rheumatism chiefly arises from exposure to damp and cold; hence its frequency in kennel dogs, and during those seasons of the year when the causes named prevail—spring and autumn.

The disease assumes an *acute* and a *chronic* form. An attack of the former frequently terminates in the latter, which may remain through life, and become increased in severity with changes of temperature; or, if the former disappears without degenerating into the latter, periodical returns of it very often occur. As in human beings, valvular disease of the heart is one of the serious complications of rheumatism which generally, sooner or later, cause the death of the animal.

Acute rheumatism has been conjectured to depend upon the presence of lactic acid in the blood.*

---

* "The acid properties of the perspiration, as manifested even by its peculiar smell—of the saliva, as tested by litmus paper—of the urine, as shown by its deposits, warrant the hypothesis that the poison which the whole disorder would seem to be an effort to discharge from the blood, is some sort of *acid*. Dr. Prout conjectured that the phenomena of acute rheumatism might depend upon the presence in the blood of *lactic* acid; and some very remarkable experiments made by Dr. Richardson lend weight and likelihood to this conjecture. Into the peritoneum of a healthy cat he introduced a solution of lactic acid in

Symptoms.—In acute articular rheumatism, the affected joints are hot, inflamed, painful, and swollen. This condition is not unfrequently mistaken for rickets, and when treated as such, it scarcely need be added that great harm is done to the patient.

The animal moves about with extreme difficulty, uttering sharp yelping cries, expressive of the torture the movements create.

Considerable constitutional disturbance is usually manifested; the pulse is rapid and jerking, the respiration increased, the breath fœtid, and the tongue loaded with fur. Constipation is generally present, and the urine is scanty and turbid.

As in the human subject, a remarkable feature of the disease is its tendency to move from place to place—a joint suddenly becomes affected, and as suddenly the disease may leave it (or continue there), and appear with the same short notice in another part; and so it goes on, mystifying those persons unacquainted with the nature of the complaint.

In lumbago, the animal walks with its back arched, and with a dragging paralytic gait; pressure or manipulation about the loins causes intense pain, there is great disinclination to move, the bowels are obstinately constipated, and the urine is high coloured, scanty, and turbid.

---

water. In two hours the action of the cat's heart became irregular. The next morning the animal was found dead. There was no peritoneal inflammation, but marked endocarditis in the left chambers of the heart. The mitral valve was inflamed and thickened, and covered on its free borders with firm, fibrinous deposits. The whole inner surface of the ventricle was highly vascular. A dog, on which a similar experiment was tried, died in two days. Unequivocal evidence of endocarditis was disclosed upon examination of the heart. The tricuspid valve was swollen to twice its ordinary size. The aortic valves, inflamed and enlarged, presented fibrinous beads along their edges; and the entire endocardial surface was red. The pericardium was simply dry. There was, however, no affection of the joints."—" Watson's Lectures on the Principles and Practice of Physic," vol. ii., p. 810.

Chest-founder, or kennel-lameness, is indicated by stiffness and pain in the shoulders, the animal has difficulty in extending its fore-legs, and when going downhill exhibits much the same appearance as a horse with navicular disease, or laminitis. If the limbs are extended outwards, or laterally, excruciating pain is caused.

In both the latter forms considerable fever is present.

Youatt observes: "This chest-founder is a singular complaint, and often a pest in kennels that are built in low situations, and where bad management prevails; where the huntsmen or whippers-in are too often in a hurry to get home and turn their dogs into the kennel panting and hot; where the beds are not far enough from the floor, or the building if it should be in a sufficiently elevated situation, has yet a northern aspect, and is unsheltered from the blast, chest-founder prevails; and I have known half the pack affected by it after a severe run, the scent breast-high, and the morning unusually cold."

Treatment.—If rheumatism is due to the presence of lactic acid, alkaline agents would appear to be those indicated in the treatment of the disease, and in the majority of cases under my own care I have found their use attended with marked benefit. The nitrate of potass, 10 to 15 grains, and bicarbonate of soda, 20 to 30 grains, in proportion to the size of the dog, should be given in a spoonful or two of water twice or three times a day.

A fixed rule of treatment, however, cannot be laid down for every case of rheumatism: some cases from time to time occur which will not yield to alkalies alone; the addition of colchicum, 2 to 5 grains, is in such instances frequently of great service. Mercury—recommended by some authorities—is, in my opinion, not a desirable agent, for not only is its use attended with susceptibility to cold in the animal it is administered to, and which in rheumatic affections should especially be avoided, but, by its depressing and salivatory effects, hinders the removal of a complaint which requires a very opposite treatment. The preparations of iodine are more suitable to chronic and articular cases.

At the onset it is advisable to clear the bowels: for this purpose saline aperients are most suitable.

With regard to local applications, warm fomentations, which may be rendered alkaline or sedative, are in severe cases (particularly of articular rheumatism) serviceable.

The patient should throughout be kept warm and dry, and a non-stimulating diet allowed. Milk and lime-water should form the chief-portion of the latter during the earlier period of the attack.

Chronic rheumatism is milder in its character than the acute form, more stationary, and less painful. An animal so affected moves stiffly, but apparently with no great suffering. Where it is articular the joints become hard, lumpy, and very much deformed.

In various changes of weather, particularly when easterly winds or wet prevails, these enlargements become hot and tender, and the animal's symptoms resemble more those of acute rheumatism.

Treatment.—The carbonate of ammonia and iodide of potassium are, perhaps, the most serviceable agents in chronic rheumatism: 3 to 5 grains of the former, 1 to 2 scruples of the latter, twice or thrice daily.

The affected parts should be stimulated with repeated hand-rubbings, or embrocations containing turpentine and ammonia. Warm baths are also very beneficial, but care should be taken that the animal is thoroughly dried, and placed in a warm and dry position afterwards.

I have already alluded to valvular disease of the heart as one of the complications of rheumatism. In such instances little can be done beyond avoiding excitement, applying counter-irritation to the left side, and reducing by medicinal agents the excessive action of the heart.—See "Heart Diseases."

RICKETS (RACHITIS).

One of the most troublesome affections to which young dogs are subject is the one termed "rickets." The larger species, and especially those highly bred, are chiefly liable to this affection, but it is by no means so common in canine pathology as many persons are led to believe. All bandy or crooked-legged whelps are not rickety, any more than are children similarly deformed from premature walking or careless nursing.

Rickets depends on, or consists in, a vitiated or abnormal condition of bone structure—in other words, defective nutrition; there is a deficiency of earthy matter and a preponderance of animal matter, and the bones, from this cause

FIG. 32.
DOG WITH RICKETS. SKETCHED FROM LIFE.

being soft, muscular action and weight bring about the various deformities met with in this disease. The morbid unhealthy state of system created by inter-breeding, has a strong influence in the production of a rachitic diathesis. The bones of the limbs, the fore ones more particularly, are those generally distorted. The facial bones are not unfrequently very prominent or bulging, giving the countenance a swollen appearance. The loins are generally narrow, the hocks bent in and enlarged, giving the hind-parts an undeveloped or wasted look (Fig. 32). The coat is staring and harsh, the mucous membranes are pallid, the sclerotic of the eye being particularly white, and the animal, taking it altogether, is an unthrifty, stunted, miserable-looking object.

I have mentioned inter-breeding as influential in the production of rickets, and in addition, or independent of this evil, may be named bad food, impure air, close confinement, and overfeeding—especially with matter deficient in bone-making properties,—or insufficient food. Remove, however, all these predisposing causes, allow good food and plentiful fresh air, and cleanliness, *but deny exercise*, and the result, *i.e.*, so far as the deformity of limbs is concerned, will be precisely the same—not from any deficiency in the structural proportion of bone, but from neglecting rules necessary for symmetrical and proportionate growth. Animals so circumstanced are like unpruned trees—the trunk is being fed and the branches allowed to grow as they may. The inclination of heavily-framed puppies to lie down, if not at liberty, is well known, and this is especially the case with mastiffs. The consequence is that the body becomes too heavy for the limbs to support; the latter, the bones of which it must be remembered are not at this age set, give way under the superincumbent weight, knuckle over or bend outwards; and it is this condition, arising from the circumstances named, which is frequently mistaken by breeders and rearers of dogs for rickets.

Rickets in the human subject involves bones other than those supporting weight, hence general deformity. This is rarely or ever the case with dogs (excepting, as mentioned, in the facial bones), more particularly as regards the ribs and spinal column; therefore it may be taken as a general rule, that canine rickets, when it does exist, only does so in a partial form. The position of the body probably exercises a considerable influence in this respect, the same weight on the spinal column being not brought to bear as in the erect position of the human being.

Treatment.—This chiefly consists in avoiding those causes which I have enumerated as giving rise to the malady. When the disease is established, then it will be necessary to adopt, in conjunction with hygienics, medical treatment. Bearing in mind that defective nutrition is the original cause, it behoves us to remedy, as far as lies in our power, the existing evil. We have seen that the bones are deficient in earthy materials; our object should therefore be to supply what is required. Mineral tonics are especially indicated. Bone-filings, pulverised egg-shells, or lime-water mixed with good oatmeal porridge, are exceedingly beneficial. Cod-liver oil is also a useful adjunct; while daily and, if need be, compulsory exercise is absolutely necessary.

COD-LIVER OIL EMULSION.

Cod-liver oil ⎫
Lime-water ⎭ aa 8 oz.

Shake well together.

Add ⎧ R. Ferri Perchlor. 4 drachms.
    ⎩ Spts. Amm. Arom. 1 ounce.

Shake well up until the whole is of an uniform consistency.

Dose.—A teaspoonful to a tablespoonful twice a day, according to age and size of dog.

Valuable in rickets and scrofula. For the latter, add 1 ounce Iod. Potass.

It is almost needless to observe that dogs of a rachitic diathesis should not be used for breeding purposes.

OSTITIS.

Ostitis, or inflammation of bone, may arise from direct injury, or be associated with constitutional disease: as scrofula, rheumatism, or mercurialism. The cancellated structure of the bone is the seat of inflammatory action.

Symptoms.—Heat, pain, swelling of the integument over the affected portion of bone; sometimes enlargement of the latter, extreme tenderness on manipulation (often mistaken for rheumatism), and the patient exhibits more or less inflammatory fever. If ostitis is confined to a limb, there is attendant lameness, or the limb is not used.

Treatment.—Perfect quietude, soft comfortable bed, hot fomentations, or linseed poultices; and, subsequently, if inflammatory action is protracted or enlargement persists, the application of iodine paint, and administration of iodide of potassium is indicated.

In 1884 I received a cross-bred mastiff dog into my infirmary, affected with cranial ostitis, caused by a violent blow with a poker, over the right parietal bone. Blisters and setons were employed, with general antiphlogistic treatment, and the patient made a good recovery.

PERIOSTITIS.

Periostitis, or inflammation of the periosteum, may be associated with ostitis, but is frequently met with in canine practice as a distinct affection. The inflamed condition of the membrane causes it to become highly vascular, thickened, and detached from the bone underneath, and, as in the case of *"splint"* on the horse's leg, osseous deposit is frequently deposited between the bone and periosteum, causing a permanent *node* or exostosis.

Periostitis in the limbs of a dog is very often caused by external violence, as a blow from a stick, stone, or kick. It occurs also in connection with the teeth and jaws, and under such circumstances is attended with acute suffering. At the present time I have a colley dog in the hospital, which has for a considerable time been a martyr to inflammation of the alveolo-dental periosteum. The removal of a molar tooth with an exostosed fang afforded immense relief, and the case is improving under the application of pure carbolic acid, frequent meals of soft warm food, and iodine paint externally.

When periostitis is associated with internal canker (otitis) the pain is most acute and agonising, and by ignorant people the symptoms manifested under such suffering have been mistaken for those of rabies. Very recently an illustration of this fact occurred in London. I fortunately saw the supposed rabid animal, and discovered severe otitis, which finally yielded to treatment.

Symptoms.—The manifestations of periostitis vary little from those attending ostitis. The pain, as in the human subject, is more superficial; the swelling, however, is more marked, and the general results less serious.

Treatment.—Remedial measures must be based on the same lines as those prescribed for ostitis. Division of the periosteum, *sub-cutaneous periosteotomy*, an operation I have frequently performed, has been practised with considerable success. Periosteal abscess must be treated on ordinary surgical principles.

SCROFULA.

Scrofula is a disease of common occurrence among the lower animals, and the canine race forms no exception to the fact.

As with human beings, so with the dog; it is usually met with in early life, and is traceable to those causes which give rise to it in our own species—such as near relationship in breeding, and certain morbid conditions of one or both parents.

Among the predisposing causes may be named insufficient and improper food, impure air, exposure to wet and cold.

Symptoms.—Animals, when so affected, are usually unthrifty and delicate; the coat is dry and harsh, the abdomen full and pendulous; the eyes are watery, the conjunctiva injected, and frequently mucus is deposited in the corner; the lymphatic glands are large and easily felt; very often the skull (especially the front portion) is unusually large. This latter is more particularly noticeable in puppyhood, and gives the idea, not unfrequently a correct one, of water on the brain.

Scrofula, when once localised, may remain latent for a long period, or gradually and manifestly developed. In an hereditary diathesis, it usually exhibits itself shortly before the animal arrives at maturity, or, as in the human subject, remains through life *in statu quo*, to become developed and distinctly marked in the offspring.

Treatment.—I need scarcely observe that the treatment of scrofula in the dog is of far less importance than are preventive measures. When treatment is adopted, it should be merely for humanity's sake, and never for the purpose of maintaining life in order to perpetuate the breed. A tainted strain of this description is neither a credit to the breeder, nor beneficial to the canine race.

The treatment is both local and constitutional. The former consists in cold baths and friction, and keeping the skin dry and warm. Cleanliness is of great importance. Animals that are allowed to live in filth, and remain unwashed, uncombed or brushed, under such circumstances are exposed to the development of strumous affections. It has been wrongly supposed that the dog does not perspire: hence perhaps one reason for negligence in attention to his body, externally. He not only perspires, but does so freely, and the arrest of such perspiration, from uncleanliness, cutaneous disease, and the like, creates serious functional derangement (from re-absorption of matters which are prevented from escaping by their natural outlet) internally, and lays the foundation for disease of a strumous character, in addition to other disorders.

With regard to constitutional treatment, iodine, iron, bark, and cod-liver oil are the agents most to be relied upon.

The first-named drug may also be used externally, in cases presenting enlarged glands or chronic abscess.

The diet should be liberal and nutritious. Daily exercise, and everything calculated to invigorate the system should be adopted.

Messrs. Gowing and Son record the following case of "Scrofula in a Puppy."

" The morbid parts forwarded are from a bull puppy between two and three months old. He was brought to me on the 9th instant, much emaciated and wasted; and from the distended, pendulous condition of the abdomen, he was apparently suffering from *ascites*. I requested the owner to leave him with me. He died some time during the night.

"*Post-mortem.*—Upon opening the abdomen, the cavity was full of serous fluid; and upon slitting open the intestines, the mucous membrane was observed to be highly inflamed through its entire course, but the peritoneal surface was only slightly discoloured in places.

" Some worms were found in the intestinal canal, which was somewhat contracted. The heart and liver I have forwarded to you, as they both give evidence of disease.

" A further history of the animal from the owner was to the effect that a fellow-pup died from the same disease, having a distended abdomen, wasting of flesh, and showing the same symptoms as the pup alluded to. The father of these pups was a fine specimen of the bull-dog, weighing upwards of forty pounds; he was of the Wallace breed, a famous strain.

" Some time ago I operated upon him for a cartilaginous growth on the cartilage of the eye; he did very well, and at that time was in good health and blooming condition. His owner gave him to a friend. Some months afterwards he was sent to me again, much wasted in flesh, with pendulous abdomen, suffering from the same disease as the pup, having a quantity of serous fluid in the abdominal cavity. Treatment was recommended; but some weeks afterwards I heard from the owner that the favourite and valuable old dog was dead. This breed of bull-dogs is, I believe, now almost extinct; they have been bred in-and-in.

"The examination of liver and heart led to the detection of a very unusual morbid change. The liver was dark in colour, speckled here and there with yellow granules. In form, the gland was almost globular; in texture it was compact, with the consistency of an ordinary fatty tumour. On section the cut surface was granular, and mottled with minute yellow specks. A small portion of the enlarged organ was examined under the quarter-inch objective, and the liver-cells were observed to be filled with globules of fat. In addition, there was a considerable quantity of deposit of the nature of tubercle.

"The heart was also much enlarged; the cavities of both ventricles were distended with coagulated blood. The walls were reduced in thickness to at least one half; and, under the microscope, the fibres were seen to be in the transition state between the nucleated cell form of the fœtal structure and the striated character of the fully developed muscle. Between the fibres there was a deposit of granular matter, identical in appearance with that observed in the liver. From the history of the case, there is good reason to believe that the puppy was the subject of scrofula, the result of hereditary transmission, intensified, and probably primarily induced, by the system of in-and-in breeding. The peculiar feature of the case is the existence of the deposit in the liver and heart—organs which are not ordinarily affected to any serious extent in tuberculosis. The lungs, spleen, and kidneys were free from disease."[*]

GLANDERS.

Fortunately, this scourge of horseflesh is but seldom met with in the dog.

---

[*] From the *Veterinarian*, November, 1881.

Mr. Fleming, in his "Veterinary Sanitary Science," on this subject, observes: "The receptivity of the dog is not very great; indeed, not many years ago, inoculations with glander virus were so unsuccessful in this animal that it was believed it could not be infected.

"Herting made experiments for several years, but they were always incomplete in their results. He fed eight dogs for a number of weeks on the raw flesh of glandered horses, but without producing the disease in them. At first, however, they were usually affected with diarrhœa, the fæces being of a dark red colour. Nordstrom produced the malady in two dogs by feeding them with this flesh; they had a bloody discharge from the nostrils, redness of the eyes, and an œdematous swelling of the head. They died.*

"Lafosse mentions the case of a dog belonging to Marshal Neil, which contracted the malady through living in the same stable with a diseased horse. Hertwig applied the nasal discharge from glandered horses to the Schneiderian membrane of six dogs, by means of a small brush. In two or three days this membrane became swollen and dark-coloured, and there was a thin glutinous discharge, with moderate tumefaction of the submaxillary lymphatic glands. When the matter was inoculated on the skin of the forehead (where the animal could not lick the wounds), in two or three days there was swelling of the eyes, redness of the conjunctivæ, and tumefaction of the submaxillary glands. The wound inflamed, suppurated for about eight days, and then, a black crust forming over it, it healed in about twenty to twenty-five days.

"Of six dogs inoculated by Renault, two became affected. One of these perished three-and-a-half months after the local development of the disease, but the other only died in the fifth month. The successful inoculation of two horses with the virus obtained from the ulcers of these dogs left

---

* "Tidskrift for Veterinairer," etc., Stockholm, 1862.

no doubt as to the nature of the malady, which appeared in a most acute form.

"Polli, of Milan, has induced the disease in dogs by depositing the virus in wounds or injecting it into the circulation. The effects were always apparent, but their intensity and gravity varied according to the mode of introduction. Prinz, Andral, Burguieres, Letenneur, Leblanc, Rayer, Saussier, and St. Cyr* have obtained results similar to those of Renault; Lafosse has also several times successfully inoculated dogs with the glanders and farcy virus; and Decroix, from the result of his experiments, came to the conclusion that acute and chronic glanders are transmissible to the carnivora by inoculation.†

"Some of the large carnivora, such as the lion, have received the disease through consuming the flesh of glandered horses."

---

* "The results of inoculations practised upon seven dogs with glander matter, by Saint Cyr, of the Lyons Veterinary School, are summed up as follows:—

"1. Glanders is not the exclusive appanage of solipeds.

"2. It can certainly be transmitted to other animals, and especially to the dog, by inoculation.

"3. In the dog, as in the horse, it manifests itself by inflammation and ulceration of the inoculated wound, swelling of the lymphatic glands in its vicinity, and nasal discharge. Chancrous ulcers are, if not always, at least generally, absent.

"4. Glanders in the dog is generally remarkably benignant, and, except in those cases in which it has been injected into the circulation, it is perhaps seldom fatal.

"5. Notwithstanding this marked benignity of 'canine glanders,' the virus none the less preserves all its activity, and, when retransmitted to the horse, inevitably produces the malady in as marked a form as when passed direct from horse to horse.

"6. Lastly, glanders in the dog, as in the horse, appears to be governed by the 'law of unicity;' for with the horse actually glandered, and the dog successfully inoculated for the first time, inoculation with the most active glander virus produces no effect. This conclusion, however, requires more experiments to corroborate it."—"Journal de Méd. Vét. de Lyon," 1866, p. 307.

† "Journal de Méd. Vét. Militaire," 1863.

SMALL-POX (VARIOLÆ CANINÆ).

Variola of the dog is by no means a frequent disease in this country, and there is but little to be found in English veterinary literature on the subject.

Youatt describes the malady as follows:

"The essential symptoms of small-pox in dogs succeed each other in the following order: the skin of the belly, the groin, and the inside of the fore-arm becomes of a redder colour than in its natural state, and sprinkled with small red spots, irregularly rounded. They are sometimes isolated, sometimes clustered together. The near approach of this eruption is announced by an increase of fever.

"On the second day the spots are larger, and the integument is slightly tumefied at the centre of each.

"On the third day the spots are generally enlarged, and the skin is still more prominent at the centre.

"On the fourth day the summit of the tumour is yet more prominent. Towards the end of that day, the redness of the centre begins to assume a somewhat grey colour. On the following days the pustules take on their peculiar characteristic appearance, and cannot be confounded with any other eruption. On the summit is a white circular point, corresponding with a certain quantity of nearly transparent fluid which it contains, and covered by a thin and transparent pellicle. This fluid becomes less and less transparent, until it acquires the colour and consistence of pus. The pustule, during its serous state, is of a rounded form. It is flattened when the fluid acquires a purulent character, and even slightly depressed towards the close of the period of suppuration, and when that of desiccation is about to commence, which ordinarily happens towards the ninth or tenth day of eruption. The desiccation and the desquamation occupy an exceedingly variable length of time, and so indeed do all the different periods of the disease. What is the least inconstant is the duration of the serous eruption, which is about four days, if it had been distinctly produced

and guarded from all friction. If the general character of the pustules is considered, it will be observed that, while some of them are in a state of serous secretion, others will only have begun to appear.

"The eruption terminates when desiccation commences in the first pustules; and, if some red spots show themselves at that period of the malady, they disappear without being followed by the development of pustules. They are a species of abortive pustules. After the desiccation, the skin remains covered by brown spots, which, by degrees, die away. There remains no trace of the disease, except a few superficial cicatrices, on which the hair does not grow.

"The causes which produce the greatest variation in the periods of the eruption are, the age of the dog and the temperature of the situation and of the season. The eruption runs through its different stages with much more rapidity in dogs from one to five months old, than in those of greater age. I have never seen it in dogs more than 18 months old. An elevated temperature singularly favours the eruption, and also renders it confluent and of a serous character. A cold atmosphere is unfavourable to the eruption, or even prevents it altogether. Death is almost constantly the result of the exposure of dogs having small-pox to any considerable degree of cold. A moderate temperature is most favourable to the recovery of the animal. A frequent renewal or change of air, the temperature remaining nearly the same, is highly favourable to the patient; consequently, close boxes or kennels should be altogether avoided.

"I have often observed that the perspiration or breath of dogs labouring under variola emits a very unpleasant odour. This smell is particularly observed at the commencement of the desiccation of the pustules, and when the animals are lying upon dry straw; for the friction of the bed against the pustules destroys their pellicles and permits the purulent matter to escape—and the influence of this purulent matter is most pernicious. The fever is increased, and also the unpleasant smell from the mouth, and that of the fæces In this state there is a disposition, which is rapidly developed in the lungs, to assume the character of pneumonia.

"This last complication is a most serious one, and almost always terminates fatally. It has a peculiar character. It shows itself suddenly, and with all its alarming symptoms. It is almost immediately accompanied by a purulent secretion from the bronchi, and the second day does not pass without the characters of pneumonia being completely developed. The respiration is accompanied by a mucous *râle*, which often becomes sibilant. The nasal cavities are filled with a purulent fluid. The dog that coughs violently at the commencement of the disease, employs himself, probably, on the following day, in ejecting, by a forcible expulsion from the nostrils, the purulent secretion which is soon and plentifully developed. When he is lying quiet, and even when he seems to be asleep, there is a loud, stertorous, guttural breathing."

Mr. James Moore, in his homœopathic work on the "Diseases of the Dog," observes with regard to it : "This disease, which is much more common on the Continent than in this country, has been fairly described by Barrier and Leblanc.

"*Symptoms.*—At first the animal is dull and depressed, and carries his head drooped ; the eyelids are half-closed and the eyes vacant in expression ; the nose is hot and dry ; the tongue furred ; the dog prefers to lie down, and when induced or compelled to get up and walk, the pace is slow and unsteady ; the bowels are confined, and the urine highcoloured ; the pulse is somewhat accelerated, and there are occasional and frequent vomitings. Sooner or later, diarrhœa comes on. The evacuations are bilious, dark, and offensive ; the countenance is expressive of anxiety and uneasiness, and there are evident indications of prostration. Four or five days from the onset, after shivering, vesicles appear on the head, and thence gradually spread to other parts of the body; these vesicles subsequently break, and the resulting scab falls off in due course.

"A pack of hounds ate the carcases of some sheep, dead of clavelée (small-pox). Seventeen of them became ill. At first, distemper was suspected, as the dogs were low-spirited, weak, paralytic in their limbs, and had a viscid, greenish discharge from their nostrils. A copious crop of 'pustules' appeared, and the disease was thereafter, rightly or wrongly, regarded as small-pox. Eleven died.

"It has been stated that some dogs were infected from sheep with this disease, during the recent Wiltshire epidemic; and that in both animals the disease was identical in its symptoms.

"In small-pox the skin is affected in the following manner: The skin of the belly, groin, etc., is redder than usual, and dotted with small roundish spots, either isolated or irregularly clustered together. Each spot gradually gets larger, and its centre becomes prominent and pointed, and contains a clear fluid, which subsequently acquires a pus-like appearance. Each spot is now flattened; the contained fluid escapes on the rupture of its envelope; scabs form from the drying of the fluid, and gradually fall off. In some parts of the body a permanent minute scar remains, and the hair is destroyed for good."

Mr. Fleming observes:* "This is a rare malady, and may be developed directly or by contagion; it is supposed to be also produced by the variola of man and of the sheep. It chiefly affects young dogs, although old animals are not exempt. One attack ensures immunity for the remainder of the dog's life.

"*Symptoms.*—The disease commences with fever, which continues for two or three days, and is followed by the appearance—over a large surface of the body, though rarely on the back and sides of the trunk—of red points,

---

* "Veterinary Sanitary Science," vol. ii. p. 98.

resembling flea-bites, which are quickly transformed into nodules, and then into vesicles. The contents of these become purulent, and finally dry into a crust, whose shedding leaves a naked cicatrix.

"In the dog, as in the sheep and pig, there are different forms of the disease, and it is benignant or malignant accordingly. Puppies nearly always succumb, and, on a necroscopical examination, it is not unusual to find variolous pustules on the mucous membrane of the respiratory and digestive organs.

"*Sanitary Measures.*—The disease being contagious, though the virus does not appear to be very volatile, it is necessary to isolate the sick, and take due precautions that the contagion is not carried from them to healthy animals.

"*Curative Measures.*—Careful dieting, a dry and moderately warm dwelling, cleanliness, and abundance of fresh air, are the essentials in the curative treatment."

An emetic in the early stage of the malady has been recommended as likely to be useful. Afterwards the treatment must be purely symptomatic.

MEASLES.

An interesting case of this nature is described in a recent report of the Epidemiological Society:

"A dog licked the hand of a child lying in bed, and on whom the measles eruption was at its height. Twelve days later the dog sickened, and suffered for two days with nasal discharge; and four days later died, with marked congestion of the throat and air-passages. It has been held by some authorities that measles in man is the analogue of distemper in dogs—indeed, it has been urged that they are the same diseases; but this case contradicts such a view, for the dog in question had, four years previously, gone through an attack of distemper; and, although second attacks of the various eruptive fevers are common enough in children, second attacks of distemper are rare amongst dogs—while such second cases, when they do occur, are invariably of a slight and temporary nature."*

TETANUS.

This disease is of rare occurrence in canine practice. It is divided into *Idiopathic, i.e.,* where no visible cause is in existence; and *Traumatic,* when it arises from injury or wound.

Tetanus consists of, or denotes, an uncontrollable spasmodic contraction of the voluntary muscles. It is exceedingly painful, and usually fatal.

The disease may assume a local or general form, *i.e.,* it may be limited to the jaws, producing *lock-jaw*; or it may extend to a part or the whole of the trunk, and give rise to partial or general rigidity.

Causes.—Changes of temperature, exposure to cold and wet, excessive fatigue; injuries by wounds or bruises; irritation to the nerve extremities, or main trunks; the presence of irritants in the stomach and intestines; strychnia.

Symptoms.—When the jaws only are affected the head is poked out, the jaws are tightly closed, the angles of the mouth are drawn back, the mouth filled with frothy saliva, and the eyes fixed in an unnatural and often hideous position.

Whatever portion of the animal is affected, this is drawn and deformed.

In general tetanus the patient, if able to walk, moves stiffly, or, as it were, *all of a piece.* The ears are pricked, the tail is carried out straight and has a quivering motion; the affected muscles have a tense corded feel, and the limbs are straight and set. During a spasm the animal falls over

---

* *Veterinary Journal*, Sept., 1876.

on its side, and presents much the same appearance as if poisoned by strychnine, uttering strange hoarse cries between fear and pain.*

Death may result from asphyxia, exhaustion, or—though I believe it to be exceedingly rare—spasmodic contraction of the heart.

Post-mortem Appearances.—These vary somewhat: most frequently the spinal cord and its membranes are congested; occasionally the brain and dura mater exhibit a similar appearance, but more particularly so in general and protracted tetanus. In cases of traumatic tetanus, this condition is more apparent in the nerve tissue near the seat of injury; while the muscles in the same locality are soft, dark, and gorged with blood. In severe cases they are sometimes ruptured.

Treatment.—A late eminent lecturer on this subject, as affecting the horse, was wont to observe, in producing a stable door-key, that that was the best measure we could adopt in this disease, and the same meaning he intended to convey is equally applicable to the dog. Perfect quietude, moderate warmth, and subdued light, should always be enforced in the treatment of canine tetanus. The person the animal is most accustomed and attached to, is the fittest attendant: the susceptibility to excitement is so intense that the presence of a stranger, rough handling, or loud

---

* I have heard it frequently argued that tetanus is not a painful disease, and that in the horse the profuse perspirations which accompany it are merely the result of absolute fear. This theory I cannot subscribe to, and never have agreed with. I do not for a moment dispute the presence of fear, or that it is a cause of perspiration; but my reply has always been that pain must be, at all events for a time, an inevitable result of sudden and inordinate stimulus by the nerves supplying the muscles so affected. Long-continued pressure may, and we know will, in time produce numbness or paralysis; but in tetanus there being remissions of convulsion, each sudden contraction when a spasm comes on must produce intense pain.

and harsh words will generally induce violent spasmodic seizures, and hasten an agonising death.

With regard to constitutional remedies, Fleming's tincture of aconite stands pre-eminent. Dose, one to two minims every two or three hours. An aperient at the onset is, if its administration is possible, very advisable; but it should be borne in mind that an attempt to give a draught to a tetanic animal is, as a rule, creative of that alarm and severe spasms at all times to be avoided. Here, then, is the benefit of aconite. If the patient is able to lap, the drug may be dropped in a little milk or water, without impregnating it with any objectionable taste. When the jaws are locked, and fluids cannot with safety be poured between the cheek and teeth, the same quantity may be given in an enema.

Counter-irritation to the spine is at times attended (chiefly in protracted cases) with benefit. Baths, warm or cold, are injudicious and useless.

If the disease is caused by a wound, this should at the same time be carefully attended to. It should be thoroughly examined to see whether any foreign or irritating matter is present; if there is, it must be at once removed. When the wound is very painful, sedative poultices afford great relief; otherwise dressing with lunar caustic, and afterwards inducing healthy suppuration, is the treatment I recommend. In traumatic tetanus, when the wound assumes a healthy condition, the constitutional symptoms usually improve with it.

The diet should be nourishing, easy of deglutition and digestion—as milk, broth, beef-tea, and such like. These may be given in the form of enemas, if necessary.

CRAMP.

Dogs subjected to violent exercise, and afterwards exposed to cold, or kennelled in cold and damp habitations, are not unfrequently affected with cramp. The same condition sometimes follows swimming, particularly in cold seasons of the year. The symptoms, though in some respects not unlike those of rheumatism, differ from them in the rapidity with which they pass off when warmth and free circulation to the part are restored. The hind parts are those generally affected. The treatment consists in brisk exercise, and friction to the part.

DISEASES OF THE HEART.

Diseases of the heart are not very frequently met with in canine practice, except as the result of complications of other maladies.

Fatty degeneration is, perhaps, the most common form met with; several instances of this I have seen when making *post-mortem* examinations of animals.

"In examining a heart thus diseased, the eye first notices the fainter tracing, or the utter absence of those transverse marks which cross the fibres of all the voluntary muscles, and less distinctly those of the involuntary muscle, the heart. In an early stage of the disease these cross-lines are dimly seen, and the fibre is studded here and there with small dark points. When the disease is more decidedly expressed the dots are more numerous and the striæ disappear. These dots are little globules of oil lying within the sheath of the fibre, they make it soft and friable.

"The parts of the heart which have undergone this change are altered in colour as well as in consistence. They are pale, like a faded leaf, or of a yellowish-brown, or a muddy-pink colour, and they commonly have a spotty or mottled appearance. The change of texture varies in degree and in extent. It may render the muscle merely soft and flabby, or it may reduce it to a state in which it feels like a wet kid glove, and can be torn as readily as wet brown paper. Every chamber of the heart is liable to this kind of disease, but most of all the left ventricle, then the right ventricle, then the right auricle, and least of all the left auricle. Generally it is more evident in the columnæ carneæ, and neai the endocardium, than elsewhere.

" Fatty degeneration of the heart may proceed from a defect of healthy nutrition throughout the body in consequence of some general disorder, or of natural decay in the decline of life. In such cases the same morbid change is commonly manifest in other parts also ; in the arteries, in the liver, in the kidneys, in the cornea.

" But fatty degeneration may be limited to the heart, and even to a small portion of the heart, and then it is owing to some local failure of nutrition ; of which, perhaps, the most common cause is a diseased condition of the coronary arteries. You are probably aware that these two vessels have no large or free communication with each other, and it is a very instructive fact, that when one of them alone is diseased, that part only of the heart frequently is found to be affected which receives its supply of blood through the unsound artery. Fatty degeneration of the heart is also met with after bygone inflammation, whether of the muscular tissue itself, or of its lining, or its investing membrane. It is no uncommon sequel of hypertrophy. In every instance the change seems ultimately traceable to deficient nutrition."*

There are no positive symptoms by which this condition of the heart can be detected during life. The pulse may be intermittent, feeble, or slow, as in other affections of the organ, and rapid exertion may produce distress. Beyond these, the practitioner has nothing to assist him until an examination after death reveals the real state of the case.

The large deposits of fat on the heart usually seen in obese animals, are usually unassociated with fatty degeneration ; though the two may exist combined, the former seldom interferes with health.

---

* Watson's " Lectures on the Principles and Practice of Physic."

Valvular disease of the heart, as I have previously, in another section, observed, is a frequent and serious complication of rheumatism. When such a condition is present, the intermittent, jerking, feeble pulse, the short, sudden inspiration and sharp cry, on violent exercise or rapid movement, frequently accompanied by a fall, as if shot, are the symptoms presented to us in this malady.

Post-mortem Appearances.—On examination, the valves are found considerably thickened, and granular on their surfaces. (In horses I have frequently observed this latter condition.) It is also not unusual to find adhesion of the pericardium to the heart, or an excess of serum, in which lymph or fibrine may be deposited.

Treatment.—Any hope of a cure in a disease of this nature must, it is almost needless to observe, be abandoned. Having reason to believe that rheumatic disease of the heart exists, it behoves us to avoid, or give instructions for the avoidance of, those causes likely to result in alarming seizures, such as I have described, or sudden death. Shocks, frights, rapid exercise, exposure to cold or intense heat, should, as far as possible, be prevented. The animal should be kept well nourished, and small doses of the iodide of iron may be given from time to time, and in severe palpitation with pain, sedatives, with counter-irritation over the left side, may be had recourse to. Constipation, diarrhœa, or, indeed, anything causing the patient to strain, must also be avoided.

The following case of heart disease, associated with rheumatism and chorea, recently came under my observation.

In December, 1877, a fox-terrier dog, about six years old, belonging to Miss Walker, of Bromley House, Penn, was brought to me for treatment. I found the animal suffering from rheumatic chorea, and I was informed by the owner that when purchased at nine months old, he at that time never stood perfectly still, but always shook slightly, especially on the fore-legs. The dog now moved with a reeling, snatching gait; the latter was particularly observable in the hind-legs. The back was also arched. When lying down or resting, the head had a tremulous, but not persistent, motion; the limbs, however, were continually twitching. I inserted a seton at the back of the ears. The same afternoon, before medicinal treatment was commenced, the animal died.

I made a *post-mortem* examination for the purpose of ascertaining the condition of the heart, as the case being of long standing, and complicated with rheumatism, I expected to find cardiac mischief. On making a section through the right ventricle, and exposing the tricuspid

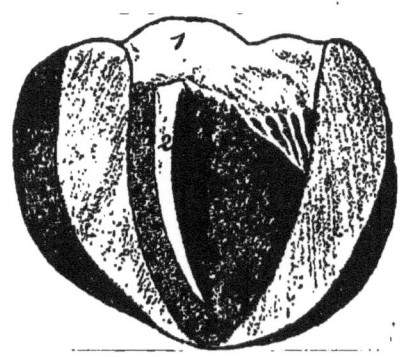

FIG. 33.

HEART OF DOG, LEFT VENTRICLE OPEN. 1. MITRAL VALVE, INFLAMED. 2. ANTE-MORTEM FIBRINOUS CLOT.

valve, I found the latter thickened and rough, beyond which there was nothing abnormal to be seen; but an examination of the left ventricle revealed the presence of an *ante-mortem* clot seven-eighths of an inch in length, wedge-shaped, tapering to a point. It was the sixteenth of an inch thick, white in colour, and fibrous, having on its upper surface a dark, recent blood-clot. This *ante-mortem* clot was immediately below and partly attached to the mitral valve, the latter being much inflamed; the tapering or pointed end was unattached.

I have endeavoured, by means of the accompanying illustration, to give a more exact idea of the appearance the heart, valve, and clot presented (Fig. 33).

The specimen was considered by several medical men to whom it was shown to be a very interesting and exceptional one.

Since writing the above, I have been informed that the dog was stolen in 1876, and nothing was seen or known of his whereabouts for a year, when he unexpectedly returned, and it is supposed by his mistress that during his absence he was roughly used, as his spirit seemed broken, and he had the appearance of being much older than he really was.

Rupture of the heart, not uncommon in the human subject, and occasionally seen in the horse, is of rare occurrence in the dog.

" A black pointer, of the Scotch breed, had every appearance of good health, except that she frequently fell into a fit after having run a little way, and sometimes even after playing in the yard. She was several times bled during and after these fits. When I examined her, I could plainly perceive considerable, and even violent spasmodic motion of the heart, and the sounds of the beating of that organ were irregular and convulsive. She was sent to the infirmary, in order to be cured of an attack of mange; but during her stay in the hospital she had these fits several times; the attack almost always followed after she had been playing with other dogs. She appeared as if struck by lightning, and remained motionless for several minutes, her gums loosing their natural appearance, and assuming a bluish hue. After the lapse of a few minutes she again rose as if nothing had been the matter. She was bled twice in eight days, and several doses of fox-glove were administered to her. The fits appeared to become less frequent; but, playing one day with another dog, she fell and expired immediately.

"The *post-mortem* examination was made two hours after death. The cavity of the pericardium contained a red clot of blood, which enveloped the whole of the heart; it was thicker in the parts that corresponded with the valve of the heart; and on the left ventricle, and near the base of the left valve of the heart, as well as the external part of that viscus, was an irregular rent two inches long. It crossed the valve of the heart, which was very thin in this place. The size of the heart was very small, considering the height and bulk of the dog. The walls of the ventricles, and particularly of the left ventricle, were very thick. The cavity of the left ventricle was very small; there was evidently a concentric hypertrophy of these ventricles; the valve of the heart was of great size.

"The immediate cause of the rupture of the valve of the heart had evidently been an increase of circulation, brought on by an increase of exercise; but the remote cause consisted in the remarkable thinness of the valve of the heart.

"This case is remarkable in more than one respect: first, because instances of rupture of the valve of the heart are very rare; and, secondly, because this rupture had its seat in the left valve of the heart, while usually, in both the human being and the quadruped, it takes place in the right, and this without doubt because the walls and the valves of the right side are thinner."*

PERICARDITIS.

Inflammation of the pericardium of heart sac is a disease, comparatively speaking, not very frequently seen, or, at all events, diagnosed in the canine species.

Pericarditis, when not the result of direct injury from crushing or penetrating wounds, is usually associated with acute rheumatism, pleurisy, or pyæmia.

---

* Youatt on "The Dog."

I have recently had two well-marked cases under treatment: the one associated with rheumatic fever, the other with pleurisy, the former patient being an aged fox terrier bitch, also affected with mammary cancer, the latter a young pug bitch.

Symptoms.—General distress, fever, pain in the region of the heart, tumultuous and jerking action of the latter, irregular pulse, considerable restlessness and anxiety of expression. Distinct valvular murmurs may be heard on auscultation.

If there is much serous effusion in the pericardium the heart-sounds will be deadened. Very frequently the patient assumes a persistent sitting posture, or stands in a fixed condition with drooping head and haggard face.

Treatment.—Both my patients made good recoveries under bromide of potassium and chloral hydrate. Externally hot linseed poultices were applied at the onset; subsequently, iodine liniment was daily painted over the cardiac region.

Diet.—Chiefly, beef-tea with port wine, and occasionally eggs and milk; during convalescence cod-liver oil and Parish's chemical food.

When there is considerable effusion in the pericardium iodide of potassium is indicated and biniodide of mercury blisters.

EMBOLISM.

Embolism in the dog is not altogether uncommon though difficult of diagnosis, the symptoms depending on the seat of the obstruction, or arrested embolus. According to Dr. Tanner, "a large clot from an inflamed vein fixed in pulmonary artery will induce immediate asphyxia; or, if able to pass on into lung, may be the cause of hæmoptysis, pleuro-pneumonia, or even gangrene. Obstruction of the chief vessel of a limb will induce mortification. Plugging of cerebral artery may cause hemiplegia and softening of portion of the brain; of renal artery albuminuria. Capillary embolism plays an important part in pyæmia and other conditions. Septic particles absorbed from a focus of unhealthy suppuration lodge in the capillaries of distant parts, and there set up secondary inflammation and abscesses."

On the 6th of June, 1883, a pointer dog, aged nine years, the property of R. C. Kettle, Esq., barrister, was brought to my infirmary, presenting the following symptoms: Deep and laboured breathing, pulse small and wavering, abdomen distended, and prominence over the hepatic region. I diagnosed the case as one of ascites, associated with enlargement of the liver and lung disease of old standing. The pulse indicated some valvular mischief in the heart. The patient was placed under treatment, and it was proposed, when prepared, to tap the abdomen. On the 16th, during my absence, Mr. Kettle took the dog away, wishing me to treat him at home; death, however, as I had prognosticated, if moved, took place soon after he reached his kennel, and, by request, I made a *post-mortem* examination the following morning.

The abdomen contained over a gallon of clear straw-coloured fluid. The liver was enlarged and congested, weighed four pounds and one ounce, and contained large deposits of medullary cancer. The valves of the heart were hypertrophied. The lungs were tuberculosed, and exhibited traces of past inflammation.

The immediate cause of death was embolism of the posterior vena cava. From the right auricle of the heart, and in a considerable portion of its passage through the liver, this vessel had become entirely blocked by a long fibro-cartilaginous granular chain-like plug, not unlike the hard roe of a fish magnified. Near to the liver this plug was purely calcareous, and could only be chipped out. A portion of the fibro-cartilaginous granular embolus which existed in the right auricle was united to the large plug by a partially fibrinous clot of blood. In the roots of the portal veins similar deposits were present, and there was more hypertrophy of the areolar framework of the liver, the lobes of the latter being united by a thick layer of lymph. Within the pulmonary artery there was also a large fibrinous clot. The lungs contained large clusters of the same granular material found in the auricle and vena cava.

Mr. Kettle informed me the dog had been in his possession for seven years, that he was his first master after his breaking, and that he had shown no signs of illness until six months previous to his consulting me, and the previous season he had galloped the hills as well as ever. The *post-mortem* examination, however, did not verify sound health so shortly before death. Doubtless many symptoms of indisposition were displayed that escaped observation prior to the first notice of his owner.

This extraordinary case is recorded, with an illustration of the embolism, in the *Live Stock Journal* for July 13th, 1883.

EMPHYSEMA.

Emphysematous swelling in the dog is usually due to the infiltration of air into the connective areolar tissue, from external injury. Pulmonary Emphysema is generally associated with asthma, and is accompanied by shortness of breath, cough, frothy expectoration, feeble husky bark, and weak pulse. Auscultation reveals wheezy sounds, with more or less cardiac palpitation. (See Asthma.)

Mr. J. S. Gould, pupil of Mr. E. Hollingham, M.R.C.V.S., of Tonbridge Wells, has kindly furnished me with the following particulars of an interesting case of Traumatic Emphysema:—

"On January 14th, 1888, we had the dead body of a deerhound bitch, the property of the Marquis of Abergavenny, brought to us for examination as to the cause of death. The bitch in question had been hunting in the afternoon, and, after running a buck, the size of her body was observed to be much increased, there was a difficulty in breathing, and frequent attempts to vomit. These conditions became rapidly more acute, and death resulted in about twenty minutes after the first noticeable symptoms of illness. It was an hour after death when we made the autopsy, the body being then an enormous size, and the loose cellular tissue under the tongue was much inflated, and protruded from the mouth in the form of a bladder, the tongue itself being of normal size. This inflated tissue pressed the tongue to the roof of the mouth, and had caused death by asphyxia. The original cause of the emphysema was a punctured wound received from the buck's antler, and in running the bitch had literally pumped herself full of air; and on the inflated cellular tissue under the tongue being pierced, the air rushed out, and the body of the hound resumed somewhat its normal proportions."

Treatment.—The treatment of Emphysema consists in making various punctures into the inflated part, so arranged as to circumscribe or localize the emphysema, and to form sufficient outlets for the imprisoned air; and it may also be desirable to enlarge the original puncture. Bandaging has been suggested as a repressive and absorbent measure.

On this subject, in Human Surgery, Gant observes:—
" Should respiration become oppressed, venesection, freely employed, will often afford the most marked and instantaneous relief."

CHAPTER XVIII.

ACCIDENTS AND OPERATIONS.

FRACTURES,
DISLOCATIONS,
AMPUTATIONS,
WOUNDS,
SPRAINS,
BURNS AND SCALDS,
UMBILICAL HERNIA,
VENTRAL HERNIA,
FEMORAL HERNIA,
FISTULÆ,
CYST EXCISION,
CHOKING,
ŒSOPHAGOTOMY,
LITHOTOMY,
URETHRAL OBSTRUCTION,
CATHETERISM,
VAGINOTOMY,
ANTI-CONCEPTION OPERATION,
SORE FEET,
SOFT CORNS,
OVER-GROWTH OF CLAWS,
REMOVAL OF DEW-CLAWS,
CROPPING,
ROUNDING,
TAILING,
WORMING,
CASTRATION,
SPAYING,
VACCINATION,
CHLOROFORM.

FRACTURES.

THESE are of very common occurrence in the dog. They are divided into compound, comminuted, and simple. Compound, when there is an external wound communicating with the fracture; comminuted, when the bone is broken into numerous fragments; simple, when the bone is broken only in one place, and without other injury. The latter may be transverse, oblique, or longitudinal.

In young animals, partial or incomplete fracture, *i.e.*,

when the outside of the bone splits away similar to a tough twig when bent to break, is occasionally met with (Fig. 34). This, in human surgery, is termed green-stick fracture, an illustration of which I once had in one of my

FIG. 34.
INCOMPLETE FRACTURE.

children, by falling from the back of a pony on to his hand and fracturing the radius in the manner described.

Fracture without separation, is when a bone is starred, as it were, and held together by the periosteum; it is rare in the dog, though common in the horse.

The long bones are those most liable to fracture, more especially those of the extremities. Fracture of the scapula, pelvis, ribs, cranium, and vertebræ are occasionally met with in the dog, and therefore demand notice in these pages.

In the human being there are various predisposing causes of fracture. In the dog they are invariably the result of direct violence. The usual symptoms of limb-fracture are: deformity, loss of muscular power, pain, swelling, and crepitus. The reparative process in the dog is remarkably rapid, and, as a rule, when the parts are placed *in situ* and the splints applied, the animal seems to understand the injured limb is not to be interfered with, and is contented to remain quiet.

The treatment of fracture consists in reducing the separated portions to their proper position and maintaining them there when so reduced by the application of splints and bandages.

Splints may be composed of wood, pasteboard, leather, or gutta-percha. The three first-named are retained in position by bandaging. The latter is rendered soft with hot water and moulded to the limb. Bandages take the place of splints when soaked in gum, starch, or plaster of Paris.

With regard to fracture of the long bones of the limbs, I have found no application equal to the wooden splint. We will suppose a case of fractured ulna or radius. The fractured edges being reduced to their relative position, and the limb held firmly in a straight line downwards, the splints, cut the length required (I always take them below the knee-joint to the foot), are applied as follows: one in front, one behind, and one on either side. The surface is smeared with pitch to maintain them better in position. A little pad of tow or cotton wool should be placed under the ends of the splints, to prevent irritation and wounds. Being thus satisfactorily arranged, a narrow bandage of calico is wound round, moderately tight, from end to end, smeared occasionally in its course with pitch. This done, the patient should be conveyed to where he is to remain : and to prevent risk, it is better to place a wire muzzle on for the first few days, or at all events until the parts have become firm.

The same treatment will apply to comminuted fracture.

A black retriever dog was brought to me, suffering from double fracture of the femur, the fractures being some distance apart; a bull and mastiff, aged, with fracture of the femur in three distinct places. Both were treated with splint-setting, and recovered perfectly, without any deformity or perceptible thickening, except on manipulation.

Fracture of a toe bone is an accident not uncommon to greyhounds when coursing, and is usually produced at the instant of making a sharp turn. Such fractures are easily set, but if not dealt with early they may be of serious moment to the animal and the interests of his owner.

I usually apply lateral adhesive splints to the broken toe, and then spread the foot on a broad splint extending a little beyond the claws. The whole is then bandaged up, and the patient kept perfectly quiet for at least a fortnight.

A month under such treatment invariably secures union. Such fractures are usually transverse or oblique.

Fracture of the scapula is occasionally met with, chiefly in small toy dogs, and is usually caused by tumbles downstairs, or from elevated positions. I have treated two (the only ones brought under my care) successfully; both were fractured at the neck of the bone.* Two pasteboard splints smeared with pitch were placed parallel, and a quarter of an

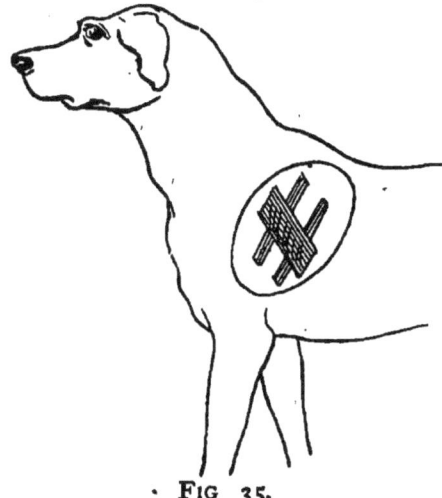

FIG 35.

FRACTURE OF SCAPULA, SHOWING POSITION OF SPLINTS AND PLASTER.

inch apart and obliquely; another was then applied crossways, and a pitch-plaster on sheep-skin covered them and the whole shoulder (Fig. 35). I then passed a bandage, commencing from the centre of the shoulder across the withers, to the other side under the brisket back again, and so on, several times securing it in its situation with pitch (Fig. 36).

On the 24th of May, 1877, a cub fox, belonging to Mrs. Boughey, five weeks old, nursed by hand, was brought to me suffering from comminuted fracture of the scapula. I set it

---

* Since writing the above I have had many cases of scapula fracture to deal with, and in following out the same principle of treatment I have had similar success.

in the same manner as above described, with one exception. The injury had taken place some days previously; in addition to the fracture, there was luxation of the shoulder-joint, which caused the limb to spread out laterally at a right angle to the shoulder. To maintain it in proper position, I cut and applied a kid glove as follows; having removed the thumb, second and fourth fingers, and the ends from the remaining ones, I inserted both fore-legs through the finger-stalls, buttoned the wrist portion over the shoulders and drew it together across the chest by means of another strip sewn on and made to button. This I found admirably

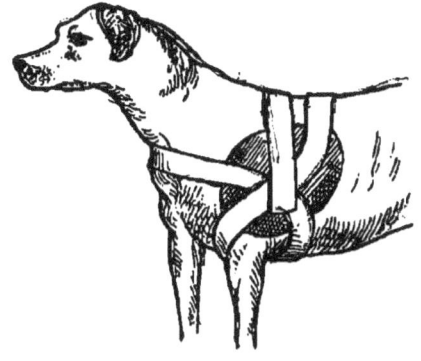

FIG. 36.

FRACTURE OF SCAPULA, WITH BANDAGE APPLIED.

answered the double purpose of keeping the limb as I wished it, and rendering displacement of the shoulder-setting more unlikely.

Within five weeks the support was removed, and I shortly after received a letter from Mrs. Boughey, informing me that the interesting little patient was able to follow her upstairs without difficulty. I have recently seen the animal, which I find in no way stunted in growth; it is perfectly straight on its limbs, and with no perceptible thickening, lameness, or defect in gait.

Fracture of the Pelvis.—In a case of this description, little can be done beyond keeping the patient quiet ; the bandage recommended for shoulder-fracture may be applied in the same way, carrying it between the hind-legs and across the loins. As a rule, however, these are far from satisfactory cases, and unless required for breeding purposes (and which then depends upon the portion of pelvis fractured) treatment is not advisable.

Mr. Percivall records a case of fracture of *the ischial portion of the pelvis* recovered by rest and nature. The situation of the injury would favour this, and even had a false joint formed, it would not have interfered with breeding.

Fracture of the Ribs usually proceeds from external violence, as blows, kicks, or being crushed. The symptoms are painful, catching respiration, pain on lifting or moving the animal, and crepitus when so doing.

The treatment consists in applying a broad bandage firmly round the chest, so as to prevent the animal dilating the thoracic walls in breathing. If the fractured end of the rib, penetrate the cavity of the chest, it is advisable that the ingress of air should be prevented as much as possible ; and the patient must be treated antiphlogistically. Perfect quietude is absolutely necessary.

Fracture of the Sternum is not a common accident, and is usually occasioned by falling from heights. The same treatment is required as for rib fracture, with the addition of a boat-shaped splint along the sternum or gutta-percha moulded to it.

Fracture of the Cranium is, under any circumstances, of serious consequence ; compression of the brain is likely to ensue, from the fractured portions bulging inwards, or from extravasation of blood on the brain.

The following case, which came under the care of Professor Simonds, is recorded by Youatt :—" Two gentlemen were playing at quoits, and the dog of one of them was struck on the head by a quoit, and supposed to be killed. His owner took him up and found that he was not dead, although dreadfully injured. It being near the Thames, his owner took him to the edge of the river, and dashed some water over him, and he rallied a little. Professor Simonds detected a fracture of the skull, with pressure on the brain, arising from a portion of depressed bone. The dog was perfectly unconscious, frequently moaning, quite incapable of standing, and continually turning round upon his belly, his straw, or his bed. It was a case of coma; he took no food, and the pulsation at the heart was very indistinct.

." I told the proprietor that there was no chance of recovery, except by an operation; and even then, I thought it exceedingly doubtful. I was desired to operate, and took him home.

" The head was now almost twice as large as when the accident occurred, proceeding from a quantity of coagulated blood that had been effused under the skin covering the skull. I gave him a dose of aperient medicine, and on the following morning commenced my operation.

" The hair was clipped from the head, and an incision carried immediately from between the eyebrows to the back part of the skull, in the direction of the sagittal suture. Another incision was made from this to the root of the ear. This triangular flap was then turned back, in order to remove the coagulated blood, and make a thorough exposure of the skull. I was provided with a trephine, thinking that only a portion of the bone had been depressed on the brain, and it would be necessary, with that instrument, to separate it from its attachment, and then with an elevator remove it; but I found that the greater part of the parietal bone was depressed, and that the fracture extended along the sagittal suture from the coronal and lamboidal sutures. At three-fourths of the width of the bone, the fracture ran parallel with the sagittal suture and this large portion was depressed upon the tunics of the brain, the dura mater being considerably lacerated.

" The depressed bone was raised with an elevator, and I found, from its lacerated edges and the extent of the mischief done, that it was far wiser to remove it entirely than to allow it to remain and take the chance of its uniting.

"In a few days the dog began to experience relief from the operation, and to be somewhat conscious of what was taking place around him. He still requires care and attention, and proper medicinal agents to be administered from time to time; but with the exception of occasionally turning round when on the floor, he takes his food well, and obeys his master's call."*

Fracture of the Vertebræ occasionally happens in dogs used for the chase. It is needless to say that such cases usually terminate in paralysis and death.

The after-treatment of fracture is very simple. Quietude and attention to the bowels and diet, are the points mainly to be observed. The bowels should be kept gently relaxed this is especially needful in fracture of the hind extremities, and particularly the pelvis, as the animal in placing himself in position for fæcal evacuation is apt, in the strain and weight almost necessarily thrown on the injured part, to displace the fracture. The diet should be plain, unstimulating, and relaxing. When an excessive amount of swelling takes place in the foot after the setting of a fractured limb, the bandages may be slit up a little distance between the splints, and the foot soaked in, or sponged with, warm water.

The removal of splints should never take place until the expiration of at least four weeks, unless they have become disarranged, or the setting is not correct.

False Joints.—When a fracture fails to unite by osseous matter, and a fibrous connection is substituted, what is termed *false joint* is established. In the long bones, treatment is more easily and satisfactorily adopted than in other situations. When it is found on the removal of the support that osseous union has not taken place, the limb should

---

* Trans. Vet. Med. Assoc., i., 51.

be again fastened up,—more firmly, if possible, than before, a liberal diet allowed, and tonics administered. If at the expiration of seven or eight weeks the false joint still exists, and there appears no prospect of its being otherwise, unless other measures are adopted, inflammatory action is to be established in the false union with the object of exciting the formation of osseous material, and this may be done by piercing the structure in various places with a sharp needle, and moving the point about when imbedded there until it is considered that sufficient irritation has been produced. The limb is then bound up as before.

Certain constitutional conditions of an animal have a tendency to retard the formation of new bone (scrofula or rickets, to wit). In such diatheses, mineral tonics and bone-

FIG. 37.
DEFORMED LIMB AFTER UNION OF FRACTURE, NECESSITATING RE-FRACTURE.

making materials should be freely exhibited; in the latter, lime-water and milk should be given to the animal to lap in the place of water.

Re-fracture.—From nature being allowed, without assistance, to effect the union of a fractured limb, or from carelessness or wrong adjustment of the splints, it frequently happens that the limb after union presents a deformed and unsightly appearance. A broken-haired terrier was recently brought to me for advice regarding the condition of a united fore-leg fractured above the knee (radius and ulna), which had been set with leather splints—the limb was bent outwards to such an extent as to be almost useless. (See Fig. 37.)

Having placed the animal under chloroform, I re-fractured the bone at the original seat; having only been done a month, this was not a difficult task. The limb being then brought into proper position, I applied the ordinary wood splints with pitch and bandages, and in five weeks afterwards I had the gratification of seeing my patient perfectly recovered, and with two straight fore-legs.

Compound Fracture is occasionally met with in the long bones of the limbs. If the end of the bone protrude through the opening, and from the smallness of the latter replacement is difficult, either the protruded bone must be removed with a fine saw or bone-nippers, or the wound enlarged. When comminution is also present, any completely detached fragments of bone should be removed, otherwise they will act as foreign bodies, create inflammation and suppuration, and prevent the healing process. In the application of splints, it will be necessary to arrange them so that the wound may be readily exposed when requisite.

Fracture with Luxation.—When fracture occurs with dislocation, the treatment is doubly difficult, as the dislocation must first be reduced; this, under the circumstances, is no easy task, and then the fracture is to be attended to. Occasionally it is necessary to have recourse to the latter first, in order to permit the extension required to reduce the dislocation; after which it is generally advisable to reset the fracture, owing to the unavoidable displacement consequent on the operation.

DISLOCATIONS.

Dislocation, luxation, or the displacement of a joint without fracture, is very commonly seen in canine practice.

The dislocations usually met with are in the shoulder, elbow, knee, hip, stifle, hock, toes.

Predisposing Causes.—Congenital deformity, elongation of the articulatory ligaments, atrophied or weak muscles, previous luxation.

FIG. 38.
DISLOCATION OF SHOULDER-JOINT.

Exciting Causes.—External violence, as falls, blows, twists, undue force in parturition, muscular action, voluntary effort.

Symptoms.—Displacement and deformity of the part; undue prominence, or the reverse, where neither should exist; shortening or elongation of the limb, generally the former; inability to perform the usual natural movements;

a tense condition, if they are not ruptured, of the muscles on the opposite side; pain on manipulation, with more or less swelling; an absence of true crepitus; an entirety of bone.

Treatment.—This consists in applying extension in the direction required for the reduction of the dislocation: in recent cases this will not be difficult. If the shoulder-joint be the seat of accident, reduction is most easily accomplished in the following manner: A strong towel or surcingle is passed underneath the brisket, between the forelegs, over the withers, round the girth, and across the front of the breast. This is held firmly, whilst an assistant steadily draws the limb in the direction required (Fig 38).

In dislocation of the elbow, the humerus should be firmly grasped by one pair of hands, while another uses steady traction on the limb below.

Dislocation of the knee is extremely rare, and when it does occur, it will be necessary, after reduction, by traction and manipulation, to place a starch bandage round it for a week or ten days.

Dislocation of the Hip.—This occurs in various forms; the head of the femur may be displaced upwards, downwards, forwards, or backwards. Reduction is performed by powerful traction above the hock, in the direction indicated by the dislocation. At the time of traction, the limb should be drawn outwardly from the upper part of the thigh, for the purpose of lifting the head of the femur over the rim of the acetabulum. Rotation will sometimes aid the operation.

Dislocation of the stifle or patella is rarely met with in canine practice. In a case which came under my own care, the bone was displaced outwardly, and could be reduced readily by the fingers, but only temporarily. The symptoms of displacement of the patella, whether outwardly or inwardly—the two forms usually met with—are an unnatural projection on the affected side, with inability to flex the joint. Reduction is effected by drawing the leg forward, and then with the fingers forcing the patella back into its place. In the case named, after reduction I fixed on an outside splint, and bound the joint round with a pitch bandage. The case did well, and no return of the luxation though three years have since elapsed, has taken place whereas previously it was continually out of position.

Mr. James Rowe, of London, reports dislocations of the patella as not unfrequent in his practice, and tells me he has successfully treated them in a similar manner to that adopted by me. One case occurred in a cat.

Dislocation of the Hock.—The same remarks made with reference to the knee will apply here.

Dislocation of the Toes.—This accident is sometimes met with, and is generally occasioned by leaping or tumbling from heights. Reduction is easily effected by extension, and the subsequent maintenance of the parts in their proper position by bandaging the whole foot, and, if need be, small splints on either side and in front of the affected toe.

Dislocation, having once taken place, is exceedingly liable to recur. For this reason, excitement and unnecessary movements should be strictly avoided. The after-treatment consists in observing much the same rules as those laid down in fracture. The patient should be kept quiet. If inflammatory symptoms, with excessive swelling round the affected joint, ensue, warm fomentations or a bran poultice may be applied, and a dose of aperient medicine administered, and if the local inflammatory action is extreme, leeches may be used. Such symptoms, however, rarely occur, except in protracted and aggravated reduction.

Dislocations should always be reduced under chloroform, both for humanity's sake, and the greater ease with which during anæsthesia, it can be accomplished.

AMPUTATIONS.

Amputation, or severation, is sometimes had recourse to in veterinary practice, when injury or disease has rendered the removal of the part or member necessary for the salvation of life.

The limbs are chiefly subjected to this operation, and although amputation of a canine leg is not of common occurrence, yet several very successful issues have followed the operation, an instance of which I recorded from my own practice in 1879.

Amputation may be accomplished by either the *flap* or *circular* method, the *modus operandi* being much the same as in human surgery. Everything should be arranged beforehand, and in readiness for the operator. It is advisable to have three assistants if possible in amputations of importance—one to administer and control the anæsthetic, one to assist in holding the limb and securing the vessels, and another to ligature. A veterinary surgeon, however, is not commonly blessed with so much professional help, and therefore has to do the best he can, often relying on the assistance of a medical friend or colleague.

In the lower animals a tourniquet is always advisable, as it ensures, if properly applied, complete pressure of the arterial branches, as well as the chief vessel. The arteries may be taken up by torsion or ligature. Unless for some special reason it is contra-indicated, chloroform or ether should always be used in amputations.

In the case I have alluded to as occurring in my practice, the necessity of amputation was due to compound comminuted fracture of the radius and ulna. Before I commenced the severation the integuments were drawn well up towards the humerus, so that upon resuming their position afterwards they might form a good covering to the stump.

A sweeping circular cut divided all tissues down to the

bones, to which it was not necessary to apply the saw except to projecting points, as sufficient fractured and detached portions were removed to keep the remaining bone-ends well away from the line of amputation. The external wound was closed by drawing the integument together with sutures.

Strict cleanliness and antiseptic dressings are necessary in the after-treatment. Should secondary hæmorrhage occur, it may be necessary to re-open the external wound, seek for and ligature the offending vessel; but moderate or slow hæmorrhage, especially if not arterial, may be allayed by astringent padding and firm compress.

In the event of sloughing or pyæmia, re-amputation is indicated.

Amputation of the hind-leg is only warranted when for particular reasons the salvation of the animal's life is desired, notably, for breeding purposes. Amputation of the tibia is conducted on the same principles as those mentioned for the fore-leg. Amputation of the toe is simple, and may with impunity be accompanied by disarticulation also. The removal of the supernumerary toe (dew-claw) will be found dealt with in another section.

WOUNDS.

I shall divide these into incised, lacerated, punctured, and contused, as these four kinds are most commonly met with in the dog.

Incised wounds are clean cut, like those produced in surgical operations, or from sharp-edged substances.

Lacerated are those in which the tissues are torn asunder.

Punctured, those produced by stabs or pricks.

Contused, by bruising or crushing.

To repair a wound, it is necessary that a process of what is termed "healing" should be gone through, and this process is accomplished in one of the following ways:

A. *First Intention;* i.e., immediate reunion of the parts without the formation of new material.

B. *Adhesive Inflammation;* or the exudation of lymph on both cut surfaces.

C. *Granulation;* or the formation of small masses of new flesh, over which a secretion of pus is continually poured.

D. *Scabbing* or *Crusting;* a covering formed by nature of dried exuded matter on the raw surface, as pus, blood, or lymph, mingled generally with dirt or dust.

The final result of either process is a scar or cicatrix, varying in character and dimensions according to the method by which the wound is healed. In our hairy-coated patients, this is not of so much moment as it is on uncovered human skin.

Incised wounds are generally most amenable to treatment. In those recently inflicted it is always advisable, if possible (unless there are diseased deep-seated structures), to obtain union by the first intention. To effect this, after the wound has been cleansed and the hæmorrhage has ceased, the lips are brought into direct apposition (taking care no hairs get between), and so maintained by sutures or plaster; the latter will necessitate the shaving off the hair before it can be applied.

The animal must then be so secured that it cannot interfere with the part. For though the dog's tongue is undoubtedly a great cleanser, it is neither a healer nor aid to apposition, and the sooner such an idea is exploded the better. Omit this precaution, and the surgeon's work will speedily be undone; the animal will persistently lick the wound, and keep it gaping open. It then heals by granulation, for it cannot do so by any other method. The result is a broad unsightly cicatrix, instead of the fine, and in time, almost inperceptible seam left from union in the first instance by direct apposition, with or without the first intention.

c c

I say, with or without the first intention, because it is not unusual for a patient to be brought some four or five days after the wound has been closed, with the sutures out and the lips apart, and we are asked to reclose it. This I seldom do, finding in the treatment of wounds in the lower animals that if the lips can be kept in apposition for the first four or five days, they will, if they then break away, resume in the final healing process the position they were originally placed in, and each suture mark will reveal the nicety or otherwise of adjustment,

The same remarks will apply to healing by adhesive inflammation,* which may be considered a kind of, if not really, first intention.

The sutures commonly used are soft wire, pins, and silk. I prefer the latter for dogs, and if dipped in a weak solution of carbolic acid they maintain their position longer, and add to the healthiness of the wound.

Granulation and scabbing are, however, the most common methods of healing in veterinary practice. When the secretion of pus takes place, its character should be examined to ascertain if it is healthy—*i.e.*, of a creamy consistency, yellowish-white, of a peculiar indescribable odour, not disagreeable or unhealthy, being ichorous or curdled, of a dirty colour, and fœtid.

Suppurating wounds require to be cleansed with tepid water at least once daily. The following liniment occasionally injected will promote a healthy discharge:—

Acid Carbolic	15 minims.
Ol. Terebinth	1 ounce.
Ol. Olivæ	6 ounces.

Where the granulations spring up too rapidly, forming what is termed "proud flesh," the application of lunar caustic is necessary; but it should be borne in mind that a

---

* It is to my mind doubtful if healing ever takes place without an exudation of lymph, at all events in the lower animals.

twofold effect follows its use, viz., a destruction of the present flesh, that which it comes in contact with, and a stimulus to growth of the future tissue. Sluggish wounds, therefore, that are occasionally treated with caustic, granulate much more rapidly than under any other treatment.

In healing by granulation care should always be taken that the wound heals from the bottom, otherwise the confined pus will burrow, and deep-seated abscess or sinuses be the result. This is particularly to be observed in punctured wounds.

Lacerated wounds must of necessity heal by granulation. In the first instance, the wound should be cleansed from clots and any foreign matters. If there is excessive hæmorrhage, it will be necessary to secure the vessel, if possible, by ligature, or pack the wound with a portion of sponge or tow, saturated with some astringent—as solution of alum or tincture of iron.

This may be removed in twenty-four hours, and if no secondary hæmorrhage occurs, the stimulating liniment before advised may be injected, and the same treatment followed as is given in wounds healing by granulation.

When no skin is removed, the edges should be brought together with sutures, and so maintained as long as possible, taking care to leave a free passage for the discharge of pus. If the sutures are tied in bows, they can be readily unfastened for the withdrawal of the packing and reclosed.

Lacerated wounds from bites should be freely cauterised.

Punctured wounds are generally very troublesome; they may be called deceptive wounds, for sometimes it is impossible to tell to what extent they go, or what foreign matters may be left behind; thorns, for instance, or the rust off a spike or nail, may, from remaining unextracted, produce pyæmia and death. Such wounds, then, should always be carefully examined, and the probe is only a safe explorer in the hands of a professional man.

As the orifice is frequently exceedingly small, the hair

around it should be cut off, so that it may not become matted and form an obstruction to the discharge of pus; this will also facilitate the daily examination and treatment of the wound. If the puncture be in the foot, and there is reason to suppose a thorn or rusty nail has produced it, a poultice is advisable, and the insertion occasionally of a little caustic. It should never be allowed to heal unless the attendant is satisfied it is sound at the bottom; otherwise, as before observed, deep-seated abscess and sinuses will result.

When the opening is small, pus has accumulated, and the swelling above extensive, it is better to enlarge the wound with a scalpel, or lance, and inject it with warm water.

Contused wounds are best treated by poulticing and fomentation; if only slight, nature herself will effect a cure.

Sloughing, more or less, may be expected if the wound is more than superficial. When the injury extends to the deeper-seated structures, and there is much extravasation of blood, scarifying and repeated fomentations are indicated. When the crushing has been so great that the textures underneath the muscles and blood-vessels are ruptured, extensive sloughing is sure to follow. Healing in such a case takes place by granulation, and the reparation needed being generally considerable, caustic applications are more frequently required, with daily cleansing, and the injection from time to time of the stimulating liniment.

Incised or torn cartilage is perhaps the most difficult structure to unite, and its union, if accomplished, is very tardy. Thus ragged or slit-eared dogs are frequently seen. An exceptional case of this description came under my notice on the 24th of January, 1887: The subject, a Dandie Dinmont terrier, the property of Cecil Kent, Esq., St. Leonard's, had its ear seized on the evening of the date named, by a bull terrier, and nearly detached in a crosswise direction from the head, the entire substance of the flap being divided more than three-quarters of its breadth.

Within half an hour of the time the injury took place the patient was brought to my house. I brought the edges o the wound, including the integument and cartilage, togethe with soft metallic interrupted sutures, allowing sufficient space between each to insert a new suture when necessary as my intention was to keep up direct apposition of the cartilaginous edges throughout the case. On either side o the wound a pad of cotton wool steeped in carbolised oi was placed, and a head bandage was employed, to keep the ear in position and immovable; the dressings were re newed almost daily. Every suture remained intact unti the 7th of February, when four intermediate ones were inserted, to counteract the relaxed condition of some of the old ones. On the 21st, three more were added, between this date and the 2nd of April (when all sutures were removed), odd ones were inserted as it was thought necessary, and one space from the margin of the flap that persistently refused to heal was pared on the edges and re united with complete success. Towards the latter part of the case zinc ointment was substituted for carbolised oil. Occasionally nitrate of silver was slightly applied. The process of healing occupied sixty-three days, and thirty-four sutures were employed. Those removed on the 2nd of April had for some days effected their purpose, and merely hung as earrings. The carriage and use of the ear after recovery was in no way affected, and all signs of such an injury and operation have become almost obliterated.

In all classes of wounds a certain amount of inflammatory fever is produced. This is best counteracted by light aperient medicine, plain unstimulating diet, and quietude.

SPRAINS.

Sprains, or undue strain of the muscular or ligamentous portion of the limbs, is of frequent occurrence in sporting dogs, and the pain attendant upon such injury is generally exceedingly acute, and accompanied with swelling and considerable febrile disturbance.

Treatment.—This should consist, until the inflammatory symptoms have subsided, in warm fomentations to the injured part (in extreme cases leeches may be applied) aperient medicine, and perfect rest. Afterwards it may be necessary to apply a splint, or starch bandage, to support the part, which usually continues weak for some considerable time.

When thickening, with chronic inflammation, remains, cold water and the following lotion can be first tried:

        Malt Vinegar .... 1 ounce.
        Spt. Vini et Camph. .... 2 ounces.
        Aqua............................. 7 „

To be used after the cold water.

This failing, the tincture of iodine, one-half the ordinary strength, may be applied daily until soreness is induced, and when this has abated, again renewed.

BURNS AND SCALDS.

Dogs are occasionally, through accident or from malicious intent, burned or scalded. The consequences, though not usually so dangerous as in human beings, are nevertheless serious, as an amount of violent inflammatory fever follows either injury. I recollect a bull-terrier, belonging to a brewer, being fearfully scalded in the following manner:—The animal had the same morning killed a rat in an empty mash-tub, and was afterwards chained up. On the arrival of his master he was as usual released, when he immediately sped to the scene of his morning's exploit, and leapt, in his excitement, not seeing the danger, into the tub, which then contained boiling water. The poor brute was extricated as quickly as possible, but with every vestige of hair removed from his body, and totally blind; not a whimper, however, escaped him. It is needless to add that, on the score of humanity, his sufferings were terminated with prussic acid, though not without some difficulty, as his savage propensities still remained, even after such a fearful ordeal.

The treatment of either burns or scalds consists in keeping down, as much as possible, inflammatory action locally, and sympathetic fever. Air should be immediately excluded from the part, the latter first being dressed with linseed oil and lime-water—three ounces of the latter to six of the former shaken together—and then covered over with cotton wool.

When sloughing commences, poultices and warm fomentations are indicated. The bowels should be kept relaxed throughout, and perfect quietude with cleanliness observed. By the latter I mean no foreign matters beyond the dressing should be allowed to come in contact with the wound. Bits of hay and straw, or the animal's hair, act as irritants and do the animal considerable mischief. During the sloughing and granulating stage, tonics and nutritious food are requisite. When the wound assumes a sluggish and unhealthy character, the application of a stimulus to its surface is required.

Blemishes must be expected to follow either a burn or scald, but in long-haired dogs these are to a great extent covered.

UMBILICAL HERNIA.

This is not unfrequently met with in toy dogs. It may be congenital, or, what is more usually the case, result from expansion of the navel cicatrix. A conical tumour is observed immediately over the navel, and into which is protruded a portion of the omentum or intestine, or both. The position of four-legged animals favours the protrusion, and consequently its increase.

Treatment.—This is exceedingly simple, and invariably successful. As soon as the animal is weaned,* being placed on his back, a conical-shaped portion of cork, with a broad base, covered or not with calico or wash-leather, should be applied to the protrusion, and secured there with strips of pitch-plaster.

If the hernia is allowed to go on until puppyhood is past, more difficulty will be experienced in dealing with it, and the chances of success will be rendered less certain.

On the 25th of June, 1877, a young pug dog, fourteen weeks old, was brought for my advice regarding a navel enlargement, which I pronounced to be hernia, and most probably *intestinal;* but I could detect no communication between the protruded portion, whatever it was, and the intestine within the abdomen, nor could any manipulation reduce it. Fasting made no difference in its appearance or feel, nor yet did a full meal. The enlargement was very much constricted at its base, and gave one the idea of an empty portion of intestine or bladder inflated and tied firmly round. To ascertain its true nature before resorting to any operation for its removal (after fasting the animal), I explored it with a suture needle; but neither blood, serum, nor any other kind of fluid, nor yet did collapse, follow the puncture. The owner then acting on my advice, chloroform was administered to the patient, and an incision made through the skin with a lancet, for the purpose of removing the protrusion by ligature, should it prove to be omentum or obliterated intestine; or if both, and the latter was not obliterated, return it and close the aperture with suture.

It was found to be the former, and removed accordingly; a couple of stitches being inserted through the lips of the divided integument and the ends of the ligature left out.

---

* Any appliance before weaning would most likely be removed by the mother's teeth.

Orders were given for the patient to be watched, so that he might not interfere with the part, and to be kept quiet. On the fifth day the ligature sloughed off, and at the end of another similar period the wound was whole.

On the 16th of the following month, July, I met the owner, and was informed that the dog was perfectly well, and that there was no mark or enlargement of any kind to be detected.

DOUBLE VENTRAL HERNIA WITH DISPLACEMENT OF THE BLADDER.

The following case is of sufficient interest and instruction to find a place in this chapter. "On the 1st of June, 1878, I received into the infirmary a white bull-terrier bitch from Mr. Coath, of the Shrubbery, Walsall. The animal in question was sent to me under the supposition she had Mammary Tumours or Cancer, and the following brief history was furnished me:—Some months previous to the above date, the bitch engaged in a fight with another dog, and, to separate the animals, a man had put his foot across the bitch as she lay on her back, whilst he tore her opponent away. At that time she was supposed to be in whelp. Shortly after the combat, these two enlargements made their appearance, and gradually increased in size On the day she was brought for my inspection, I found them firm, smooth, and glistening, and situated in the neighbourhood of the two posterior mammæ, the latter appearing to be involved. The left side was much the greater, the tumour being as large as a goose-egg, and extending to the groin. That on the right was about one-third the size. The bitch being gross, I ordered a dose of castor oil, and light unstimulating diet, until her condition was such as to warrant an operation being performed, if necessary. On frequent examinations made between the 1st and 21st, I found the tumours varied somewhat in their condition : at one time being softer and lower in temperature, at another the reverse. The presence of fluid was always evident. On the latter date I made a most careful examination, the patient being then considerably reduced in flesh. The left tumour was at this time exceedingly tense, hot, and larger than it had ever been ; moreover, the bitch evinced pain, especially on manipulating it, and had not been observed to micturate with her usual frequency. I at once determined to explore this particular tumour with a fine trochar. This I inserted at the right of the nipple, and when withdrawn there came through the canula a full stream of hot urine, altogether nearly a breakfast cupful. With this evacuation the enlargement entirely disappeared, and nothing remained but the mammary gland. The other tumour also became less, owing, doubtless, to removal of the pressure consequent on the distended bladder. All doubt now as to the nature of the tumours was at an end. It was clearly a case of double rupture ; the sac tapped contained the greater portion of the bladder, with probably a small knuckle of intestine, while the opposite tumour was entirely intestinal. The peritoneal rupture on either side—which it was previously, notwithstanding careful manipulation, owing to the size and fulness of the enlargements, impossible to detect—could now be distinctly felt.

The following morning the same state of affairs existed, and again I passed the trochar with a similar result, repeating the operation for two or three days. In the meantime she was prepared for an operation, which I performed on the 28th ; Mr. C. A. Newnham, surgeon, who kindly assisted me, also his son, and several gentlemen who took an interest in the case.

The bitch being put under the influence of chloroform, and placed on her back, and the hind parts lifted a little off the table to facilitate the reduction of the hernia, I made a longitudinal incision to the right of the nipple. On dividing the sac, intestine alone was visible, and the absence of

bladder was accounted for by its having been empti
before the operation; otherwise it would have occupied t
entire sac.

Having fully reduced the hernia, I closed the periton
rent, which was a little less than two inches, with unint
rupted catgut suture, and the external wound w
interrupted silk sutures. A light wire muzzle was th
put on the patient, to prevent her gnawing or licking t
parts, and she was made as comfortable as possible.

The diet for the first fortnight was sweetened milk a
water, subsequently pure milk; and, finally, bread a
milk, until the part was well. The case proceeded tc
perfectly satisfactory conclusion. The last external sut
came away on the twenty-third day, and within four we
all was thoroughly healed, and no enlargement appare
or anything to denote what had been amiss beyond a f
seam where the incision had been made.

Having allowed the patient a month to recover condit
and establish the firmness of the part, I proceeded
prepare her for the second operation; viz., the reduct
of the hernia on the opposite side. This took place
the 11th of August, in the presence of Messrs. Newnh
and Manby, surgeons, and others. The operation v
conducted under chloroform, in precisely the same man
as on the first occasion. I should observe that t
rupture, which in the first instance was comparativ
small, had increased considerably in size, and was n
larger than the one already operated on. This I attribu
to the pressure brought to bear on it from reducing
opposite large one, which must necessarily have hac
tendency to force the smaller one further out. As may
imagined, I did not feel so sanguine about the resul
the second operation as the first; for I had grave dou
whether, in reducing this *increased* rupture, the oppo
one would not break through again. However, I operat
the hernia was intestinal, the peritoneal rent was not

long as in the other, but the hernial sac was considerably thicker, and more numerous in its layers. On the 25th, exactly a fortnight afterwards, the last stitch was removed, and on the 10th of September the bitch was perfectly well, in good condition, and in excellent spirits.

The diet was the same as that prescribed after the first operation. Probably it would have been considered more scientific had I pared the edges of the ruptured peritoneum; but I preferred—as I do in similar cases in other animals—trusting to lymph effusion, and its subsequent organization, rather than incurring the risk of producing general and acute peritonitis, which paring an old ruptured peritoneum would tend to do.

It is perhaps scarcely necessary to point to the obvious cause of this double rupture; viz., that the peritoneum was broken in the act of tearing away the other dog, while the man's foot across the bitch's abdomen held her firmly down; a cruel, but I trust an unintentional, procedure.

Since the above record, many cases of ventral hernia have come under my notice.

DOUBLE FEMORAL HERNIA.

Last autumn, 1887, I was requested to attend a bitch in London, stated to have been ruptured on both sides, and with an inverted womb. She had previously at various times been under my treatment for bronchial asthma. Besides being asthmatical, she was aged and very obese. On my arrival, I found a large femoral hernia close to the groin on either side; but no uterine inversion. A vaginal prolapse had probably been observed when straining, and mistaken for the womb. The abdomen, being very large and its walls thin at the seat of rupture, had most likely given way, in a violent paroxysm of coughing.

The age of the animal, the enormous obesity, and we[ak] condition of the heart precluded the administration [of] chloroform, and the usual method of reduction: so I h[ad] a suitable truss applied, which the patient continues [to] wear.

FISTULA.

Fistulæ, or sinus wounds, occur in different position[s] but are all, more or less, due to some local irritation, ver[y] often abscess, and present the same structural characte[r] *i.e.*, a narrow constricted passage lined by thickene[d] membrane, which secretes a variable unhealthy puruler[t] discharge.

Fistula in ano has already been described in Chapter V[.]

A troublesome form of fistula is that affecting th[e] lachrymal apparatus (*Fistula Lachrymalis*), which mos[t] frequently originates in some persistent obstruction in th[e] nasal or lachrymal duct. In 1886 I received a case of thi[s] description into my hospital. The external opening wa[s] about an inch and a half below the eye, through which th[e] lachrymal secretion freely passed. The treatment consiste[d] in astringent injections, and the application of nitrate [of] silver,—the process of healing occupied seven week[s]. Sometimes it is necessary to slit up the canaliculus, an[d] maintain for a period an open wound.

Fistula Parietal Abdominalis may result from a[n] imbedded thorn or other punctured wounds, or abscess[.] Last year a Yorkshire terrier was brought to me for advic[e] as to an old standing sore which the animal persistentl[y] licked. An examination revealed a fistulous wound in th[e] abdominal parietes. The opening was opposite and abou[t] an inch to the left of the prepuce, the sinus running back wards for some three inches, and obliquely towards th[e] penis. The treatment consisted in a free incision of th[e] sinus, carried backwards from the opening, and the sub[-] sequent application of nitrate of silver; the part was perfectly healed in seventeen days.

Mammary Fistula is most frequently associated with cancer. It has been mentioned in connection with mammitis under the heading of *Lacteal Fistula*, but such cases are very exceptional. The surgical treatment, when the disease is not associated with cancer, is much the same as in other forms of fistula. Injections of iodine are sometimes useful.

Fistula in the Teat, though common in bovines, seldom occurs in the bitch, and when it does so, the opening usually takes place at the base of the teat. Lactation retards the treatment, and if the patient is suckling, it may be necessary to wean the puppies, or wait until the bitch is dry before adopting direct surgical treatment.

Gastric and Biliary Fistulæ being purposely promoted for experimental purposes, need no description in this work.

EXCISION OF SEROUS CYST.

In the early part of 1883 I was consulted by Mr. H. E. Marston relative to a swelling in front of the throat of a small, smooth white terrier called "The Colonel." The enlargement proved to be a *serous cyst*, or abscess. The contents were then evacuated with a trochar and canula, and as I was informed it had previously been opened and had refilled, I gave instructions with a view of preventing the latter result. On the 14th of January, 1884, I received another visit from Mr. Marston and "The Colonel," and the old story of evacuation and refilling was once more told. An examination revealed considerable enlargement of the fruitful cyst, and, as a final measure, I recommended its complete excision. So, on the 16th, "The Colonel" came to my infirmary, and submitted with a nerve of iron to the knife, the operation proving a long and tedious one.

I found the cyst firmly attached to the skin in fron[t] especially in the locality where it had been so frequentl[y] lanced or tapped. This adhesion being removed, it becam[e] then necessary to separate its further attachments, whic[h] as the knife steadily proceeded, revealed more and mo[re] complications.

Leaving the jugular veins and carotid arteries by almo[st] a hair's breadth, and fully exposed, I came at last in vie[w] of the trachea, and here it was found that the injury ha[d] arisen which gave rise to the formation of the cyst, the[re] having been a fracture of some of the cartilaginous ring[s] which Mr. Marston informed me he attributed to a kic[k] the dog received in the neck. Having got well to th[e] base of the tumour, the patient was placed on his feet, i[n] order that it might hang pendulent whilst a ligature wa[s] drawn round it, and it was then finally excised, bein[g] about the size of an orange, and containing two ounces an[d] a half of tenacious, glairy matter. I closed the extern[al] wound with sutures, applied antiseptic dressing with bandage, and, like a little warrior, "The Colonel" we[nt] away, evidently satisfied with the result of the somewh[at] bloody operation he had encountered.

The four following days he came for surgical attentio[n] to the wound, each visit showing a satisfactory conditio[n] of the part operated upon, and he left Wolverhampton o[n] the 23rd with every prospect of soon being well, whic[h] prognosis a subsequent letter from his master confirmed.

In such a situation, and so intricate in its attachment[s] the excision of this cyst required the most careful, patien[t] delicate, and watchful dissection, the more so as th[e] administration of chloroform was not admissible; and th[e] heroic manner in which this animal behaved during th[e] painful period adds one more link to the chain of testimon[y] recorded of the courageous attributes of the canine race.

CHOKING.

Dogs very frequently get choked, especially ravenous feeders. A portion of bone or solid matter, too large, or from its shape impossible to be passed down the œsophagus, becomes fixed, it may be in the upper portion of the throat, the pharynx, or some distance down the tube.

Treatment.—If the obstruction is not deeply lodged, and can be seen or felt, an attempt should be made to extract it

FIG. 39.

THROAT FORCEPS.

with forceps. An ingenious instrument for this purpose is sold by Arnold and Sons, London. (See Fig. 39.)

When, however, the substance is too low for extraction a whalebone probe, having a portion of sponge fastened on the end and dipped in oil, may be gently passed down to the obstruction and then steadily pushed onwards. Before, however, attempting this measure, it is advisable to manipulate externally with the fingers, as the substance may be of such a nature that external pressure may break it down and facilitate its onward passage. Pins, needles, and other sharp substances may be removed by moving the probe about, rotating it, and then withdrawing it.

Considerable irritation often ensues after choking, and when the lining membrane of the œsophagus has been lacerated, a great degree of inflammatory action is sure to follow; to subdue both, and act as local sedative, warm bread and milk and broths should for some days afterwards form the sole diet of the animal.

ŒSOPHAGOTOMY.

This operation is sometimes necessary, when the means named in the previous section for relief in choking have failed. Mr. A. E. Macgillivray, V.S., Banff, records a case recently, in which œsophagotomy was performed by a medical gentleman :—" The animal being properly and conveniently secured on a table, was put under chloroform, and Dr. J. C. Hirschfeld operated. After making a pretty large cuticular incision, and cutting cautiously through the subjacent dermal muscle, the doctor dissected down between the sterno-maxillary and mastoido-humeral muscles of the left side, and thus on to the obstructed œsophagus behind the trachea ; and here it may be remarked that this was the more easily accomplished, owing to the absence in the dog of the omo or subscapulo-hyoidean muscle, which passes (partly crosswise) along the outside of the trachea. Having arrived at and laid bare the obstructed part of the gullet, a pretty free incision was made in the same, and, with much difficulty the doctor extracted two of the coccygeal vertebræ of an ox ! One of these vertebræ measured about two inches across the transverse processes, and nearly an inch and a half vertically ; the other was a little less in size.

" Dr. Hirschfeld closed up the wound in the œsophagus with continuous sutures of prepared catgut, and the external wound with interrupted sutures of horse-hair. The stitching of the gullet was an extremely difficult job, but was very successfully done.

" The dog was restricted to entirely fluid sustenance for several days, and the wound kept clean and dressed outside and inside with a weak solution of carbolic acid.

"A most satisfactory and complete recovery soon ensued, the animal being, apparently, not a whit the worse for the very serious operation."[*]

---

[*] "Veterinary Journal," January, 1878.

Peuch and Toussaint (whose recent work I have at hand) have twice performed œsophagotomy on the dog, once with a successful issue.*

The operation has, so far, been a rare one, but with the results, both in human and veterinary practice, hesitation when life rests upon it, should no longer exist.

LITHOTOMY.

The following newspaper report of removal of vesical calculi from the dog was published in the veterinary journals in September, 1881 :—

"Mr. J. Woodroffe Hill, veterinary surgeon, of Wolverhampton, removed by the operation of lithotomy two hundred and two stones from the bladder of the well-known St. Bernard bitch "Mab," winner of numerous prizes. The stones vary from the size of a millet-seed to a potato, the four largest weighing respectively three ounces, two ounces, one ounce, and half an ounce, and the lot in bulk nine ounces. They are chiefly triangular in shape, perfectly smooth, and white. The operation, which was performed under chloroform, was witnessed, amongst others, by the owner of "Mab," Mr. J. C. Tinker (of Harborne), Mr. C. A. Newnham (surgeon), Mr. J. T. Phillips, M.R.C.V.S., and other gentlemen. No unfavourable symptoms have yet resulted from this formidable operation, but Mr. Hill scarcely anticipates a favourable issue. Under any circumstances the case is unique in canine surgery."—*Wolverhampton Evening Express.*

With regard to the above extraordinary case the following particulars were appended :—I was first consulted about "Mab" on August 18th, 1880, chiefly as to her not breeding, and a continual irritation of the urino-generative organs. On examination I then discovered she had, in connection with her last pregnancy, sustained a vaginal

---

* Peuch et Toussaint: "Précis de Chirurgie Veterinaire."

injury close to the mouth of the uterus, and for which I gave instructions as to treatment. Stone at this time was not suspected. After this I did not see her again until April, 1881, when her owner informed me she had visited the dog, and I examined her as to pregnancy. Careful abdominal manipulation, whilst the bitch was on her back, revealed a movable substance, but of its nature there was some doubt. On Saturday morning, June 26th, the day of the operation, the patient was again brought to me. She was this time continually straining and passing blood and urine in small quantities. Placing her upon her back, I found the enlargement previously felt had considerably increased in size, and, on grasping it, crepitus was both felt and heard. I then diagnosed the case as one of cystic calculi, though strong adverse opinions were expressed by other professionals. As the poor creature was in evident and acute pain, at the wish of the owner, and in accordance with my own feelings about the case, I at once operated by the cæsarian method ; and, although it was scarcely possible a successful issue could result therefrom, especially in her obese condition, yet I felt it was justifiable when such a valuable life was in the balance, as it resolved itself into a question of relief by the only method in canine surgery possible, or otherwise letting her linger on in agony, I advocated a preparation for the ordeal, but as the owner was leaving home for a fortnight, and the patient would not have lived until his return, I had no alternative but to perform the operation. As it was impossible to dilate the urethra sufficiently, and vagino vesical lithotomy was out of the question, I decided upon the cæsarian section. A quantity of fat omentum had to be removed to expose the bladder. The largest stone was discovered fixed in its neck, and when released by incision, all the others followed. Many besides those collected were lost in the straw upon which she lay. The incised bladder was carefully united with carbolised cat-gut, and the external wound closed by the ordinary method, the strictest after-precautions being taken. Unfortunately the unfavourable prognosis I gave was realised, and poor "Mab" succumbed on Sunday night, patient and grateful to the last moment, extending herself for fomentation, &c., and licking my hand.

A *post-mortem* examination revealed another large stone in the left kidney, surrounded by gangrenous structure and pus. This stone was of a ragged nature, and weighed half an ounce; and the kidney, which was only an apology for one, merely forming a thin sac for the stone, weighed barely another half ounce. The opposite kidney, which had been doing all the work, weighed six ounces. The bladder was considerably hypertrophied, its walls being thickened to the extent of three-quarters of an inch, and cartilaginous. Its neck, in which the stone weighing three ounces had lodged, was enormously distended. Altogether the organ weighed a trifle over eight ounces. The process of healing in those parts cut in the operation, including the bladder, was well established, and had not peritonitis set in (which I believe was due to my instructions as to after treatment being disregarded) the patient would have undoubtedly recovered from it, though her span of life afterwards would have been of brief duration, owing to other organic disease.

As observed in the newspaper report, the case is unique in canine surgery; and though a severe loss, apart from pecuniary consideration, has fallen upon Mr. Tinker, a gain to lovers of the canine race, and to the animals themselves, may be the result, inasmuch as cystic calculus (which undoubtedly dogs suffer from more frequently than is suspected) may be more studiously sought for, and successfully removed.

Accidents and Operations.

URETHRAL OBSTRUCTION CAUSED BY CALCULI.

On 2nd Dec., 1882, I received several urgent telegr[ams] from Brighton, concerning the inability of a dog to urin[ate]. I advised the use of the catheter, but was informed it c[ould] not be passed, and a final message implored me to g[o at] once. Unfortunately my visit was made too late, d[eath] having taken place shortly before I arrived. A *post-mo[rtem]* examination of the dog, which was a valuable Fre[nch] Poodle, the property of Captain Henry Boughey, reve[aled] acute inflammation and rupture of the bladder, due to obstructed passage of urine arising from the accumula[tion] of small stone in the urethral canal. The bladder of [the] poor sufferer had been enormously distended with confi[ned] and continually secreted urine prior to its rupture. I [re]moved nearly a quart from the abdominal cavity. [This] case once more illustrates the value of the catheter [in] canine practice. Had even an attempt been made to p[ass] the instrument, the obstruction would have been detec[ted], and failing the passage of the cartheter beyond it, [the] stones could have been forced back into the bladder [by] syringing the urethra with oil; or, as a *dernier resso[rt]* peritoneal incision into the urethra might have b[een] adopted with success.

CATHETERISM.

The passage of the catheter in the canine subject [is a] matter of extreme simplicity, though, singularly, for y[ears] it has erroneously been considered by some individuals, [out]side canine practice, an impossibility.

The animal to be operated on may be either placed [on] its back or side; the penis is then made to protrude [by] placing the forefinger between the prepuce and [the] abdomen, and pressing the sheath backwards, at the s[ame] time keeping the thumb firmly across the body of the penis immediately behind the erectile enlargements.

A gum elastic catheter, according to the size required, having been dipped in oil, is inserted into the urethral canal and gently passed backwards. Very often a sudden check will be felt, which is due to spasmodic contraction at the base of the *penial* bone, but if the operator pauses a moment or two, relaxation takes place, and the final passage into the bladder is accomplished without further obstacle. In some instances the instrument is more easily passed without the wire or *vice versâ*.

Catheterism can also be performed in the bitch.

VAGINOTOMY.

In protracted or chronic cases of vaginal inversion, it becomes necessary at times to remove the protruded portion by amputation (vaginotomy). The operation is not difficult, and is usually successful. In 1884 an aged toy bitch was sent to my infirmary from a considerable distance, with instructions to remove a polypus, the owner having consulted, as he stated, "his doggie book on the matter." My examination revealed it to be a chronic case of inversion. The usual treatment of plugging was resorted to, but owing to the advent of "œstrum" shortly afterwards, it was necessary in a few days after the return of the inversion and insertion of the sponge, to remove the latter, when the protrusion speedily followed. I subsequently wrote to the owner, informing him that amputation was the only measure to effect a permanent cure, the vagina having very little contractile power, and the protrusion having existed so long. At the same time I warned him of a certain amount of risk that would attend the operation. He decided to have the bitch back as she was, and then upon the day fixed for her return consented to the operation, which I

performed under chloroform. Having drawn out
inversion as far as possible, I enclosed the mass i[n]
carbolized tight ligature. On the third day the tum[or]
came away, and was followed by a slight discharge
matter; a little carbolized glycerine and water was pou[red]
into the vagina, and nothing further done. The b[itch]
manifested no distress or irritation during the presence
the ligature, or after sloughing was accomplished, but
and was as lively as usual, and was fit to return ho[me]
within a week.

ANTI-CONCEPTION OPERATION.*

Bitches on "heat" (œstrum) but too frequently go ast[ray]
and much disappointment, often attended by seri[ous]
pecuniary loss results from connection with some ill-b[red]
cur. Not only, in such a case, is a good litter lost, bu[t]
there be disparity of size, the male being disproportiona[tely]
large, the life of the bitch is often forfeited. On the o[ther]
hand the unfortunate sequel of "throwing back," or sh[ow]
ing in future litters the stain of the *mésalliance*, [very]
frequently follows, mental impression being in ca[nine]
females exceedingly strong (see section on breeding).
have noticed precisely the same results in the equine spe[cies]
—one notably a bay mare, was served for the first t[ime]
with a chestnut stallion, and all her future progeny v[were]
chestnuts, though she was put to different coloured hor[ses]

Knowing a bitch "in season" to have gone astray, v[hat]
measure likely to be of any service to prevent breeding
be adopted? Only one! and that is syringing out
womb with a rather strong solution of alum, using for
purpose the human enema pipe with the vaginal [tube]
attached. The sooner the operation is performed a[fter]
disconnection the better, and more likely chance of suc[cess]
but even twelve hours afterwards it may prove preven[tive]

---

* This subject, which should have found a place in Chapter
was by mistake omitted.

and especially if the bitch is in the early period of œstrum I will give one illustration out of many that have come under my notice. Last autumn a valuable red Dachshund bitch was brought to me that had gone astray to a cur the previous day. I thoroughly syringed the womb with warm soap and water, repeated in three hours, and again the following morning. Three days afterwards I obtained the services of a good red Dachshund dog, and the bitch threw four beautiful self-coloured puppies, two with red noses like herself, and two with black like the father, without a stain, at the proper period from the last connection.

I advise this measure to veterinarians and canine fanciers as the most simple and effectual I know. Warm soap and water is better than alum if a subsequent connection at that " œstrum " is intended, as it stimulates the function whereas alum checks it.

SORE FEET.

This is often a troublesome complaint with dogs. Those that travel long distances, following carriages, or accompanying sportsmen, are frequently affected. The thick cuticle covering the sole or pad of the foot becomes worn down, the deeper-seated structures are in consequence bruised, and the foot becomes swollen, hot, and painful.

Treatment.—This consists in warm fomentations and poultices—bran, or bran and bread scalded together, are the best agents for the latter ; *linseed is too drawing.* Where the inflammatory action is excessive and the pain extreme, the surface may be pricked in two or three places, and leeches applied.

If suppuration takes place, the matter should be evacuated by lancing, and subsequently treated as for abscess.

Aperient medicine is advisable, *with rest.* To prevent the animal tearing off the poultice, a wire muzzle should be worn. The return to exercise should be gradual, and take place on soft ground.

SOFT CORNS.

These are not unfrequently met with in canine practi[ce]. They are situated between the toes, and very often gi[ve] rise to ulceration, and if then neglected the bones or joi[nt] may become involved, and permanent lameness result.

In greyhounds, this is a very serious matter, and one [I] have occasionally had to deal with.

Friction and moisture favour the presence of soft cor[ns] and encourage their persistence.

Treatment.—I usually touch the surface of the corn wi[th] nitrate of silver, particularly so if there is any ulcerati[on] after which cotton wool smeared with zinc ointment [is] packed between the toes, and a foot bandage applied, [to] keep the dressing fixed, and prevent the patient licking [or] interfering with it. The ointment should be applied daily[.]

If the corn has existed long, its removal by excision [is] the most effectual method.

OVERGROWTH OF CLAWS.

The claws occasionally (especially in dogs which have b[ut] little walking exercise) become considerably elongate[d] and, curving underneath, sometimes penetrate the pad [of] the foot, causing intense pain and inflammation.

Treatment.—This consists in shortening the claw wi[th] sharp-cutting nippers, and poulticing the foot if injure[d]. It is not advisable to reduce the claws too much at fir[st] but to repeat the operation in a fortnight's time. The pr[e]vention of a recurrence of such an abnormal condition [is] in allowing the animal a sufficient amount of liberty a[nd] exercise, so as to produce the wear necessary for the [ir] proper length and shape.

Occasionally the nail of the fifth toe (*dew-claw*) grows [in] a complete circle, and its point becomes embedded in t[he] flesh of the toe, creating considerable pain, inflammato[ry] action, and suppuration. Numerous patients have bee[n] brought to me as to their suffering, and constantly licking a limb, without the true cause being suspected.

Treatment.—This simply consists in dividing the nail with strong scissors or claw-cutting forceps, and drawing forth the imbedded point, when immediate relief will be afforded. Poulticing for a few days is often advisable, especially if there is much swelling and suppuration. Unlike the other nails, these, through their position, have no wear, and therefore their condition should be watched.

REMOVAL OF DEW-CLAWS.

The dew-claws, or supplementary toes, grow above the foot, on the inside of the leg, and are apparently of but little use. Youatt observes : " They are simply illustrations of the uniformity of structure which prevails in all animals, so far as is consistent with their destiny." This view, however, will not hold good generally. Until recently, the St Bernard was considered imperfect without double dew-claws, yet such an endowment was simply superfluous, and much akin to a second thumb on the human hand, defacing, or detracting from the uniformity of structure and creating an eyesore to admirers of perfection.

Doubtless double dew-claws became hereditary, or were encouraged to become so by breeding only with dogs possessing them.

Now, wisely, St. Bernards without dew-claws can pass muster, and hold their own in the show ring. Lately, however, the elongation of the dew-claw on the hind leg, so as to form a kind of fifth toe, has been made a point of excellence, but one, unless I am much mistaken, that will be generally discarded as an attempt to foster and develop a monstrosity.

The presence, however, of dew-claws, especially in sporting dogs, is generally regarded as an eyesore, and as they are frequently torn, and impede the animal's duties in cover work, they are usually removed. For my pa[rt] I never in any of my own dogs interfere with them.

If they are to be removed, it should always be accor[m]plished when the animal is very young; their excisio[n] being easily effected with a sharp pair of scissors, fir[st] dividing the skin, and the dew-claw being drawn to o[ne] side before it is detached, in order that the skin may afte[r]wards cover the wound. But if the operation is performe[d] a day or two after birth, these precautions are not nece[s]sary,—they can be simply snipped straight off.

CROPPING.

Youatt observes: "This is an infliction of too muc[h] torture for the gratification of a nonsensical fancy; an[d] after all, in the opinion of many, and of those, too, who a[re] fondest of dogs, the animal looks far better in his natur[al] state than when we have exercised all our cruel art upon hir[m]

Blaine, on this subject, wisely remarks: "Nature ga[ve] nothing in vain; some parts being intended for use, ar[d] some for beauty. That must, therefore, be a false tas[te] which has taught us to prefer a curtailed shape to a perfec[t] without gaining any convenience by the operation."

Fashion, however, unfortunately, in this as with man[y] other matters relating to the lower animals, steps in an[d] countenances what is to all intents and purposes an act [of] wanton cruelty, and until she is overruled we can only rel[y] on those, and I trust there are yet among us many suc[h] who prefer Nature to a piece of silver gained throug[h] creating an imperfection in her work, to gratify the taste [of] a *whimsical or fashionable judge.*

It does not appear to have entered into the minds of thes[e] wiseacres, that one great function of the external ear is th[e] protection of the more delicately arranged internal structur[e]. Have they ever observed a long-eared dog enter a rabbi[t] hole? Does he scramble through the sand with his ear[s] full cock? A negative answer should suffice.

Again the ears are full of expression. Alarm, excitement, joy, watchfulness, are each denoted by their different attitudes; remove them, and the beauty of the countenance is lost.

I shall not take up space in this book, which is devoted to worthier, and I trust more interesting subjects, in describing the manner and time of operating. If any of my readers are desirous of obtaining such information, I refer them to those works wherein it is mentioned.

ROUNDING.

This may be termed cropping in another form, and unless absolutely necessary, as in the extension of cartilaginous disease in canker, it is equally to be condemned with the former. That it is a prevention of canker is purely imaginary. Such an idea is on a par with cutting off a leg to prevent its being broken. True, the part that is removed cannot become diseased, but what is left can, and is very likely to, after such unwise measures. And then, as Mayhew has it, "the wretched beast is rounded a second time," and so on until he has little or no ear left. The operation is generally performed with a rounded iron, but however done, it is cruel and unnecessary.

TAILING.

This also is a dictate of fashion; shortening this appendage is not necessarily a cruel operation. It should always be performed, when intended, a few days after birth, while the parts are tender, easily and instantaneously removed, and with but little hæmorrhage or subsequent disturbance to the animal. Drawing the tendons is not requisite except when a fine or tapering tail is required, and then it decidedly has that effect. For dividing the tail and then drawing it, a pair of the ordinary flat-nosed sharp-edged pincers are best adapted, and avoids the otherwise filthy habit of biting the required length off.

The operation, however, is not a humane one, and therefore unworthy of further notice in these pages.

WORMING.

This absurd and cruel practice is, I am thankful to s[ay] not frequently, as compared with the past, adopted.

This so-called "worming" consists in removing one [of] the cords or tendons of the frænum, which, when remov[ed] and released from tension, is in its movements said [to] resemble a dying worm. Ignorant people are thus impos[ed] upon by pretenders of equal ignorance, and with whi[ch] barbarity is mingled.

Two prevalent ideas regarding the operation are that [it] is a preventive of rabies and mischievous disposition, bo[th] of which are equally absurd and, I need scarcely ad[d,] erroneous.

CASTRATION.

Castration is now rarely performed on the dog, exce[pt] for certain conditions of the testicles which render the removal necessary. Emasculated dogs have a gre[at] tendency to become obese, idle, and, so far as sports a[re] concerned, comparatively useless. In all animals, a loss [of] energy, physical strength, and acuteness of the sense[s] generally results from castration.

It has been argued that animals, particularly dogs, [in] this state are more affectionate and faithful—the last resul[t] so far as nature is concerned, that could be expected [to] follow such an operation. Slaves they may be. Disincl[i]nation to fraternise with their own species, and mo[re] especially those of the opposite sex, is a natural cons[e]quence of emasculation, and therefore the supposed *hom[e] affection and faithfulness* are but the result of the unenviable state.

The operation, which should be performed under chloro[o]form, is a simple one. An incision is made through th[e] scrotum on either side of the median line. The testicle being protruded, a thread or silk ligature is placed round the spermatic cord about an inch above the testicle, and the latter is then removed a little below the ligature with a scalpel or sharp scissors. Other methods are adopted, as torsion, scraping, or the hot iron. An aperient, and warm fomentations, are generally all that is necessary in the after-treatment.

SPAYING.

Spaying, or removal of the ovaries of the bitch, is now almost unheard of, and I trust the time is not far distant when it will be discontinued in other animals. The operation is both *inhuman and useless*. I am thankful to say I have never seen it performed in canine practice, and will therefore quote from another authority. Youatt observes :

"In performing this operation an opening is made into the flank on one side, and the finger introduced ; one of the ovaries is laid hold of and drawn a little out of the belly ; a ligature is then applied round it, just above the bifurcation of the womb, and it is cut through, the end of the ligature being left hanging out of the wound. The other ovary is then felt for and drawn out, and excised and secured by a ligature. The wound is then sewed up, and a bandage is placed over the incision. Some farriers do not apply any ligature, but simply sew up the wound, and in the majority of cases the edges adhere, and no harm comes of the operation, except that the general character of the animal is essentially changed. She accumulates a vast quantity of fat, becomes listless and idle, and is almost invariably short-lived.

The female dog, therefore, should always be allowed to breed. Breeding is a necessary process, and the female prevented from it is sure to be affected with disease sooner or later ; enormous collections and indurations will form, that will inevitably terminate in scirrhus or ulceration."*

* Youatt : "The Dog," p. 225.

VACCINATION.

Vaccination is very largely adopted for the preventio of distemper, and, so far as its beneficial effects are cor cerned, it might just as well be practised for the sam purpose with regard to other canine diseases. Betwee distemper and smallpox (variola) there is not the slighte: analogy. However, the operation is a harmless one, an(as the latter disease does occasionally attack the do; it may be attended with good results.

The usual places selected for vaccination are the bac of the neck, the inside of the forearms, and the ears. I the latter, care should be taken that disease of the cartilag is not occasioned.

CHLOROFORM

Little need be said here on the well-known value (chloroform in surgical operations on the lower animal In veterinary practice it is now, I am thankful to sa; extensively used. In the dog it is of especial value ; indee(an operation of any consequence on the larger breeds, an those of a savage disposition, could not be performed wit any degree of comfort or safety without the employment (an anæsthetic. Of course there are circumstances in whic its administration would be attended with risk—as in son diseases of the respiratory organs and the heart. I hav only witnessed one fatal result, and that occurred : removing a mammary cancer from an old and inordinate. fat spaniel bitch. She had received every preparatio medicinal and otherwise ; the cancer was removed in a fe minutes under chloroform, and she immediately afterwar(ceased to breathe. A *post-mortem* examination reveal(hypertrophy of the heart, with extensive valvular diseas and thus death was readily accounted for.

On the score of humanity, however, chloroform chief demands our attention, and with the knowledge that v are not inflicting pain is gained strength of nerve, confiden in ourselves, and, probably, a more successful issue to our patient.

When, then, we have such a powerful instrument at hand, easy of application, and, with care, harmless in its results, there surely can be no excuse for wanton torture. Indeed, to the right-minded man, the *unavoidable* infliction of pain must ever be a source of regret. Away with the *theory* that dumb animals are devoid of imagination, which, it has been observed, adds so much to the torment of human pangs. They are not only imaginative, but their imagination is acutely sensitive, and in the dog and the horse this is particularly the case.

Rather, therefore, than we should *stretch our imagination* with so unreasonable a theory, let us use the means placed within our reach to allay suffering, and to afford to those animals which are the firm, faithful friends and companions of man the best and most humane treatment we are capable of bestowing. So that, as recently remarked by a noble member of my profession, " we may be a blessing to that lower portion of God's creation for which we are so deeply responsible." We must ever remember that the most sacred duty of the Veterinary Surgeon is to prevent or alleviate pain and distress in animals ; and we must also recollect that, in addition to their companionship, they possess—

> "Many a good
> And useful quality, and virtue too—
> Attachment never to be weaned or changed
> By any change of fortune ; proof alike
> Against unkindness, absence, and neglect ;
> Fidelity that neither bribe nor threat
> Can move or warp; and gratitude for small
> And trivial favours, lasting as the life,
> And glistening even in the dying eye."

POISONS AND THEIR ANTIDOTES.

ARSENIC.

THIS drug is very frequently, and I might also add, indiscriminately, prescribed in the columns of certain papers for canine ailments.

Actions and uses.—Administered in excess it is an irritant poison. Medicinally it is an alterative, tonic, and antiseptic. Externally, it is useful in skin diseases, and for the removal of warts and tumours.

"Quantities of from three to ten grains, mixed with water, and administered to dogs, caused in a few minutes nausea, vomiting, short moaning, difficult breathing, a wiry rapid pulse of 120 or upwards, and black evacuations made with considerable pain. These symptoms were accompanied by a look of extreme anguish; blunted perception; and death with convulsions followed in from six to thirty hours."—*Finlay Dun.*

Post-mortem Appearances.—Stomach (according to the quantity of poison received) more or less inflamed, softened and thickened, and presenting extravasated blood-spots and erosions. In slow poisoning the latter are most marked, the mucous membrane being also universally purple. Some weeks after death, bright yellow spots, as observed in the human subject, have been found inside the stomach. The lungs are usually congested. A peculiarity of arsenic is its mummifying effects on the body after death; instead of putrefaction taking place, the carcase becomes dry and shrivelled.

Antidotes.—Moist hydrated peroxide of iron; magnesia. Certain mechanical antidotes, in the absence of those agents just mentioned, may be used with advantage, viz., insoluble powders, as charcoal and clay, together with oleaginous and mucilaginous matters. Diuretics are subsequently useful in removing the absorbed poison from the system.

Doses.—$\frac{1}{15}$ to $\frac{1}{10}$ of a grain.

ANTIMONY.

The form chiefly used in canine practice is that known as **Tartar Emetic**, and is nearly exclusively administered for emetic purposes.

Actions and Uses.—Alterative, antiphlogistic, sedative, and emetic. Externally, it is a counter-irritant, and when absorbed produces the same effects in the dog as when administered by mouth.

Antidote.—Tannic acid.

Doses.—As an alterative, antiphlogistic, and sedative, $\frac{1}{8}$ to 2 grains.

Emetic, 1 to 3 grains.

NUX VOMICA—STRYCHNINE.

This drug is probably the most frequent source of poisoning in dogs.

Actions and Uses.—In excessive doses, a deadly poison. Medicinally it is a tonic and nerve-stimulant, being especially valuable in cases of paralysis, chorea, and amaurosis. Excessive doses produce general rigidity, trembling, spasmodic muscular twitchings, extending to the glottis, diaphragm, and muscles of respiration, hence death by asphyxia.

Post-mortem Appearances.—Redness and inflammation of the stomach and intestines (more particularly present when the animal has survived some time). In some cases, engorgement of the lungs, right side of the heart, and large bloodvessels; in others, an absence of blood in the latter, rigidity of the involuntary muscles, flaccidity of the voluntary ones. Congestion of the brain and membranes of the spinal cord. For some hours after death the body is stiff and straight, the limbs rigidly extended, the head thrown backwards towards the spine, the ears erect, and the tail carried straight out.

Antidotes.—Decoction of tobacco; extract of hemlock; chloroform.

Doses.—Nux vomica pulv., 2 grains.

Nux vomica extract, $\frac{1}{2}$ to 1 grain.

Strychnia, $\frac{1}{30}$ to $\frac{1}{10}$ of a grain.

Liquor strychnia,* 3 to 10 minims.

OPIUM.

Actions and Uses.—In large doses, a narcotic poison. Medi-

---

* Two fluid drachms of liquor strychnia contain one grain of the strychnia.

cinally, stimulant, sedative, narcotic, anodyne, antispasmodic a astringent.

Post-mortem Appearances.—"On opening the bodies of anim poisoned by large doses of opium, the brain and lungs are fou gorged with dark-coloured fluid blood, which does not, howev yield on analysis any indication of the presence of opium. T stomach and intestines are occasionally slightly reddened. T body passes very rapidly into a state of putrefaction."—*Fin. Dun.*

Antidotes.—Stimulants, as brandy, ammonia, compulse exercise, artificial respiration, syringing the body with cold wat applying ammonia, cayenne-pepper fumes, or strong acetic a to the nostrils, and artificial respiration.

Doses.—1 to 3 grains. Laudanum, 10 to 30 minims.

DIGITALIS.

Actions and Uses.—In excessive doses, an irritant and sedati poison. Medicinally, diuretic, sedative, and anodyne. Bei liable to accumulate in the system, its action requires watching.

"Doses of about one to two drachms given to dogs cause nause and when vomiting is prevented, moaning and expression abdominal pain, feebleness of the pulse, diarrhœa, gene weakness, shivering, slight convulsions, contraction of the pupi and diminution of common sensibility. As might be expect from such symptoms, inflammation and its consequences are fou after death throughout most parts of the alimentary canal. Co gestion of the lungs, a spotted appearance of the heart, occasiona injection of the membranes of the brain and spinal cord, and fluid condition of the blood, are also observed. Digitalis produc its effects by whatever channel it enters the body, and appears destroy life by depressing the action of the heart. Its effects the circulation, however, are not very uniform, being modified various circumstances, and especially by the dose employed. W large doses, the pulse becomes much accelerated, irregular, a intermittent."—*Finlay Dnn.*

Antidotes.—Stimulants internally and externally.

Doses.—2 to 4 grains.

BELLADONNA.

Actions and Uses.—In excessive doses, a narcotic acrid poisc Medicinally, sedative, anodyne, and antispasmodic, Its effect all doses, and by whatever channel it enters the body, is to cau dilatation of the pupil.

EE—2

"Half an ounce of the ordinary watery extract is fatal to dogs in about thirty hours, when given by the mouth; half that quantity in twenty-four hours when introduced into a wound; and even smaller doses than these are more speedily fatal when injected into the jugular vein."—*Christison.*

Post-mortem Appearances.—"In animals poisoned by belladonna, death results partly from paralysis, partly from coma; the blood remains fluid, and putrefaction sets in very early; the lungs, and sometimes also the brain and its membranes, are congested; but no inflammatory appearances can in general be detected."—*Finlay Dun.*

Antidotes.—Same as for opium.

Doses.—Powdered leaves 2 to 5 grains.

Extract, 1 to 3 grains.

ACONITE.

This drug is chiefly used, in canine practice, homœopathically.

Actions and Uses.—In large doses, a cerebro-spinal poison, paralyzing the nervous functions. Medicinally, it is a sedative, antispasmodic, and anodyne, especially valuable in tetanus. When given in excess, active and continued vomiting takes place, followed by exhaustion and paralysis of the hind parts. A drachm of Fleming's tincture has speedily destroyed dogs. Diluted with eight or ten parts of water, it has been found efficacious in allying skin-irritation and hastening the cure of eczema.

Antidotes.—Emetics; stimulants externally and internally.

Doses.—Fleming's tincture, 1 to 2 minims.

CHLOROFORM.

This most useful drug—a boon alike to men and animals—may, through unforeseen circumstances, prove a fatal agent.

Actions and Uses.—In excess, a narcotic poison. Medicinally, an anæsthetic stimulant, and antispasmodic, and externally, an antiparasitic agent.

Post-mortem Appearances.—"In animals destroyed by the inhalation of chloroform, the *post-mortem* appearances are variable. The lungs are usually congested; the heart continues to beat for a considerable time after respiration has ceased, its left side being nearly empty, but its right filled with semi-solid, dark-coloured blood. The veins of the head, neck, and chest are distended with black fluid venous blood; and the membranes of the brain are sometimes congested."—*Finlay Dun.*

Antidotes.—Fresh air, stimulants, and artificial respiration.

Doses.—By inhalation in admixture with air, 1 to 4 drachms.

Internally as a stimulant and antispasmodic, 5 to 10 minims.

PRUSSIC ACID.

This is the most deadly and instantaneous poison we come in contact with, and for that reason is most frequently used for the destruction of animals.

Actions and Uses.—Fatal in doses of one to four drops, either placed on the tongue, within the eyelids, or injected into the jugular vein. Medicinally (diluted) it is sedative, antispasmodic, and anodyne.

"To the dog, in obstinate vomiting, two grains of the acid with ten grains of carbonate of soda and one ounce of water may be administered every hour. One drachm of the acid with about a quart of water, employed slowly as an enema two or three times a day, lessens muscular contractions in tetanus. *Externally*: To allay pain and irritation in chronic skin affections, especially in dogs, two or three drachms of the acid are mixed with a pint of distilled or rain water."—*Tuson.*

Post-mortem Appearances.—"There is more or less venous congestion. The blood in all parts of the body is fluid, of a bluish appearance, and evolves the peculiar odour of the acid, which is sometimes also perceptible in the contents of the stomach, and in various of the secretions, especially that of the serous cavities. This odour, however, can seldom be detected where life has been prolonged for some time after the poison has been given. When the strong acid has been administered, some experimenters find that the voluntary muscles and those of the intestines lose their contractility, and that the heart also loses its irritability, and becomes gorged with dark grumous blood. There is, however, much difference of opinion concerning the state of the heart, and the appearances reported are not at all uniform. The villous coat of the intestines is sometimes red, shrivelled, and easily removed, and the nervous centres are usually congested."—*Finlay Dun.*

Antidotes.—Cold affusion over the head and neck, bleeding inhalation of ammonia or chlorine, fresh air; hydrated peroxide of iron in conjunction with an alkali, as, carbonate of potash.

Doses—Medicinal acid, 1 to 3 minims.

CARBOLIC ACID.

Not unfrequently dogs become poisoned either from the absorption of this agent when too freely used in skin-dressings, or from licking the same.

Actions and Uses.—In excessive doses, an irritant poison. Medicinally, sedative, anodyne, astringent, and antiseptic. Externally, antiseptic, deodorizer, disinfectant, caustic, and styptic.

Antidotes.—Albumen; soap; demulcent drinks.

Doses.—Crystals, 1 to 5 grains.

ERGOT OF RYE.

Ergot of rye is a poison, but neither so powerful nor so certain in its effects on the lower animals as on man.

Actions and Uses.—" When given in single large doses, it causes local irritation of the parts with which it comes in contact, and subsequently affects the nervous system, especially the spinal cord. When given to dogs, it produces vomiting, tenesmus, and after a variable but generally short time, dulness, prostration of muscular power, and spasms, chiefly of the diaphragm. These effects are produced in small dogs by doses of from six to twelve drachms. Twenty-four drachms proved fatal to a terrier bitch in twenty-four hours. When injected into the veins of the dog in quantities of from two to six drachms, dissolved in several ounces of water, it causes, first, great excitement and excessive acceleration of the pulse; and then, after a variable time, depression, paralysis, especially of the hinder extremities, spasms, and coma. Death ensues, generally from paralysis of the heart, in from five minutes to two hours. When injected into the arteries, it acts still more rapidly. If placed underneath the cellular tissue, or in contact with a recent wound, it causes much irritation and inflammation, the formation of fœtid unhealthy pus, and great depression of the vital powers."—*Finlay Dun.*

Medicinally, a parturient; styptic in pulmonary hæmorrhage, and also externally.

Doses.—½ to 1 drachm.

CANTHARIDES.

Actions and Uses.—In large doses, an irritant poison, producing gastro-enteritis, nephritis, inflammation of the bladder, coma, convulsions, and death. Orfila "found that a drachm and a half of a strong oleaginous solution, injected into the jugular vein of a dog, killed it in four hours with symptoms of violent tetanus; that three drachms of the tincture with eight grains of powder suspended in it caused death in twenty-four hours, if retained in the stomach by a ligature on the gullet, insensibility being then the chief symptom ; and that forty grains of the powder killed another dog in four hours and a half, although he was allowed to vomit. In all the instances in which it was administered by the stomach, that organ was found much inflamed after death, and generally fragments of the poison were discernible if it was given in the form of powder. When applied to a wound, the powder excites surrounding inflammation ; and a drachm will in this way prove fatal in thirty-two hours, without any constitutional symptom except languor."—*Christison on Poisons.*

Medicinally, stimulant, diuretic, and tonic. *Externally*, counter-irritant, vesicant, and stimulant.

Antidotes.—Mucilaginous substances, per mouth and rectum; and to allay pain and inflammation, bleeding and opiates.

Doses.—2 to 3 grains.

TURPENTINE.

This being a favourite vermifuge, may be given in excess or undiluted, and produce death.

Actions and Uses.—In large doses, an irritant poison. Medicinally, stimulant, antispasmodic, astringent, cathartic, anthelmintic, diuretic, and diaphoretic. Externally, counter-irritant and stimulant.

Antidotes.—Mucilage, and oil.

Doses.—An as anthelmintic, 1 to 2 drachms in a tablespoonful of olive oil.

CALOMEL.

Actions and Uses.—In excessive doses an irritant poison. Given continually it produces ptyalism. In medicinal doses it is a cathartic, stimulant, sedative, alterative, cholagogue, diuretic, diaphoretic, antiphlogistic, anthelmintic.

Antidotes,—These will be found fully discussed in chapter iii. section, Salivation.

Doses.—1 to 3 grains.

LEAD (ACETATE).

Actions and Uses.—Corrosive and irritant. Medicinally and externally. Astringent and sedative.

Antidotes.—Sulphuretted hydrogen, sulphuric acid, iodide of potassium.

Doses.—2 to 5 grains.

ZINC.

Actions and Uses.—In excess an irritant and emetic. Medicinally, astringent and tonic. Externally, astringent, mild, caustic and desiccant.

Antidotes.—Oil muclage, chalk.

Doses.—Oxide, 10 to 15 grains.
    Sulphate. Emetic, 8 to 10 grains. Medicinally, 2 to 3 grains.

HENBANE.

Actions and Uses.—In large doses a narcotico-acrid poison. Medicinally, anodyne, calmative, and antispasmodic.

Antidotes.—Same as for opium.

Doses.—Extract, 5 to 10 grains.
    Tincture, 40 to 50 minims.

INDEX.

	PAGE
ABSCESS.	288
nature of	288
descriptions of.	288
causes of	288
structures especially liable to	289
symptoms of	289
treatment of	289
Abscess (chronic)	290
animals usually seen in	290
character of	290
treatment of	290
Abscess (internal)	290
symptoms of	290
Absence of Milk	166
Acarus of itch disease	200, 204
Accidents and operations	370
Administration of medicine	12, 13
Agalactia	166
Age, indications of the	48, 49
Air-passages, internal parasites in the	35
pentastomum tænioides	35
situation of	35
first discovered in the frontal sinuses of the horse and dog by Chobart	36
experiments with	36
nature and character of the parasite	36
mode of invasion	36
symptoms produced by the worm	37
treatment	37
Alopecia	215
animals most frequent in	215
causes of	216
treatment of	216

	P.
Amaurosis	
nature of	
causes of	182,
symptoms of	
treatment of	
Amputations	
methods of	
case of	
after treatment of	
Anasarca	
Anæmia	
causes of	333,
symptoms of	
cases of (by D'Arbor)	
post-mortem examinations	334,
treatment of	
Ani, prolapsus	
symptoms of	
treatment of	
Ano, fistula in	
causes of	
symptoms of	
treatment of	87,
Anthelmintics	2
Anti-conception operation	4
Aphthæ of the mouth	
causes of	
symptoms of	
treatment of	
Apoplexy	2
predisposing causes	2
exciting causes	2
symptoms of	2
treatment of	269, 2
Apoplexy, parturient	1
case of	1
pathology of	1
causes of	1

425

Index.

	PAGE
Apoplexy, parturient	166
symptoms of	166
treatment of	166, 167
Appetite	3
Ascites (active)	327
causes of	327
pathology of	327-329
Ascites (passive)	329
dogs commonly seen in	329
causes of	329
how differing from active	329, 330
symptoms	330, 332
treatment of	332
Asthma (congestive)	37
character of dog chiefly affected	37
Asthma, predisposing causes of	37
exciting causes of	37
symptoms of	37
treatment of	38
Asthma (spasmodic)	38
predisposing causes of	38
exciting causes of	38
symptoms of	38
treatment of	38, 39
BALANITIS	129
causes of	129
symptoms of	129
treatment of	129, 130
Baldness	215
Beer, use of, medicinally	6
Biliary calculi	107
Biscuits	5
Bladder, displacement of the	393
Bladder, paralysis of the	127
causes of	127, 128
treatment of	128
Bladder, inflammation of the	113
Blain	55
seasons most frequently seen in	55
symptoms of	55
treatment of	55, 56
Bones, value of	4
Bowels, diseases of the	71
inflammation of the	79
Brain, compression of the	276
causes of	276
symptoms of	276
treatment of	276
Brain, concussion of the	275
causes of	275
symptoms of	275

	PAGE
Brain, reatment of	275,
Brain, inflammation of the	276
membranes of the	279
Breeding	142
necessity of properly mating in	142
mental impression, the influence of, on the offspring	142
re-conception	143
close relationship, objectionable	144
age for breeding	144
number of visits necessary for conception	144
symptoms of pregnancy	144, 145
period of pregnancy	146
Breeding, to prevent	407
Bronchitis (acute)	20
causes of	20
symptoms of	20, 21
Bronchitis, treatment of	21, 22
Bronchitis (chronic)	22
symptoms of	22
treatment of	22
Bronchitis, verminous	22
symptoms of	23, 24
pathology of	25
eight cases, autopsies of	25-31
Strongylus canis bronchialis	31
illustrations of, male and female	31
general and specific chaters of	31, 32
differs from the parasitic bronchitis of other domestic animals	32
origin of the disease	32
duration of	33
mode of invasion	33
age at which it is most prevalent	34
reason of its fatality in youth	34
Bronchocele	296
causes of	296
symptoms of	296
treatment of	296, 297
interesting case of	297-299
Brushing	9
benefit derived from	9
Burns and scalds	390

	PAGE		PA
Burns and scalds treatment of	391	Cataract	. I
		descriptions of	. I
CÆSAREAN section	159-163	causes	. I
Calculi, biliary.	. 107	symptoms of	. I
symptoms of	. 107	treatment of	. I
treatment of	107, 108	Catarrh	
Calculi, cystic.	118, 402	symptoms of	15,
congestion and distension		treatment of	
of the bladder resulting		Catarrh, gastric	
from	. 119	causes of	
urine, retention of, result-		symptoms of	
ing from	. 122	treatment of	64, 65,
Calculi, gastric	. 70	Catheterism	. .
treatment of	. 70	how performed	. 405,
Calculi, renal	. 111	Chest-founder (see "Rheu-	
symptoms of	. 112	matism")	. 338,
treatment of	. 113	Chest, dropsy of	. 40,
Calculi, urethral	110, 125	Choking	
symptoms of	110, 125	causes of	
treatment of	. 125	treatment of	
Cancer (so called)	. 177	Chorea	
nature of	. 177	causes of	
causes of	. 177	symptoms of	. 270,
symptoms of	177, 178	treatment of	. 271,
treatment of	178, 179	Chloroform	
Cancer proper.	. 294	value of	
encephaloid	. 295	arguments in favour of	
gum	. 296		415,
medullary	. 295	Claws, over-growth of	
melanotic	293, 294	causes of	
osteoid	. 295	treatment of	. 409,
scirrhous	. 295	Cold	
Canker of the ear (external)	. 190	Colic	
description of dog affected	190	causes of	
causes of	. 190	symptoms of	
symptoms of	190, 191	treatment of	
treatment of	. 191	Colic, liability of puppies to	
Canker (internal)	. 192	treatment of	
causes of	. 192	Combing	
symptoms of	. 192	Constipation	
treatment of	192, 193	natural tendency to, in the	
ditto, by Coculet	. 194	dog	
Canker of the mouth	. 53	causes of	
causes of	. 53	symptoms of	
symptoms of	. 53	treatment of	
treatment of	. 53	diet in	
Canine Lactation	. 164	daily exercise, necessity	
Cartilaginous Wounds	. 388	of, in	
case of	388, 389	Consumption	
Castration	. 413	predisposing causes of	
when necessary	. 413	exciting causes of	
effects of	. 413	symptoms of	
ideas concerning	. 413	treatment of	
methods of	413, 414	in relation to breeding	

	PAGE
Cornea, hairy tumours on the	186
cases of	186, 187, 188
treatment of	186, 187
Corns, soft	409
Cramp	359
causes of	359
symptoms of	360
treatment of	360
Crooked limbs	342
causes of	342
Cropping	411
why adopted	411
why undesirable	411
Cyst excision	398
case of	398, 399
Cystic calculi	118, 402
Cystitis (acute)	113
causes of	113
symptoms of	113, 116
treatment of	116, 117
diet in	117
Cystitis (chronic)	117
causes of	117
symptoms of	117, 118
treatment of	118
DEAFNESS	198
causes of	198, 199
treatment of	199
Decayed teeth	51
Dementia	283
case of	283, 284
Dentition	48, 51
Dew-claws, removal of	410
how removed	410, 411
Diarrhœa	72
liability of puppies to	72
causes of	72
treatment of	72, 73
diet in	73
Digestive powers of the dog	1
Diphtheria	299
Diphtheria, class of dog affected	299
symptoms of	299, 300
post-mortem examinations	300, 301
preventive measures,	302, 303
outbreak of, in Tasmania.	304
transmission from man to dog	303
cases of	304, 307
post-mortem examinations	308, 309

	PAGE
Diphtheria, experimental inoculation	305, 307
histological examination	308, 310
conclusions drawn from	310
Diseases, general	288
Disinfection	11, 12
Dislocations	380
usual situations	380
predisposing causes	380
exciting causes	380
symptoms of	380, 381
treatment of	381
of the shoulder	381
of the elbow	381
of the knee	381
of the hip	381
of the patella	381
of the hock	382
of the toes	382
Distemper	310
nature of	311
class of animal most frequent in	311
not a necessary disease	311
complications of	311
causes of	311, 312
incubation period of	312
symptoms of	313
treatment of	313, 315
associated with bronchitis and pneumonia	315
symptoms of	315
treatment of	316
necessity of ventilation	316
associated with jaundice	317
symptoms of	317
treatment of	317, 318
associated with diarrhœa	318
treatment of	318
associated with fits	318, 319
treatment of	319
Distemper, vesicular eruption in	319
symptoms of	319
what owing to	320
treatment of	320
associated with chorea and paralysis	321
treatment of	321, 322
preventive measures for distemper	322, 323
vaccination, uselessness of in	322

Index. 429

	PAGE
Distemper, inoculation, value of	322
Distemper and human typhoid fever, no identity between	323, 324
Distemper, malignant	324
symptoms of	325
post-mortem appearances	325
causes of	326
treatment of	326
Draughts, how to administer	13
Dropsy	327
usual forms of	327
Dysentery	73
nature of	73
causes of	74
symptoms of	74
treatment of	74
diet in	74
Dyspepsia	61
EAR, diseases of the	190
Ear, polypus in the	195
character of	195
causes of	195
symptoms of	195
ditto (Mercer)	195, 198
treatment of	198
Ear, serous abscess of the	194
causes of	194
symptoms of	194
treatment of	194
Ears, scurfy	199
causes of	199
treatment of	199
Eclampsia, parturient	167
cases of (Mauri)	167, 171
ditto (Laffitte)	170
Eczema	207
nature of	208
causes of	208, 209
treatment of	209
Eczema (chronic)	209
treatment of	209, 210
Eczema mercuriale	210
symptoms of	210
Embolism	366
effects of	366, 367
case of	367
symptoms of	367
post-mortem appearances	367, 368
Emphysema	368
causes of	368

	PAGE
Emphysema, case of	368
post-mortem appearances	369
treatment of	369
Encephaloid cancer	295
Enteritis	79
tissues involved in	79
causes of	79
Enteritis, symptoms of	79
how distinguished from other affections, especially colic	79
general symptoms of	79, 80
terminations of	80
how denoted	80
treatment of	80, 81
diet in	81
Entozoa	219
treatment for	221, 222, 223
Epilepsy	266
confounded with rabies	267
susceptible periods for	267
predisposing causes of	267
exciting causes of	267
symptoms of	267, 268
associated with distemper	268
treatment of	269, 270
Epileptic rabies a fallacy	266
Erythema	211
symptoms of	211
treatment of	211
Exercise	6
necessity of	6, 7
means of taking	7
Eye, diseases of the	180
extirpation of the	185
when necessary	185
how performed	185
subsequent treatment	185, 186
Eye-ball, protrusion of the	185
causes of	185
treatment of	185
FALSE-JOINT	377
Fatness, excessive	337
Fatty degeneration, liver	103
heart	360
ovaries	140
Fatty substances, influence of, as food	105
Feeding, time of	2
system of	2
health in relation to	2
Feet, sore	408
causes of	408

	PAGE
Feet sore, symptoms of	408
treatment of	408, 409
Femoral hernia	396
Fistula	397
nature of	397
Fistula in ano	87
Fistula lachrymalis	397
parietal abdominalis	397
mammary	398
lacteal	398
teat	398
biliary	398
gastric	398
Flatulency	61
Flatulency, treatment of	62
Fleas	217
treatment for	217
ditto (Gamgee)	217
protective measures	217
Food	1
quantity of	3
Food, kind of	3, 4, 5
Foreign bodies in the stomach	70
Founder (chest)	338, 340
Fractures	370
descriptions of	370, 371
bones most liable to	371
causes of	371
treatment of	371
of long bones	372
of the scapula	373, 374
of the pelvis	374, 375
of the ribs	375
of the sternum	375
of the cranium	375, 377
of the vertebræ	377
false joint	377
treatment of	377, 378
re fracture	378, 379
compound fracture	379
fracture with luxation	379
GASTRIC calculi	70
Gastritis (acute)	66
terminations of	66
causes of	66
symptoms of	66, 67
post-mortem appearances	67
treatment of	67, 68
Gastritis (chronic)	68
causes of	68
symptoms of	68
treatment of	68

	PAGE
Gastro-enteritis	82
causes of	82
symptoms of	82
treatment of	82
Gastro-hysterotomy	159, 163
General diseases	288
General management	1, 14
Generative organs, diseases of	129
functions of the	141
Glanders	349
cases of (Fleming)	350, 351
Glossitis	54
causes of	54
symptoms of	54
treatment of	54
Glossy coat, means of obtaining	8
Grooming	8
Grooming, benefit derived from	9
Gum cancer	296
HÆMATURIA	110
causes of	110
symptoms of	110
treatment of	111
Haw, enlargement of the	184
causes of	184
symptoms of	184
treatment of	184, 185
Heart, diseases of the	360
Heart, fatty degeneration of the	360
pathological anatomy	360, 361
causes of	361
symptoms of	361
Heart, valvular disease of the	361
symptoms of	361
post-mortem appearances of	361
treatment of	361
case of, associated with rheumatic chorea	362, 364
Heart, rupture of the	364
symptoms of	364
post-mortem examination	365
cause of	365
why remarkable	365
Hepatitis (acute)	89
predisposing causes of	89
exciting causes of	89
symptoms of	89
terminations of	89
treatment of	90

Hepatitis (chronic)	90
causes of	90
symptoms of	90
treatment of	90, 91
terminations of	91
Hernia (femoral)	396
case of	396
cause of	396
treatment of	397
Hernia (umbilical)	391
causes of	391
symptoms of	391
treatment of	392
Hernia (uterine)	137
symptoms of	137
treatment of	138
Hernia (ventral)	393
case of	393
symptoms of	393, 394
treatment of	394, 396
Husk	64
Hydrargyria	210
Hydrocephalus	277
causes of	277
symptoms of	277
treatment of	277, 278
Hydrophobia (so called)	240
Hydrophthalmia	188
causes of	188
symptoms of	188
treatment of	189
Hydrothorax	40
tapping in	42
Hydrophthalmia, congenital	189
Hysteria & Hydrophobia	242, 266
ICTERUS	91
Indigestion	61
Indigestion, causes of	61
symptoms of	61
treatment of	61, 62
diet	62
Inflammation of bladder	113
bone	344
bowels	79
brain	279
bronchial tubes	20
claws	409
ear	190, 192
eye	180
feet	408
kidney	109
larynx	18
liver	89

Inflammation of lungs	42
mammary gland	175
pericardium	365
periosteum	345
peritoneum	82
pharynx	57
pleura	39
prepuce	129
spleen	108
stomach	66
tongue	54
uterus	166
Influenza	16
causes of	17
symptoms of	17
treatment of	17, 18
Internal parasites	219
Intestines, worms in the	76
symptoms of	76
Intus-susception	74
character of	74
intestines involved	75
termination of	75
cases of	75
autopsies	75
symptoms of	76
treatment of	76
Inversion of the stomach	68
Iritis	183
causes of	183
symptoms of	184
treatment of	184
Itch	200
JAUNDICE	91
causes of	91, 92
symptoms of	92
terminations of	92
associated with pregnancy	92
treatment of	92, 93
diet in	93
Jaundice, Weber, M., his paper on Jaundice	94, 100
Trasbot, ditto, translated by Fleming	100, 103
KENNEL arrangement	9, 10, 11
construction of	10, 11
cleansing of	10
Kennel-lameness (see "Rheumatism")	338
Kidney, inflammation of the	109
LACTEAL Tumours	176
Laryngitis (acute)	18
predisposing causes of	18

Index.

	PAGE
Laryngitis, exciting causes of	18
symptoms of	18
treatment of	18, 19
Laryngitis (chronic)	19
symptoms of	19
treatment of	19, 20
Larynx, inflammation of the.	18
Legs, crooked.	342
causes of	342
Leukæmia	332
nature of	332
diseases associated with	332
cases recorded (Innorenza)	333
Lice	218
how hatched	218
treatment for	218
Lips, warts on the	216
Lithotomy	402
case of	402, 404
Liver, diseases of the	89
Liver, fatty degeneration of the.	103
symptoms of	103
treatment of	103, 104
post-mortem examination	104
Liver, inflammation of the	89
Liver and spleen, diseases of the.	89
cancerous deposit in the	106, 295
post-mortem examinations	106, 295
Lungs, inflammation of the	42
Lumbago (see "Rheumatism")	338, 339
MAMMARY gland, diseases of the.	175
Mammitis (acute)	175
causes of	175
symptoms of	175
treatment of	175, 176
Mammitis (chronic)	176
causes of	76
symptoms of	176
treatment of	176
Management, general	1
Mange (follicular)	204
cause of	204
symptoms of	205
treatment of	205, 206, 207

	PAGE
Mange (Sarcoptic	200
diseases analogous to	200
cause of	200
symptoms of	201
treatment of	202, 203, 204
Marasmus	336
causes of	336
symptoms of	336
treatment of	336
Measles	356
case of	356
symptoms of	356
Measles, parasitic	236
symptoms of	237, 238
Medicine, administration of methods of	12, 13
Medullary cancer	295
Melanosis	293
Meningitis	279
disease usually associate with	279
symptoms of	279
treatment of	279
case of (Leblanc)	279, 280, 281
symptoms of	280
post-mortem examination	281
case of (Gowing)	281
symptoms of	281, 282
treatment of	282
post-mortem examination	282, 283
Mental emotion, effects of on canine lactation	164, 165
Metritis	134
Milk fever	166
Mouth-canker of the	53
diseases of the.	48
Mouth and Tongue, diseases of the	48
NEPHRITIS	109
causes of	109
symptoms of	109
treatment of	109, 110
Nervous system, diseases of the	239
Neuralgia	286
symptoms of	286, 287
treatment of	287
Nose, polypus in the	46
Nostomania	255
causes of	286
treatment of	285, 286

Index. 433

	PAGE
ursing	13
good, necessity of, in sickness	13, 14, 285
ursing, in medical treatment	13, 14
OBESITY	337
causes of	337
treatment of	337, 338
Obstruction of the bowels	74
Œsophagotomy	401
how performed	401
after treatment	401
Œstrum	141
time of appearance	141
signs of	141
treatment during	142
Operations	370
Ophthalmia	180
causes of	180
symptoms of	180, 181
treatment of	181
Ophthalmia, chronic, or constitutional	181
symptoms of	181, 182
treatment of	182
Osteoid cancer	295
Ostitis	344
causes of	344
symptoms of	345
treatment of	345
Ovaries, fatty degeneration of the	140
Overgrowth of claws	409
Ozæna	46
causes of	46
symptoms of	46
treatment of	46, 47
PARALYSIS	272
causes of	272
diseases connected with	273
symptoms of	273
treatment of	273, 274, 275
of the bladder	127
of the tongue	56
Parasites (external)	200
Parasites (internal)	219
Ascaris marginata	220, 221, 222
Bothriocephalus latus	233
B. cordatus	233
B. dubius	233

	PAGE
Parasites, B. fuscus	233
B. reticulatus	233
Cysticercus cellulosus	236, 237, 238
Cysticercus piciformis	238
Cysticercus tenuicollis	230
Distoma conjunctum	220
Dochmius trigonocephalus	225
Echinococcus veterinorum	230
Estrongylus gigas	224
Filaria hæmatica	225
Filaria hepatica	225
Filaria, immitis	223
Parasites, Filaria trispinulosa	
Hæmatozoon subulatum	225
Holostoma alatum	220
Maw worms	234
Pentastoma tæmoides	35, 36, 37, 234
Spiroptera sanguinolenta	224, 225
Strongylus canis bronchialis	31
Tænia cœnurus	227
Tænia cucumerina	226
Tænia echinococcus	230
Tænia marginata	229
Tænia serrata	233
Trichina spiralis	225
Tricocephalus depressiusculus	225
Trichosoma plica	225
Parturient apoplexy	166
Parturient eclampsia	167
Parturition	145
symptoms of approaching labour	146
assistance, when needed	147
warm bath, value of	147
uterine stimulants	148
management after parturition	148
Parturition, diseases immediately connected with	146
Parturition, unnatural	148
means used to deliver in	148-158
Penis, warts on the	130
causes of	130
treatment of	130
Pericarditis	365
causes of	365

F F

434 Index.

	PAGE
Pericarditis, symptoms of	365
treatment of	365
diet in	365
Peritonitis (acute)	82
cause of	82
symptoms of	82, 83
post-mortem appearances	83
treatment of	83, 84
terminations of	84
Peritonitis (chronic)	84
symptoms of	84
chronic, post-mortem appearances	84
treatment of	84
Periostitis	345
causes of	345
symptoms of	345
mistaken for rabies	345
treatment of	345
Pharyngitis	57
causes of	57
symptoms of	57
terminations of	57
treatment of	57
Pharyngitis, abscess in	57, 58
treatment of	58
Pharyngitis stricture in	58
Pharyngitis, treatment of stricture in	58
Pharynx, inflammation of	57
Piles	84
nature of	84
causes of	85
symptoms of	85
treatment of	85, 86
Pills, how to administer	12, 13
Plethora	336
dogs most liable to	336
associated with fits	337
symptoms of	337
treatment of	337
Pleurisy (acute)	39
predisposing causes of	39
exciting causes of	39
symptoms of	39, 40
terminations of	40
post-mortem examination	40
treatment of	40, 41, 42
ventilation, necessity of, in	41
Pleurisy (chronic)	42
symptoms of	42
treatment of	42

	PAG
Pleuro-pneumonia	3
Pneumonia	4
predisposing causes of	4
exciting causes of	4
symptoms of	43, 4
treatment of	4
regenerative process in	4
Polypus, aural	195-19
nasal	4
vaginal	13
Prolapsus ani	8
Puppies, feeding of	
RABIES	23
etymology of	240, 24
parliamentary enquiry	24
nature of	24
causes of	241-24
spontaneity	241, 24
incubation, period of	246, 247, 24
duration of	24
symptoms of (furious)	250-25
ditto (dumb)	25
maternal affection in	25
post-mortem appearances in	256-26
innocuousness of the milk in	262, 263, 26
treatment of	264-26
preventive measures	26
Rabies, epileptic, a false allegation	26
Rachitis	34
Removal of dew-claws	41
Renal calculi	11
Respiratory organs, diseases of the	1
Retention of urine	12
Rheumatism (acute)	33
descriptions of	33
causes of	33
forms of	33
symptoms of	339, 34
treatment of	340, 34
Rheumatism (chronic)	34
symptoms of	34
treatment of	34
Ribs, fracture of	37
Rickets	34
causes of	34
symptoms of	342, 34

	PAGE
Rickets, treatment of	344
Ringworm	211
vegetable parasite due to	211
causes of	212
symptoms of	212
incubation, period of	212
treatment of	212, 213
Ringworm (Honeycomb)	213
vegetable parasite due to	213
causes of	213
symptoms of	213, 214
treatment of	215
Rounding	412
when necessary	412
how performed	412
Russian bath, preventive of rabies	265
Rye, ergot of, use in parturition	148
SALIVATION	58
causes of	58
symptoms of	58, 59
treatment of	59, 60
Sarcoptes canis	201
Scalds	390
treatment of	391
Scapula, fracture of	373
Scirrhous cancer	295
Scrofula	346
causes of	346
symptoms of	346, 347
treatment of	347, 348
case of (Gowing)	348
post-mortem	349
Scrotal irritation	130
Scrotal irritation, causes of	130
symptoms of	130, 131
treatment of	131
Scurfy ears	199
Septikæmia puerperalis	172
causes of	172
symptoms of	172
post-mortem examination	172, 173
treatment of	173, 174
Shoulder-joint, dislocation of	381
Skin, diseases of the	200
Skull, fracture of	375
Small-pox	352
symptoms of	353, 354, 355
Small-Pox, sanitary measures	356
curative measures	356
Soft corns	409
treatment of	409
Sore feet	408
Spaying	414
inhumanity and uselessness of	414
methods of	414
reasons why not indicated	414
results	414
Spirits, use of, medicinally	6
Spleen, diseases of the	89
inflammation of the	108
Splenitis	108
in connection with other diseases	108
symptoms of	108
treatment of	108
Sprains	389
symptoms of	390
treatment of	390
Stomach, calculi in the	70
character of	70
treatment of	70
diseases of the	61
foreign bodies in the	70
associated with rabies	70
causes of	70
Stomach, inflammation of the	
Stomach, inversion of the	68
case of	68
symptoms of	69
autopsy	69
Stomach, worms in the	63
symptoms of	63, 64
species of worm	64
treatment of	64
Stone in the bladder	118, 404
St. Vitus's dance	272
Swelling of the ears	190
TAILING	412
age when done	412
method of	412
Tape-worm	225
Tapping the chest	42
Tartar, on the teeth	52
prejudicial to health	55
treatment of	52, 32

	PAGE
Teeth, decayed	51
cause of disease	52
associated with feeding	52
extraction of	52
hæmorrhage from	52
treatment of	52
Testicles, enlarged	131
symptoms of	131
causes of	131
treatment of	132
Tetanus	357
nature of	357
causes of	357
symptoms of	357
cause of death	358
post-mortem appearances	358
treatment of	358, 359
diet in	359
Ticks	218
treatment for	218
Tongue, affections of the	54
paralysis of the	56
causes of	56
symptoms of	56
treatment of	56, 57
worming	413
TUMOURS	290
Calcareous	292
situations of	292
treatment of	292, 293
Fatty	290
situations of	291
character of	291
diagnosis	291
treatment of	291
Fibro-cystic	291
situations of	292
treatment of	292
Fibrous	291
causes of	291
situations of	291
diagnosis	291
treatment	291
Tumours—*Lacteal*	176
causes of	176
symptoms of	176
treatment of	177
Melanotic	293
symptoms of	293
post-mortem examination	294
treatment of	294

	PAGE
Osseous	293
situations of	293
treatment of	293
Rectal	84
symptoms of	85
treatment of	85, 86
Turnside	278
causes of	278
symptoms of (Youatt)	278
post-mortem examination	278, 279
Turkish Bath	265
ULCERS on the tongue	55
causes of	55
treatment of	55
Umbilical hernia	391
Urethra, worm in the	127
Urethral calculi	110, 125, 405
Urinary organs, diseases of the	109
Urine, retention of the	125
causes of	125
symptoms of	126
treatment of	126, 127
Séon, M., records a singular case of	127
Uteris, inflammation of the	134
causes of	134
symptoms of	134, 135
treatment of	135
Uterus, *inversion* of the	136
causes of	136
symptoms of	136
treatment of	136
Uterus, *ulceration* of the	136
causes of	137
symptoms of	137
treatment of	137
Uterus, *hernia* of the	137
symptoms of	137, 138
treatment of	138
Uterus, *dropsy* of the	139
causes of	139
symptoms of	139
case of	139
VACCINATION	415
why adopted	415
where performed	415
Vagina, inversion of the	132
causes of	132
symptoms of	132

	PAGE		PAGE
Vagina, treatment of	133	Warts, character of	216
Vagina, polypus in the	134	treatment of	216, 217
symptoms of	134	Washing	8
treatment of	134	frequency of	8
Vaginotomy	133, 406	method of	8
Variolæ caninæ	352	Water, allowance of	6
Vermifuges	235, 236	Wine, use of medicinally	6
Vertigo	270	Worming	413
symptoms of	270	what it consists in	413
causes of	270	ignorant ideas concerning	413
treatment of	270	Worm expellants	235
Vomiting	62	Worms in the intestines	76
susceptibility to, in dogs	63	in the stomach	6?
indication of	63	Wounds	384
character of	63	descriptions of	384
treatment of	63	methods of healing	385
		treatment of	385-389
WARTS	216		
situations favourable to growth of	216	YELLOWS, the	91, 317

www.ingramcontent.com/pod-product-compliance
Lightning Source LLC
Chambersburg PA
CBHW051236300426
44114CB00011B/762